"An immediacy and a sense of reality...
which no latter-day historian
can hope to contrive."

Thus writes famed Civil War authority
Bruce Catton in his memorable introduction to
these unforgettable eye-witness accounts of the
years of bitter battle and bloody carnage
known as the War Between the States.

Sometimes the narrator is an enlisted man,
sometimes an officer, but always he is a man
who knows not only the cold facts but the living
feel of combat. There have been many books on
the Civil War—but there has never been one to
equal this in its stunning authenticity, its
wonderful immediacy.

With a running commentary that establishes
the background and chronology
of each combat account.

COMBAT

The

EDITED AND WITH COMMENTARY BY
DON CONGDON
INTRODUCTION BY
BRUCE CATTON

Civil War

THE CLIMACTIC YEARS

A DELL BOOK

514999

Published by
DELL PUBLISHING CO., INC.
750 Third Avenue
New York, New York 10017

Originally published in one volume by Delacorte Press

Reprinted by arrangement with
Delacorte Press
New York, N.Y.

Printed in the U.S.A.

First Dell printing—July 1968

ACKNOWLEDGEMENTS

"Gettysburg: Second Day" from *The Twentieth Maine*, by John J. Pullen. Copyright © 1957 by John J. Pullen. Reprinted with the permission of J. B. Lippincott Company.

SELECTIONS WERE ALSO TAKEN FROM THE FOLLOWING BOOKS:

Decisive Battles of the Civil War by Colonel Joseph B. Mitchell. Copyright 1955 by Joseph B. Mitchell. Reprinted by permission of G. P. Putnam's Sons.

The Growth of the American Republic, Fifth Edition, by Samuel Eliot Morison and Henry Steele Commager. Copyright © 1962 by Oxford University Press, Inc. Reprinted by permission of the publisher.

The Coming Fury by Bruce Catton. Copyright © 1961 by Bruce Catton. Reprinted by permission of Doubleday & Company, Inc., and, for the British Commonwealth, Victor Gollancz, Ltd.

Terrible Swift Sword by Bruce Catton. Copyright © 1963 by Bruce Catton. Reprinted by permission of Doubleday & Company, Inc., and, for the British Commonwealth, Victor Gollancz, Ltd.

Never Call Retreat by Bruce Catton. Copyright © 1965 by Bruce Catton. Reprinted by permission of Doubleday & Company, Inc., and, for the British Commonwealth, Victor Gollancz, Ltd.

The Blue and the Gray by Henry Steele Commager. Copyright 1950 by the Bobbs-Merrill Company, Inc. Reprinted by permission of the Bobbs-Merrill Company, Inc.

This Hallowed Ground by Bruce Catton. Copyright © 1955, 1956 by Bruce Catton. Reprinted by permission of Doubleday & Company, Inc., and, for the British Commonwealth, Victor Gollancz, Ltd.

CONTENTS

MAPS

ILLUSTRATIONS

COMBAT: *The Civil War*

WE WILL HAVE TO FIGHT HERE

THE BATTLE OF ANTIETAM ENDED with the Federals in possession of the field, and the Confederates in retreat, so despite
the extremely heavy bluecoat casualties it was technically at
least, a northern victory. Abraham Lincoln certainly considered Antietam a victory; he used it to justify the issuance
of his greatest document, the Emancipation Proclamation,
which in effect ended slavery in America. But Little Mac
was not one to accept success gladly. Lincoln and Halleck
pressed him to pursue Lee and force a decisive battle, but
October passed with no significant movement, other than
the embarrassment of another cavalry raid by Jeb Stuart
around the Union army. At last, on November 7, McClellan
was relieved and General Ambrose Everett Burnside
replaced him as commander of the Army of the Potomac.

With Richmond as his objective, Burnside moved
southeast to the Rappahannock opposite Fredericksburg,
where he hoped to cross the river before Lee could arrive on
the opposite bank.

Confederate General James Longstreet says: "About the
18th or 19th of November, we received information through
our scouts that Sumner, with his grand division of more than
thirty thousand men, was moving toward Fredericksburg.
Evidently he intended to surprise us and cross the Rappahannock before we could offer resistance. On receipt of
the information, two of my divisions were ordered down to
meet him. We made a forced march and arrived on the hills
around Fredericksburg about three o'clock on the afternoon
of the 21st. Sumner had already arrived, and his army was
encamped on Stafford Heights, overlooking the town from
the Federal side.

"About the 26th or 27th it became evident that
Fredericksburg would be the scene of a battle, and we advised the people who were still in the town to prepare to

leave, as they would soon be in danger if they remained. The evacuation of the place by the distressed women and help-less men was a painful sight. Many were almost destitute and had nowhere to go, but, yielding to the cruel necessities of war, they collected their portable effects and turned their backs on the town. Many were forced to seek shelter in the woods and brave the icy November nights to escape the ap-proaching assault from the Federal army.

"Very soon after I reached Fredericksburg the remainder of my corps arrived from Culpeper Court House, and as soon as it was known that all the Army of the Potomac was in motion for the prospective scene of battle Jackson was drawn down from the Blue Ridge. In a very short time the Army of Northern Virginia was face to face with the Army of the Potomac.

"At a point just above the town, a range of hills begins, ex-tending from the river's edge out a short distance and bearing around the valley somewhat in the form of a crescent. On the opposite side are the noted Stafford Heights, then occu-pied by the Federals. At the foot of these hills flows the Rap-pahannock River. On the Confederate side nestled Fredericksburg, and around it stretched the fertile bottoms from which fine crops had been gathered and upon which the Federal troops were to mass and give battle to the Con-federates. On the Confederate side nearest the river was Taylor's Hill, and south of it the now famous Marye's Hill; next, Telegraph Hill, the highest of the elevations on the Confederate side (later known as Lee's Hill, because during the battle General Lee was there most of the time), where I had my headquarters in the field; next was a declination through which Deep Run Creek passed on its way to the Rappahannock River; and next was the gentle elevation at Hamilton's Crossing, not dignified with a name, upon which Stonewall Jackson massed thirty thousand men.

"The hills occupied by the Confederate forces, although over-crowned by the heights of Stafford, were so distant as to be outside the range of effective fire by the Federal guns, and, with the lower receding grounds between them, formed a defensive series that may be likened to natural bastions. Taylor's Hill, on our left, was unassailable; Marye's Hill was more advanced toward the town, was of a gradual as-cent and of less height than the others, and we considered it the point most assailable, and guarded it accordingly.

"This was the situation of the 65,000 Confederates

massed around Fredericksburg, and they had twenty-odd days in which to prepare for the approaching battle.

"On the morning of the 11th of December, 1862, an hour or so before daylight, the slumbering Confederates were awakened by a solitary cannon thundering on the heights of Marye's Hill. Again it boomed, and instantly the aroused Confederates recognized the signal of the Washington Artillery and knew that the Federal troops were preparing to cross the Rappahannock to give us the expected battle. The Federals came down to the river's edge and began the construction of their bridges, when Barksdale opened fire with such effect that they were forced to retire. Again and again they made an effort to cross, but each time they were met and repulsed by the well-directed bullets of the Mississippians. This contest lasted until 1 o'clock, when the Federals, with angry desperation, turned their whole available force of artillery on the little city, and sent down from the heights a perfect storm of shot and shell, crushing the houses with a cyclone of fiery metal. From our position on the heights we saw the batteries hurling an avalanche upon the town whose only offense was that near its edge in a snug retreat nestled three thousand Confederate hornets that were stinging the Army of the Potomac into a frenzy. It was terrific, the pandemonium which that little squad of Confederates had provoked. The town caught fire in several places, shells crashed and burst, and solid shot rained like hail. In the midst of the successive crashes could be heard the shouts and yells of those engaged in the struggle, while the smoke rose from the burning city and the flames leaped about, making a scene which can never be effaced from the memory of those who saw it. But, in the midst of all this fury, the little brigade of Mississippians clung to their work. At last, when I had everything in readiness, I sent a peremptory order to Barksdale to withdraw, which he did, fighting as he retired before the Federals, who had by that time succeeded in landing a number of their troops. The Federals then constructed their pontoons without molestation, and during the night and the following day the grand division of Sumner passed over into Fredericksburg.

"About a mile and a half below the town, where the Deep Run empties into the Rappahannock, General Franklin had been allowed without serious opposition to throw two pontoon-bridges on the 11th, and his grand division passed over and massed on the level bottoms opposite Hamilton's Crossing, thus placing himself in front of Stonewall Jackson's corps. The 11th and 12th were thus spent by the Federals in crossing the river and preparing for battle."*

Fredericksburg†

BY THE SURVIVORS OF THE 118TH PENNSYLVANIA VOLUNTEERS

THERE HAD BEEN FREQUENT PRELIMINARY ORDERS to be in readiness to move immediately, to move at a moment's notice, to move at once, to move without delay. It was the usual phraseology then so familiar and aroused but little comment, as a soldier was about as ready to move at one time as another. They were accompanied by directions to carry five days' cooked rations, and the orders, following each other so closely, kept that supply continually on hand.

The thunder of heavy cannonading about four o'clock on the morning of the 11th of December, followed promptly by the "general," dissipated the flippant treatment with which the preliminary directions had been received, and, amid some bustle and confusion, the regiment was without delay in line, awaiting the order to march.

The sun, great and round, rose ominously red. Camp-fixtures were to remain standing and the troops to be equipped in light-marching order only. The soldiers had not yet conceived that much was intended beyond a reconnoissance in heavy force. This, though, was one of those hopeful conceptions to drive off the notion that there would be a fight.

The company cooks were metamorphosed, that is, these professional gentlemen had been promoted to the ranks, exchanged their ladles for muskets and cartridge-boxes, and were given an opportunity to pepper the enemies of their country instead of the bean soup. One of them, whose rotund form and unctuous face made his usual occupation unmistakable, hearing the boom of the heavy guns, asked what the noise was.

He was answered: "The rebel artillery."

* "Battle of Fredericksburg," *Battles and Leaders*, III, 70, 72, 73, 75.
† From *The History of the 118th Pennsylvania Volunteers*.

Taylor's Hill

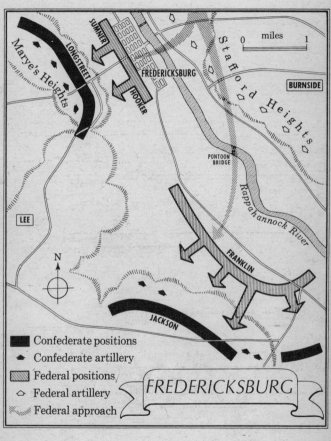

miles
0   1

Stafford Heights

BURNSIDE

SUMNER

LONGSTREET

Marye's Heights

FREDERICKSBURG

HOOKER

PONTOON
BRIDGE

Rappahannock River

LEE

N

FRANKLIN

JACKSON

■ Confederate positions
◆ Confederate artillery
▨ Federal positions
◇ Federal artillery
〰 Federal approach

FREDERICKSBURG

"You fellers needn't think you can fool me. I've heard that noise too often in Philadelphia; they're unloading boards somewhere."

Afterward, when the man of pots and pans heard the screech of the shells and saw them falling in the river near the engineers who were laying the pontoons, he went lumbering to the rear as though he had forgotten something, and his oleaginous form faded in the distance.

At seven o'clock the column was in motion, not in the familiar direction towards Hartwood Church, but by the shortest and most practicable route to Falmouth and the Rappahannock. Evidences were everywhere abroad of preparation for desperate and bloody work. Ambulance trains were parked in every direction; every safe and readily accessible location was occupied by hospital tents. Stretchers in unlimited supply were being hurried to the front for immediate use. Fresh, clean straw, neatly bundled had been distributed where the wounded were to be brought for treatment. The thunder of the guns continued in uninterrupted roar.

The march was soon accomplished. The whole of the Centre Grand Division was massed on "Stafford Heights," the prominent bluffs on the left bank of the river, commanding a full view of the city of Fredericksburg, the stream and the lowlands and hills upon the other side. Line upon line, shoulder to shoulder, this closely packed body of men awaited, in quiet resoluteness, the order that should send them forward to measure strength and courage with their adversaries. It was a martial sight.

The stream, inconsiderable in width, is navigable for steamboats. The water-front of the city extended about a mile, with streets at right-angles, lined with substantial brick and stone buildings reaching back from the water about half that distance. The city lay on a plain away below the heights which overlooked it. At the distance of half a mile arose a formidable hill, of easy, gentle slope, then modestly known by its owner's name as Marye's Heights. It was to become famous as the scene of most desperate and valorous assaults. Marye's Heights were lined with earthwork, planned and constructed by skilled engineers, defended by soldiers tried in battle, mounted with guns handled by the best artillerists. They appeared almost impregnable. The enemy's cannon answered in active response to the Union guns. All this was in full view, and as the column passed over the bluffs and down to the bridges, all those "thinking bayonets" could not but conclude that a direct assault would be hopeless.

Whilst the infantry massed about the heights suffered but little annoyance from the enemy's artillery, the engineers and pontooniers were at a difficult and perilous task. Every house on the river-bank had its riflemen, and small earthworks had been constructed for others whom the houses could not shelter. Each attempt to lay the boats was met with terrific and fatal volleys; the loss was appalling. In sheer desperation, the afternoon well spent, the engineers, resting from their labor, had sought such shelter as could be found at the foot of the bluffs and on the edge of the river. The pontoon boats, dismounted from their wagons, lay useless on the shore. Suddenly bodies of men, pelted as relentlessly as were the engineers, rushed to the shore. With commendable precision, regardless of their terrible loss, they took the places allotted them in the boats and pushed them into the stream. They were rapidly pulled across, the galling fire continuing until a landing effected upon the other side in a measure silenced it. The laying of the bridges soon followed, but it was late in the afternoon before they were fitted for a passage.

It did not fall to the lot of our division to cross that night, and about five o'clock it retired a mile or so for a bivouac near a spot designated as "White House"; but whence it derived its name is inconceivable, as no settlement was thereabouts and nothing observable but a solitary whitewashed shanty.

Mr. Henry K. Jewell, a well-known citizen of Philadelphia and an acquaintance of many of the officers of the regiment, opportunely appeared during the afternoon. He was connected in some civic capacity with the Commissary Department. The soldier rarely knows much that is reliable, except what is occurring immediately around him. He gathers his information afterwards when the newspapers reach the front. Mr. Jewell said the cause of the delay in attacking Fredericksburg was the nonarrival of the pontoons, and also told of General Sumner's demand, through General Patrick, on General Lee, to surrender the city, and its refusal. The story of both circumstances subsequently appeared fully in the newspapers, and is now historically recorded. The delay in forwarding the pontoons has been the frequent subject of severe comment and harsh criticism, and it has fallen mostly upon General Halleck, on whom it was alleged the responsibility rested.

Jewell was a thoughtful fellow. He had loaded himself with canteens, all he could carry, filled to the brim with an excellent quality of ardent spirits. He freely and cheerfully distributed this among his friends who had the conveniences at hand to carry it. It was carefully husbanded, and proved a priceless *jewel* in the next day's engagement, when it was judiciously dispensed to many a wounded sufferer.

At eight o'clock on the morning of the 12th the regiment returned to the same spot it had held on the day before. All day long the big guns on the bluffs and the field-batteries tore away persistently at the enemy's works on Marye's Heights. The roar was continuous, but apparently little damage followed the cannonading; certainly none to the entrenchments, though it probably caused some loss among the soldiery. Smoke in great volumes hung over everything, lifting occasionally, when there was a lull in the firing, to permit a cursory observation.

All day long Sumner's Right Grand Division was pouring over the pontoons amid a storm of the enemy's shells. The enemy seemed to have a pretty fair knowledge of where the bridges were, and were tolerably successful in securing the range. So close, indeed, did the shells from the Confederate batteries fall to the pontoons that the crossing soldiers were frequently splashed with the water that flew up from the places where they struck the river. It was cooling, but not refreshing.

From the Phillips House, a most pretentious mansion, which was General Burnside's head-quarters, staff-officers, at frightful pace, were continually coming and going. Night settled before things were in complete readiness, and the regiment rested where it was, awaiting the breaking of the portentous morn.

Saturday, the 13th, dawned in an almost impenetrable fog, so dense that it, with the smoke of the battle, made objects close at hand scarcely distinguishable. It was of such density that there was a fear that in a close engagement friends might be mistaken for foes. To avoid such a contingency the very unusual precaution of a word of recognition was adopted, and the watchword "Scott" was given to be used in such an emergency.

Between nine and ten o'clock the fog lifted a little, and unfolded a scene thrilling in its inspiration and awful in its terror. The streets of the city were literally packed with soldiers. Glistening rifle-barrels, sombre blue, surged in undistinguishable columns, pressing for the open country to seek some relief from the deadly plunge of cannon-shots dealing mercilessly their miseries of wounds and death. But the same batteries on Marye's Heights were again encountered, more frowning and formidable than ever, and wicked in their renewed determination to punish the termerity that dared assault these formidable entrenchments. With such gunnery, fog and smoke settled again and the scene was lost to view from Stafford Heights, the continuing noise alone indicating the progress of the battle.

Amid all these stirring scenes four officers of the regiment indulged in a game of euchre. Intent upon their amusement, they were lost to the terrors around them, and apparently heedless of the greater dangers they were soon to face when it should be their turn to be active participants in the pending combat. As the game progressed and the interest increased it was suddenly interrupted by orders that started the command on its way to where the battle was the hottest. The game was resumed from time to time at the frequent halts that occur in the movements of large bodies of troops across narrow bridgeways, and it was not completed until the near approach to the action stiffened every nerve to its highest tension.

Then the custody of the *deck* became a subject for consideration. Every one of the quartet tried to convince every other one that the best possible thing for him to do was to carry it. Unanimously, and finally, it was concluded that, as they were fighting for the existence of a republic, it would not be seemly, should they fall, to have it transpire that they had been taking care of kings and queens. Royalty and knavery were, consequently, allowed to float down towards the sea on the waters of the Rappahannock.

In these peaceful days, and to those unacquainted with army life during an active campaign, this amusement in the face of danger might seem stolid and reckless indifference. Not so. It passed away the wretched time of waiting, every minute of which would otherwise seem an hour, and quieted the nerves which would be thrilling with excitement if the mind had nothing to dwell upon but the possibilities of the pending battle.

About one o'clock the regiment was called to attention and, with the division, began the movement to the bridges.

It was tedious, halting and hesitating. The bridges were crowded and the streets jammed from the slow deployments under the withering fire which met the fresh victims fed to the slaughter, as the troops in advance reached the open country. It was but a short distance to the bluffs and then the battle in all its fury was spread out to view. Upon the slope of Marye's Heights were long lines of blue formed with regularity, moving with precision, disappearing as speedily as they were seen before the furious cannonade and the deadly musketry. Thought was rife and expression free with the selfish hope that some effective service might be done by those already in to save others from the terrible ordeal, revealed in ghastly horror everywhere, into the very jaws of which the regiment was about to plunge. The futility of open assaults was manifest. The disasters which had been plainly seen to follow each other so rapidly were woefully dispiriting. But all such hopes were vain.

About two o'clock the regiment entered the town. It had been reported that $65,000 worth of tobacco, in boxes, had been thrown overboard from the wharf near the pontoons. Some of the men belonging to the regiments already in the town were diving for and bringing up the tobacco, which they sold to their comrades by the box or in job-lots to suit the pocket. A cool transaction in December and under the enemy's fire. Sergeant Conner, of G, invested $25 in these speculative "job lots," and, placing them in his knapsack, essayed to carry his purchase until a fitting opportunity was afforded to realize. But his venture proved unsuccessful, as he abandoned his knapsack when the regiment assaulted the heights beyond the lines.

The view from the other side of the river gave but a faint conception of what was within the town. On every hand were ruin and pillage. The city had been rudely sacked, household furniture lined the streets. Books and battered pictures, bureaus, lounges, feather-beds, clocks and every conceivable article of goods, chattels and apparel had been savagely torn from the houses and lay about in wanton confusion in all directions. Fires were made for both warmth and cooking with fragments of broken furniture. Pianos, their harmonious strings displaced, were utilized as horse-troughs, and, amid all the dangers, animals quietly ate from them. There was a momentary, irresistible desire to seek some shelter from the havoc of the guns in the deserted houses. It was manfully conquered and the men heroically held to their places.

The march was continued under all the dreadful shelling along what was apparently the main thoroughfare, which ran at a right angle to the river, to a street that crossed it parallel with the stream, and on towards the farther edge of the city. Turning into this street there was a halt for some time in line of battle, closed well up to the sidewalk. Upon the side of the street nearest the enemy some protection was afforded from the shower of death-dealing missiles that had poured down so relentlessly from the moment of entering the town; but bricks, window-shutters and shingles, struck by the shells and solid shot, flew around unceasingly. Opposite the centre, in the rear, was a house that had been most roughly handled. It was evidently the residence of some person of culture and refinement. Several solid shots had passed through the upper rooms and a shell, bursting in the library, had made bricks, mortar and books a heap of rubbish. A tastefully bound copy of "Ivanhoe" which had escaped the wreck tempted the literary tastes of an officer, and he picked it up, intending that it should help to while away an hour of loneliness in some quieter time. Light as was the load, he soon became weary of it and his book was abandoned.

The dashing charge over the level plain, the determined advance against breastworks lined with threatening bayonets, the splendid resistance to columns of assault, are tests of courage and endurance of frequent occurrence. It is seldom, however, that the mettle of men is tested in column in the crowded streets, where there can be no resistance, into which, from unseen positions, the artillery strikes its rapid, telling blows, and will not and can not be silenced. Courageous men, well fitted to meet in a conflict, the purpose of which is seen, an adversary behind his own entrenchments, at his own guns, may well quake when submitting unresistingly to continuous punishment in mass, where The march was continued under all the dreadful shelling parently hopeless confusion. So, when the soldiers of the Right and Centre Grand Divisions passed through such a bitter experience of war in the streets of Fredericksburg, and then valiantly assailed the formidable heights beyond, they proved that the Union soldiery possessed a tenacity and courage equal to any standard vaunted in Anglo-Saxon song or story.

There is scarcely any situation which, however serious,

cannot sustain the ludicrous. Never do colored servants, except in rare individual instances, follow when soldiers are exposed to such dangers as the regiment had passed through, and which still surrounded it where it had last halted, near the outskirts. A romping, rollicking little darkey, who had been christened Scipio Africanus, because his qualities were the very opposite of those of that distinguished Roman general, was standing upon a door which had fallen from its hinges and lay upon the pavement, and was grinning and chippering, exposing his pearl-white teeth till they resembled, embedded in his ebony jaws, chalk upon a blackboard. He was in full view of the entire command, who were hugely enjoying his guffaws, wondering whether such unusual hilarity, in such a trying situation, was not assumed. Suddenly a solid shot whizzed wickedly over head, struck the front of a brick house upon the opposite side of the street, glanced, flew up into the air and, returning, struck violently the other end of the door upon which the boy was standing. Up, away up, bounded the darkey, unhurt, but scared apparently beyond the recollection that aught was left of him.

It was a ridiculous sight. Shouts and laughter from the whole line greeted him as he landed some ten or fifteen feet from where he started. He waited for no comments, but, with his face changed almost to a deadly pallor, evidently with no conception that he was yet moving of his own volition, disappeared somewhere to safer quarters, not even catching the quaint remark which followed him as he flew away: "What's de matter wid you, honey? You's been foolin' wid a torpedo, ha?"

The same shot upset a wooden step and platform in front of a house and exposed three small boxes of tobacco that had been hidden underneath. There was a rush by the men to secure the plunder.

During the halt Colonel Gwyn exercised the regiment for some time in the manual of arms, at the conclusion of which it was ordered to load.

The crucial moment was fast approaching. The brigade moved off, passing its brigade commander, who was intently observing the temper and bearing of his soldiers, back into the main highway from which it had been withdrawn for a little rest and less exposure. The head the column must have been seen; the rapidity of the firing increased; the roar was deafening; shot and shell screeched in maddening sounds;

they fell thicker and faster, dropping with wonderful accuracy right into the midst of the column. Every gun seemed trained upon this very street; and so they were, for it was afterwards learned that batteries, specially planted for the purpose, raked every highway leading from the river. Soldiers, some malingerers, some skulkers, often demoralized, stood behind houses at the corners watching the column. Some had been in and had withdrawn discomfited and dejected; others were of the class who generally manage to elude danger. Sullen and silent, their conduct was no incentive and their presence no encouragement to those not of the sterner sort, who had not yet felt the hot blast of the musketry. Two brass guns in action at the end of the street were pounding away vigorously and effectively at the enemy, the gunners holding heroically to their places in spite of the severe punishment they were receiving.

The Confederate shells performed some curious and fanciful gyrations. One in particular fell obliquely, striking in the centre of the hard, solid roadway, then ricocheted, struck a house, flew up the wall, tore off a window-shutter, then crossed over to the other side, striking the house opposite, down again into the street, passed back to the other side over the heads of Company H, and finally fell upon the steps of the house it had first struck and lay there without exploding. This was fortunately the case with much of their ammunition, which appeared to be remarkably faulty.

It is not to be supposed that the column moved upon the highway with the steadiness of a parade occasion. There was hesitancy and some unsteadiness, but no dropping out, no skulking, no concealment.

Avoiding the middle of the street, where it was soon observed the fire was the most direct, and closing to the pavement, the men held their places with reasonable accuracy and moved under the trying circumstances with commendable precision.

As the regiment debouched from the town, upon the edge of the closely built thoroughfare, was a sign, in large black letters; "Van Haugen's Variety Store." It had scarcely come into view when a shell burst and tore it to fragments. The pieces of the shell and sign fell into the ranks of Company K. Their loss was not so serious as that of the 1st Michigan, in the rear, where, at about the same time, another shell burst, killing or maiming some sixteen of its soldiers, whose startled shrieks could be heard above the din and roar of the battle. The column now plunged into and waded through the mill-race. This was done as quickly as possible, for the Confederates had trained a battery on this spot. In the mill-race were noticed very many solid shot and unexploded shells, which had evidently rolled back into the water after striking the side of the embankment. Private John Mensing was carrying his piece at "arms port": a shell struck and shivered it to fragments, but beyond a severe cut on his right hand he was not injured. Another tore off the right arm of Private John Fisher just below the elbow and knocked down four sergeants in one company. They were more or less bruised and hurt, but none of them seriously.

The right of the brigade had now reached an open level space on the left of the road, some four hundred yards in width, as well as observation could estimate it. At its farther edge the ground rose abruptly, as if the earth had been cut away. This perpendicular rise or cut was the extreme base of the slope that approached and terminated in the guncapped Marye's Heights. The artillery played with unintermitting vigor.

The usual rotations brought the regiment on the right of the brigade, on the 13th. It had about covered its front from where the right first struck the open plain, where by the "forward into line" the left was extended into the plain. It was intended that the right should rest on the road. There was some confusion attending the formation, but a line was ultimately established pressed close up to the edge of the abrupt rise, over which and beyond to the top of the hill everything was in full view. Beyond the summit was another elevation, and just below it a stone fence, lined with rebel infantry, whence the musketry rolled unceasingly.

A board fence, with some of the boards displaced, others torn from the top, stood between the abrupt rise and the stone fence, nearer to the latter. It had evidently greatly retarded the previous advances and what was left of it was yet in the road to impede others.

Humphrey's division had just charged up the hill, and, although they had failed to carry the heights, hundreds of men lay prone upon the ground in fair alignment, apparently too spirited to withdraw entirely from their futile effort. It seems scarcely credible, but a closer inspection showed all these men, apparently hundreds in number, to be killed or too seriously wounded to move.

The regiment still hugged the ground closely where it had

first established its line. Instinctively, in taking up a movement indicated by an advance by another portion of the line,
for the terrible roar drowned the voice of command, it began
its desperate work of assault. Under the appalling musketry
and amid great disorder, the advance was maintained with
reasonable regularity to a brick-yard, with its kiln standing,
through which tore shot and shell, and from which bricks
flew in every direction. The little shelter afforded by the kiln
had enticed the wounded within its reach to crawl to it for
cover, and their mangled, bleeding forms lay strewn
everywhere, closely packed together. Sweeping by this, right
into the very mouth of the cannon, upward and onward the
advance continued to the board fence. The fence was about
five feet high, of three boards, with intervals between them.
Opposite the centre and right, the boards had been torn
off down to the one nearest the ground. The fatality that
had followed the delay in their removal was marked by the
bodies of the dead lying there, one upon another. To the
left, the boards still remained; the men heroically seized
and tore them all away, some climbing over. Thinned out,
exhausted, with energies taxed to their limit, in the face of
such fearful odds, instinctively the line halted.

Major Herring here received a ball in his right arm. He
was sitting on his horse at the time. As the ball struck him,
some one said, "This is awful!" "This is what we came here
for," quietly replied the major, as he dismounted. Subsequently, another ball passed through his left arm, and buck-
shot through his coat. At nightfall, his wounds needing
surgical attention, he was forced to go to the hospital for
treatment. He made several efforts to reach the front again,
but his strength failed him. It was feared amputation would
be necessary, but he insisted upon conservative surgery, and
it saved him his arm. The absence of his strong directing
mind at such a critical time was a serious misfortune.

From the place of the halt to the stone fence, behind
which belched the deadly musketry, was between two and
three hundred feet. At that distance, halted with little or no
cover, such punishment was unbearable.

There was still about two hours of daylight. Some two
hundred yards to the left, but no greater distance from the
stone fence, there was decidedly better cover, and to this un-
dulation, broad enough to include the entire regimental
front, the command was moved within a few moments from
the time it had halted. Colonel Barnes, commanding the

brigade, rode the full length of the line before it started, calling to the men to fall in. Although in full view of the Confederates, and the target for their shots, he escaped injury.

It seems remarkable that men could live at all that close to the enemy's lines, but there the regiment remained all that night, all of Sunday's daylight and well into the night, suffering but few casualties, and those happening principally when necessity forced exposure, or temerity prompted rashness. But safety was only found in hugging the ground as tight as a human body could be made to hold on to the earth. Darkness was a relief from the stiff and uncomfortable postures, but during those ten or twenty hours of that winter's daylight, there was no safety except with bodies prone and flattened to their fullest length. A raise of the head, or a single turn not unfrequently proved fatal.

Just as the day was closing a regiment advanced immediately to the rear of where the command lay. It had been ordered to charge the works, and had got thus far on its mission, but had no one to conduct it farther. All its officers had disappeared; its men, hopeless as was their task were even yet anxious to fulfil it. Colonel Gwyn, informed of its situation, and understanding its anxiety to still go forward, valiantly stepped to its front and centre, and gallantly tendered his services to lead it on. Colonel Barnes, comprehending the fruitless purpose of the undertaking, forbade it, and ordered the regiment to retire to some convenient shelter and await the further direction of its brigade commander. This it was not disposed to do, but mingled with the others on the front line, and remained with them until they were withdrawn.

The combat ceased with the night. Its lengthening shadows were gratefully hailed as a relief from the terrors of a day of suffering and death.

In getting to the front, one of Company H's men had been severely wounded, but had managed to crawl up to his company. After nightfall some of his comrades got a stretcher and carried him into the town. Leaving him at one of the improvised hospitals, the men started in search of quarters, intending, for one night at least, to sleep with a roof over their heads. A corner store, with a dwelling above, seemed a suitable place. But doors and windows were fastened. An entrance, by the aid of a couple of bayonets, was soon effected. A newspaper was produced and lighted, dropping pieces of half-burned paper as the party passed through the store into the back room, searching for a candle. One was found in a candlestick, lighted, and a reconnoissance in force was made, to discover what the enemy had left. Returning to the store, the party found, right in the track of the burned paper, an unexploded shell. The precious thing was picked up very carefully, and put tenderly away in a closet. An iron teakettle was found in the house, a well in the yard, and clapboards on the building. These helping, a steaming pot of coffee was made and drunk. Then, alternately mounting guard, the party indulged in a luxurious sleep, with bare boards for feathers, and starting betimes, reached the front again before daylight.

Sunday morning broke bright and clear. Just as the day dawned the men at the front, who had been sleeping as best they could, rose and walked up and down briskly to warm their chilled blood. The whole line seemed to be in motion. Suddenly, without the least warning, the Confederates poured in upon them a heavy volley. Every man promptly dropped to the ground. In one place they were crowded together too closely for comfort. Beyond, a man who, with the cape of his overcoat over his head, was apparently asleep, there was room for two or three.

"Wake him up, and tell him to move along," some one cried. The soldier next to him gave him a shake, and said:

"I can't, he's too fast asleep."

"You must."

The soldier pulled the overcoat cape back, intending to give him a vigorous shake. As he uncovered the head, the colorless side-face, and a triangular hole in the neck told the tale. He was sleeping his last sleep. He must have been struck by a shell the day before, and fallen just where he lay, and some comrade's hand had thrown the cape over his head to hide the ghastly wound.

If there was remembrance of the Christian Sabbath there was no recognition of its religious observances. The city was a charnel-house, its churches and its dwellings hospitals, and its streets rumbling with vehicles and crowded with stretcher-bearers carrying the wounded sufferers.

The cannonading ceased. The cannon, that for three days had thundered so incessantly, had opportunity to cool, and the gunners rested from their unceasing toil. The quiet—there was no noise save from the occasional discharge of a musket—was in striking contrast to the continuous roar that had preceded it.

Fortunately the rigors of winter weather had not yet arrived. Save from the constrained position of their bodies, and the want of water, the men of the regiments in the front line suffered no discomfort and but little loss. There was still sufficient in the haversacks for nourishment, but all looked longingly for the night to come. There was scarcely any firing from the Union side, save where some one more daring than his fellows would rise in his place, discharge his piece, and quickly seek cover again. They frequently suffered for their exposure.

Sergeant Geo. W. Stotsenberg, of Company K, turned the cartridges out of his box into his cap, loaded, knelt upon one knee, waited, and, whenever a head appeared above the stone wall, blazed away at it, and reloaded. He kept his position for more than two hours, and though the bullets sang about his ears and ploughed little furrows in the ground before him, he was not even touched.

Captain Crocker could not long brook this forced restraint. He had suffered greatly from his close confinement. Angered beyond endurance at the foe who kept him thus confined, he threw a taunting menace in their teeth. About noon, saying naught to any one, he rose suddenly from his place, seized the colors, advanced with them a few paces to the front, and jammed the staff well into the ground, shaking his fist angrily and firing a round of epithets in no polite or cultured strain. His greetings were responded to in language equally cultured, accompanied by a volley of balls. His temerity lost him nothing except the emptying of his canteen, which was struck. Lieutenant Kelley, who was close beside him, observed the contents escaping to the ground, and before Crocker was aware of what he was losing, rose to his knees, placed the hole to his lips, and drained whatever remained to the dregs. Kelley got a "ball," if Crocker did not.

Captain Bankson was not to be outdone by this daring feat of Crocker's, and he followed with one of like temerity. He left his place, proceeded to where the colors had been planted, seized them, waved them several times defiantly at the enemy, and then returned. A similar salute of musketry greeted him, but he, too, escaped unharmed.

It has been observed that the human voice was sometimes so drowned by the din of battle that the utterance of commands was useless. Successful obedience only followed close observance and apt attention. Any inattention or failure to comprehend what was likely to be done frequently separated the best of soldiers from their commands. A misunderstanding resulting from this condition of things happened in the regiment at its halt just beyond the board fence. The attention of some was momentarily distracted, more particularly by the casualties that there befell some of the best men. In what appeared but an instant, the regiment had moved by the left flank to a position three hundred yards away, where it remained during the rest of the engagement. Those who had not observed the movement were left where they were. The first conclusion was that the regiment had withdrawn entirely. There was considerable confusion, and the soldiers of one command intermingled with others. Nor was it possible to distinguish organizations, as the men were flattened tight to the earth, with their faces downward. They might recognize any one standing up, especially because few were in such position, but for one who stood to recognize those who were lying, was an impossibility. This impossibility of recognition was a further difficulty in the way of removing the conviction that there had been a formal withdrawal.

In the full assurance that their belief was well founded, those who had been left retired for a better cover to the rear of the brick-kiln. There, rumors from the town that the regiment had been seen in the city confirmed their belief, and they remained awaiting a favorable opportunity to rejoin it. To attempt it just then was an invitation for a volley, and a great personal risk, which, as the regiment was believed not to be engaged, the occasion did not seem to demand.

As the detachment lay behind the kiln, an officer was noticed approaching them, oblivious to all the dangers around him, shot at by volleys, aimed at singly, coolly stopping to examine the faces of the dead he passed, moving with deliberation and ease. He finally safely reached the cover of the kiln wall. It was Lieutenant William Wilson, of Company A. He reported that as the regiment left the city he had become separated from it, and had ever since been employed in a hopeless search for it. He was told of the misfortune which had happened to the detachment, the conviction that the regiment had been withdrawn, and the apparent confirmation by the stories that had come from the town, and he was advised to remain where he was. This did not, however, satisfy him. He said he had met a number of the men, but had not yet seen the field-officers and colors, and as he had pretty faithfully hunted the city, he was determined to prosecute his search further at the front.

In a few moments he left and was again exposed to the same startling dangers. Volleys upon volleys greeted him, but alone, bold and erect, a most inviting target, bent upon his purpose, he continued his errand and disappeared from view still unhurt. It was an exhibition of splendid heroism. By mere accident he reached the position which the regiment occupied, but was unaware of it until he was recognized and hailed by his name.

As has been noticed, when the brick-kiln was passed on the advance, wounded, more than could be covered, were in indiscriminate confusion about it, and since then the number had sensibly increased. If there were any on hand to administer relief the force was wholly inadequate to the occasion. Strangely, large numbers of blocks of ribbon were scattered around. How they came there was inconceivable, nor was there any disposition to inquire. Their usefulness was soon apparent. Generous hands quickly unwound the blocks, and tenderly, it may be awkwardly, applied the ribbon to wounds gaping, exposed and yet untreated, and bandaged hurts, possibly nearing fatality from want of care. But whether life was saved or not, it was a comfort and consolation for kindly hands to minister to those pressing needs.

During the time the detachment was at the brick-kiln another advance appeared, moving up the hillside. One regiment, with its commandant gallantly riding in its front, maintained a most excellent alignment. It preserved its shapely formation until just in rear of the brick-yard, when the commanding officer fell seriously wounded. Three of his soldiers bore him away and his command then seemingly disappeared entirely.

With this advance appeared a battery of twelve-pound Napoleons. It had scarce unlimbered before every horse and rider fell. The men left without firing a shot. The officers remained a moment gesticulating violently, apparently endeavoring to enforce the return of their men, and then they too disappeared and the deserted guns alone remained. No guns could be served at such a point and no gunners could live in such exposure. It seemed madness to have ordered a battery in action there.

The detachment at the brick-kiln gradually drew off to the city and collecting about the outskirts moved after dark to the river-bank, where it bivouacked for the night. After daylight communication with the front was again wholly cut off and it was impossible for them to rejoin their fellows; nor was it necessary, as the fight had subsided to an indifferent sort of a skirmish, with no prospect of an assault by the enemy. The bivouac was consequently maintained until the command was retired from the front line.

Shortly before ten o'clock on Sunday night the regiment was relieved from its perilous and trying post at the extreme front and withdrawn to the bivouac on the river-bank, where the missing detachment was. Here it remained during Monday. A little after noon General Burnside and his staff rode down to the bridge and passed over. There was always a kindly feeling for Burnside, but now his presence stirred no enthusiasm; his appearance aroused no demonstration. It may have been a coincidence that, as he rode by, he drew his hat further down over his face. Unuttered throughts were rife that somebody had seriously blundered. But sadly and silently the men viewed their commander, with the deepest consideration for the anxiety and solicitude which at that moment must have almost overwhelmed him.

At dusk the brigade started for the front again. It took a position on the highway at the farther end of the city, as it was subsequently learned, to cover, with other troops, the withdrawal of the entire army to the other side of the river. Absolute quiet was cautioned and conversation forbidden. That silence might be maintained strictly, the rattling of the tin-cups was prevented by removing them from the belts. It was a weird night. The wind blew a gale, fortunately directly from the enemy, and, with the extreme quiet prevailing in our lines, voice and noise were distinctly audible in theirs. Window-shutters banged and rattled, and shots rang out frequently on the picket-line. An attack was momentarily expected and every one was ready to resist the anticipated assault.

In the rear of the centre of the regiment was J. H. Roy's drug store. Within all was impenetrable darkness, but there came from it continually the sound of breaking glass. All the dangers could not deter the pilfering soldier. Groping about for something desirable, a whole shelf of bottles would fall at once, creating a tremendous rattle, penetrating in the extreme quiet, scattering their contents in every direction. Repeated orders were given to arrest these purloiners, but the seizure of one would speedily be followed by the approach of another in the darkness readily eluding the guard. His presence would soon be known by another smashing of glassware. An officer, annoyed beyond restraint, rushed in himself and seized a marauder with a bottle in his hand. Violently shaking himself loose and escaping, the man left a bottle in the officer's hand which, on bringing to the street, he discovered to be labelled "Ayer's Cherry Pectoral." This he put in his pocket, but, soon forgetting it, resumed his place on the cellar-door, where he had been previously resting, and shivered the bottle to fragments. The contents, of a sticky consistency, soaked his clothing.

About four o'clock in the morning there was a sudden call to attention and a rapid movement to the lower end of the town. The officer who brought the order to retire indicated the wrong direction. Pretty much everything had been withdrawn and all movements required alacrity, but, reaching the river at the point where the officer conveying the order directed, the bridge, which had been there was found to have been removed. The brigade was the last to cross; daylight was close at hand and the mistake threatened disaster. The column was counter-marched with amazing rapidity and headed for the centre bridge. It, too, was in course of removal, but the engineers hurriedly replaced the planks and, in the midst of a drenching rain, which then began to fall, the column crossed to the other side. Day was just breaking when the movement was completed.

Fredericksburg was fought and lost. The Army of the Potomac, battered about and abused, had become indifferent to results. A victory, where the enemy was pursued, routed or brought to terms, had never been theirs to achieve. After a battle it therefore accepted a withdrawal or advance with equal complacency, maintaining the consciousness that it had done all men could do to accomplish a designated purpose. But always before it had administered punishment commensurate with what it had received. There was a conviction, at least with the troops thrown against the works on Marye's Heights, that such was not the result at Fredericksburg. It was too apparent, even to the obtuse observer, that the heavy sufferers on that fatal hillside were the soldiers who assaulted, and not the soldiers who defended. It was too plain that for the multitude of dead and wounded who covered its slope no corresponding number of disabled soldiery lay behind the powerful entrenchments.

There is no need of any comments, only such as suggest

themselves to any soldier. Burnside is dead. We all admired his frank and manly character. His assumption of all blame for the defeat is worthy of him. But it will not atone for the slaughter of so many brave men.

After this battle there remained in the army little confidence in his capacity for this command. He has since been reported as saying: "No one will ever know how near I came to achieving a great success," and to this we will add, *"No one ever will."*

The loss of the Federal army was 1,180 killed, 9,028 wounded, and 2,145 missing, and on the part of the Confederates it was 5,309 killed, wounded and missing.

HOOKER MAKES HIS MOVE

BURNSIDE'S TROOPS HAD TAKEN A SEVERE BEATING at Fredericksburg, but Burnside stubbornly refused to admit it. He ordered a new attack on Lee's position. Aghast, his generals finally convinced him of his folly. The Army of the Potomac retreated across the Rappahannock, having suffered more than 12,000 casualties—more than twice the Confederate loss.

The weather continued to be unusually mild, and the Virginia roads were dry and acceptable for marching. Burnside, hoping to redeem himself, decided to risk a sudden change to bad weather and ordered the army to make another crossing of the Rappahannock. The troops moved out of camp on January 20, and as they began their march, the skies clouded over and then rain began to fall. The army bogged down in the mud and cold, but Burnside insisted that the troops push on to the river.

Once there, the exhausted men could look across the river and see the Confederates leaning on their rifles, waiting for them to attempt the crossing. The attack was doomed before it could begin; this time, Burnside wisely ordered a return to camp. Winter had set in with a vengeance, and almost as many troops were lost through exhaustion, exposure, and sickness as if they had fought. This second debacle brought Burnside's relief, and the command was given to General "Fighting Joe" Hooker.

By the time spring arrived, Hooker had injected new life in the troops and they were ready to do battle again. Reinforcements swelled the army to 134,000, more than double the size of Lee's army across the river. "The position of the Confederates on the other side of the Rappahannock had not changed since the battle of Fredericksburg. As then, they occupied at the end of April the line of fortified heights extending from Skenker's Creek to the point where they touched the river above Falmouth. On this side, however, they had extended their lines by covering, with fortifications occupied with troops, the only two feasible crossings between Falmouth and the point where the Rapidan empties into the Rappahannock: Banks and United States fords. And these two fords were passable only in the summer. Everywhere else the steep and wooded banks of the two rivers presented a barrier which could not be passed. It was a stretch of twenty to twenty-five miles to defend. The rebel army did not number more than sixty thousand in front of Hooker, when, on April 27, the latter began his movement on Chancellorsville.

"Chancellorsville is not a village, or even a hamlet. It is a solitary house in the midst of a cultivated clearing, surrounded on all sides by woods, which have given that region the name of *Wilderness*. A veritable solitude, impenetrable for the deploying or quick manœuvring of an army. So that it was not there that Hooker had planned to give battle. But it was a well chosen point for concentrating his forces, three or four miles southeast of United States Ford. From that point he could strike the enemy, taken in reverse, or, at least, force him to come out of his position, as weak from the rear as it was strong from the front. If the Confederate army fell back on Richmond, it presented its flank to our attack, and, if he were stopped or delayed by some obstacle and pursued at the same time by a force strong enough to vigorously press his rearguard, his retreat might be changed to a rout. If, on the contrary, he marched towards Chancellorsville to meet us, he was forced to accept battle in the open field, in unforeseen conditions, exposed to attack by a pursuing army as much as on the Richmond road. Attacked at the same time both in front and rear, Lee ran the chance of being cut in pieces, and would be very fortunate if he saved the remnant of his forces.

"Such was Hooker's well concerted plan, the secret of which was confided to no one, not even to his most intimate friends amongst the officers.

"The point on which everything depended for success was to be able to assemble the army at Chancellorsville before the enemy could oppose him at that point. This part of the plan was as admirably executed as it had been ably conceived, and it can be truly said that up to that point General Hooker showed himself to be an able tactician.

"In the first place, he detached all his cavalry, under the orders of General Stoneman, to cut the enemy's lines of communication with Richmond. The undertaking was not very dangerous, for Stoneman took with him more than ten thousand horse, who could meet with no serious resistance. Under his instructions, after crossing the Rappahannock, he was to divide his force into two columns: one, under command of General Averill, was to threaten the force the enemy might have at Culpeper and Gordonsville, while the other, led by Stoneman himself, would attempt to accomplish the main object of the expedition. Both columns were to come together at a given point, to attack the enemy in case he retreated directly towards Richmond, and to harass him if he took the road to Gordonsville.

"At the same time that the cavalry started, the Eleventh and Twelfth Corps (Howard and Slocum) marched for Kelly's Ford, above the mouth of the Rapidan and twenty-seven miles distant from Fredericksburg. There, on the 28th, they were met by Meade's corps (the Fifth), which was to join them. The passage of the Rappahannock was made that night without opposition. On the 29th, that of the Rapidan was effected happily, in two columns, and, the movement continuing with a promptness of good augury, the three corps arrived at Chancellorsville on the afternoon of the 30th. Their advance opened United States Ford, behind which the Second Corps (Couch) was waiting, in order to throw across a pontoon bridge and join the other corps, which was done before night. Hooker himself arrived at the appointed rendezvous, to finish up the work he had so brilliantly commenced.

"While these important movements were being accomplished on one side, the attention of the enemy was concentrated in the opposite direction, towards what seemed to him to be a prelude to an attack in force. In fact, on the 29th, at daybreak, while our right, having already crossed the Rappahannock, was advancing towards the Rapidan, a bridge of boats was established by force at the same point where, on the 13th of December preceding, Franklin had passed the river, and the Sixth Corps (Sedgwick) after having driven back the enemy's sharpshooters, advanced into the plain below Fredericksburg. A little further down, the First Corps (Reynolds) did the same thing, and finally, the Third Corps (Sickles) took position in reserve, ready to cross over in its turn if necessary. This was the force designed to hold the enemy in his intrenchments by the menace of an immediate attack, or to pursue him, if, discovering the danger which threatened him, he should abandon his position.

"During that day the demonstration succeeded to our best wishes. The enemy appeared only to prepare his defence on the side where it was not intended to attack him.

"The next day, the 30th, the Confederates not stirring, Hooker called the Third Corps to Chancellorsville. We started immediately, making a forced march in order to arrive in time for the decisive attack. That night we made our fires at a short distance from the bridge across which the Second Corps had marched in the morning.

"So there, on the 30th, at night, the Confederates, still motionless in their positions in rear of Fredericksburg, prepared for an attack on their right, indicated by the movements of the two corps of Sedgwick and Reynolds, while in rear of their left four other corps were already united, and about to be joined by a fifth. On one side, Sedgwick, with forty thousand men, including Gibbon's division of the Second Corps, which, having its camp in full view of the enemy, had not yet moved; on the other, Hooker, with about seventy thousand men in a position which seemed an assurance, in advance, of a victory. 'Now,' said he, in an order of the day to the army, 'the enemy must flee shamefully or come out of his defences to accept a battle on our ground, where he is doomed to certain destruction!' And every one repeated, 'He is in our power!' Nobody doubted that, before two days, all our past reverses would be effaced by the annihilation of Lee's army."*

Chancellorsville*

BY COLONEL REGIS de TROBRIAND

What hooker called "our ground" to give battle on was about half-way from Chancellorsville to Fredericksburg, outside of that region covered with almost impenetrable woods, where we were at that time. On that side the country was open and favorable for the manœuvering of an army. It

* From Regis de Trobriand, *Four Years with the Potomac Army.*
* *Ibid.*

was then important to get there at the earliest possible moment. Two broad roads led to it, coming together near a church called Tabernacle, while a third road, running near the river, led to Banks Ford. By these three roads, Hooker renewed his movement in advance, on Friday morning, May 1. Slocum, with the twelfth Corps, held the right by the plank road; Sykes, with a division of the Fifth Corps, supported by Hancock's division of the Second Corps, advanced in the centre, along the principal road, called the Macadamized road (although it was not); and Meade led the column composed of Humphreys' and Griffin's divisions along the road near the river. The three other corps, the Second, the Third, and the Eleventh, were to follow the movement, so as to come into line of battle outside of the forest, at two o'clock in the afternoon.

But before Hooker had left Chancellorsville Lee had started to meet him. Informed, the evening before, of the true state of affairs, he had collected his forces in all haste, and leaving behind him only Early's division reënforced by one brigade, he had hurried forward all the rest at midnight, in the direction of Chancellorsville. Between ten and eleven o'clock in the morning, his advance guard encountered our cavalry skirmishers, and forced them back. But behind them Sykes had already deployed his division. He charged the enemy resolutely, drove them back in his turn, and established himself in the position which had been assigned to him by his instructions.

Everything went well with us. On the right, Slocum had encountered no opposition; on the left, Meade had arrived in full view of Banks Ford, without the least obstacle. He had only to form promptly in order of battle. The corps in the rear would have had time to get into line while the enemy made his disposition on his side, on the ground where General Hooker had "devoted him to certain destruction."

Well, as if Heaven wished to take up that arrogant defiance to adverse fortune, it was at this time and at this very place that General Hooker virtually lost the battle of Chancellorsville by an error as unexpected as inexplicable.

Instead of supporting Sykes' division strongly, and pushing his forces forward, he hurriedly sent the order to the three columns to return to the positions they had occupied the night before. Amongst the general who were in position to judge for themselves, I know not one who considered the measure otherwise than deplorable. Couch, before withdrawing Hancock's division, sent to pray the general-in-chief to countermand the order; Warren, who commanded the corps of topographical engineers, and who was in the advance, hurried himself to headquarters with the same errand. Nothing availed. The decision was maintained. The columns fell back uneasy, astonished above all that the first order given by Hooker as general in command in front of the enemy was to retreat without fighting. That did not at all resemble Hooker commanding a division.

The position which we voluntarily abandoned to the enemy was excellent; the position which we took in place of it was detestable. In the first, we could deploy and fight, well connected together on a crest of ground running in the direction of our lines; in the second, we were as if penned up in the midst of natural obstacles, on low and flat ground, which neutralized any advantage in numbers by the difficulty of movement. In the first, we barred to the enemy the only three routes by which he could penetrate into the Wildnerness; in the second position, we gave up to him the plank road, and it will soon be seen what use he made of it against us. Finally, in the first case we preserved all the material and moral advantage of the offensive; in the second, we subjected ourselves to all the disadvantage of a defensive accepted without necessity, as it was without preparation.

The enemy took possession immediately of the position which we so benevolently abandoned to him. He planted his guns there, and followed our retreating troops closely. The afternoon was passed on his side in feeling of our lines at several points by direct demonstrations; on our side, by protecting ourselves by abatis, by regulating the position of the different corps, and awaiting events.

Towards four o'clock, the Third Corps, which had remained in reserve between Chancellorsville and the river, received orders to advance. In the woods, on the right and left we passed a great number of troops, massed without apparent order and filling all the small clearings. Soon we came out on the Fredericksburg road, in front of which stretched our line of battle. Berry's division, which had preceded ours, deployed in the open ground around the farm. As we turned to the right, to take position further on, the skirmishing fire told us that the enemy extended along our front, on the other side of some great woods, which concealed his movements from us. He had his batteries already in position on that side, for the shells and balls reached the troops while they were deploying. One struck a colonel of the Excelsior Brigade. We saw him fall from his horse, without letting go his bridle rein, although he was dead. His men hastened to him and carried off his body.

To discover the enemy's movements, five or six daring men had climbed to the top of the highest trees, from which they had a view over the surrounding woods. The position was very dangerous, for they might become targets for the rebel sharpshooters. In order to guard against it as much as possible, they kept up a continual shaking of the trees in which they were; they could be seen thus balancing in the air more than a hundred feet above the ground, braving the double danger of the enemy's bullets and a fall—death in either event.

Firing ceased a little after dark. The moon rose calm and smiling, and nothing troubled the tranquility of the night.

The next morning, May 2, an order was sent to the First Corp, to join us. Sedgwick then remained alone below Fredericksburg with the Sixth Corps and Gibbon's division of the Second; twenty-six to twenty-seven thousand men in all.

At Chancellorsville our line was disposed in the following order: On the left, the Fifth Corps and Hancock's division extended from the vicinity of the river to the turnpike, facing towards Fredericksburg; in the centre, the Twelfth Corps, forming an obtuse angle with the left, and covering the road in front and parallel to which it stretched; then, in the same direction, Birney's division of the Third Corps; finally, the Eleventh Corps on the right. Two divisions of the Third Corps (Barry and Whipple) and one division of the Second Corps (French) were held in reserve.

In the morning, the enemy contenting himself with attacking Hancock's pickets, without approaching his line, Hooker began to be troubled about what was passing in our front, beyond the curtain of woods, which limited our view in that direction. He sent forward the troops of the twelfth Corps, who, being received by a deadly fire, could not force their way, and were compelled to fall back, leaving the general commanding in the same uncertainty as before. But almost immediately, through an opening in the woods before the Twelfth Corps, there appeared a column of rebels marching rapidly from the left to the right, and which consequently presented its flank to our whole line of battle.

This movement threatened our right, which appeared to be unprepared for it. As it was the opposite side from that by which the enemy had advanced from Fredericksburg, less disposition was made against an attack there than elsewhere. The whole Eleventh Corps prolonged the general line parallel to the road. But a small brigade thrown back barred this road with two guns, resting on nothing, leaving our extreme right completely in the air.

General Hooker had visited that part of the line in good season, without prescribing any change. Only, when the movement of the enemy revealed to him the possibility of an attack from that direction, he sent some additional instructions to General Howard, which had no other effect than to cause an advance of the pickets. There was no change made in the disposition of the troops. The fact is that General Hooker did not believe in the danger of such an attack, and that he preferred to regard the movement as a retreat of the army of Lee on Gordonsville. Otherwise he would not have telegraphed a few hours later to General Sedgwick: "Take Fredericksburg and everything you find there and pursue the enemy vigorously. *We know that he is in full retreat,* endeavoring to save his trains. Two of Sickles' division are upon him."

General Slocum was far from sharing that confidence. Towards noon I met him visiting our front to see how we were placed, and examining attentively the position of the Eleventh Corps.

"Let me recommend you to fortify yourself as well as possible," he said to me. "The enemy is massing a considerable force on our right. In two or three hours he will fall on Howard, and you will have him upon you in strong force. You had better protect yourself as well as possible, at least by an abatis on your front."

I was about to follow his advice when the division received orders to advance. We moved forward out of the woods, and crossed the open ground which extended in our front. It was an effort to cut in two the column of the enemy, which continued to defile before us, and to sweep away what must be his rearguard.

Our advance was delayed in the woods. We had to build or rebuild some bridges over some brooks. We had to cut our way painfully through the thick underbrush, a network of branches and briars. But these detentions afforded the Second Division time to support us. Finally, by main force, our first regiments reached the crossroads on which the rear of the enemy's column was marching. A brisk fire was opened immediately; our men charged upon the enemy surprised at seeing an attack made upon them from a thicket which they thought absolutely impenetrable. They fell into confusion. Some fled, others surrendered; the Twenty-seventh Georgia resisted stoutly; but it was soon surrounded and compelled to lay down its arms. More than five hundred prisoners remained in our hands, and were immediately sent to the rear.

We had in this way, continually on the run, reached some abandoned furnaces. Birney had just formed the division in a square across the road by which the enemy had disappeared, and he waited the arrival of the Second Division, reënforced by two brigades, one from the Eleventh and one from the Twelfth Corps. The men took breath, laid off their knapsacks, and reloaded their pieces. The officers laughed and conversed together, relating the different episodes of the combat.

Suddenly the noise of a distant firing came through the air. Our ranks became silent, as if by magic. Each one listened, and turned his head towards Chancellorsville. There is no more doubt; there is where the fight will be made. The musketry fire increases and rolls uninterruptedly. Soon the roar of cannon breaks out like a clap of thunder, at first by a volley of batteries, then by shots hurried, furious, as in combat *à outrance*.

In a moment the aids passed at a gallop along the front of our regiments. The command rang out, from one end of the division to the other. *Forward!* Double quick! March! And we were soon swiftly returning on the run by the road over which we had just come. Hurry up! Jackson has crushed our right; the Eleventh Corps is in an utter rout. Hurry up! Quick! or we will be cut off!

Harassed and out of breath, yet in good order, we finally reached the edge of the open ground that we had first crossed on leaving our lines. Our artillery was still there, but turned against the same woods we had occupied a few hours before. Firing had ceased. Jackson's troops filled the intrenchments which the Eleventh Corps had raised, and the rebel flag floated behind the abatis which, in the morning, had protected the front of our division. Evening had come. We silently formed in line of battle near the artillery, and awaited the fate which the night had in store for us.

We then heard a detailed account of what had happened in our absence.

General Lee, having found our lines too strong to be carried on our left or centre, had agreed to Stonewall Jackson's proposition to lead an attack on our extreme right. The movement was not without risk, for, in order to do it, it was necessary to march on one single road, at a short distance from our front, a long column of twenty-five thousand men, and to divide in two parts an army which, altogether, was yet inferior in number to ours. But the position taken since the evening by General Hooker was so absolutely defensive, the difficulty of moving so as to get out of it so manifest, that the general commanding the enemy thought that a few demonstrations would suffice to keep him on the defensive. Jackson commenced his movement early in the morning, and although the head of his column had been noticed between nine and ten o'clock, he continued to march with impunity along our front the greater part of the day. When, at last, in the afternoon, our division was sent to cut him in two, we were only able to reach his rearguard, which merely hastened his march.

Jackson, having gone beyond the point where our lines extended, turned to the right, by a road which led into the turnpike, near an inn known as Old Wilderness Tavern, and massed his forces there for one of those terrible attacks which have rendered his name celebrated in this war. This movement was made known to General Devens, who commanded the last division in that direction, and to General Howard, his corps commander, by two soldiers sent out to reconnoitre. Several times a brisk fire was opened upon the line of pickets of the Eleventh Corps, showing the presence of the enemy's skirmishers. Yet, notwithstanding all that, no new measure was taken, and the small brigade across the road remained alone, with two regiments in reserve, to meet an attack against our right, already turned.

About five o'clock, the picket firing was suddenly renewed, then redoubled, and came nearer. Soon the men appeared falling back hurriedly on both sides of the road. A moment more, and the enemy, emerging from the woods in deep masses, with the rebel yell, threw himself upon the few regiments which were opposing him. The latter endeavored to resist, but they were quickly swept away and beaten down. The remainder of the division, taken in flank, melted away, was broken, and rolled upon the next division, which it carried with it; while along the road, in the midst of the fleeing multitude, the wagons, the ambulances, horses and mules, which had been imprudently left in that part of the field, were precipitated pell-mell. In vain, a few superior officers endeavored to stop the flight. In order to meet the attack it was necessary to change front to the rear, and, during this movement, their ranks were broken and carried along with the torrent. It was not an engagement, it was a rout, in the midst of which a few regiments, keeping their order, endeavored to hold together. Two brigade commanders, Schimmelpfennig of Schultz's division, and Bushbeck of Steinwehr's division, succeeded in effecting their change of front, and fought until, overwhelmed and carried away by numbers, they were compelled to fall back on the Twelfth Corps. All the rest went on in the greatest confusion towards Chancellorsville and the road to the Rappahannock.

In the midst of the rout and tumult, Hooker hurried up. Very fortunately, he found at hand, back of the road on which the enemy was sweeping everything before him, Berry's division, the one which he had so long commanded. "Forward!" he cried, "with the bayonet!" The division, supported by Hay's brigade of the Second Corps, advanced, with a firm and steady step, cleaving the multitude of disbanded men as the bow of a vessel cleaves the waves of the sea. It struck the advance of the Confederates obliquely, and stopped it with the aid of the Twelfth Corps artillery.

Jackson's attack, arrested on the left and in front, was thrown towards the right, that is to say, into the woods between the road and the intrenchments abandoned by the Eleventh Corps. It was drawing near the position that Birney had occupied in the morning, and thus a new, terrible, and imminent danger presented itself to us. In the open ground, and in front of the woods, and two or three hundred yards from the intrenchment, the division had left its artillery without protection, while advancing towards the furnaces. The guns were there on low ground, in full view, under the guard of the cannoneers only. Multitudes of flying men had taken this direction, to escape more quickly, and wagons, ambulances, and pieces of artillery rolled at a gallop across the field, in the hope of finding, further on, an opportunity to get back into our lines. The moment was most critical. Who should save the guns from almost certain capture?

At this instant, General Pleasonton, who had accompanied us in our forward movement, returned with two regiments of cavalry, which he had found it impossible to use to advantage in the midst of the thickets. While marching, one of his aids, who had gone on in advance, came back in haste to announce that the Eleventh Corps was fleeing in disorder, and that cavalry was necessary to stop it. Pleasonton put his columns at a gallop, and, on arriving, recognized at a glance the imminence of the peril. Then, consulting only his inspiration in the responsibility he was about to take, he assumed the direct command of the artillery at that point.

To put it in position, he must have at least ten or twelve minutes, minutes more than precious in such a case. He called Major Keenan of the Eighth Pennsylvania, and said to him: "Major, charge into the woods with your regiment and hold the rebels in check until I can get these pieces into position. It must be done at all hazards."

"General, I will do it," simply replied Major Keenan.

It was nearly certain death. He knew it; but the honor of the duty assigned, and the importance of the service to be done, lighted up his features with a noble smile. He had but four or five hundred men. Riding at their head, he charged furiously at the enemy, advancing victoriously, and fell lifeless on the line whose advance he seemed to still bar with his dead body. This intrepid charge caused the attack to hesitate for a short time, and Pleasonton gained the ten minutes which he required.

All he had to do more was to clear the ground of stragglers and vehicles, and to put in position, near the two batteries of the division, the one he had brought with him, and a few pieces of the eleventh Corps, which had retired in that direction. When remains of the Eighth Pennsylvania cavalry had fallen back to the right and left, Pleasonton had twenty-two guns in line, loaded with double charges of canister, and ready to open fire. In the rear, the Seventeenth Pennsylvania, half concealed by a roll of the ground, awaited the moment to charge in its turn, in case of necessity.

Soon the wood was full of rebels. A moment later, their flags appeared behind the intrenchment; a volley of musketry lighted up the top of the works, and a mass of men bounded over with a fierce yell. Now was the time. Twenty-two pieces made but one detonation, followed by a deep silence. When the smoke rose, everything had disappeared. The mass of men had been swept away at a stroke, and, as it were, annihilated.

This lightning stroke marked the limit of Stonewall Jack-

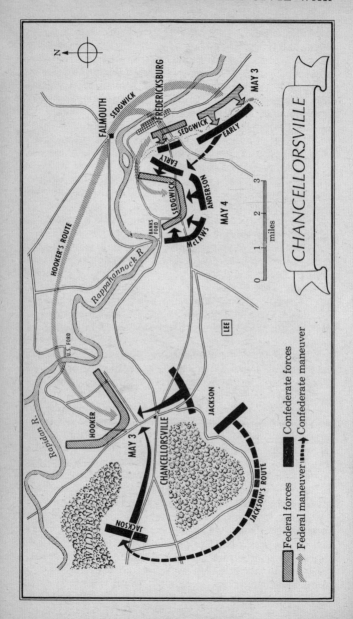

CHANCELLORSVILLE

Federal forces
Confederate forces
Federal maneuver
Confederate maneuver

son's success. The firing still continued behind the cover of the intrenchments, and some attempts were even made to renew the charge against the guns; but the crushing power of their fire, and, probably, also the uncertainty as to what might be concealed by the swell of the ground where were the cavalry and the teams, prevented the enemy from advancing out of the woods. Sickles soon arrived, followed by Whipple's division. Birney's division came back in its turn, and the contest ceased on both sides.

All was not over, however, for the day. It was to be closed by the fifth act of the drama, in which Birney's division was to play the principal role.

It was ten o'clock at night. The moon, high in the heavens, gave but an uncertain light through the vapors floating in the atmosphere. No fire was lighted in the woods or on the plain. Federals and Confederates concealed in the shadows the secret of their respective positions.

The brigade commanders were called to General Birney to receive their instructions. When Ward returned, the colonels assembled around him. We learned that a night attack had been determined on. The plan was to charge into the woods with the bayonet, striking down the enemy where we found him, and, marching right before us, to join Berry's division on the turnpike. The troops were disposed as follows: Ward's brigade deployed in the first line without intervals between the regiments; Graham and Hayman's brigades in the second line, breaking by the right of companies in advance. It was expressly forbidden to reload the muskets after the first fire.

The colonels communicated their orders in a low voice to their company officers, the latter to the sergeants, and on to the soldiers. The preliminary dispositions were made without noise. The higher officers were on foot behind the file-closers. When everything was ready and nothing was stirring along the line, the signal was awaited in a silence so profound that one could have heard the flight of a nighthawk. The moon looked on with its usual serenity.

After a few minutes of waiting which appeared long a movement ran along the line. General Ward had, in a steady and measured tone, ordered, *Forward!* which was repeated in low murmurs from one to another. We started at a quick step, gun on shoulder, neither hurried nor loitering.

There were perhaps two hundred yards to pass over before reaching the woods, whose dark line appeared in front of us. All eyes vainly sought to penetrate the silent obscurity. Every one instinctively hurried his step, and we could soon distinguish the outline of the intrenchments sketched out by us in the morning. Each one said to himself: "They are there, taking aim, with the finger on the trigger. They are letting us come near, to be the more sure of their fire. At twenty paces they will fire their volley. But those of us not struck down will be upon them before they can reload their guns, and then—"

The nearer we approached, the lower dropped the point of the bayonets of the front rank.

At a distance of twenty steps there was no sign of movement. Well, it was said, the contest will be at bayonets' point; so much the better.

In such moments one has an excessive delicacy of hearing. A cracking of branches and a footstep on the dead leaves were heard on our right. It was the Ninety-ninth Pennsylvania, which was advancing into the woods without encountering any one. In an instant, we were there in our turn. The enemy—I do not know why, even now—had neglected to occupy the border of the woods. He was farther back, in a line of intrenchments more complete and on higher ground. Perhaps, also, we surprised him in the midst of some movement preparatory for the next day's battle. However that might have been, profiting by the fortunate accident, without seeking the cause, we continued to advance through the thicket, but not in as good order.

We had moved forward about fifty yards, and my regiment was crossing a rough and muddy ravine, when a voice cried out, "Halt! who goes there?" Nearly at the same time one shot, then ten, twenty, a hundred; the word *Forward!* was heard on all sides; a loud hurrah responded, and the bloody contest commenced.

The ground on which we found ourselves was not only very wooded, but also very rough. There were unequal little hillocks and small winding ravines, at the bottom of which crept or stagnated the water from springs or from rainfall. The trees grew very irregularly, scattered, here high, there brushy, and covered with thorns. The line of the brigade was broken in an instant: the regiments obliqued to the right or the left, led astray by the slope of the ground. The companies were mingled together while crossing the obstacles; the left of the Ninety-ninth Pennsylvania was thrown over into my right. The Third Maine, on the other hand, was separated from my left. My regiment itself was divided into two parts. We ran to one side to reëstablish order, and on the other the companies dashed forward on the run. Some carried the intrenchments before them without firing a shot; others recoiled before a deadly fire. The defence was as confused as the attack. Terrible at some points, at others it was a mere nothing. But, instead of ceasing, the fire redoubled on our side. In spite of orders, the men reloaded their pieces, some while marching, others posted behind trees.

The second line, entering in its turn into the woods, carried away by the noise of the firing, began to fire also. A hundred voices were immediately raised above the noise of the tumult: "Stop firing there below! You are firing on us!" A few men fell, struck from the rear. Then all dashed forward, pellmell, as they were able. The enemy, broken already at several points, did not await the shock. They disappeared, running, leaving not a man in the intrenchments.

The confusion was extreme. I had around me about a hundred men of the Thirty-eighth, mingled with others of different regiments. They were brave men. They marched with mine, without thinking of profiting by the opportunity to slip away. For the rest, I did not trouble myself about the companies out of my sight. I knew they were well commanded, and all inflamed with honorable rivalry between those of the right, belonging to the old Thirty-eighth, and those of the left, belonging to the old Fifty-fifth. I had but one thing to fear, which was that the desire of each to surpass the others might carry them too far.

However, the repeated hurrahs showed clearly that the Third Maine had advanced farther than we had. We hurried forward to rejoin them, the more eagerly inasmuch as four of my companies would be with it. The ranks being reformed as well as possible, we again took up our march, crossing obliquely a second hollow. We had scarcely commenced to ascend the opposite slope, when, at a distance of fifty yards, the crest burst into a flame like a volcano, and sent us a hail of bullets. Happily for us, the enemy, deceived by the darkness, had fired too soon. The avalanche of lead passed, whistling, over our heads. Hardly a man was hit. We fell back towards the left, to turn the position, following the curve of the ravine, and there we found a fire by file from the same quarter where the Third Maine must have passed. Where was the enemy? Where were our men? We could not tell anything about it. In this obscure labyrinth of ravines and hillocks, of dwarfed thickets and giant trees, we had lost our direction.

How could we find it again? We were fired on from all sides; from the front, from the right, from the left, and even from the rear, where the fragments of the second line, scattered like ours, marched at hazard, and fired in the same manner. The moon was hidden; we could not see ten steps. Around me, men fell or disappeared. The part of the wood where we were had become the focus to which all the firing converged. The bullets struck the trees all around us; shells crossed their sparks from all directions, and filled the air with the noise and flash of their bursting. The groans of the wounded, the orders of the officers, the oaths of the soldiers, the whistling of the balls, the roaring of the conical projectiles, the crackling of the branches, the rolling of the fusillade, the thunder of the artillery—everything united in a concert infernal.

I was there joined by Colonel Pierson, of the First New York. He belonged to the second line, and had hardly twenty men with him. He endeavored to lead forward those who were giving way. Half a dozen of the latter had taken refuge behind an epaulement, where they were cowering. We tried to make them march; but it was of no use, and I had no time to lose.

With a handful of men, who still followed me, I turned my steps towards a point where the firing seemed to have ceased. All at once, I felt the ground moving under my feet, and cries issuing from it. It was a square hole, from which the dirt had been taken out, without doubt, for the intrenchments. Five or six poltroons had lain down there flat on the ground, literally packed like sardines in a box. We passed over them, and continued our advance.

In the midst of a clearing, there was growing a great tree. Around its trunk five men were crowded, thinking they were protected from the fire. There were two on one side, and three on the other. The precaution was of little use, where the balls came from all quarters.

A few steps further on I met an officer, going in the opposite direction. He was alone, and appeared to be looking for his company.

"Have you seen any men of the Thirty-eighth?" I asked him.

"I do not know; I saw some troops in that direction; but they belonged to the Twelfth Corps, and we were fired upon.

A nice mess!" grumbled he. "The devil himself would not know where he was."

Nevertheless, the information was useful to me. It served to set me right. Knowing the position occupied by General Slocum, I turned immediately to the left. I walked as fast as possible, putting aside the small branches with the point of my sabre. I thought I recognized a path which must lead to the turnpike. I immediately took it, hoping to find my lost companies there.

Passing around a thick bush, a man ran against me. He wore a light blue jacket (color of the uniform of the old Fifty-fifth), trimmed with black on the sleeves. The man recognized me immediately.

"Don't go that way, colonel," said he to me. "The rebels are in force a few steps away. They hold the line of the road by which we advanced out of the woods this morning, and are picking up all who pass. They have taken a good many prisoners from us, and I came near being gobbled up myself. A wounded man warned me in time, and told me that General Ward had been taken, with two or three officers of his staff."

While listening to him I had turned about to retrace my steps. I saw that I was alone with my informant. The last men who had followed me had taken a different direction.

It appeared quite improbable to me that General Ward had been taken prisoner at the extreme left of his brigade, in the very direction where, as he well knew, the greater part of the force of the enemy was. But, if the report were true, the command devolved upon me, and, without believing it, I resolved to find out about it. The melee had finished, evidently to our advantage. The two lines of rifle-pits taken from the enemy were vacant. To the continual fusillade had succeeded the occasional shot, and the shells burst only at intervals. Soldiers were going back and forth looking for their regiments, or helping the wounded. The dead were lying alongside of the living.

On returning towards the edge of the woods, I recognized my lieutenant-colonel walking behind me.

"Colonel Allason," I said to him, immediately, "where are our men?"

"All around, colonel; at least, I suppose so. The companies of the right have just gone out of the woods, where the Fourth Maine occupies a part of the intrenchments taken from the enemy. Two or three other regiments have the same orders that we have, to reform near the guns. But five companies are lacking, of whom I have no news since the commencement of the action. Were you with them?"

"No," I told him. "They took the lead from the beginning, and must have reached the main road where Berry's division is."

On the open ground we found, in fact, one half of the regiment, around which rallied, from time to time, the men strayed away during the contest. General Ward was near there, inquiet about two officers of his staff who were missing. We did not know whether they were dead or prisoners. The latter supposition was the true one. This was, without doubt, what had given rise to the report I had heard.

By inquiring of every one, and sending out in search of them, I finally found out what had become of my missing companies.

Three of them, belonging to the old Fifty-fifth, finding the ground easier than elsewhere, had advanced under the command of Captains Williams and Demasure and Lieutenant Suraud. But they had not advanced faster than the company of the Thirty-eighth, commanded by Captain Brady. They charged the intrenchments together, overcame the force they found there, and, after a moment's halt, saw a short distance away the flashing of the fire from a battery of artillery. The idea of carrying the battery came to them immediately, and, with one accord, they took that direction. We must believe that, in the tumult, the cannoneers did not hear them approach, or that, if they were seen, the direction from which they came caused the gunners to hesitate. However that may be they advanced right up to the mouths of the guns.

One of the first to leap into the battery was a great German, nearly six feet high, named Johann. He wore in the front of his cap a red lozenge, the distinguishing mark of the First Division, Third Corps.

"Hello! who are you?" cried one of the cannoneers.

"Thirty-eighth New York," cried Johann, brandishing his bayonet.

"Hold on! don't fire!" cried a score of voices at once. "This is the Twelfth Corps, General Slocum."

And my men, completely mystified, recognized General Slocum himself, in the midst of the artillerymen, revolver in hand, ready to be slain at his pieces rather than not defend them at all risks. The general complimented the officers on the vigor with which they had led the charge, and the four companies were put in line to defend the artillery they had so nearly attacked.

The last company to hear from was one belonging to the old Thirty-eighth, commanded by Captain Althouse. The captain, without troubling himself about what was going on elsewhere, or turning to right or left, had marched straight ahead, with well closed ranks. He fortunately crossed the two intrenched lines, and continued his march without stopping. Reaching a piece of woods thicker than the rest, he saw himself surrounded and summoned to surrender. All resistance was useless. He had advanced directly into what appeared to be the enemy's lines. The captain, with chagrin, was about to surrender his sabre when a joyous voice called out, in a shout of laughter, "Well, that is a good joke! This is the First Division."

The Company was in the midst of a brigade of Berry's division. It was the only one, to my knowledge, which arrived at its destination.

At that time we were still ignorant of the most important event of that nocturnal combat. We had taken two rows of rifle-pits from some of the enemy's regiments, but at a very heavy cost to us. But what gave the engagement the importance of a victory gained for us was the fact that Stonewall Jackson, the most to be dreaded of our adversaries after Lee, had fallen, mortally wounded, a few steps from us in the same woods, a witness of a melee as bloody as it was confused.

Encouraged by the day's success, full of confidence in the fortunes of the morrow, Jackson had made his disposition to throw himself on our rear, and cut off our line of retreat to United States Ford. After having himself overlooked some changes in the disposition of his troops, he had advanced out of his lines, with a few officers of his staff, in order to see himself the exact position we occupied. In this way he reached the turnpike, where he had before him Berry's division, where the atttack commenced against the most advanced of his regiments in the woods. In an instant he recognized that it was something more serious than a skirmisher's alarm. He turned his horse to reënter his lines, and took the most direct road. His troops were under arms, eyes and ears open, as may be imagined. At the noise of horses galloping, they thought it was a charge of cavalry, and fired. Jackson fell, struck by several bullets, one of which broke his arm. Two or three of his officers were killed or wounded. The others made themselves known. A litter was hastily brought. The general was placed thereon, and they hurried to get him into his own lines. They had scarcely started when one of the bearers fell, struck by a ball or by a piece of shell. The general was roughly thrown to the ground. The fall aggravated his wound, and doubled his suffering.

Thus ended the second day of May, 1863.

We had about two hours of repose. Before daybreak the brigade was assembled, and we received an order to form line behind the artillery, in the field which extended between the Chancellorsville house and the woods which we had swept clean of living rebels, while leaving there a large number of our own dead. It was on that side a renewed attack was expected. By leaving Birney's division where it was, along with Whipple's, we would have had an excellent defensive position at that point, for we should have taken the enemy between two fires, both in front and in flank. It was deemed preferable to draw back the whole Third Corps between the house and the woods, perpendicular to the main road. The result was that the enemy, finding the ground free, which we had just quitted, promptly took possession of it, and placed his artillery there, giving him a converging fire, without hindrance, upon the centre of our position. And yet the retreat of our corps was not made without difficulty. Although the day had hardly broken, the brigade which brought up the rear was attacked as soon as it was put in motion. But General Graham, who commanded it, held back forces much superior to his own, and effected a retreat in good order, without breaking.

Then began a desperate battle, the brunt of which the Third Corps had still to bear. The enemy advanced in three lines sustained by strong reserves, between the main road and the ground where his guns replaced those which Pleasonton had so well defended. The movement then was simply the continuation of that which, the evening before, had swept away the Eleventh Corps. The resistance was terrible as the attack was desperate. The musketry and artillery fire mowed down the Confederate ranks; but the more they fell the more came on, and they continued to advance, crying: "Remember Jackson!"

During this time Ward's brigade was receiving blows without being able to return them. The bullets ricocheted in our ranks, shells burst around us, and the balls which passed over the first line found a mark in the second. As we were without cover, we had caused the men to lie down, to avoid useless losses; the officers alone remaining standing. In spite of this precaution, the number of wounded increased more and more, when we received an order to throw ourselves rapidly on the other side of the road, where a violent fire had broken out, and extended into the thicket.

In order not to return to the first phase of the day's action, I will say that, up to this time, the troops of the Third Corps had to sustain alone the furious attack of which we have just spoken. They defended the ground foot by foot, until they had fired their last cartridge, and were compelled to fall back to the rest of the army, saving their artillery, but abandoning that part of the plateau of Chancellorsville to the enemy.

During the fight, General Hooker had been wounded on the threshold of the Chancellorsville house. He was standing under a verandah, watching the approach of the Confederates, when he was violently knocked down by one of the columns sustaining the roof, which had been struck by a cannon ball. The shock was so great that he remained unconscious during the most of the battle, and did not appear to have recovered his faculties during the rest of the day—which, I think, explains many things, and especially why the Third Corps received neither support nor reënforcements at the time when it had the most urgent need of them.

Let us return now to the woods where our brigade had just disappeared.

Generally, on reading the description of a battle, one witnesses, as it were, from the upper air, as formerly the Olympian divinities witnessed the heroic combats of the Greeks and Trojans. We see the movement of the right, the left, and the centre of each army; we see the reënforcements arrive, the reserves put in action, and in that view of the whole, well pictured, the details are of little account. But to a colonel who is in the action matters are presented under an entirely different aspect. Of the general field he sees nothing; of the details very little. Unless good fortune gives him an exceptional position, his visual horizon does not extend beyond his brigade, and is often bounded by the line of his regiment. Where he receives the order to go, there he goes; forward, backward, to the right, to the left. His sphere of action is limited to take his regiment in on a charge; to hold it steady on a retreat; in every event to execute rapidly and correctly the changes of position which he is directed to make. Aside from that, the battle may be won or lost; he knows nothing about it. He will learn that later. What happens elsewhere is none of his business.

As an example, here is a copy of my pencil notes, May 3, during the battle of Chancellorsville, from the time when I left off my story:

"Being able to penetrate the thicket only on foot, I turned my horse over to Couillou (a sapper), with orders to bring him to me by a detour, to a clearing towards which we were going. Arriving there, neither man nor horse was to be seen. The fire continued with extreme violence. It must be Berry's division which stops the enemy's movements on this side. They are firing through the thickets, without being able to charge. Our men hold firm. No hurrahs, but a deafening noise of musketry. What the devil has become of Couillou?

"The firing came nearer and stronger at the centre. Clearly the enemy was driving us back at that point.

"We are not on the left centre, near the Twelfth Corps. We have hurried forward with our utmost ability. It seems that the time is critical. We formed our line twenty or thirty paces from the first, which, after all, had not given way. In this direction, the rebels are giving voice to their sharp yell, and our men reply by distinct hurrahs, as if there were not enough noise without that! As we had a great number of wounded, we were made to fall back to the edge of a road, where the men can at least lie down in the ditch. The bullets do us much less injury; the shells continue to trouble us. A great column of black smoke towards our left, then sheets of flame; the Chancellorsville house is burning. At the rate they are going on in our front, they will soon use up all their ammunition, and it will be our turn to take their place. The wounded are continually passing through our lines. One of them, half naked, is as black as a Negro. He runs shrieking towards the ambulances. It is an artilleryman, wounded by the explosion of a caisson. Couch passes by at a light trot, a little switch in his hand, as usual. Sickles goes by in his turn at a walk, with a smiling air, smoking a cigar. 'Everything is going well,' said he, in a loud voice, intended to be heard. Then, in a lower tone, giving me his hand, he whispered in my ear a congratulation and a promise. It would appear that I won a star in the fight by moonlight, the night before.

"We returned to the right, always on the double quick. The enemy's artillery rains projectiles upon us. Our lot for to-day is to receive blows from all sides, without being able to return them. A lieutenant of the Third Maine is cut in two by a shell bursting in his body; legs thrown to one side, the trunk to the other. One of our batteries has silenced the one which troubled us so much. General Berry has just been killed near us. An excellent man and a brave soldier. An hour of respite. It is as hot as summer; my cloak oppresses me, and I have no horse! Nothing in my stomach for twenty-four hours, but a cup of black coffee and a big swallow of whiskey, which a staff officer gave me a short time ago.

"Fifth change of position to the rear. Interval employed in covering ourselves with light intrenchments. This time, we are in the front line. The two other brigades of the division return at last to join us. General Mott is wounded. Colonel MacKnight, of the One Hundred and Fifth Pennsylvania, is killed; also Colonel Shylock, of the Fifth Michigan. In General Birney's staff, two officers are wounded, Clarke and Walker. The latter, division inspector, belongs to my regiment. He is said to be maimed for life.

"Two batteries have just come into position on our line. At half after four, the firing recommences, and stops at five o'clock.

"We learn that the first Corps arrived last night, coming from Fredericksburg, and that the Sixth carried the heights above the city this morning."

One can judge by this extract how much a colonel sees and knows about a battle in which he has all the time manœuvred his regiment. Here, now, is what occurred:

Every effort of the enemy was against the Third Corps. When that corps, out of ammunition, began to fall back to the rear, from the right to the other side of the road, Stuart, who succeeded Jackson, extended his attack on his left, hoping to take us in reverse, and reach our line of retreat towards the Rappahannock. There he struck French's division of the Second Corps, which not only held its ground, but even compelled its assailants to fall back. It was to sustain him that Ward's brigade had been ordered into the woods.

In this part of the field, our right was facing to the west, while our centre looked south, and our left east.

In the meanwhile, Lee, having learned of the success of Stuart on our right, and seeing us all engaged in that direction, attacked our left centre vigorously, so that for a moment it was in danger of being broken. Upon which our brigade was hurried over to reënforce the Twelfth Corps.

The danger past, Stuart returned to the charge, reënforced by new troops, and now forced French to retire. This was the reason for our precipitate return near the clearing where we had first taken position.

But our comrades of the Third Corps were not yet out of the difficulty, notwithstanding their having fallen back and changed front. The enemy, who just effected a junction of his two wings on the plateau of Chancellorsville, and who had not been able to force, at the angle to our left, the intrenched line of our advanced posts admirably defended by Colonel Nelson A. Miles, now commenced again the attack against Sickles with renewed vigor. Our men, short of ammunition, had no other resource than the bayonet. They availed themselves of it brilliantly and with great success. The New Jersey brigade, amongst others, commanded by General Mott, broke the first line of the Confederates, and, advancing, took flags and trophies from their second line.

General Hooker, recovering from his unconsciousness, although still feeling the effects of the accident, had resumed the command of the army, left for some hours to General Couch. He gave the order to retire to a stronger line of defence which he had had traced out the night before by the engineer officers. There the other two brigades of the division came to join us.

Thus ended the third day of May, 1863.

Our new position rested, at one end, on the Rappahannock, the other on the Rapidan. On the left it faced southeast, on the right southwest, making a very open angle, at whose apex, opposite the enemy's centre, was formed a great trilateral work. This was the point occupied by the Third Corps. As the army made no further movement until it repassed the river, we can leave it behind its breastworks and join the corps at Fredericksburg.

On the afternoon of the 2d, Hooker, seeing his right broken in, and the Third Corps compromised by Jackson's attack, had thought immediately of making a diversion from the other side, which would turn Lee. He sent an order to General Sedgwick to cross the Rappahannock as quickly as possible, and march out on the Chancellorsville road, attacking and destroying whatever force might bar his way. Sedgwick received the despatch about midnight, having already crossed the river by virtue of a preceding order directing him to take the Bowling Green road and "any other." He immediately changed his dispositions, and marched on Fredericksburg without loss of time. His instructions were: "You will leave your train behind you, except the mules carrying ammunition, and will march so as to be in the neighborhood of the general in command at daylight. You will probably strike the rear of the forces commanded by General Lee, and, between you and the major-general commanding, the latter hopes to make a finish of his adversary."

The silence as to the fortified heights seemed to imply that the general-in-chief supposed that they had been stripped of troops since the morning; without that, the contest to be entered on at that position should have entered explicitly into the calculation in reference to the time allowed to Sedgwick to reach the neighborhood of Chancellorsville. Now, not a company had been withdrawn by the enemy from that strong position, which was still defended by Early's division, reënforced by a brigade.

The Sixth Corps was surrounded by a cordon of rebel pickets, whose firing gave warning of the march as soon as it began. Early, forewarned, prepared for an attack. Immediately, on entering Fredericksburg, Sedgwick sent four regiments to try the heights; they were received with a deadly fire, and were compelled to retire. The preparations for a final assault occupied the last hours of the night. It would appear that they were not moved with the promptness which circumstances demandèd, for it was not till eleven o'clock in the morning that the two columns of attack charged the intrenchments. Colonel Spear of the Sixty-first Pennsylvania, who led the right, was killed. Colonel Johns of the Seventh Massachusetts, commanding the left, was severely wounded; but, in spite of the vigor of the defence, Marye's Heights were carried by main force. At the same time Howe's division carried the enemy's position on the left, and the whole line was ours, with a part of the artillery and a large number of prisoners.

Without loss of time, the troops reformed, and the Sixth Corps advanced on the Chancellorsville road, leaving Gibbon's division of the Second Corps at Fredericksburg, as the order of General Hooker had directed. Those of the enemy who had retired in that direction were driven back without stopping to Salem Heights, in front of Banks Ford. There Brooks' division, which had the advance, met with a determined resistance. It was then about four o'clock in the after-

Chancellorsville: *Hooker's men under heavy Confederate pressure*

noon (Sunday, May 3). We note the hour, for at this moment the army under the immediate command of Hooker was already inclosed behind the second intrenched line, and the battle there was virtually finished, entirely to the advantage of Lee.

Leaving in front of us what troops were necessary to hold us in our lines, in the cramped position which we occupied, hardly able to move, Lee sent MacLaws' division, strengthened by Mahone's brigade, against Sedgwick. These forces reached Salem in time to reënforce Wilcox's brigade, which, abandoning the guard of Banks Ford, had hurried on to bar the road against the Sixth Corps. The enemy was, at first, driven back from the heights he occupied, but, when his reënforcements reached him, he retook them, notwithstanding an obstinate resistance, forcing Brooks and Newton to fall back. Sedgwick's advance was arrested, when night came to put an end to the engagement.

Behold us now, on Monday, May 4. What has become of the plan so ably conceived, so happily executed in the beginning? That plan which would leave to Lee's army only the alternative of a shameful flight or certain destruction? Hooker lost the benefit of everything he had done up to that time when, on the 1st of May, he had abruptly stopped a series of fine offensive manœuvres, to take up a purely defensive attitude on his first meeting the enemy. From that moment he no longer attacked. He simply stood on the defensive, and he defended himself badly.

On the 2d his right was swept away. That the Eleventh Corps, composing the right, had fought poorly or not at all; that some regiments had fled, leaving their arms stacked, or throwing them away so as to run faster, is a fact that must unfortunately be acknowledged. But would all this have happened if the Eleventh Corps had been prepared to receive the attack from the side on which it was absolutely defenceless? We must judge matters coolly. The facts prove that the attack had not been foreseen either by General Howard or by General Hooker. The latter visits and examines that part of the line in the morning, and when General Howard asks him if the dispositions made are satisfactory he replies in the affirmative, in the presence of General Devens, commanding the division placed on the extreme right. Only, on his return to headquarters, he sent a note to the commanders of the Eleventh and Twelfth Corps to direct them to "examine the ground and decide what positions they must take in the eventuality of an attack on the flank, in order to be prepared to receive the enemy from whatever direction he might present himself." That done, as if to clear his conscience, and without assuring himself that any modification was made of the defective dispositions of the Eleventh Corps, he stripped his lines himself by sending Sickles with two divisions to run after the tail of the enemy's column, when it had nearly all passed by. To support it, he detached a brigade from Slocum's command, another from that of Howard; then he ordered General Pleasonton to follow with his cavalry, and do the enemy, "who was marching in the direction of Gordonsville," all the injury he could. We know the result of it.

The following night is devoted partly to firing on ourselves. It might have been more profitably employed.

On the 3d the enemy continued to force back our right, and to press us strongly on our centre. He found before him only the Third and Twelfth Corps, each supported by a division of the Second. No combinations, no manœuvres. Each one defends himself as best he can, and in the position he is occupying, some by firing, others by the bayonet. And, all this time, one half the army remains inactive in the rear. The First, the Fifth, and the Eleventh (which must have been eager to make amends for the evening before) move only to fall back when the whole line retires to a position more crowded, and still more on the defensive.

Thus we find the army paralyzed at the very time when the capture of Fredricksburg Heights by Sedgwick, and his approach to the rear of Lee, should have been the signal to us for a redoubling of efforts, the decisive moment to throw the First Corps on the flank of Stuart, with the Fifth and the Eleventh Corps strike the centre of Lee, weakened by the loss of the troops he had been compelled to send against the Sixth Corps, and crush these forces between the two mills of iron and fire. Everything could yet have been saved; but all was lost. Hooker was no longer Hooker. The blow of the miserable piece of wood which had stretched him senseless across the sill of the Chancellorsville house had left him completely shattered, and as though there was a cloud over his faculties.

When General Warren, arriving from Salem, where he had assisted in the fight, came to report to Hooker, and asked him if there were any instructions to send to Sedgwick, Hooker replied, "None."

However, the Sixth Corps could not be left there in danger of being cut in pieces without a knowledge of the state of affairs. Warren took upon himself to write to Sedgwick: "We have drawn our lines in somewhat, and repulsed the last assault easily. General Hooker wishes that the Confederates would attack him to-morrow, if they so desire. He does not wish you to attack them as yet in force, unless he attacks at the same time. He says that you are too far from him for him to direct your movements. Look well to the safety of your corps, and keep your communications open with General Benham at Banks Ford, and with Fredericksburg. You may retire on either point, if you think it better to cross the river. Banks Ford would bring you within supporting distance of the rest of the army, and would be preferable to a retreat on Fredericksburg."

But when Sedgwick received that despatch (on the 4th) he had no longer any choice. Early advanced from the direction of Fredericksburg, reënforced by the troops which Lee, left free by Hooker's inaction, had sent to envelop the Sixth Corps. Threatened from two sides at once, Sedgwick was compelled to fight in a disadvantageous position. Howe's division, attacked from the direction of the river, defends itself vigorously, facing to the rear. After giving way a moment on the left, it gains the advantage, and ends by decidedly repelling the enemy, while, from the direction of the road, Brooks holds his position without much difficulty.

And, during that whole afternoon, we heard the cannon roaring without stirring ourselves, or even making any pretence of moving. Did Hooker, with six army corps, expect that Sedgwick, with seventeen or eighteen thousand men, was coming to deliver him from the false position in which he had placed himself? Or, rather, did he have any other idea than that of recrossing the Rappahannock without further fighting?

As soon as night came on, Sedgwick took advantage of it to draw back his three divisions on Banks Ford, and the morning's sun found the Sixth Corps safe and sound on the left bank of the river. Perhaps Lee, freed from all embarrassment in that direction, would have tried a general attack on us, with his whole force, if a rain in torrents, which came on in the afternoon, had not forcibly delayed his preparations until the following day. But Hooker did not wait for the attack which he had desired the evening before. In the night of the 5th the whole army recrossed the river, without hindrance, and, for the second time in five months, returned beaten to its encampment.

The victory cost the enemy only thirteen thousand men; defeat cost us seventeen thousand. The Third Corps and the Sixth, together, bore half the loss. The other half was shared principally between the Second, the Eleventh, and the Twelfth. As to the first and Fifth, they lost enough only to mention it.

Except the small force commanded by General Pleasonton, the cavalry had poorly performed its mission. Stoneman had scattered his column in every direction, without any appreciable result, except a lively alarm in the neighborhood of Richmond. Averill had not led his troops further than the Rapidan.

So that we were completely beaten—beaten on account of the general-in-chief, who, after having prepared for his army the best opportunity for being victorious which it had ever had, threw to the winds all his advantage. For one moment he had held the enemy in his hand; he had only, so to speak, to stretch it forth, to crush him; and he had not only allowed the enemy to escape, but had delivered himself up to him, by falling backward in such a manner as to paralyze his own movements. By one fault after another, and one error after another, he lost the opportunity to repossess himself of fortune's favors, and condemned one-half of his army to a fatal inaction, even to the humiliating extremity of escaping by night from a position yet formidable, before forces decidedly inferior to his own.

LEE INVADES PENNSYLVANIA

STONEWALL JACKSON'S ARM WAS AMPUTATED and his health seemed to improve, until, still suffering exhaustion from shock and exposure, he contracted pneumonia. This disease, a greater killer those days than now, had its way with Jackson. On May 10, the South lost its most famous general; General Lee said, "I have lost my right arm."

At Chancellorsville, the Federals had once again taken a licking at the hands of Lee and Jackson. Although General Hooker had had a decided advantage over Lee when the fighting began, he did not see in time, as Federal generals before him had not seen, the vulnerability of Lee's army, especially when Jackson took off on his end run to hit the Federal right flank. Nor had Sedgwick moved quickly enough to put pressure on Lee's rear. Sedgwick's troops had captured the heights above Fredericksburg, but because of poor communications with Hooker he had fought Lee not knowing the rest of the Union troops had already drawn back on the Rappahannock to insure their escape route. Sedgwick made no headway, for Lee could now deal solely with Sedgwick's attack. Both Hooker and Sedgwick retreated across the river.

Lee's Army of Northern Virginia had shown itself to be a superb fighting force and Lee was seriously considering a new invasion of the North. He had the backing of most of the Confederate leaders, who clung to the belief that a victory on Union soil would bring recognition from England and France and the accompanying prestige and power resulting therefrom. Such a victory also would encourage the antiwar party in the North in their efforts to persuade the rest of the Union that continuation of the war was futile. And surely an invasion that threatened Washington would bring the Army of the Potomac rushing north, thus moving the war out of Virginia.

A minority opinion existed in the South (as evidenced by General Longstreet) that part of Lee's army should be detached and sent west to help defend Vicksburg and the Mississippi valley. Lee resisted such a move and his record of success was sufficient for him to withstand opposition and keep his army intact.

Lee divided his 70,000 men into three corps. First Corps remained with Lieutenant General James Longstreet. Second Corps was given to Richard Ewell, and Third Corps went to A. P. Hill, both of whom were appointed Lieutenant Generals.

Early in June, General Ewell's corps swung northwest into the Shenandoah Valley, then marched north into Maryland, heading for Pennsylvania. Longstreet and Hill followed soon after. Once in Pennsylvania, Ewell sent off two attack columns, one of which captured York and Wrightsville, while the other threatened Harrisburg.

General Hooker had received news that Lee was heading north, but he proposed to Washington that the Army of the Potomac strike for Richmond, pointing out that any such move should bring Lee rushing back to Virginia. But Stanton, who was dissatisfied with Hooker, ordered him to turn around and march north, keeping his men between Lee and the capital.

Getting rid of Hooker presented a problem to Stanton and Lincoln. They had decided to replace him but feared that an outright removal would cause political repercussions. Stanton set out to frustrate and irritate Hooker to a point where, in a rage, he would offer his resignation. At the end of June, Hooker did just that, and the offer was promptly accepted. General George Meade, who had commanded the V Corps in the Army of the Potomac, took over the command on June 28.

As the Army of the Potomac continued its march north toward Harrisburg, it advanced on a front, according to Catton, "35 to 40 miles from tip to tip." Progress was slow while Union cavalry under General John Buford searched for Lee's army. At Gettysburg on June 30, Buford finally made contact with Confederate patrols. That night he occupied a position on Seminary Ridge northwest of the town and, believing that Lee's army was near, sent out scouts to locate it.

For once the Federals were better informed than the Confederates. Since June 25, Stuart had been riding in a long cast around the Army of the Potomac (from east to west), expecting to meet forward elements of Lee's army in southern Pennsylvania. By cutting to the east of the Army of the Potomac he could take a short cut and molest the Federals' supply routes. But Stuart kept running into Federal troops. This slowed his progress, thus depriving Lee of news of Meade's activities. When Lee finally discovered the federals hot on his heels he ordered Ewell, Longstreet, and Hill to converge at Gettysburg. Divisions from both Hill to the west and Ewell in the north began arriving in Gettysburg on July 1.

At daybreak Buford's cavalry pickets saw Confederate troops marching directly toward their positions on Seminary Ridge. Buford placed his troops, now dismounted, in battle formation. He hoped to delay the Confederates long enough for the main body of Federal troops approaching from the south to reach Gettysburg.

As more and more Confederate troops appeared over the western ridge Buford sent couriers to hurry the Federal divisions. The first to arrive was General Reynolds' I Corps. They went into position with Buford on Seminary Ridge.

In the early stages of the battle the Federals successfully stood off the forward elements of Hill's corps, but when the main body arrived the Federals were outnumbered. "The battle lines grew and grew until they formed a great semicircle west and north of the town. . . . Another Yankee corps, the XI, came up and went through the town on the double, colliding head on with Confederates who were marching south. . . . These Confederates cut around both flanks of the XI Corps' line, crumpled them, punched holes in the line, and late in the afternoon drove the survivors back through the village in rout; then the line west of town caved in, and by evening the Federals who were left (they had had upwards of 10,000 casualties) were reassembling on the high ground south and east of Gettysburg, grimly determined to hold on until the rest of the army came up, but not at all certain that they could do it."*

Federal troops were marching hard and fast. One of the approaching columns was part of the V Corps, and one of its regiments, the 20th Maine, would have a vital role to play the next day.

"Off to the west there were disturbances of the atmosphere, as though someone was beating a rug, far over

* Bruce Catton, *This Hallowed Ground*, p. 251.

the horizon. Late in the afternoon they went into bivouac near Hanover, then right out of bivouac again, for a lathered horseman arrived with bad news that soon spread through the entire corps. The report said that the First Corps and the Eleventh Corps had run into Lee at a place called Gettysburg, fourteen or fifteen miles to the west, and had been hurt badly. General Reynolds, the First Corps commander, had been killed; the two corps had been driven back through the town of Gettysburg and now were dug in on some hills this side of the town, waiting for the rest of the army to arrive.

"This meant that the march of the Fifth Corps would continue into the night. The bugles sounded 'Forward!' and they were pushing westward again. In midevening, the moon came up, illuminating the countryside with a clear blue light, and suddenly a phantom was riding ahead of them. 'At a turn of the road a staff officer, with an air of authority, told each colonel as he came up that McClellan was in command again, and riding ahead of us on the road,' Colonel Chamberlain reported. And Private Theodore Gerrish of the 20th Maine wrote, 'Men waved their hats and cheered until they were hoarse and wild with excitement.' No one knew how the false rumor got started, but for a time that evening they marched believing that their beloved McClellan was once again leading them into battle. The men were intensely keyed up. Later there would be a rumor that the spirit of George Washington was accompanying them, riding on a white horse.

"It was a night that Gerrish always remembered. He wrote, 'The people rushed from their homes and stood by the roadside to welcome us, men, women, and children all gazing on the strange spectacle. Bands played, the soldiers and the people cheered, banners waved, and white handkerchiefs fluttered from doors and windows, as the blue, dusty column surged on.'

"But as the evening wore on, excitement gave way to weariness. The cheering died away. Many of the men began to stagger, half asleep on their feet. They had now marched over twenty-five miles. Some time after midnight a halt was called and they got two or three hours' sleep, lying in the dust and the dew beside the road.

"Around four-thirty the sun came up red, indicating another hot day. They arose, dazed and stiff, and continued the march. Arriving on some level, open ground, the two divisions of the Fifth Corps then present formed as though pieces at the right shoulder. Detail cleared away fences in front, and they advanced in formation—great blocks of dusty blue, with the flags and the shimmer of steel over them in the morning light. There was a remarkable stillness in the ranks, broken only by low-voiced commands and the swishing of legs through growing grain, hay, and low bushes. Coming to the crest of a knoll, they saw a group of rough, wooded hills ahead, with the brown scars of earthworks on them . . . wagon and artillery parks . . . rows of stacked muskets where troops were resting . . . other evidences that they were in the rear of a battle line.

"East of the hills, the Fifth Corps division maneuvered into a line facing generally north, and there was a lot of waiting and standing around. Officers got out in front of their regiments and read an order from General Meade. A number of phrases filtered through to tired brains . . . 'enemy are on our soil . . . whole country now looks anxiously to this army to deliver it . . . homes, firesides and domestic altars are involved.' It sounded pretty serious. And then came a grim and remarkable sentence that made them realize just how serious it was. 'Corps and other commanders are authorized to order the instant death of any soldier who fails in his duty at this hour.'

"Later in the forenoon the corps moved, crossed a creek, and went into a reserve position in a field just off the Baltimore Pike near an orchard. The town and the scene of yesterday's fighting were not visible, being hidden by the hills and some woods on high ground west of them. They could see a lot of activity. Ambulances coming up. Staff officers riding furiously on mysterious errands. Wagons distributing ammunition. But aside from the occasional boom of a cannon, it seemed mighty peaceful for a battlefield.

"The men stretched out and got some much needed rest. It felt good to have the earth pressing against the back instead of the feet. They dozed off. From off behind the hills and the woods, someone began popping corn. First one kernel went pop. Then others softly—pop, pop, pop, pop, p-p-p-popopopopopopop—the sound of musketry, muffled by heat, distance and intervening terrain. The sound started in the northwest, then ran around to the west and finally died away. A few eyes opened, then closed. It was just skirmish firing. The men of the 20th Maine dozed and slept. The for a grand review, with colors unfurled, lines dressed, scent of trampled and crushed grass rose around them. Summer breathed hot on their upturned faces. It was quiet at Gettysburg."*

Gettysburg: Second Day**

BY JOHN P. PULLEN

WHILE THE TIRED SOLDIERS of the 20th Maine slept behind Powers Hill, the stage was being set for their entrance, and various actors were moving about in the wings.

Chief of these was Major General George Gordon Meade, former Fifth Corps commander, now commanding general of the Army of the Potomac. Meade was not a spectacular leader but he was a safe one, and a man of character—not given to throwing soldiers' lives away needlessly. This seems to have been a virtue that had impressed the men of the 20th Maine. Private Theodore Gerrish described Meade thus: "He had not the dashing appearance of many other generals, but when we saw that tall, bowed form, enveloped in a great brown overcoat, riding to the front, we always felt safe." Gerrish also remembered that Meade appeared to be continually bent over by the great burdens placed upon his shoulders; as the General rode along "he always seemed to be looking upon the ground, at a point about twenty yards in advance of him."

This overborne appearance, combined with sharp eyes, a deeply lined face, and a large Roman nose, usually gave Meade the look of a tired eagle, but on this morning of July 2, somewhere between eight and nine o'clock, as he came out of the little house in the rear of Cemetery Ridge serving as his headquarters, he was wearing a cheerful face, relatively speaking. Captain George Meade, his son and aide, said that "to one who was familiar with the general's manner and tones of voice in different moods he seemed in

* From John J. Pullen, *The Twentieth Maine*, pp. 95, 96, 97.
** From Pullen, *op. cit.*

excellent spirits, as if well pleased with affairs as far as they had proceeded."

And well he might be pleased. In falling back from their defeat west and north of the town on the previous day, the First Corps and the Eleventh Corps had occupied and held excellent ground. Arriving on the field shortly after midnight, General Meade had found them dug in and reinforced on hills south of Gettysburg. Now the rest of the army, with the exception of one corps, had arrived and had occupied more of the high ground.

The line, as planned by Meade that morning, looked like a big fishhook. The hook itself, with point to the east, lay on a group of rather steep hills just south of the village. The long shank of the hook ran south along a ridge known as Cemetery Ridge. The eye of the shank was supposed to rest upon a rough, rocky hill called Little Round Top. Opposite Cemetery Ridge, on Seminary Ridge about a mile to the west, and curving through the town of Gettysburg, lay the Confederate line. It was longer than the Union line; troops had to be moved farther in any maneuvers along it. With higher ground, with shorter interior lines. Meade had the advantage.

But things started to go wrong for him, and there were hints of trouble early in the day. The southernmost corps in line was the Third Corps, commanded by Major General Daniel E. Sickles. Sickles was a brave officer, affectionately regarded by his men, but he was a "political general," and the West Pointers were inclined to look upon him with a certain amount of suspicion. General Meade told his son, Captain Meade, to go down and see what Sickles was doing. Captain Meade rode down the Taneytown Road and came upon the temporary headquarters of the Third Corps in a patch of woods west of the road. He was told that General Sickles had been up all night and was now in his tent resting; that the Third Corps was not in position; and that General Sickles didn't know exactly where he was supposed to go.

Captain Meade thereupon galloped hastily back to army headquarters and told his father of this seeming indecision on the part of General Sickles. In Meade's mind the picture was clear; the shank of the fishhook was to run straight south; half that shank was the Second Corps; and below it, resting its left upon Little Round Top, the Third Corps. Sharply and decisively, he told Captain Meade to gallop back to Sickles again and tell him that his instructions were to go into position on the left of the Second Corps. His right was to connect with the Second Corps and he was to prolong the line of that corps, occupying the "position that General Geary had held the night before."

Back down the Taneytown Road rode Captain Meade once more. At General Sickles' headquarters, he found the tents struck, staff officers hustling about, and a movement of some sort under way. General Sickles, a thick-set man with a large head, full round face and heavy moustache, was sitting on his horse. There are good days and bad days, depending on your name, and for the name Dan Sickles July 2, 1863, wasn't going to be a good day. It was starting wrong already. The commanding general of the army had assigned his corps to an area that he, Sickles, considered completely indefensible. Cemetery Ridge was no ridge at all here. It sank away into low ground, with high ground a few hundred yards in front, where Sickles believed the enemy could plant artillery and make his own position untenable.

And now here was this young whippersnapper of an aide telling him something about getting into a position held by General Geary on the night before, and implying that he ought to be quick about it. However, it is politic to be civil to a general's aide, particularly if the aide is the general's son, and Sickles told young Meade that his troops were then moving and would be in position shortly. But he also muttered that General Geary had no battle position the night before; his troops were merely massed in that vicinity. Captain Meade rode back to army headquarters, where it was assumed that Sickles now knew where he was supposed to place his men, and was acting accordingly.

Around eleven o'clock, General Sickles appeared briefly at Meade's headquarters. He was fussing about his position. Meade went over it again with him, explaining that Sickles' corps was to prolong the line of the Second Corps down toward Little Round Top. Reference was apparently made again to the position as that held by General Geary the night before and Sickles said Geary hadn't had any position, and so on and so on. Sickles wanted to know if he couldn't use his own judgment in posting his corps and Meade said, "Certainly, within the limits of the general instructions I have given you; any ground within those limits you choose to occupy, I leave to you."

Sickles then got General Hunt, the army chief of artillery,

to accompany him back to his area to have a look at the ground. A Confederate attack would be—Sickles thought —disastrous if he remained where he was. What did Hunt think about that ridge of high ground out in front? Wouldn't that be a better position for Sickles' artillery? Shouldn't Sickles move his corps out there? Hunt advised him to wait for orders before making any such move. Later Hunt went back to army headquarters and reported that the good points and some bad ones—and that if he were the commanding general he wouldn't put troops out there until he had gone and looked it over for himself. About this time there was a disturbance over to the right, and this seems to have given Meade and Hunt something else to think about.

At about the same time—farther to the south, out to the west and southwest of the Round Tops—another loose end was coming unraveled. Here General John Buford was patrolling with two brigades of cavalry. Buford and his men had brought the Confederates to their first halt on the day before and had stood them off until the Union infantry corps arrived. They had continued to fight beside the infantrymen all day, taking heavy losses. Now they were out of rations and forage. Many of the horses had thrown their shoes and were unfit for service.

Buford had sent word of all this to his superior, General Alfred Pleasonton, the cavalry chief. Pleasonton, and General Dan Butterfield, now army chief of staff, had apparently given Meade the impression that other cavalry was immediately available to replace Buford. Pleasonton now reported that Buford wanted to go to the rear and refit, since the rest of the army was nearly all up. All right, said Meade, let Buford go as a guard with the army trains back to Westminster and refit there. Meade assumed that Pleasonton would substitute other cavalry for Buford's, so that this watchful and protective screen in front of the army's left would be maintained. This Pleasonton failed to do. And Butterfield—fine composer of bugle calls, great designer of badges and banners, but right at this moment somewhat lacking in the qualities of a desirable chief of staff—failed to see that Pleasonton had slipped up.

So Buford moved back and no one went out in his place. From this area, out beyond the Round Tops, the Union left was now open to surprise and to a sudden, smashing attack of troops in mass.

The blow was on the way. It had been under consideration for several hours, and it was the first move over which Robert E. Lee exercised personal direction. The fight of the day before had been one that had boiled up from a chance encounter when advanced elements of the two armies had run into one another near Gettysburg. But now General Lee was taking charge. And if one would believe Longstreet's account, Lee was like a man who saw a fateful struggle ahead of him, and who knew that he could postpone it, perhaps to a more favorable time and place, but who found further waiting intolerable. Arriving at Gettysburg at five o'clock on the afternoon of July 1, Longstreet had found his chief on Seminary Ridge, watching the Union forces taking positions on the opposite height of land after their initial defeat. Lee had pointed out the Union positions. Longstreet had raised his glasses and studied the landscape for five or ten minutes, intently, for there were questions of life and death in every patch of woods, every ridge or hollow of the ground, and if men were going to get killed out there, they had better get killed advantageously. It seemed to Longstreet that the big decision hinged on a couple of round-topped hills that stuck up starkly on the south end of what appeared to be the Union line.

Longstreet lowered his glasses and proposed a plan: Move way around those hills. Get behind the Union left. Get between Meade's army and Washington, in a strong defensive position. Then Meade would attack, and on ground of Lee's expert choosing the Union army could be badly beaten. Or if Meade did not attack immediately, they could pick another strong position nearer Washington and move to it at night. Then Meade—and Washington too—would be frantic. The Union army would be forced to attack, into some trap of the terrain that Lee could set.

But Robert E. Lee, ordinarily as composed as steel and stone, had been gripped in a fixity of purpose that, for the good gray general, seemed almost like a passion. Lee had struck the air with his clenched fist and declared, "The enemy is there, and I am going to attack him there."

Once again Longstreet had urged his scheme, pointing out that the move around the Union left would give Lee control of the roads to Washington and Baltimore. But Lee had vehemently declared, "No; they are there in position, and I am going to whip them or they are going to whip me."

And again on the following morning—July 2—Longstreet

had proposed that the army move all the way around the Round Tops to Meade's left and rear. But the great commander still would not listen.

Lee's plan was to attack frontally with part of his army, while Longstreet's Corps made a concealed movement to the right, falling upon the Union left flank and driving it in. Once in position on Meade's flank, Longstreet was to attack in a northeasterly direction, guiding his left on the Emmitsburg Road.

After a long delay—Longstreet waiting for one of his brigades, Law's, to come up—the flanking move finally got under way around eleven o'clock in the forenoon. Longstreet was lacking Pickett's Division, but with the two big divisions of Hood and McLaw's he still had a massive force. The corps started moving south, keeping behind Seminary Ridge and other high ground in order to avoid observation from Union signal units on Little Round Top. Longstreet was in a bad mood, deeply resenting the fact that his recommendations had been disregarded. He was further exacerbated when it began to appear that the route reconnaissance, performed by one of Lee's engineer officers, had been done badly, resulting in many halts and countermarches. And Longstreet had another grumble. Stuart, who with his cavalry was supposed to be the eyes and ears of the army, was off galloping around somewhere miles away from Gettysburg. The little cavalry that remained with the army was elsewhere on the field. Here where Lonstreet was making his move, not so much as one trooper was available to precede him. In the absence of cavalry, Longstreet ordered General Hood, one of his division commanders, to send out picked scouts in advance, so that the infantry would not be walking into the area entirely blind.

With many troublesome delays, Longstreet's column moved south. It got to be one and two and three o'clock, and they still had not arrived at the attack position.

Back at the little house behind Cemetery Ridge, Meade's headquarters, a conference was called, to assemble shortly after three. The battle of Gettysburg was a great one for conferences and consultations on the Union side, and the corps commanders were arriving to talk things over. But the conference didn't last long. Major General Gouverneur K. Warren, Meade's chief of engineers, came in with a report to the effect that General Sickles had advanced his corps and was

way out of position. Warren made this startling disclosure to
General Meade.

It was now somewhere around three-thirty. Longstreet's
sweating infantrymen were coming into position on a low
ridge slanting across the Emmitsburg Road. Ahead of them
on their right, they saw the Round Tops. Ahead, and much
closer on their left, a peach orchard, and here there was a
surprise—Yankee guns and infantry in the orchard, also extending up the Emmitsburg Road. From the peach orchard,
the Union line seemed to angle back toward the Round
Tops. It was Sickles' Corps, thrust out in a salient, with one
arm facing generally west, the other southwest. If Sickles'
move had seemed questionable to Meade's staff officers, it
now seemed devilishly inconvenient for the Confederate
commanders. Their orders were to attack up the Emmitsburg Road. But here was a strong force of bluecoats to
overcome before they could even start.

The situation began to look more favorable, however,
when reports came back from the scouts that Hood had sent
out. The reports said that the Round Tops were unoccupied,
and this whole area seemed to be lightly, if at all, defended.
The scouts had climbed Big Round Top and looking down,
had seen Union wagon trains parked just east of the hills.

General Hood now urged Longstreet to alter the course of
the attack so as to move around Big Round Top and come in
on the Union left and rear. This was, substantially, what
Longstreet had wanted Lee to do with the whole army. But
Longstreet was now sullen—and stubborn. Lee's orders
were to attack up the Emmitsburg Road. Well, then, they
would attack up the Emmitsburg Road.

With McLaws' Division preparing to advance on the
peach orchard, Hood took his division far to the right in
order to envelop the southward-facing arm of Sickles' salient
and be in position to strike at the undefended Round Tops.

At headquarters, Army of the Potomac, the conference of
corps commanders had broken up with explosive sud-
denness. First had come Warren's report of Sickles' new and
highly original position. Then from far over on the left, cannonading and a few rattles of musketry had been heard. And
now to the conference came General Sickles, having previously been detained. Meade told him not to get off his
horse. He told General George Sykes, the fifth Corps commander, to go get his corps and move it over there to the left.

General Sykes, a little man with a big nose and a fine suit of whiskers, flew off to rouse up the Fifth Corps, still resting in rear of Powers Hill. Meade then told General Sickles to get back to his corps and he would follow him and see just what the situation was. Even though prepared by Warren's report, Meade was shocked, when he arrived, to see how far forward Sickles had actually posted the Third Corps—entirely disconnected from the rest of the army and far out beyond the possibility of support from existing positions.

General Sickles was deeply sorry. He said that he would withdraw his troops. Meade replied, "Yes, you may as well, at once. The enemy will not let you withdraw without taking advantage of your position, but you have to come back, and you may as well do it at once as at any other time."

General Sickles turned to give the necessary orders; just then Longstreet's cannoneers pulled their lanyards and the sky smashed over the Emmitsburg Road. It was now too late to withdraw. Meade told Sickles to hold on and do the best he could and that some way or other he would be supported. A projectile shrieked past. Meade's mount reared, plunged and went crazy. Meade was carried from the scene on a runaway horse—the final touch of frustration. It was now around four o'clock.

Meanwhile, General Gouverneur K. Warren had arrived on the summit of Little Round Top to play his big part, on his Big Day in history. A slight, dark, intense officer who bore a faint resemblance to Edgar Allen Poe, Warren had come to this elevated point to see what was going on out there beyond the Round Tops to the west. The hill was unoccupied except for a few signalmen. Since he was a military engineer, Warren presumably had recognized the importance of Little Round Top long before this. But he had not realized that it was completely undefended, and this discovery was highly disturbing. He also saw that off to the west there was a long line of woods, which made an excellent concealment for the enemy. Acting on a sudden inspiration, Warren sent word down to a battery emplaced on a smaller hill below (Devil's Den) where Sickles line ended, and asked the artillerymen to fire a shot into the woods. The projectile, flying among the trees, caused the Confederate infantrymen to look upward, and the corresponding gleam of reflected sunlight on shifting rifle barrels and bayonets revealed their position to Warren. It also gave him a nasty shock. For here was a long line of battle that would far outflank the Union left when it advanced. With a thrill of mortal danger, Warren saw what would happen. The right of Longstreet's attack would sweep over Little Round Top. With this point in their possession, the Confederates would have the key to the battlefield. Starting here they could enfilade and roll up the Union line in a wholesale disaster. Troops here would be in command of the vital Taneytown Road. And if Meade's troops were routed, Lee would be between them and Washington, a most embarrassing possibility, in the light of Meade's orders from that city.

There was only one thing to do: get some soldiers up here as soon as the Lord would let him. Warren sent an aide flying off to find Meade and request at least a division. He sent another down to Sickles asking for a brigade. Sickles had to say no. He had enough fighting to do right where he was. By now the attack had begun and Longstreet was starting to smash in his salient with an overwhelming violence that was to cost Sickles his corps and his right leg. (The Third Corps was practically destroyed. The leg shattered by a shell, had to be amputated. General Sickles sent it to the Army Medical Museum, where the bones can be seen today. Sickles used to visit the museum and stand for minutes at a time, looking at his bones and thinking—no doubt—about the day that was not his day at Gettysburg.)

So there was no help to be expected from Sickles. But help was at hand from another source—the Fifth Corps which General Sykes had started forward at Meade's order. The reconnaissance officers and advance elements of the Fifth Corps were now appearing, passing north of Little Round Top, and going out to the support of Sickles.

The leading brigade was Vincent's, and right near the front was the 20th Regiment Infantry, Maine Volunteers.

Summoned to support the unhooked and unhinged salient of General Sickles, the 1st Division of the Fifth Corps had marched rapidly toward the firing. The 20th Maine, near the head of the column in Vincent's Brigade, reached the edge of a wheatfield, where the brigade halted momentarily to await instructions.

The woods ahead, beyond the field and out toward the Emmitsburg Road, was roaring and smoking; tiny flashes of lightning winked over the treetops, changing instantly to lazily drifting puffballs; the ground shook, and underneath was the sound of musketry, the shrill piping of far-off yells and the almost human screams of horses being struck in the short-range artillery duel.

But Colonel Chamberlain and his Maine soldiers didn't have long to look, or listen. Warren's call for help was being directed to Colonel Vincent, their brigade commander. A staff officer came dashing up to Vincent, and the focus of attention suddenly shifted to the left and rear. There was a great deal of shouting and pointing at Little Round Top—an ugly, rock-strewn hill with woods all over it except on the western face. Vincent turned his horse and made for the hill with an urgent squeak of saddle leather, leaving word for the brigade to follow. His standard-bearer galloped after him. Chamberlain and the others saw the two horsemen try to ride up the northwest face of Little Round Top but it was too rough; they couldn't make it. They then skirted the northern foot of the hill and disappeared in the woods behind the crest. The triangular flag with its red Maltese cross flashed once or twice between the trees. Near it, a shellburst blossomed with a growling roar. The Confederates, too, had their eye on Little Round Top. The artillery fire intensified as the brigade, following Vincent, scrambled up the lower gradient of the hill. In this movement, the 20th Maine now came last. Three Chamberlain brothers were riding abreast: Colonel Joshua; Tom, now a lieutenant acting as adjutant; and another brother, John Chamberlain, who had arrived at Gettysburg with the Christian Commission and who had chosen to go along with the 20th Maine to help the chaplain and the ambulance men. A large, unseen object swished past their faces. Said the Colonel, "Boys, I don't like this. Another such shot might make it hard for mother. Tom, go to the rear of the regiment, and see that it is well closed up! John, pass up ahead and look out a place for our wounded."

The regiment scrambled up the northern face of the hill under a heavy artillery fire from the Confederates. Shells were bursting among the trees and on the rocks and there were miserable slashing and humming sounds in the air—fragments of iron and splintered stone flying, sliced-off branches tumbling down. Mounted officers got off their horses, sending the animals to sheltered positions in the rear. The Maine men turned south behind the summit, getting some protection from the crest, and on the southern slope of the hill they found Colonel Strong Vincent putting the brigade into line of battle.

Within the fifteen minutes or so available, Vincent was doing one of the war's best jobs of reconnaissance, selection and occupation of position. His regiments were following him in this order:

> 44th New York
> 16th Regiment
> 83rd Pennsylvania
> 20th Maine

Vincent had chosen a line of defense that would start on the west slope of Little Round Top and continue around the hill in a quarter circle—not on the crest, but well below it. As the regiments arrived, he put them into line carefully, even taking time to defer to a whim voiced by Colonel James C. Rice, commander of the 44th New York. The 44th and the 83rd Pennsylvania were known as Butterfield's Twins, and going into line in the order in which they were arriving, the two regiments would be separated by the 16th Michigan. Colonel Rice had a seizure of superstition or sentiment, and he said to Vincent, "Colonel, the 83rd and 44th have always fought side by side in every battle, and I wish they may do the same today."

He was accommodated. The 16th marched past the 44th and took position first, on the west slope. The Twins, following, went into line side by side, curving around the hill. Coming up last in the column, the 20th Maine extended the formation to the east, and Vincent told Chamberlain, "This is the left of the Union line. You understand. You are to hold this ground at all costs!"

Chamberlain ordered his regiment in "on the right by file into line." This was a slow maneuver, made even more awkward by the rough ground, rocks and trees, but it anchored the right of the 20th firmly to the left of the 83rd, and each man was ready to commence firing as soon as he came into position. They now saw that they were on the brink of a smooth shallow valley, lightly forested and strewn with rocks. Across this valley to the south, facing them: Big Round Top, gigantic, covered with forest and huge boulders, apparently impassable. On their right, the rest of the brigade.

On the left, nothing!

Chamberlain was looking off in that direction, studiously. To his men it afterward seemed that the Colonel had the ability to see through forests and hills and to know what was coming. This apparently magical gift of great infantry officers was something that Chamberlain had caught on to; it was merely a matter of studying the terrain closely, imagining all kinds of horrible things that might happen, and planning countermeasures in advance.

Knowing that he had no support on the left, Chamberlain sent Company B, commanded by Captain Walter G. Morrill, out in that direction to guard his exposed flank and act as the necessities of the battle would require. Chamberlain didn't know quite what these necessities would be, but he knew Morrill and he was the sort of fellow who would do something and probably do it right.

Holding the left of the entire four-or-five mile Union line, the 20th Maine had stepped, all unawares, into the spotlight of history. Off to the west, Sickles' salient was caving in. Up from the south was coming the powerful right hook of Longstreet's attack. If this point failed, the Confederates would be smashing into the rear of a Union line that was already wildly confused by a massive frontal attack. Robert E. Lee and the Confederacy were never so close to victory.

So here on this hidden corner of the battlefield, one of the world's decisive small-unit military actions was about to begin. And upon this spot were converging many chains of cause and effect- starting from previous events that had seemed, in their time, unimportant.

When Hood's Division swung across the Emmitsburg Road and prepared to attack, its right brigade, Law's Alabamians, had already marched twenty-eight miles since 3 A.M. In the 15th Alabama, canteens were empty and the men were thirsty. A detail of twenty-two men collected all the canteens and started for a well a hundred yards or so to the rear to fill them and return. But before they could get back the advance started. As the Alabama brigade approached Big Round Top, the men saw near the western foot of the hill what appeared to be a small regiment in an advanced position. These Yankees were beyond good shooting range, but puffs of smoke appeared from among them and Alabama soldiers began to fall in alarming numbers. Later they were to learn that this regiment was the 2nd U. S. Sharpshooters.

Including a company of Maine marksmen, as well as sharpshooters from other states, this was a group of men who could each put ten consecutive shots into a target at six hundred feet with an average distance from the center of less than five inches. Against this deadly fire, one of Law's regiments almost broke, but they rallied and the brigade swept on, a long line of veterans in sun-bleached gray, bayonets shining, color staffs slanting forward, the flags of the Confederacy flickering above them. When they got to where they could start giving it back to the Yankees, the sharpshooters suddenly withdrew; part of them went back to a little hill on the left (Devil's Den) and the other part ran up Big Round Top and disappeared among the trees and boulders.

From this position the sharpshooters began sniping again at the right flank of the Confederate advance. On this wing in command of the 15th Alabama, with the 47th Alabama also acting under his direction was Colonel William C. Oates, a mustachioed and bewhiskered officer who was both courageous and perceptive. Not wanting to go on and leave the hornet's nest of sharpshooters in his rear, Oates ordered the advance to extend to the right, up over Big Round Top, to clear his flank. It was a brutal climb. (It's an exhausting climb today on the smooth path the Park Service has built.) For infantrymen who had already marched twenty-eight miles, who had to climb over boulders and through brush, who were laden with arms and ammunition, and who had to fight deadshot Yankees on the way, it was an ordeal. Several fainted in the heat. But the sharpshooters finally disappeared, and the right of the 15th Alabama reached the top, where Colonel Oates told them to stop and rest.

Here they hoped the water-carriers would catch up with them. But the canteen party was destined never to arrive; it had walked into a concealed party of sharpshooters and had been captured to a man. The men of the 15 Alabama always thought that the loss of this water detail had a lot to do with losing the battle of Gettysburg.

During the break, Colonel Oates found a place on the summit from which he could peer through the heavy July foliage and get some idea of where he was, and what was going on. He was amazed at the prospect. He could see Gettysburg in the distance. He could see the battle smoke drifting up from Devil's Den and hear the racket of the fighting that was starting around Little Round Top. He realized that he was on the highest point in the neighborhood. It was like sitting high in a box seat, overlooking the flank of the Union line.

Oates also realized that he held what could be the key of the battlefield. Drag up some artillery, cut down a few trees to clear a field of fire, and he could command not only Little Round Top, but the whole Union line all the way up Cemetery Ridge. Oates was entranced with the idea of a position here on Big Round Top. He thought . . . "within half an hour I could convert it into a Gibraltar that I could hold against ten times the number of men that I had." A staff officer from Law, now acting division commander, came up and Oates urged a halt for the purpose of occupying Big Round Top; that, clearly, was the thing to do. The staff officer admitted that Oates was probably right, but their orders were to find and turn the left of the Union line, and the left of the Union line was not up here, it was down there on Little Round Top. And there was no time to go back and find someone with authority to change those orders. (The absence of general officers on this critical right end of the Confederate line was a deficiency that Oates was to deplore to his dying day.) But orders were orders, and so Oates told his weary men to get up and start down the slope of the hill toward Little Round Top.

As they were descending, Oates saw, only a few hundred yards away, the Federal trains, including an extensive park of ordnance wagons. If he could work his way a little farther east, he would be completely in the rear of Meade's army. By the time he reached the bottom of the hill, Oates had moved his troops by the right flank and had them in a column of fours. Rapidly, the column headed eastward through the thinly wooded valley between the Round Tops. As soon as he got past the Union flank, Oates would bring his command to a "front" and go crashing into the Yankee rear in an attack that ought to start the Union left falling like a row of tenpins.

Back on Little Round Top, the men of the 20th Maine had been waiting. These minutes of inactivity would be almost intolerable, but blind instinct would be getting their bodies ready—blood seeming to beat harder and faster through the arteries; lungs seeming to dilate deep down, reaching for more oxygen; stomach and intestines shrinking and stopping all movement; and tension rising to the point where it could shake a man like the passage of a powerful electric current.

When it came, any kind of action would be a relief—and the reaction would be explosive.

The Maine men had watched Morrill's Company B disappear into the trees on their left front, walking warily, rifles held high. Now they turned their attention to the right front, where the shallow valley opened out toward Devil's Den. There was a great commotion in that direction. Minié balls began to whistle through the branches overhead, twigs and leaves falling around them. An order ran along the line: *Come to the ready . . . take good aim. . . .* They heard volleys crash out from the rest of Vincent's Brigade on their right, followed by the frantic rattling of ramrods and the "thugging" of leaden cones being driven home in rifle barrels. They heard something else that raised the hair on the backs of their necks. It was a shrill, undulating yell—sharp and chilling as a winter wind, full of hate, exultation, and "Let's go get 'em!" It was the rebel yell, and they were coming on with a rush.

The order-in-line of the forces about to confront each other was as follows:

LAW'S BRIGADE (Plus 4th and 5th Texas)

CONFEDERATE RIGHT
15th Ala., 47th Ala., 4th Ala., 5th Tex., 4th Tex., 48th Ala., 44th Ala.

VINCENT'S BRIGADE

UNION LEFT
20th Maine, 83rd Pennsylvania, 44th New York, 16th Michigan

Neither was an actual straight line. The Union regiments were in a quarter circle around part of the hill. Of the Confederate regiments, the 15th Alabama and the 47th Alabama were behind the others, retarded by their climb over Big Round Top. The two Texas regiments didn't belong with Law's Brigade, but had got into the middle of it in a shuffle during the advance. The 44th Alabama did not come all the way to Little Round Top, but turned off and attacked Devil's Den.

The first troops the 20th Maine caught sight of were those of the 4th Alabama—fierce, lean men who were charging up

the hill on their right, then drawing back as the fire of the
rest of the Union brigade came out at them, then extending
farther up the valley. They soon reached the right front of
the 20th Maine and the regiment opened fire. Confined in
the rocky valley, the noise became a continuously re-echo-
ing roar, punctuated with the spanging of soft lead on stones
and the yowling of ricochets. The attacking force gradually
covered the entire front of the 20th Maine, and the smoke
of the firing grew thick, hanging in the sultry air.

But this fighting had no more than started when Lieutenant James H. Nichols, commanding Company K, ran up
to tell Colonel Chamberlain that something very strange was
going on *behind* the attacking Confederate line. Mounting a
rock, Chamberlain saw a solid gray mass advancing along
the valley toward his left, partially screened by the smoke
and the fighting already in progress on his front.

This was Oates and his flanking column. By itself, it was a
large force, outnumbering the 20th Maine almost two to
one, and the sight gave Chamberlain a real jolt. What did
the book say to do, in a situation like this?

The order-in-line of the 20th Maine companies (less
Company B, detached as skirmishers and now presumably
cut off by the Confederate flanking column) was as represented here:

Colors
Left G C H A F D K I E

In the face of the impending flank attack, the obvious
countermove was to change front with the whole regiment,
in order to face to the left and thus guard the flank of the
brigade against the heavy assault that would presently be
coming in from that direction. But Chamberlain quickly saw
that this wouldn't work. The 20th Maine was on a spur of
high ground extending out from Little Round Top. In
changing front, in order to keep his right in contact with the
83rd Pennsylvania, Chamberlain would have to swing the
whole regiment back. This would relinquish part of the high
ground to the enemy. Also, much of the 20th Maine was
already participating in the fire-fight that had involved the
rest of the brigade.

Rejecting the obvious maneuver, Chamberlain called his
company commanders and gave them instructions that were
completely fantastic, considering the fact that the regiment

was already under fire. Chamberlain decided to move the left wing (left half) of the regiment to the left and rear, facing it at right angles with the original line. Meanwhile the right wing would extend itself by taking intervals to the left and forming a single rank, so that the regiment would stand thus:

```
F  D  K  I  E
A
H
C
G
```

As the left wing moved, the right wing was instructed to stay in contact with it, the men taking side steps to the left, meanwhile keeping up their fire to the front, without regard to the effect or whether or not the fire was needed. This would tend to conceal the movement.

The plan was executed in a way that never thereafter ceased to be a source of wonder to the officers of the 20th Maine. With bullets smashing into it, and the roar of gunfire making commands inaudible, the regiment writhed and twisted into the new formation like a single, living organism responding to a sense of imminent danger. Or—it was almost as though every man had been party to a quiet conference, where everything had been diagrammed and perfectly understood. On the right wing, men were firing, shouting, dodging from rock to rock and tree to tree, and gradually forming a single rank that covered the entire original front of the regiment. Chamberlain remembered that while this was going on there seemed to be no slakening of fire on that front.

Meanwhile the men of the bent-back wing were forming a solid line facing to the left, taking what concealment they could find behind rocks and undergrowth. Their presence came as a grievous surprise to the 15th Alabama.

When the Alabamians came to a front and charged up on what had been a few moments before an unguarded flank, the Maine men rose above the rocks and a volley flashed out that lighted all the fires of hell in that hot, shadowed backyard of the battle. At close range, it was a deadly blast, followed by hoarse screams, the sound of bodies falling in the bushes, the clatter of rifles dropped on the rocks by stricken men. Broken by the fire, the Alabama charge stopped momentarily. But

these were hard men and they came on again, this time right
up into the Maine line. Squads of them bayoneted their way
through and had to be disposed of in horrid hand-to-hand
grappling. The Maine men hadn't fixed bayonets; they clubbed their muskets and chopped with them like axes.

No one could ever describe this part of the fight
coherently, or tell just how long it lasted. From here on
everything was a medley of monstrous noises and a blur . . .
muzzle-flashes blazing . . . gray forms appearing through the
smoke . . . faces looming up with red, open, yelling mouths
ringed with the black of cartridge biting . . . strangled animal
sounds . . . and the queer-sounding resonances of skulls
struck by musket butts. Chamberlain remembered that "the
edge of conflict swayed to and fro, with wild whirlpools and
eddies. At times I saw around me more of the enemy than of
my own men; gaps opening, swallowing, closing again with
sharp convulsive energy; squads of stalwart men who had
cut their way through us, disappearing as if translated. All
around, strange, mingled roar. . . ."

Somehow, the line held, in one form or another, although
the fighting was raging up and down in such a way that often no definite line could be seen. Nearly everyone but the
hospital attendants of the 20th Maine were in ranks, and all
were fighting like madmen. One young fellow was cut down
with a ghastly wound across the forehead, and Chamberlain, thinking that he might be saved with prompt attention, sent him to the rear. Soon he saw him in the fight again
with a bloody bandage around his head.

George Washington Buck, a boy who had been unjustly
reduced to private at Stoneman's Switch, made sergeant
again. Chamberlain came across Private Buck lying on his
back, tearing his shirt away from his chest. What he saw
convinced him—and the Colonel—that there wasn't much
time left. Chamberlain bent over him and told him that he
was promoting him to sergeant on the spot. Sergeant Buck
was carried to the rear and died shortly afterward.

There were other transformations in the flame of battle.
Two mutineers from the 2nd Maine, who were being held
with the regiment as prisoners awaiting court-martial, chose
this moment to return to duty. Picking up rifles, the two 2nd
Mainers waded into the fray and laid about them so lustily
that Chamberlain resolved to get the charges against them
dropped if he survived.

And the Colonel saw something else he was always to remember—a grouping that could have been a model for the sort of heroic statuary that came out of the war to adorn village squares. "I saw through a sudden rift in the thick smoke our colors standing alone. I first thought some optical illusion imposed upon me. But as forms emerged through the drifting smoke, the truth came to view. The cross-fire had cut keenly; the center had been almost shot away; only two of the color guard had been left, and they fighting to fill the whole space; and in the center, wreathed in battle smoke, stood the color-sergeant, Andrew Tozier. His color staff planted in the ground at his side, the upper part clasped in his elbow, so holding the flag upright, with musket and cartridges seized from the fallen comrade at his side he was defending his sacred trust in the manner of the songs of chivalry."

The fight was seen through many eyes, but all seem to have seen it through the same red, smoky haze. Private Gerrish described the action where Company H was fighting, out on the bent-back wing. "If a rock promised shelter, down went a man behind it, and a rifle barrel gleamed and flamed above it. Every tree was also utilized, but a great majority of the troops were not thus provided for. As the moments passed the conflict thickened; the cartridge boxes were pulled around in front and left open; the cartridges were torn out and crowded into the smoking muzzles of the guns with a terrible rapidity. The steel rammers clashed and clanged in barrels heated with burning powder."

Gerrish saw the first sergeant, Charles W. Steele, stagger up to the company commander with a big hole in his chest. "I am going, Captain," the sergeant reported. In reply, Captain Joseph F. Land shouted, "My God, Sergeant!" and sprang to catch him, but too late, and Steele was dead by the time his body struck the ground. Another sergeant, Isaac N. Lathrop—a giant of a man—went crashing down with a mortal wound. Gerrish recalled that "of twenty-eight of that company, fifteen were either killed or wounded, and in other companies the slaughter had been equally as great. Not only on the crest of the hill, among the blue coats, was blood running in little rivulets and forming crimson pools, but in the gray ranks of the assailants there had also been a fearful destruction."

The 20th Maine had sixty rounds per man, and in the relatively short time of an hour or an hour and a half, they fired nearly every round. This meant that over twenty thousand bullets went out, and many more than that came back, slashing across the valley, flattening on rocks and flying in tearing ricochets.

Trees on the slope were gashed and peppered with white scars up to a height of six feet. One three- or four-inch tree in front of the left of Company F was gnawed completely off about two feet off the ground, the ragged edges of the cut showing that it had been made by bullets and not by a shell.

Everywhere, men going down . . .

Colonel Oates of the 15th Alabama saw a bullet strike Captain J. Henry Ellison in the head. "He fell upon his left shoulder, turned upon his back, raised his arms, clenched his fists, gave one shudder, his arms fell, and he was dead."

And then more of his officers falling . . . "Captain Brainard, one of the bravest and best officers in the regiment, in leading his company forward, fell, exclaiming, 'O, God! that I could see my mother' and instantly expired. Lieutenant John A. Oates, my dear brother, succeeded to the command of the company, but was pierced through by a number of bullets, and fell mortally wounded. Lieutenant Cody fell mortally wounded, Captain Bethune and several other officers were seriously wounded, while the carnage in the ranks was appalling."

And later, "My dead and wounded were then nearly as great in number as those still on duty. They literally covered the ground. The blood stood in puddles in some places on the rocks. . . ."

There were charges and countercharges up and down the slope. Colonel Oates believed that he drove the Federals from their position five times, and each time they rallied and drove back, twice coming to the point of hand-to-hand combat. He remembered that once "a Maine man reached to grasp the staff of the colors when Ensign Archibald stepped back and Sergeant Pat O'Connor stove his bayonet through the head of the Yankee, who fell dead."

Then came a lull when the Confederates drew back temporarily, and the Maine soldiers could have agreed with Oates that the scene had taken on a decidedly reddish tinge. The 20th had lost almost a third of its strength. They saw their dead and wounded out in front of them, mingled with those of the enemy. During the countercharges they had been scattered all the way down the slope to the very feet of the enemy, now rallying for another attempt.

Across the valley, a Confederate soldier saw Colonel Chamberlain standing by himself, in the open, behind the center of the 20th Maine's line. It was evident from Chamberlain's uniform and his actions that he was an important officer, well worth a careful shot. The soldier found himself a place between two big rocks, rested his rifle over one of them and looked at Chamberlain over the sights, taking steady aim. When he started to pull the trigger, a queer feeling came over him and he stopped. Ashamed of himself, he once again lined up his sights, but for some reason that he couldn't explain, he was unable to pull the trigger. Years later, he wrote to Chamberlain saying he was glad that he hadn't fired and he hoped that Chamberlain was too.

Over on the right of the 20th Maine, the rest of Vincent's Brigade had been holding its own. The right wing had almost broken once but was rallied by Colonel Vincent himself, and the 140th New York had arrived in time to hurl back the Confederate attack at this point. But Vincent had fallen with a bullet in his left groin, saying as they carried him back, "This is the fourth or fifth time they have shot at me, and they have hit me at last." On this western part of Little Round Top, Hazlett's Battery had also arrived, and the men of the 20th Maine could hear Hazlett's guns pounding, with heavy musketry also telling of desperate fighting. There was no hope of assistance from that quarter. The left of the 20th Maine had now been bent so far back that bullets from the attacking Confederates were falling into the rest of the brigade from the rear. The acting adjutant of the 83rd Pennsylvania came dodging and scrambling over to Chamberlain, wanting to know if his left had been turned.

Chamberlain sent word to Captain O. S. Woodward, commander of the 83rd, that the enemy was pushing his left back almost double upon his right and asked for a company. Woodward replied that he couldn't spare a company, but if the 20th Maine would pull its right companies to the left, he would move over and fill up the gap.

This move was made and brought some relief, but the 20th Maine had been bent back so far that it was in the rear of the army, in rear of the brigade, and in rear of itself. Let it give way in another Confederate charge, and Lee might be rolling up the Army of the Potomac like a rug.

And that was not the worst. There were hoarse cries of "Ammunition!" up and down the line, and soldiers were scrambling around looking for cartridges in the boxes of the dead and wounded. Chamberlain saw men fire their last rounds and then look back at him as if to say, "What now?"

The Colonel's alert brain ticked off the alternatives. The Confederates were gathering for another assault, but the 20th Maine couldn't withdraw; its orders were to hold the ground at all costs. He knew that they could not withstand another charge. And they couldn't continue the fire-fight for the reason that they had run out of ammunition. (Later Chamberlain figured that this was a good thing, for if they had continued, the enemy with superior numbers would have finished them off on a musket-to-musket basis.) Chamberlain decided that there was only one thing to do: fix bayonets and charge down into the Alabamians, hoping that surprise and shock action would drive them.

But here, too, there was a serious difficulty. With the left of the 20th Maine bent back so far, a charge might disperse the regiment or cause it to split in two at the angle. The left wing therefore had to begin the charge and swing around abreast of the right before the whole line could move forward. Colonel Chamberlain limped along the line, giving the necessary instructions. (His right instep had been cut by a flying shell fragment or rock splinter, and his left thigh had been badly bruised when a Minié ball bent his steel scabbard against it.)

As Chamberlain was returning to the center, Lieutenant Holman S. Melcher of Company F came up to him and asked permission to go out and get some of his wounded who lay between the 20th and the enemy line. To Melcher's surprise, the Colonel said, "Yes, sir. Take your place with your company. I am about to order a right wheel forward of the whole regiment."

Chamberlain stepped to the colors and his voice rang out. "Bayonet!" There was a moment of hesitation along the line, an intaking of breath like that of a man about to plunge into a cold, dark river. But along with it there was a rattling of bayonet shanks on steel. Intent on his wounded, Lieutenant Melcher sprang out in front of the line with his sword flashing, and this seems to have been the spark. The colors rose in front. A few men got up. Then a few more. They began to shout. The left wing, which was fighting off an attack at the time, suddenly charged, drove off its opponents and kept on until it had swung around abreast of the right wing. Then the regiment plunged down the slope in a great right wheel, Captain A. W. Clark's Company E holding the pivot against the 83rd Pennsylvania. To an officer of the 83rd, the 20th Maine looked as though it were moving "like a great gate upon a post."

The Confederate troops at the bottom of the slope were taken completely off guard. There were, perhaps, physical as well as psychological reasons to explain the apparent miracle that followed. The Confederates had been weakened by their strenuous approach march, thirst, and their efforts during the fighting. There was no time to fire a decisive volley and the Maine bayonets were shining in their faces almost before they knew what had happened. For a moment they fought in a daze. Then, before this roaring, downward-lunging assault, they gave backward and the affair took on the qualities of a dream. With one hand an Alabama officer fired a big revolver in Colonel Chamberlain's face, missed, and promptly handed over his sword with the other hand. Men were running, tripping, falling. The Confederate line broke up in confusion.

Farther on, the Alabamians made a stand with squads of the formidable 4th and 5th Texas, and it might have gone badly with the 20th Maine had there not been a fortuitous intervention. Even as the 20th Maine had been saving the army's left flank, so now it was itself about to be aided by one of its own fragrants. This was Captain Morrill's Company B. After moving out as a skirmish party, Company B had not been heard from. Supposedly it had been cut off or captured by the sudden advance of the Alabamians. But the men of Company B had been very much alive all the while, hidden behind a stone wall. Now, having been joined by some of the sharpshooters that Oates had driven over Big Round Top, they rose up and fired a volley into the Confederate rear, at the same time making a loud demonstration.

The exhausted and staggered Alabamians were being pressed back by the charging Maine regiment in front—back so far that they were also receiving fire from the rest of the Yankee brigade on their left. And now, suddenly, bullets were coming from their right and rear. Morrill and his men had unleashed one of the most fearsome weapons of war—surprise, which explodes in the brain and destroys the power to reason. Oates saw a dreadful thing: men being shot in the face, while others beside them were being shot in the back, and still others were being struck by bullets coming simultaneously from two or three different directions. The growing panic that set in is traceable in the reports coming to Oates from his company commanders. In one of these reports Morrill's little band was magnified into two regiments. Another report had it that there was a line of dismounted Union cavalrymen in the Confederate rear, although there is no record of cavalrymen in the Little Round Top fight, either mounted or dismounted. Oates believed that he was completely surrounded, and his regiment would have to cut its way out. "I . . . had the officers and men advised the best I could that when the signal was given that we would not try to retreat in order, but every one should run in the direction from whence we came. . . . When the signal was given we ran like a herd of wild cattle, right through the line of dismounted cavalrymen. . . . As we ran, a man named Keils, of Company H, from Henry County, who was to my right and rear, had his throat cut by a bullet, and he ran past me breathing at his throat and the blood spattering."

In spite of their numbers, their courage, and their almost superhuman exertions, the Confederate troops had suffered a baffling defeat.

Part of the reason had been superb handling of a regiment by a college professor who had been in the army less than a year. And part had been—well, everything going against them, events combining in a way that might not happen again in a thousand years.

To find any parallel, it would almost be necessary to go back to Second Kings, 7, wherein the four leprous men had said to one another, "Why sit we here until we die?" and had then risen up and advanced into the camp of the Syrians, the Lord at the proper moment causing the Syrians to hear "a noise of chariots, and a noise of horses, even the noise of a great host," so that they all fled for their lives.

After sweeping the front of the brigade clear and rounding up an estimated four hundred prisoners, the 20th Maine returned to its original position on Little Round Top, and it was a triumphant but a sobering walk. The slaughter had been sudden, prodigious—and sickening, now that there was time to look at the results. As Oates had noted, the ground was literally covered with bodies. Some moaning and moving and bleeding. Others silent, lying in the ridiculous, rag-doll postures of the dead. They were scattered everywhere, among rocks, behind trees. The 20th

Maine had suffered 130 casualties, including forty killed or mortally wounded. Mingled with these were around 150 dead and wounded Confederates.

In his official report Colonel Chamberlain stated, "We went into the fight with 386, all told—358 guns. Every pioneer and musician who could carry a musket went into the ranks. Even the sick and footsore, who could not keep up in the march, came up as soon as they could find their regiments, and took their places in line of battle, while it was battle, indeed."

Now that there was time to stop and think about what had happened, it was enough to give a man the shakes.

The thing that was most frightening about it was how the weight of a momentous battle could have come to rest so disproportionately upon just a few ordinary men—farmers, fishermen and woodsmen. Seldom if ever before had one small regiment fought so fantastically. The maneuver whereby the double line of battle had stretched itself out into a single line, extending and bending back under fire with the noise making ordinary commands impossible, was something out of a dream.

The charge, the swinging and straightening of the left wing back into line, the plunge down the slope had succeeded simply because it had been so improbable.

And if the Maine men had been in any mood to reflect, they might have mused upon the workings of a Providence that had brought them past Antietam, Fredericksburg and Chancellorsville to arrive at this spot with the unfit weeded out, but with the lean fighting muscle of the regiment largely unimpaired.

It was immediately clear to a lot of people that one of the most important actions of the war had just been fought. Corporal William T. Livermore recorded the day's events in his diary. "The Regiment we fought and captured was the 15th Alabama. They fought like demons and said they never were whipped before and never wanted to meet the 20th Maine again. . . . Ours was an important position, and had we been driven from it, the tide of battle would have been turned against us and what the result would have been we cannot tell."

But the man who had seen the Confederacy's lost opportunity more clearly than anyone else was Colonel Oates. Roll call that night revealed that less than half of this once-great regiment remained. In later years he would reflect, "There

never were harder fighters than the Twentieth Maine men
and their gallant Colonel. His skill and persistency and the
great bravery of his men saved Little Round Top and the
Army of the Potomac from defeat. Great events sometimes
turn on comparatively small affairs."

And later, for this day's work, would come the Congres-
sional Medal of Honor for Joshua Chamberlain.

It was, as Maine men would say, "*a caution!*" But right
now, with nostrils filled with the sulphurous, sick-sweet
smell of burned gunpowder, heads dazed, and ears ringing,
they weren't saying or thinking much of anything.

The smoke settled and the shadows deepened in the little
valley. Westward, trees turned black against a sultry purple
sunset. To the west and north, the roar of battle died away
in a slow, rumbling diminuendo. Darkness came, and in
barns and other buildings where the wounded had been
taken, the surgeons were working desperately by
candlelight.

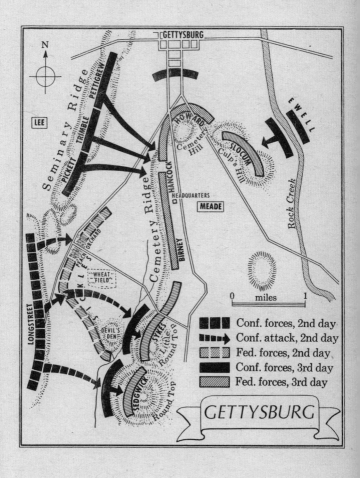

GETTYSBURG

THE LULL BEFORE THE STORM

THE DAY BEGAN WITH A FIGHT between Confederate troops who controlled the lower half of Culp's Hill on the Federal right flank. Fierce fighting surged back and forth as the Confederates tried to reach the top of the hill from which they could threaten the whole Union right flank and rear. By 10:30 A.M. they had worn themselves out in frontal charges, and an ominous quiet settled over the battlefield.

Robert E. Lee had failed to turn either Federal flank. Now he was considering an assault on the Federal center at Cemetery Ridge. General Longstreet felt the attack would be a disaster and he said so, emphatically, without effect. Lee ordered Longstreet to send the Conferate divisions into battle.

Not until 2 P.M. was the silence of the battlefield broken. Then: "rebel artillery, from all points, in a circle radiating around our own, began a terrific and concentrated fire on Cemetery Hill. A flock of pigeons, which not ten minutes previously had darkened the sky above, were scarcely thicker than the flock of horrible missiles that now, instead of sailing harmlessly above, descended on our position. The storm broke upon us so suddenly that soldiers and officers—who leaped, as it began, from their tents and from lazy siesta on the grass—were stricken in their rising with mortal wounds, and died, some with cigars between their teeth, some with pieces of food in their fingers, and one at least—a pale young German from Pennsylvania—with a miniature of his sister in his hands, which seemed more fit to grasp an artist's pencil than a musket. Horses fell, shrieking awful cries. The boards of fences flew in splinters through the air. The earth, torn up in clouds, blinded the eyes of hurrying men."

And: "holes like graves were gouged in the earth by exploding shells. The flowers in bloom upon the graves at the

* From a reporter for the New York *World*, as reported in *The Rebellion Record*, Vol. VII.

Cemetery were shot away. Tombs and monuments were knocked to pieces, and ordinary gravestones shattered in rows."†

The men on Cemetery Ridge had expected a fight this day, but they were not prepared for the onslaught to come.

Gettysburg: Third Day*

BY COLONEL FRANK HASKELL

AT FOUR O'CLOCK ON THE MORNING OF THE THIRD, I was awakened by General Gibbon's pulling me by the foot and saying: "Come, don't you hear that?" I sprang up to my feet. Where was I? A moment and my dead senses and memory were alive again, and the sound of brisk firing of musketry to the front and right of the Second Corps, and over at the extreme right of our line, where we heard it last in the night, brought all back to my memory. We surely were on the field of battle, and there were palpable evidences to my reason that to-day was to be another blood. Oh! for a moment the throught of it was sickening to every sense and feeling! But the motion of my horse as I galloped over the crest a few minutes later, and the serene splendor of the morning now breaking through rifted clouds and spreading over the landscape, soon assured me. Come day of battle! Up Rebel hosts, and thunder with your arms! We are all ready to do and to die for the Republic!

I found a sharp skirmish going on in front of the right of the Second Corps, between our outposts and those of the enemy, but save this—and none of the enemy but his outposts were in sight—all was quiet in that part of the field. On the extreme right of the line the sound of musketry was quite heavy; and this I learned was brought on by the attack of the Second Division, Twelfth Corps, General Geary, upon the enemy in order to drive him out of our works which he had sneaked into yesterday, as I have mentioned. The attack was made at the earliest moment in the morning when it was light enough to discern objects to fire at.

† From Warren L. Goss, *Recollections of a Private.*
* From *The Battle of Gettysburg.*

The enemy could not use the works, but was confronting Geary in woods, and had the cover of many rocks and trees, so the fight was an irregular one, now breaking out and swelling to a vigorous fight, now subsiding to a few scattering shots; and so it continued by turns until the morning was well advanced, when the enemy was finally wholly repulsed and driven from the pits, and the right of our line was again re-established in the place it first occupied.

The heaviest losses the Twelfth Corps sustained in all the battle occurred during this attack, and they were here quite severe. I heard General Meade express dissatisfaction at General Geary for making this attack, as a thing not ordered and not necessary, as the works of ours were of no intrinsic importance, and had not been captured from us by a fight, and Geary's position was just as good as they, where he was during the night. And I heard General Meade say that he sent an order to have the fight stopped; but I believe the order was not communicated to Geary until after the repulse of the enemy.

Late in the forenoon the enemy again tried to carry our right by storm. We heard that old Rebel Ewell had sworn an oath that he would break our right. He had Stonewall Jackson's Corps and possibly imagined himself another Stonewall, but he certainly *hankered* after the right of our line—and so up through the woods, and over the rocks, and up the steeps he sent his storming parties—our men could see them now in the day time. But all the Rebel's efforts were fruitless, save in one thing, slaughter in his own men.

These assaults were made with great spirit and determination, but as the enemy would come up, our men lying behind their secure defenses would just singe them with the blaze of their muskets, and riddle them, as a hail-storm the tender blades of corn. The Rebel oath was not kept, any more than his former one to support the Constitution of the United States. The Rebel loss was very heavy indeed, here, ours but trifling.

I regret that I cannot give more of the details of this fighting upon the right—it was so determined upon the part of the enemy, both last night and this morning—so successful to us. About all that I actually saw of it during its progress, was the smoke, and I heard the discharges. My information is derived from officers who were personally in it. Some of our heavier artillery assisted our infantry in this by firing, with the piece elevated, far from the rear, over the heads of our men, at a distance from the enemy of two miles, I suppose. Of course they could have done no great damage. It was nearly eleven o'clock that the battle in this part of the field subsided, not to be again renewed. All the morning we felt no apprehension for this part of the line, for we knew its strength, and that our troops engaged the Twelfth Corps and the First Division, Wadsworth's, of the First, could be trusted.

For the sake of telling one thing at a time, I have anticipated events somewhat, in writing of this fight upon the right. I shall now go back to the starting point, four o'clock this morning, and, as other events occurred during the day, second to none in the battle in importance, which I think I saw as much of as any man living, I will tell you something of them, and what I saw, and how the time moved on.

The outpost skirmish that I have mentioned soon subsided. I suppose it was the natural escape of the wrath which the men had during the night hoarded up against each other, and which, as soon as they could see in the morning, they could no longer contain, but must let it off through their musket barrels, at their adversaries. At the commencement of the war such firing would have awaked the whole army and roused it to its feet and to arms; not so now. The men upon the crest lay snoring in their blankets, even though some of the enemy's bullets dropped among them, as if bullets were harmless as the drops of dew around them. As the sun arose to-day, the clouds became broken, and we had once more glimpses of sky, and fits of sunshine—a rarity, to cheer us.

From the crest, save to the right of the Second Corps, no enemy, not even his outposts could be discovered, along all the position where he so thronged upon the Third Corps yesterday. All was silent there—the wounded heroes were limping about the field; the ravages of the conflict were still fearfully visible—the scattered arms and the ground thickly dotted with the dead—but no hostile foe. The men were roused early, in order that the morning meal might be out of the way in time for whatever should occur. Then ensued the hum of an army, not in ranks, chatting in low tones, and running about and jostling among each other, rolling and packing their blankets and tents.

They looked like an army of rag-gatherers, while shaking these very useful articles of the soldier's outfit, for you must know that rain and mud in conjunction have not had the effect to make them clean, and the wear and tear of service have not left them entirely whole. But one could not have told by the appearance of the men, that they were in battle yesterday, and were likely to be again to-day. They packed their knapsacks, boiled their coffee and munched their hard bread, just as usual—just like old soldiers who know what campaigning is; and their talk is far more concerning their present employment—some joke or drollery—than concerning what they saw or did yesterday.

As early as practicable the lines all along the left are revised and reformed, this having been rendered necessary by yesterday's battle, and also by what is anticipated to-day.

It is the opinion of many of our Generals that the Rebel will not give us battle to-day—that he had enough yesterday—that he will be heading towards the Potomac at the earliest practicable moment, if he has not already done so; but the better, and controlling judgment is, that he will make another grand effort to pierce or turn our lines—that he will either mass and attack the left again, as yesterday, or direct his operations against the left of our center, the position of the Second Corps, and try to sever our line. I infer that General Meade was of the opinion that the attack to-day would be upon the left—this from the disposition he ordered, I know that General Hancock anticipated the attack upon the center.

The dispositions to-day upon the left are as follows:

The Second and Third Divisions of the Second Corps are in the position of yesterday; then on the left come Double-day's—the Third Division and Col. Stannard's brigade of the First Corps; then Colwell's [Caldwell's]—the First Division of the Second Corps; then the Third Corps, temporarily under the command of Hancock, since Sickles' wound. The Third Corps is upon the same ground in part, and on the identical line where it first formed yesterday morning, and where, had it stayed instead of moving out to the front, we should have many more men to-day, and should not have been upon the brink of disaster yesterday. On the left of the Third Corps is the Fifth Corps, with a short front and deep line; then comes the Sixth Corps, all but one brigade, which is sent over to the Twelfth. The Sixth, a splendid Corps, almost intact in the fight of yesterday, is the extreme left of our line, which terminates to the south of Round Top, and runs along its western base in the woods, and thence to the Cemetery. This Corps is burning to pay off the old scores made on the 4th of May, there back of Fredericksburg.

Note well the position of the Second and Third Divisions of the Second Corps—it will become important. There are nearly six thousand men and officers in these two Divisions here upon the field—the losses were quite heavy yesterday, some regiments are detached to other parts of the field—so all told there are less than six thousand men now in the two Divisions, who occupy a line of about a thousand yards. The most of the way along this line upon the crest was a stone fence, constructed of small, rough stones, a good deal of the way badly pulled down, but the men had improved it and patched it with rails from the neighboring fences, and with earth, so as to render it in many places a very passable breastwork against musketry and flying fragments of shells.

These works are so low as to compel the men to kneel or lie down generally to obtain cover. Near the right of the Second Division, and just by the little group of trees that I have mentioned there, this stone fence made a right angle, and extended thence to the front, about twenty or thirty yards, where with another less than a right angle it followed along the crest again.

The lines were conformed to these breastworks and to the nature of the ground upon the crest, so as to occupy the most favorable places, to be covered, and still be able to deliver effective fire upon the enemy should he come there. In some places a second line was so posted as to be able to deliver its fire over the heads of the first line behind the works; but such formation was not practicable all of the way. But all the force of these two divisions was in line, in position, without reserves, and in such a manner that every man of them could have fired his piece at the same instant. The division flags, that of the Second Division, being a white trefoil upon a square blue field, and of the Third Division, a blue trefoil upon a white rectangular field, waved behind the divisions at the points where the Generals of Division were supposed to be; the brigade flags, similar to these but with a triangular field, were behind the brigades; and the national flags of the regiments were in the lines of their regiments. To the left of the Second Division, and advanced something over a hundred yards, were posted a part of Sannard's Brigade, two regiments or more, behind a small bush-crowned crest that ran in a direction oblique to the general line. These were well covered by the crest, and wholly concealed by the bushes, so that an advancing enemy would be close upon them before they could be seen. Other troops of Doubleday's Division were strongly posted in rear of these in the general line.

I could not help wishing all the morning that this line of the two divisions of the Second Corps was stronger; it was, so far as numbers constitute strength, the weakest part of our whole line of battle. What if, I thought, the enemy should make an assault here to-day, with two or three heavy lines—a great overwhelming mass; would he not sweep through that thin six thousand?

But I was not General Meade, who alone had power to send other troops there; and he was satisfied with that part of the line as it was. He was early on horseback this morning, and rode along the whole line, looking to it himself and with glass in hand sweeping the woods and fields in the direction of the enemy, to see if aught of him could be discovered. His manner was calm and serious, but earnest. There was no arrogance of hope, or timidity of fear discernible in his face; but you would have supposed he would do his duty conscientiously and well and would be willing to abide the result. You would have seen this in his face. He was well pleased with the left of the line to-day, it was so strong with good troops. He had no apprehension for the right where the fight now was going on, on account of the admirable position of our forces there. He was not of the opinion that the enemy would attack the center, our artillery had such sweep there, and this was not the favorite point of attack with the Rebel. Besides, should he attack the center, the General thought he could reinforce it in good season. I heard General Meade speak of these matters to Hancock and some others, at about nine o'clock in the morning, while they were up by the line, near the Second Corps.

No further changes of importance except those mentioned were made in the disposition of the troops this morning, except to replace some of the batteries that were disabled yesterday by others from the artillery reserve, and to brace up the lines well with guns wherever there were eligible places, from the same source. The line is all in good order again, and we are ready for general battle.

Save the operations upon the right, the enemy, so far as we could see, was very quiet all the morning. Occasionally the outposts would fire a little, and then cease. Movements would be discovered which would indicate the attempt on the part of the enemy to post a battery. Our Parrotts would send a few shells to the spot, then silence would follow.

At one of these times a painful accident happened to us, this morning. First Lieutenant Henry Ropes, 20th Massachusetts, in General Gibbon's Division, a most estimable gentleman and officer, intelligent, educated, refined, one of the noble souls that came to the country's defense, while lying at his post with his régiment, in front of one of the Batteries, which fired over the Infantry, was instantly killed by a badly made shell, which, or some portion of it, fell but a few yards in front of the muzzle of the gun. The same accident killed or wounded several others. The loss of Ropes would have pained us at any time, and in any manner; in this manner his death was doubly painful.

Between ten and eleven o'clock, over in a peach orchard in front of the position of Sickles yesterday, some little show of the enemy's infantry was discovered; a few shells scattered the gray-backs; they again appeared, and it becoming apparent that they were only posting a skirmish line, no further molestation was offered them. A little after this some of the enemy's flags could be discerned over near the same quarter, above the top and behind a small crest of a ridge. There seemed to be two or three of them—possibly they were guidons—and they moved too fast to be carried on foot. Possibly, we thought, the enemy is posting some batteries there. We knew in about two hours from this time better about the matter.

Eleven o'clock came. The noise of battle has ceased upon the right; not a sound of a gun or musket can be heard on all the field; the sky is bright, with only the white fleecy clouds floating over from the West. The July sun streams down its fire upon the bright iron of the muskets in stacks upon the crest, and the dazzling brass of the Napoleons. The army lolls and longs for the shade, of which some get a hand's breadth, from a shelter tent stuck upon a ramrod. The silence and sultriness of a July noon are supreme. Now it so happened that just about this time of day a very original interesting thought occurred to General Gibbon and several of his staff, that it would be a very good thing and a very good time, to have something to eat. When I announce to you that I had not tasted a mouthful of food since yesterday noon, and that all I had had to drink since that time, but the most miserable muddy warm water, was a little drink of whiskey that Major Biddle, General Meade's aide-de-camp, gave me last evening, and a cup of strong coffee that I gulped down as I was first mounting this morning, and further, that, save the four or five hours in the night, there was scarcely a moment since that time but that I was in the saddle, you may have some notion of the reason of my assent to this extraordinary proposition. Nor will I mention the doubt I had as to the feasibility of the execution of this very novel proposal, except to say that I knew this morning that our larder was low; not to put too fine a point upon it, that we had nothing but some potatoes and sugar and coffee in the world. And I may as well say here, that of such, in scant proportion, would have been our repast, had it not been for the riding of miles by two persons, one an officer, to procure supplies; and they only succeeded in getting some few chickens, some butter, and one huge loaf of bread, which last was bought of a soldier, because he had grown faint in carrying it, and was afterwards rescued with much difficulty and after a long race from a four-footed hog, which had got hold of and had actually eaten a part of it. "There is a divinity," etc.

Suffice it, this very ingenious and unheard of contemplated proceeding, first announced by the General, was accepted and at once undertaken by his staff. Of the absolute quality of what we had to eat, I could not pretend to judge, but I think an unprejudiced person would have said of the bread that it was good; so of the potatoes before they were boiled. Of the chickens he would have questioned their age, but they were large and in good *running* order. The toast was good, and the butter. They were those who, when coffee was given them, called for tea, and vice versa, and were so ungracious as to suggest that the water that was used in both might have come from near a barn. Of course it did not. We all came down to the little peach orchard where we had stayed last night, and, wonderful to see and tell, ever mindful of our needs, had it all ready, had our faithful John. There was an enormous pan of stewed chickens, and the potatoes, and toast, all hot, and the bread and the butter, and tea and coffee. There was satisfaction derived from just naming them all over. We called John an angel, and he snickered and said he "knowed" we'd come.

General Hancock is of course invited to partake, and without delay we commence operations. Stools are not very numerous, two in all, and these the two Generals have by common consent. Our table was the top of a mess chest. By this the Generals sat. The rest of us sat upon the ground, cross-legged, like the picture of a smoking Turk, and held our plates upon our laps. How delicious was the stewed chicken. I had a cucumber pickle in my saddle bags, the last of a lunch left there two or three days ago, which George brought, and I had half of it. We were just well at it when General Meade rode down to us from the line, accompanied by one of his staff, and by General Gibbon's invitation, they dismounted and joined us. For the General commanding the Army of the Potomac, George, by an effort worthy of the person and the occasion, finds an empty cracker box for a seat. The staff officer must sit upon the ground with the rest of us. Soon Generals Newton and Pleasonton, each with an aide, arrive. By an almost superhuman effort a roll of blankets is found, which upon a pinch, is long enough to seat these Generals both, and room is made for them. The aides sit with us. And fortunate to relate, there was enough cooked for us all, and from General Meade to the youngest second lieutenant we all had a most hearty and well relished dinner. Of the "past" we were "secure."

The Generals ate, and after, lighted cigars, and under the flickering shade of a very small tree, discoursed of the incidents of yesterday's battle and of the probabilities of today. General Newton humorously spoke of General Gibbon as "this young North Carolinian," and how he was becoming arrogant and above his position, because he commanded a corps. General Gibbon retorted by saying that General Newton had not been long enough in such a command, only since yesterday, to enable him to judge of such things. General Meade still thought the enemy would attack his left again to-day towards evening; but he was ready for them. General Hancock thought that the attack would be upon the position of the Second Corps. It was mentioned that General Hancock would again assume command of the Second Crops from that time, so that General Gibbon would again return to the Second Division.

General Meade spoke of the Provost Guards, that they were good men, and that it would be better to-day to have them in the works than to stop stragglers and skulkers, as these latter would be good for but little even in the works; and so he gave the order that all the Provost Guards should at once temporarily rejoin their regiments. Then General Gibbon called up Captain Farrell, First Minnesota, who commanded the provost guard of his division, and directed him for that day to join the regiment. "Very well, sir," said the Captain, as he touched his hat and turned away. He was a quiet, excellent gentleman and thorough soldier. I knew him well and esteemed him. I never saw him again. He was killed in two or three hours from that time, and over half of his splendid company were either killed or wounded.

And so the time passed on, each General now and then dispatching some order or message by an officer or orderly, until about half-past twelve when all the Generals, one by one, first General Meade, rode off their several ways, and General Gibbon and his staff alone remained.

We dozed in the heat, and lolled upon the ground, with half-open eyes. Our horses were hitched to the trees munching some oats. A great lull rests upon all the field. Time was heavy, and for want of something better to do, I yawned, and looked at my watch. It was five minutes before one o'clock. I returned my watch to my pocket, and thought possibly that I might go to sleep, and stretched myself upon the ground accordingly. *Ex uno disce omnes*. My attitude and purpose were those of the General and the rest of the staff.

What sound was that? There was no mistaking it. The distinct sharp sound of one of the enemy's guns, square over to the front, caused us to open our eyes and turn them in that direction, when we saw directly above the crest the smoke of the bursting shell, and heard its noise. In an instant, before a word was spoken, as if that was the signal gun for general work, loud, startling, booming, the report of gun after gun in rapid succession smote our ears and their shells plunged down and exploded all around us. We sprang to our feet. In briefest time the whole Rebel line to the West was pouring out its thunder and its iron upon our devoted crest. The wildest confusion for a few moments obtained sway among us. The shells came bursting all about. The servants ran terror-stricken for dear life and disappeared. The horses, hitched to the trees or held by the slack hands of the orderlies, neighed out in fright and broke away and plunged riderless through the fields. The General at the first had snatched his sword, and started on foot for the front. I called for my horse; nobody responded. I found him tied to a tree, nearby, eating oats, with an air of the greatest composure, which under the circumstances, even then struck me as exceedingly ridiculous. He alone, of all beasts or men near, was cool. I am not sure but that I learned a lesson then from a horse. Anxious alone for his oats, while I put on the bridle and adjusted the halter, he delayed me by keeping his head down, so I had time to see one of the horses of our mess wagon struck and torn by a shell. The pair plunge—the driver has lost the reins—horses, driver and wagon go into a heap by a tree. Two mules close at hand, packed with boxes of ammunition, are knocked all to pieces by a shell. General Gibbon's groom has just mounted his horse and is starting to take the General's horse to him, when the flying iron meets him and tears open his breast. He drops dead and the horses gallop away. No more than a minute since the first shot was fired, and I am mounted and riding after the General.

The mighty din that now rises to heaven and shakes the earth is not all of it the voice of the rebellion; for our guns, the guardian lions of the crest, quick to awake when danger comes, have opened their fiery jaws and begun to roar—the great hoarse roar of battle. I overtake the General half way up to the line. Before we reach the crest his horse is brought by an orderly. Leaving our horses just behind a sharp declivity of the ridge, on foot we go up among the batteries. How the long streams of fire spout from the guns, how the rifled shells hiss, how the smoke deepens and rolls. But where is the infantry? Has it vanished in smoke? Is this a nightmare or a juggler's devilish trick? All too real. The men of the infantry have seized their arms, and behind their works, behind every rock, in every ditch, wherever there is any shelter, they hug the ground, silent, quiet, unterrified, little harmed. The enemy's guns now in action are in position at their front of the woods along the second ridge that I have before mentioned and towards their right, behind a small crest in the open field, where we saw the flags this morning. Their line is some two miles long, concave on the side towards us, and their range is from one thousand to eighteen hundred yards. A hundred and twenty-five rebel guns, we estimate, are now active, firing twenty-four pound, twenty, twelve and ten-pound projectiles, solid shot and shells, sperical, conical, spiral.

The enemy's fire is chiefly concentrated upon the position of the Second Corps. From the Cemetery to Round Top, with over a hundred guns, and to all parts of the enemy's line, our batteries reply, of twenty and ten pound Parrotts, ten-pound rifled ordnance, and twelve-pound Napoleons, using projectiles as various in shape and name as those of the enemy. Captain [John G.] Hazard commanding the artillery brigade of the Second Corps was vigilant among the batteries of his command, and they were all doing well. All was going well. All was going on satisfactorily. We had nothing to do, therefore, but to be observers of the grand spectacle of battle. Captain Wessels, Judge Advocate of the Division, now joined us, and we sat down behind the crest, close to the left of Cushing's Battery, to bide our time, to see, to be ready to act when the time should come, which might be at any moment.

Who can describe such a conflict as is raging around us? To say that it was like a summer storm, with the crash of thunder, the glare of lightning, the shieking of the wind, and the clatter of hailstones, would be weak. The thunder and lightning of these two hundred and fifty guns and their shells, whose smoke darkens the sky, are incessant, all pervading, in the air above our heads, on the ground at our feet, remote, near, deafening, ear-piercing, astounding; and these hailstones are massy iron, charged with exploding fire. And there is little of human interest in a storm; it is an absorbing element of this. You may see flame and smoke, and hurrying men, and human passion at a great conflagration; but they are all earthly and nothing more. These guns are great infuriate demons, not of the earth, whose mouths blaze with smoky tongues of living fire, and whose murky breath, sulphur-laden rolls around them and along the ground the smoke of Hades. These grimy men, rushing, shouting, their souls in frenzy, playing the dusky globes and the igniting spark, are in their league, and but their willing ministers. We thought that at the second Bull Run, at the Antietam and at Fredericksburg on the 11th of December, we had heard heavy cannonading; they were but holiday salutes compared with this. Besides the great ceaseless roar of the guns, which was but the background of the others, a million various minor sounds engaged the ear. The projectiles shriek long and sharp. They hiss, they scream, they growl, they sputter; all sounds of life and rage; and each has its different note, and all are discordant. Was ever such a chorus of sound before? We note the effect of the enemies' fire among the batteries and along the crest. We see the solid shot strike axle, or pole, or wheel, and the tough iron and heart of oak snap and fly like straws. The great oaks there by Woodruff's guns heave down their massy branches with a crash, as if the lightning smote them. The shells swoop down among the battery horses standing there apart. A half a dozen horses start, they tumble, their legs stiffen, their vitals and blood smear the ground. And these shot and shells have no respect for men either. We see the poor fellows hobbling back from the crest, or unable to do so, pale and weak, lying on the ground with the mangled stump of an arm or leg, dripping their life-blood away; or with a cheek torn open or a shoulder mashed. And many, alas! hear not the roar as they stretch upon the ground with upturned faces and open eyes, though a shell should burst at their very ears. Their ears and their bodies this instant are only mud. We saw them but a moment since there among the flame, with brawny arms and muscles of iron, wielding the rammer and pushing home the cannon's plethoric load.

Strange freaks these round shot play! We saw a man coming up from the rear with his full knapsack on, and some canteens of water held by the straps in his hands. He was walking slowly and with apparent unconcern, though the iron hailed around him. A shot struck the knapsack, and it and its contents flew thirty yards in every direction, the knapsack disappearing like an egg thrown spitefully against a rock. The soldier stopped and turned about in puzzled surprise, put up one hand to his back to assure himself that the knapsack was not there, and then walked slowly on again unharmed, with not even his coat torn. Near us was a man crouching behind a small disintegrated stone, which was about the size of a common water bucket. He was bent up, with his face to the ground, in the attitude of a Pagan worshipper before his idol. It looked so absurd to see him thus, that I went and said to him, "Do not lie there like a toad. Why not go to your regiment and be a man?" He turned up his face with a stupid, terrified look upon me, and then without a word turned his nose again to the ground. An orderly that was with me at the time told me a few moments later, that a shot struck the stone, smashing it in a thousand fragments, but did not touch the man, though his head was not six inches from the stone.

All the projectiles that came near us were not so harmless. Not ten yards away from us a shell burst among some small bushes, where sat three or four orderlies holding horses. Two of the men and one horse were killed. Only a few yards off a shell exploded over an open limber box in Cushing's battery, and at the same instant, another shell over a neighboring box. In both the boxes the ammunition blew up with an explosion that shook the ground, throwing fire and splinters and shells far into the air and all around, and destroying several men. We watched the shells bursting in the air, as they came hissing in all directions. Their flash was a bright gleam of lightning radiating from a point, given place in the thousandth part of a second to a small, white puffy cloud, like a fleece of the lightest, whitest wool. These clouds were very numerous. We could not often see the shell before it burst; but sometimes, as we faced toward the enemy, and looked above our heads, the approach would be heralded by a prolonged hiss, which always seemed to me to be a line of something tangible, terminating in a black globe, distinct to the eye, as the sound had been to the ear. The shell would seem to stop, and hang suspended in the air an instant, and then vanish in fire and smoke and noise.

We saw the missiles tear and plow the ground. All in rear of the crest for a thousand yards, as well as among the batteries, was the field of their blind fury. Ambulances, passing down the Taneytown road, with wounded men, were struck. The hospitals near this road were riddled. The house which was General Meade's headquarters was shot through several times, and a great many horses of officers and orderlies were lying dead around it. Riderless horses, galloping madly through the fields, were brought up, or down rather, by these invisible horse-tamers, and they would not run any more. Mules with ammunition, pigs wallowing about, cows in the pastures, whatever was animate or inanimate, in all this broad range, were no exception to their blind havoc. The percussion shells would strike, and thunder, and scatter the earth and their whistling fragments; the Whitworth bolts would pound and ricochet, and bowl far away sputtering, with the sound of a mass of hot iron plunged in water; and the great solid shot would smite the unresisting ground with a sounding "thud," as the strong boxer crashes his iron fist into the jaws of his unguarded adversary. Such were some of the sights and sounds of this great iron battle of missiles. Our artillerymen upon the crest budged not an inch, nor intermitted, but, though caisson and limber were smashed, and guns dismantled, and men and horses killed, there amidst smoke and sweat, they gave back, without grudge, or loss of time in the sending, in kind whatever the enemy sent, globe, and cone, and bolt, hollow or solid an iron greeting to the rebellion, the compliments of the wrathful Republic.

An hour has droned its flight since the war began. There is no sign of weariness or abatement on either side. So long it seemed, that the din and crashing around began to appear the normal condition of nature there, and fighting man's element. The General proposed to go among the men and over to the front of the batteries, so at about two o'clock he and I started. We went along the lines of the infantry as they lay there flat upon the earth, a little to the front of the batteries. They were suffering little, and were quiet and cool. How glad we were that the enemy were no better gunners, and that they cut the shell fuses too long. To the question asked the men, "What do you think of this?" the replies would be "O, this is bully," "We are getting to like it." "O, we don't mind this." And so they lay under the heaviest cannonade that ever shook the continent, and among them a thousand times more jokes than heads were cracked.

We went down in front of the line some two hundred yards, and as the smoke had a tendency to settle upon a higher plain than where we were, we could see near the ground distinctly all over the fields, as well back to the crest where were our own guns as to the opposite ridge where were those of the enemy. No infantry was in sight, save the skirmishers, and they stood silent and motionless—a row of gray posts through the field on one side confronted by another of blue. Under the grateful shade of some elm trees, where we could see much of the field, we made seats of the ground and sat down. Here all the more repulsive features of the fight were unseen, by reason of the smoke. Man had arranged the scenes, and for a time had taken part in the great drama; but at last, as the plot thickened, conscious of his littleness and inadequacy to the mighty part, he had stepped aside and given place to more powerful actors. So it seemed; for we could see no men about the batteries. On either crest we could see the great flaky streams of fire, and they seemed numberless, of the opposing guns, and their white banks of swift, convolving smoke; but the sound of the discharges was drowned in the universal ocean of sound. Over all the valley the smoke, a sulphury arch, stretched its lurid span; and through it always, shrieking on their unseen courses, thickly flew a myriad iron deaths. With our grim horizon on all sides round toothed thick with battery flame, under that dissonant canopy of warring shells, we sat and heard in silence. What other expression had we that was not mean, for such an awful universe of battle?

A shell struck our beastwork of rails up in sight of us, and a moment afterwards we saw the men bearing some of their

wounded companions away from the same spot; and
directly two men came from there down toward where we
were and sought to get shelter in an excavation near by,
where many dead horses, killed in yesterday's fight, had
been thrown. General Gibbon said to these men, more in a
tone of kindly expostulation than of command: "My men, do
not leave your ranks to try to get shelter here. All these matters are in the hands of God, and nothing that you can do
will make you safer in one place than in another." The men
went quietly back to the line at once. The General then said
to me: "I am not a member of any church, but I have always
had a strong religious feeling; and so in all these battles I
have always believed that I was in the hands of God, and
that I should be unharmed or not, according to his will. For
this reason, I think it is, I am always ready to go where duty
calls, no matter how great the danger."

Half-past two o'clock, an hour and a half since the commencement, and still the cannonade did not in the least
abate; but soon thereafter some signs of weariness and a little slacking of fire began to be apparent upon both sides.
First we saw Brown's battery retire from the line, too feeble
for further battle. Its position was a little to the front of the
line. Its commander was wounded, and many of its men
were so, or worse; some of its guns had been disabled, many
of its horses killed; its ammunition was nearly expended.
Other batteries in similar case had been withdrawn before to
be replaced by fresh ones, and some were withdrawn afterwards. Soon after the battery named had gone, the
General and I started to return, passing towards the left of
the division, and crossing the ground where the guns had
stood. The stricken horses were numerous, and the dead and
wounded men lay about, and as we passed these latter, their
low, piteous call for water would invariably come to us, if
they had yet any voice left. I found canteens of water
near—no difficult matter where a battle has been—and held
them to livid lips, and even in the faintness of death the
eagerness to drink told of their terrible torture of thirst. But
we must pass on. Our infantry was still unshaken, and in all
the cannonade suffered very little. The batteries had been
handled much more severely. I am unable to give any figures.
A great number of horses had been killed, in some batteries
more than half of all Guns had been dismounted. A great
many caissons, limbers and carriages had been destroyed,
and usually from ten to twenty-five men to each battery had

been struck, at least along our part of the crest. Altogether the fire of the enemy had injured us much, both in the modes that I have stated, and also by exhausting our ammunition and fouling our guns, so as to render our batteries unfit for further immediate use. The scenes that met our eyes on all hands among the batteries were fearful. All things must end, and the great cannonade was no exception to the general law of earth. In the number of guns active at one time, and in the duration and rapidity of their fire, this artillery engagement, up to this time, must stand alone and pre-eminent in this war. It has not been often, or many times, surpassed in the battles of the world. Two hundred and fifty guns, at least, rapidly fired for two mortal hours. Cipher out the number of tons of gunpowder and iron that made these two hours hideous.

Of the injury of our fire upon the enemy, except the facts that ours was the superior position, if not better served and constructed artillery, and that the enemy's artillery hereafter during the battle was almost silent, we know little. Of course, during the fight we often saw the enemy's caissons explode, and the trees rent by our shot crashing about his ears, but we can from these alone infer but little of general results. At three o'clock almost precisely the last shot hummed, and bounded and fell, and the cannonade was over. The purpose of General Lee in all this fire of his guns—we know it now, we did not at the time so well—was to disable our artillery and break up our infantry upon the position of the Second Corps, so as to render them less an impediment to the sweep of his own brigades and divisions over our crest and through our lines. He probably supposed our infantry was massed behind the crest and the batteries; and hence his fire was so high, and his fuses to the shells were cut so long, too long. The Rebel General failed in some of his plans in this behalf, as many generals have failed before and will again. The artillery fight over, men began to breathe more freely, and to ask, What next, I wonder? The battery men were among their guns, some leaning to rest and wipe the sweat from their sooty faces, some were handling ammunition boxes and replenishing those that were empty. Some batteries from the artillery reserve were moving up to take the places of the disabled ones; the smoke was clearing from the crests. There was a pause between the acts, with the curtain down, soon to rise upon the great final act, and catastrophe of Gettysburg. We have passed by the left of the Second

Gettysburg: *High tide of the Confederacy, July 3, 1863*

Division, coming from the First; when we crossed the crest the enemy was not in sight, and all was still—we walked slowly along in the rear of the troops, by the ridge cut off now from a view of the enemy in his position, and were returning to the spot where we had left our horses. General Gibbon had just said that he inclined to the belief that the enemy was falling back, and that the cannonade was only one of his noisy modes of covering the movement. I said that I thought that fifteen minutes would show that, by all his bowling, the Rebel did not mean retreat. We were near our horses when we noticed Brigadier General Hunt, Chief of Artillery of the Army, near Woodruff's Battery, swiftly moving about on horseback, and apparently in a rapid manner giving some orders about the guns. Thought we, What could this mean? In a moment afterwards we met Captain Wessels and the orderlies who had our horses; they were on foot leading the horses. Captain Wessels was pale, and he said, excited: "General, they say the enemy's infantry is advancing." We sprang into our saddles, a score of bounds brought us upon the all-seeing crest. To say that men grew pale and held their breath at what we and they there saw, would not be true. Might not six thousand men be brave and without shade of fear, and yet, before a hostile eighteen thousand, armed, and not five minutes' march away, turn ashy white?

None on that crest now needs be told that *the enemy is advancing*. Every eye could see his legions, an overwhelming resistless tide of an ocean of armed men sweeping upon us! Regiment after regiment and brigade after brigade move from the woods and rapidly take their places in the lines forming the assault. Pickett's proud division, with some additional troops, hold their right; Pettigrew's (Worth's) their left. The first line at short interval is followed by a second, and that a third succeeds; and columns between support the lines. More than half a mile their front extends; more than a thousand yards the dull gray masses deploy, man touching man, rank pressing rank, and line supporting line. The red flags wave, their horsemen gallop up and down; the arms of eighteen thousand men, barrel and bayonet, gleam in the sun, a sloping forest of flashing steel. Right on they move, as with one soul, in perfect order, without impediment of ditch, or wall or stream, over ridge and slope, through orchard and meadow, and cornfield, magnificent, grim, irresistible.

All was orderly and still upon our crest; no noise and no

confusion. The men had little need of commands, for the survivors of a dozen battles knew well enough what this array in front portended and, already in their places, they would be prepared to act when the right time should come. The click of the locks as each man raised the hammer to feel with his fingers that the cap was on the nipple; the sharp jar as a musket touched a stone upon the wall when thrust in aiming over it, and the clicking of the iron axles as the guns were rolled up by hand a little further to the front, were quite all the sounds that could be heard. Capboxes were slid around to the front of the body; cartridge boxes opened, officers opened their pistol-holsters. Such preparations, little more was needed. The trefoil flags, colors of the brigades and divisions moved to their places in rear; but along the lines in front the grand old ensign that first waved in battle at Saratoga in 1777, and which these people coming would rob of half its stars, stood up, and the west wind kissed it as the sergeants sloped its lance towards the enemy. I believe that not one above whom it then waved but blessed his God that he was loyal to it, and whose heart did not swell with pride towards it, as the emblem of the Republic before that treason's flaunting rag in front.

General Gibbon rode down the lines, cool and calm, and in an unimpassioned voice he said to the men, "Do not hurry, men, and fire too fast, let them come up close before you fire, and then aim low and steadily." The coolness of their General was reflected in the faces of his men. Five minutes has elapsed since first the enemy have emerged from the woods—no great space of time surely, if measured by the usual standard by which men estimate duration—but it was long enough for us to note and weigh some of the elements of mighty moment that surrounded us; the disparity of numbers between the assailants and the assailed; that few as were our numbers we could not be supported or reinforced until support would not be needed or would be too late; that upon the ability of the two trefoil divisions to hold the crest and repel the assault depended not only their own safety or destruction, but also the honor of the Army of the Potomac and defeat or victory at Gettysburg. Should these advancing men pierce our line and become the entering wedge, driven home, that would sever our army asunder, what hope would there be afterwards, and where the blood-earned fruits of yesterday? It was long enough for the Rebel storm to drift across more than half the space that had at first separated us. None, or all, of these considerations either depressed or elevated us. They might have done the former, had we been timid; the latter had we been confident and vain. But, we were there waiting, and ready to do our duty—that done, results could not dishonor us.

Our skirmishers open a spattering fire along the front, and, fighting, retire upon the main line—the first drops, the heralds of the storm, sounding on our windows. Then the thunders of our guns, first Arnold's then Cushing's and Woodruff's and the rest, shake and reverberate again through the air, and their sounding shells smite the enemy. The General said I had better go and tell General Meade of this advance. To gallop to General Meade's headquarters, to learn there that he had changed them to another part of the field, to dispatch to him by the Signal Corps in General Gibbon's name the message, "The enemy is advancing his infantry in force upon my front," and to be again upon the crest, were but the work of a minute. All our available guns are now active, and from the fire of shells, as the range grows shorter and shorter, they change to shrapnel, and from shrapnel to canister; but in spite of shells, and shrapnel and canister, without wavering or halt, the hardy lines of the enemy continue to move on. The Rebel guns make no reply to ours, and no charging shout rings out to-day, as is the Rebel wont; but the courage of these silent men amid our shots seems not to need the stimulus of other noise. The enemy's right flank sweeps near Stannard's bushy crest, and his concealed Vermonters rake it with a well-delivered fire of musketry. The gray lines do not halt or reply, but withdrawing a little from that extreme, they still move on.

And so across all that broad open ground they have come, nearer and nearer, nearly half the way, with our guns bellowing in their faces, until now a hundred yards, no more, divide our ready left from their advancing right. The eager men there are impatient to begin. Let them. First, Harrow's breastworks flame; then Hall's; then Webb's. As if our bullets were the fire coals that touched off their muskets, the enemy in front halts, and his countless level barrels blaze back upon us. The Second Division is struggling in battle. The rattling storm soon spreads to the right, and the blue trefoils are vying with the white. All along each hostile front, a thousand yards, with narrowest space between, the volleys blaze and roll; as thick the sound as when a summer hailstorm pelts the city roofs; as thick the fire as when the incessant lightning fringes a summer cloud. When the Rebel infantry had opened fire our batteries soon became silent, and this without their fault, for they were foul by long previous use. They were the targets of the concentrated Rebel bullets, and some of them had expended all their canister. But they were not silent before Rorty was killed, Woodruff had fallen mortally wounded, and Cushing, firing almost his last canister, had dropped dead among his guns shot through the head by a bullet. The conflict is left to the infantry alone.

Unable to find my general when I had returned to the crest after transmitting his message to General Meade, and while riding in the search having witnessed the development of the fight, from the first fire upon the left by the main lines until all of the two divisions were furiously engaged, I gave up hunting as useless—I was convinced General Gibbon could not be on the field; I left him mounted; I could easily have found him now had he so remained—but now, save myself, there was not a mounted officer near the engaged lines—and was riding towards the right of the Second Division, with purpose to stop there, as the most eligible position to watch the further progress of the battle, there to be ready to take part according to my own notions whenever and wherever occasion was presented. The conflict was tremendous, but I had seen no wavering in all our line.

Wondering how long the Rebel ranks, deep though they were, could stand our sheltered volleys, I had come near my destination, when—great heaven! were my senses mad? The larger portion of Webb's brigade—my God, it was true—there by the group of trees and the angles of the wall, was breaking from the cover of their works, and, without orders or reason, with no hand lifted to check them, was falling back, a fearstricken flock of confusion! The fate of Gettysburg hung upon a spider's single thread! A great maginficent passion came on me at the instant, not one that overpowers and confounds, but one that blanches the face and sublimes every sense and faculty. My sword, that had always hung idle by my side, the sign of rank only in every battle, I drew, bright and gleaming, the symbol of command. Was that not a fit occasion, and these fugitives the men on whom to try the temper of the Solingen steel? All rules and properties were forgotten; all considerations of person, and danger and safety despised; for, as I met the tide of these rabbits, the damned red flags of the rebellion

began to thicken and flaunt along the wall they had just
deserted, and one was already wavering over one of the guns
of the dead Cushing. I ordered these men to "halt," and
"face about" and "fire," and they heard my voice and
gathered my meaning, and obeyed my commands. On some
unpatriotic back of those not quick of comprehension, the
flat of my sabre fell not lightly, and at its touch their love of
country returned, and, with a look at me as if I were the
destroying angel, as I might have become theirs, they again
faced the enemy. General Webb soon came to my assistance.
He was on foot, but he was active, and did all that one could
do to repair the breach, or to avert its calamity. The men
that had fallen back, facing the enemy, soon regained confidence in themselves, and became steady.

This portion of the wall was lost to us, and the enemy had
gained cover of the reverse side, where he now stormed with
fire. But Webb's men, with their bodies in part protected by the abruptness of the crest, now sent back in the
enemies' faces as fierce a storm. Some scores of venturesome
Rebels, that in their first push at the wall had dared to cross
at the further angle, and those that had desecrated Cushing's guns were promptly shot down, and speedy death met
him who should raise his body to cross it again. At this point
little could be seen of the enemy, by reason of his cover and
the smoke, except the flash of his muskets and his waving
flags. These red flags were accumulating at the wall every
moment, and they maddened us as the same color does the
bull. Webb's men are falling fast, and he is among them to
direct and to encourage; but, however well they may now
do, with that walled enemy in front, with more than a dozen
flags to Webb's three, it soon becomes apparent that in not
many minutes they will be overpowered, or that there will
be none alive for the enemy to overpower. Webb has but
three regiments, all small, the 69th, 71st and 72nd Pennsylvania—the 106th Pennsylvania, except two companies, is
not here to-day—and he must have speedy assistance, or
this crest will be lost.

Oh, where is Gibbon? where is Hancock?—some
general—anybody with the power and the will to support
that wasting, melting line? No general came, and no succor!
I thought of Hays upon the right, but from the smoke and
war along his front, it was evident that he had enough upon
his hands, if he stayed the in-rolling tide of the Rebels there.
Doubleday upon the left was too far off and too slow, and on

another occasion I had begged him to send his idle regiments to support another line battling with thrice its numbers, and this "Old Sumter Hero" had declined. As a last resort I resolved to see if Hall and Harrow could not send some of their commands to reinforce Webb. I galloped to the left in the execution of my purpose, and as I attained the rear of Hall's line, from the nature of the ground and the position of the enemy it was easy to discover the reason and the manner of this gathering of Rebel flags in front of Webb. The enemy, emboldened by his success in gaining our line by the group of trees and the angle of the wall, was concentrating all his right against and was further pressing that point. There was the stress of his assault; there would he drive his fiery wedge to split our line.

In front of Harrow's and Hall's Brigades he had been able to advance no nearer than when he first halted to deliver fire, and these commands had not yielded an inch. To effect the concentration before Webb, the enemy would march the regiment on his extreme right of each of his lines by the left flank to the rear of the troops, still halted and facing to the front, and so continuing to draw in his right, when they were all massed in the position desired, he would again face them to the front, and advance to the storming. This was the way he made the wall before Webb's line blaze red with his battle flags, and such was the purpose there of his thick-crowding battalions.

Not a moment must be lost. Colonel Hall I found just in rear of his line, sword in hand, cool, vigilant, noting all that passed and directing the battle of his brigade. The fire was constantly diminishing now in his front, in the manner and by the movement of the enemy that I have mentioned, drifting to the right. "How is it going?" Colonel Hall asked me, as I rode up. "Well, but Webb is hotly pressed and must have support, or he will be overpowered. Can you assist him?" "Yes." "You cannot be too quick." "I will move my brigade at once." "Good." He gave the order, and in briefest time I saw five friendly colors hurrying to the aid of the imperilled three; and each color represented true, battle-tried men, that had not turned back from Rebel fire that day nor yesterday, though their ranks were sadly thinned. To Webb's brigade, pressed back as it had been from the wall, the distance was not great from Hall's right. The regiments marched by the right flank. Colonel Devereux cooly commanded the 19th Massachusetts. His major, Rice, had already been wounded and carried off. Lieutenant Colonel Macy, of the 20th Massachusetts, had just had his left hand shot off, and so captain Abbott gallantly led over this fine regiment. The 42d New York followed their excellent Colonel Mallon. Lieutenant Colonel Steele, 7th Michigan, had just been killed, and his regiment, and the handful of the 59th New York, followed their colors. The movement, as it did, attracting the enemy's fire, and executed in haste, as it must be, was difficult; but in reasonable time, and in order that is serviceable, if not regular, Hall's men are fighting gallantly side by side with Webb's before the all important point. I did not stop to see all this movement of Hall's, but from him I went at once further to the left, to the 1st brigade. General Harrow I did not see, but his fighting men would answer my purpose as well. The 19th Maine, the 15th Massachusetts, the 32d New York and the shattered old thunderbolt, the 1st Minnesota—poor Farrell was dying then upon the ground where he had fallen—all men that I could find I took over to the right at the *double quick.*

As we were moving to, and near the other brigade of the division, from my position on horseback I could see that the enemy's right, under Hall's fire, was beginning to stagger and to break. "See," I said to the men, "See the *chivalry!* See the gray-backs run!" The men saw, and as they swept to their places by the side of Hall and opened fire, they roared, and this in a manner that said more plainly than words—for the deaf could have seen it in their faces, and the blind could have heard it in their voices—*the crest is safe!*

The whole Division concentrated, and changes of position, and new phases, as well on our part as on that of the enemy, having as indicated occurred, for the purpose of showing the exact present posture of affairs, some further description is necessary. Before the 2d Division the enemy is massed, the main bulk of his force covered by the ground that slopes to his rear, with his front at the stone wall. Between his front and us extends the very apex of the crest. All there are left of the White Trefoil Division—yesterday morning there were three thousand eight hundred, this morning there were less than three thousand—at this moment there are somewhat over two thousand; twelve regiments in three brigades are below or behind the crest, in such a position that by the exposure of the head and upper part of the body above the crest they can deliver their fire in the enemy's faces along the top of the wall. By reason of the disorganization incidental in Webb's brigade to his men's having broken and fallen back, as mentioned, in the two other brigades to their rapid and difficult change of position under fire, and in all the division in part to severe and continuous battle, formation of companies and regiments in regular ranks is lost; but commands, companies, regiments and brigades are blended and intermixed—an irregular extended mass—men enough, if in order, to form a line of four or five ranks along the whole front of the division. The twelve flags of the regiments wave defiantly at intervals along the front; at the stone wall, at unequal distances from ours of forty, fifty or sixty yards, stream nearly double this number of the battle flags of the enemy. These changes accomplished on either side, and the concentration complete, although no cessation or abatement in the general din of conflict since the commencement had at any time been appreciable, now it was as if a new battle, deadlier, stormier than before, had sprung from the body of the old—a young Phoenix of combat, whose eyes stream lightning, shaking his arrowy wings over the yet glowing ashes of his progenitor.

The jostling, swaying lines on either side boil, and roar, and dash their flamy spray, two hostile billows of a fiery ocean. Thick flashes stream from the wall, thick volleys answer from the crest. No threats or expostulation now, only example and encouragement. All depths of passion are stirred, and all combatives fire, down to their deep foundations. Individuality is drowned in a sea of clamor, and timid men, breathing the breath of the multitude, are brave. The frequent dead and wounded lie where they stagger and fall—there is no humanity for them now, and none can be spared to care for them. The men do not cheer or shout; they growl, and over that uneasy sea, heard with the roar of musketry, sweeps the muttered thunder of a storm of growls. Webb, Hall, Devereux, Mallon, Abbott among the men where all are heroes, are doing deeds of note. Now the loyal wave rolls up as if it would overleap its barrier, the crest. Pistols flash with the muskets. My "Forward to the wall" is answered by the Rebel counter-command "Steady, men!" and the wave swings back. Again it surges, and again it sinks. These men of Pennsylvania, on the soil of their own homesteads, the first and only to flee the wall, must be the first to storm it.

"Major ———, *lead* your men over the crest, they will follow." "By the tactics I understand my place is in rear of the men." "Your pardon, sir; I see *your* place is in rear of the men. I thought you were fit to lead." "Captain Sapler, come on with your men." "Let me first stop this fire in the rear, or we shall be hit by our own men." "Never mind the fire in the rear; let us take care of this in front first." "Sergeant, forward with your color. Let the Rebels see it close to their eyes once before they die." The color sergeant of the 72d Pennsylvania, grasping the stump of the severed lance in both his hands, waved the flag above his head and rushed towards the wall. "Will you see your color storm the wall alone?" One man only starts to follow. Almost half way to the wall, down go color bearer and color to the ground—the gallant sergeant is dead. The line springs—the crest of the solid ground with a great roar heaves forward its maddened load, men, arms, smoke, fire, a fighting mass. It rolls to the wall—flash meets flash, the wall is crossed—a moment ensues of thrusts, yells, blows, shots, and the undistinguishable conflict, followed by a shout universal that makes the welkin ring again, and the last and bloodiest fight of the great battle of Gettysburg is ended and won.

General Meade rode up, accompanied alone by his son, who is his aide-de-camp, an escort, if select, not large for a commander of such an army. The principal horseman was no bedizened hero of some holiday review, but he was a plain man, dressed in a serviceable summer suit of dark blue cloth, without badge or ornament, save the shoulder-straps of his grade, and a light, straight sword of a General or general staff officer. He wore heavy, high-top boots and buff gauntlets, and his soft black felt hat was slouched down over his eyes. His face was very white, not pale, and the lines were marked and earnest and full of care.

As he arrived near me, coming up the hill, he asked, in a sharp, eager voice: "How is it going here?" "I believe, General, the enemy's attack is repulsed," I answered. Still approaching, and a new light began to come in his face, of gratified surprise, with a touch of incredulity, of which this voice was also the medium, he further asked: *"What! Is the assault already repulsed?"* his voice quicker and more eager than before. "It is, sir," I replied. By this time he was on the crest, and when his eye had for an instant swept over the field, taking in just a glance of the whole—the masses of prisoners, the numerous captured flags which the men were derisively flaunting about, the fugitives of the routed enemy, disappearing with the speed of terror in the woods—partly at what I had told him, partly at what he saw, he said, impressively, and his face lighted: "Thank God." And then his right hand moved as if it would have caught off his hat and waved it; but this gesture he suppressed, and instead he waved his hand, and said "Hurrah!" The son, with more youth in his blood and less rank upon his shoulders, snatched off his cap, and roared out his three "hurrahs" right heartily.

The General then surveyed the field, some minutes, in silence. He at length asked who was in command—he had heard that Hancock and Gibbon were wounded—and I told him that General Caldwell was the senior officer of the Corps and General Harrow of the Division. He asked where they were, but before I had time to answer that I did not know, he resumed: "No matter; I will give my orders to you and you will see them executed." He then gave direction that the troops should be re-formed as soon as practicable, and kept in their places, as the enemy might be mad enough to attack again. He also gave directions concerning the posting of some reinforcements which he said would soon be there, adding: "If the enemy does attack, charge him in the flank and sweep him from the field; do you understand?" The General then, a gratified man, galloped in the direction of his headquarters.

When the prisoners were cleared away and order was again established upon our crest, where the conflict had impaired it, until between five and six o'clock, I remained upon the field, directing some troops to their position, in conformity to the orders of General Meade. The enemy appeared no more in front of the Second Corps; but while I was engaged as I have mentioned, farther to our left some considerable force of the enemy moved out and made show of attack. Our artillery, now in good order again, in due time opened fire, and the shell scattered the "Butternuts," as clubs do the gray snow-birds of winter, before they came within range of our infantry. This, save unimportant outpost firing, was the last of the battle.

CHICKAMAUGA

ON JULY 4, LEE BEGAN HIS RETREAT to the Potomac. The river was high from heavy rains. The last Confederate did not cross until July 13, but Mead's pursuit was too slow to cause trouble. Lee had left a third of his army on the field of Gettysburg, but Meade's own casualties of 25,000 helped reinforce his natural caution. Both armies had been through hell.

To the people in the North, however, the news of Lee's repulse and the fall of Vicksburg, both received on the Fourth of July, were cause for jubilant celebration. Then on July 9, Port Hudson fell, and "the Father of Waters flowed unvexed to the sea." The noose was drawing ever tighter around the Confederacy, but there were still plenty of trouble spots for the Union. General Grant describes one which concerned him greatly in the summer of 1863:

"After the fall of Vicksburg I urged strongly upon the Government the propriety of a movement against Mobile. General Rosecrans had been at Murfreesboro, Tennessee, with a large and well-equipped army from early in the year 1863, with Bragg confronting him with a force quite equal to his own at first, considering that it was on the defensive. But after the investment of Vicksburg, Bragg's army was largely depleted to strengthen Johnston, in Mississippi, who was being reënforced to raise the siege. I frequently wrote to General Halleck suggesting that Rosecrans should move against Bragg. By so doing he would either detain the latter's troops where they were, or lay Chattanooga open to capture. General Halleck strongly approved the suggestion, and finally wrote me that he had repeatedly ordered Rosecrans to advance, but that the latter had constantly failed to comply with the order, and at last, after having held a council of war, replied, in effect, that it was a military maxim 'not to fight two decisive battles at the same time.' If true, the maxim was not applicable in this case. It would be bad to be defeated in two decisive battles fought the same day, but it would not be bad to win them. I, however, was fighting no

battle, and the siege of Vicksburg had drawn from Rosecrans's front so many of the enemy that his chances of victory were much greater than they would be if he waited until
the siege was over, when these troops could be returned Rosecrans was ordered to move against the army that was detach-
ing troops to raise the siege. Finally, on the 24th of June,
he did move, but ten days afterward Vicksburg surrendered,
and the troops sent from Bragg were free to return. . . .

"Soon it was discovered in Washington that Rosecrans
was in trouble and required assistance. As fast as transports
could be provided all the troops except a portion of the Seventeenth Corps were forwarded under Sherman, whose
services up to this time demonstrated his superior fitness for
a separate command. I also moved McPherson, with most of
the troops still about Vicksburg, eastward, to compel the
enemy to keep back a force to meet him. Meanwhile Rosecrans had very skillfully manœuvred Bragg south of the
Tennessee River, and through and beyond Chattanooga. If
he had stopped and intrenched, and made himself strong
there, all would have been right, and the mistake of not
moving earlier partially compensated. But he pushed on,
with his forces very much scattered."

Rosecrans thought Bragg was retreating. He sent three
Union corps under Thomas, McCook and Crittenden fan-
ning out south of Chattanooga. Because of mountainous terrain and the lack of lateral roads, the three corps became
widely extended, forty miles separating the right and left
wings. If Bragg could catch a single corps by itself he could
easily destroy it.

Bragg, meanwhile, was twenty-five miles south of Chattanooga. Not only was he no longer retreating, he was trying
to get his generals to mount an attack, and he was receiving
substantial reinforcements. By the time Bragg was ready to
move on September 18, Rosecrans had sensed the danger
and ordered his three corps to come together. McCook and
Thomas wheeled north to form a defensive line south of
Chattanooga and west of Chickamauga Creek.

Bragg's plan of attack was to smash into the Federal left,
drive between Rosecrans and Chattanooga, and roll the
Union forces into the mountains, where they could be cut up
piecemeal. First Bragg would cross the Chickamauga,
march north along its banks, then wheel eastward, where he
would assault the Union positions which were facing south.
According to Catton, if Bragg could cut "the north-south

road that ran from Lafayette to Chattanooga Rosecrans' army would be done for.

"That was what Bragg planned, and he probably would have got it if he had been able to start the fighting twenty-four hours earlier. On September 18 the Federal left rested at Lee and Gordon's Mills, where the Lafayette road crossed the Chickamauga, and nobody but Crittenden was there to hold it. The country off to the northeast, downstream, across which Bragg proposed to attack, was empty except for cavalry, Thomas and McCook were still coming in from the distant right, and Confederate infantry could have marched straight to the Lafayette road, deep in the Federal rear. But on September 18, while this balky Confederate army was moving down its side of the river, driving Yankee cavalry away from the crossings and getting itself properly organized, Thomas' four divisions were making a prodigious hike. They left their camp in the afternoon and they kept on marching all night, setting fences on fire to light the way, infantry stumbling with fatigue but plowing on regardless; and by the morning of September 19, when Bragg's army at last opened its offensive, Thomas had most of his people in line east of the Lafayette road several miles north of Crittenden, drawn up squarely in the path of the Confederate divisions that were coming west from the river.

"So the Yankee army was not where Bragg thought it was. It was still highly vulnerable, to be sure; if the left ever gave way the whole army would be lost, and Bragg's army had shown at Stone's River that when it struck a blow it struck with bonecrushing power. But Bragg's army could no longer win by maneuver. It would have to fight for everything it got, and although at last it got a good deal it did not get what it needed most. The battle of Chickamauga went by nobody's plan, once the first shots were fired. A Federal brigadier summed it up perfectly when he wrote that it was 'a mad, irregular battle, very much resembling guerrilla warfare on a vast scale, in which one army was bushwhacking the other, and wherein all the science and the art of war went for nothing.' The Confederate Senator G. A. Henry of Tennessee called the turn before the battle began when he told President Davis that the Army of Tennessee needed better leadership and warned him: 'As sure as you are born, that army is better than its commanders.' Both armies were.

"It began a little west of the Chickamauga on that morning of September 19, when Bedford Forrest's cavalry—ad-

vancing dismounted, as competent foot-soldiers as any infantry—collided with one of Thomas' brigades near Reed's bridge. Confederate infantry moved up to help, and before long both armies were heavily engaged. Rosecrans brought McCook's weary corps in on Thomas' right and pulled Crittenden back from Lee and Gordon's, and all day long his army fought desperately to keep the Confederates away from the Lafayette road, with Thomas' corps drawn up in a long shallow crescent and taking most of the pressure. The country was full of trees and underbrush, with little clearings here and there; nobody could see much of his enemy's position, it was almost impossible to move artillery along the narrow country lanes, both armies were sodden with weariness, drinking water was hard to find, casualties were extremely heavy, and by nightfall all anyone could be sure of was that there had been a terrible fight and that it would be worse tomorrow.

"That night there was a full moon, lighting the smoky fields and woods where lay so many thousands of dead and wounded men. In each army, generals who went to headquarters to report and compare notes felt a pervading air of depression and uncertainty; it was the hard fighting men, John B. Hood and Phil Sheridan, who were most struck by it. Rosecrans got a dozen of his chief lieutenants into a cramped log cabin owned by a lady who comes down in history simply as 'the Widow Glenn'; there was a cot for the commanding general to rest on, and a camp chair for General Thomas, but everyone else sat on the floor or lounged against the wall. A fire flickered in the fireplace, and some aide lit a candle, with an inverted bayonet for a candelholder. The generals were subdued, and the innumerable small noises of the surrounding camp could be heard in the little room; for some reason, when men spoke they spoke in low tones or even in whispers. Thomas was practically torpid for want of sleep. He kept dozing in his chair, rousing himself now and then to say, 'I would strengthen the left,' and then drowsing again.

"His advice was sound. The Federal army held a long, irregular line facing eastward, in front of the Lafayette road. The Confederates had tried all day to crush the northern end of that line—the left, held by Thomas—so that they could get in between Rosecrans and Chattanooga, and they were certain to renew the pressure in the morning. Rosecrans had some thought of shifting his troops into a position from which he could make a counterattack, but he felt that the men were too exhausted to be disturbed. The most he could do was to tell McCook and Crittenden to contract their lines in the morning so that they could send additional help over to Thomas in case he needed it.

"A few miles away, on the Confederate side of this most dismal of battlefields, in a country so tangled that a general could get lost making a simple trip to his superior officer's headquarters, Bragg was revising his command arrangements. It was natural that he should do this, in view of the way some of his generals had performed, although it was a risky thing to do in the middle of a big battle; one suspects that he was trying to find a way to make full use of the talents of General Longstreet, who reached the scene that evening, ready for action even though only five of his brigades were on hand. At any rate, Bragg divided his army into two wings, giving the right wing to Polk and the left to Longstreet. Polk was to make an all-out assault on Thomas at daybreak, and Longstreet was to apply pressure at the other end of the Federal line, making a full-scale attack of his own as soon as Polk's offensive showed progress.

"As usual, there was a hitch. Polk's attack did not get under way until somewhere around nine o'clock in the morning, for reasons now indecipherable: Bragg blamed Polk, Polk blamed D. H. Hill, Hill proclaimed his utter innocence, and probably the real trouble was simply that the chain of command was distressingly loose and that the units of this unhappy army moved with a time-lag much like the one that was habitual in the Army of the Potomac. At any rate, the attack on Thomas was badly delayed, and the delay may have saved the life of the Union army because when at last Polk's troops attacked they struck with enormous force and if they had come in before Rosecrans could send reinforcements from his right Thomas' corps would probably have been overpowered.

"The attack flamed all along his front, overlapping his left as he had feared, and men from McCook's and Crittenden's corps were sent to the left, where Thomas touched the edge of final disaster, once, when John Breckinridge broke past his flank with his division and put two brigades squarely on the vital Lafayette road; these brigades swung around, astride that fateful sandy highway, and came charging south straight into the Union rear, and for a time part of Thomas' line was under attack from two sides at once. By a prodigious effort, the Federals broke these brigades and drove them away, mangling them so badly that they had to be taken out of action altogether; but after they were gone another Confederate corps came in their place, and the fight had to be made all over again, and Thomas notified Rosecrans that he had to have more help.

"The unexpected result of this pressure on the Union left was that the Union right collapsed. In the hot confusion of battle, army headquarters at last lost track of the shifting and counter-marching that had been ordered, and Rosecrans finally pulled the division of Major General Thomas J. Wood out of Crittenden's line and sent it off to the left. This left a big gap in the line, and before anyone could fill it Longstreet made his own attack, striking with five divisions at the precise spot that had just been vacated, handling his men with the cold professional competence that prevailed in Lee's army. A third of Rosecrans' army was crumpled and driven off to the west, Sheridan's entire division and most of Jeff Davis', with elements from other commands, going all the way beyond the lower end of Missionary Ridge and shambling in disorganized rout toward the crossroads of Rossville, five miles north of battlefield. With them went Rosecrans himself and two of his corps commanders, McCook and Crittenden. Since the last word the unhappy Rosecrans had from Thomas indicated that the left was in dire straits, Rosecrans seems to have assumed now that the entire army had been broken up, and he himself went all the way to Chattanooga in the belief that the commander of a beaten army ought to return to his base and make arrangements for a last-ditch stand.

"That left Thomas to pick up the pieces and save the army, and Thomas did all any soldier could have done. He contacted his original lines and formed a long extension on Snodgrass Hill to the west, getting his men into a huge horseshoe-shaped formation, determined to hold on until dusk and make the final withdrawal an orderly one. He was powerfully helped by two circumstances: Polk's wing had been so roughly handled in the morning's fighting that it was unable to renew the assault until late in the day, and a Federal reserve corps under Major General Gordon Granger, three brigades that had been stationed east of Rossville, came hurrying down to buttress the lines on Snodgrass Hill."*

* Bruce Catton, *Never Call Retreat*, pp. 245, 246, 247, 248, 249.

General Granger's reserve corps had been "distributed over a long stretch of country,† its rear at Murfreesboro and its van on the battlefield of Chickamauga. These troops had been posted to cover the rear and left flank of the army (of the Cumberland.). During September 19, the first day of the battle, they were engaged in some skirmishing and stood at arms expecting an attack. On the evening of the 19th every indication pointed to a renewal of the battle early the next day. The night was cold for that time of the year. Telltale fires were prohibited. The men slept on their arms. All was quiet save in the field hospitals in the rear. A bright moon lighted up the fields and woods. Along the greater part of a front of eight miles the ground was strewn with the intermingled dead of friend and foe. The morning of Sunday, the 20th, opened with a cloudless sky, but a fog had come up from the warm water of the Chickamauga and hung over the battle-field until 9'clock. A silence of desertion was in the front. This quiet continued till nearly 10 o'clock; then, as the peaceful tones of the church-bells, rolling over the land from the east, reached the meridian of Chickamauga, they were made dissonant by the murderous roar of the artillery of Bishop Polk, who was opening the battle on Thomas's front. Granger, who had been ordered at all hazards to hold fast where he was, listened and grew impatient. Shortly before 10 o'clock, calling my attention to a great column of dust moving from our front toward the point from which came the sound of battle, he said. 'They are concentrating over there. That is where we ought to be.' The corps flag marked his headquarters in an open field near the Ringgold road. He walked up and down in front of his flag, nervously pulling his beard. Once stopping, he said, 'Why the——does Rosecrans keep me here? There is nothing in front of us now. There is the battle'—pointing in the direction of Thomas. Every moment the sounds of battle grew louder, while the many columns of dust rolling together here mingled with the smoke that hung over the scene.

"At 11 o'clock, with Granger, I climbed a high hayrick near by. We sat there for ten minutes listening and watching. Then Granger jumped up, thrust his glass into its case, and exclaimed with an oath:

" 'I am going to Thomas, orders or no orders!'

† The following narrative of Granger's reinforcement of Thomas is by J. S. Fullerton, from Vol. III of *Battles and Leaders*, pp. 665 to 667.

" 'And if you go,' I replied, 'it may bring disaster to the army and you to a court-martial.'

" 'There's nothing in our front now but ragtag, bobtail cavalry,' he replied. 'Don't you see Bragg is piling his whole army on Thomas? I am going to his assistance.'

"We quickly climbed down the rick, and, going to Steedman, Granger ordered him to move his command 'over there,' pointing toward the place from which came the sounds of battle. Colonel Daniel McCook was directed to hold fast at McAfee Church, where his brigade covered the Ringgold road. Before half-past 11 o'clock Steedman's command was in motion. Granger, with his staff and escort, rode in advance. Steedman, after accompanying them a short distance, rode back to the head of his column.

"Thomas was nearly four miles away. The day had not grown very warm, yet the troops marched rapidly over the narrow road, which was covered ankle-deep with dust that rose in suffocating clouds. Completely enveloped in it, the moving column swept along like a desert sandstorm. Two miles from the point of starting, and three-quarters of a mile to the left of the road, the enemy's skirmishers and a section of artillery opened fire on us from an open wood. This force had worked round Thomas's left, and was then partly in his rear. Granger halted to feel them. Soon becoming convinced that it was only a large party of observation, he again started his column and pushed rapidly forward. I was then sent to bring up Colonel McCook's brigade, and put it in position to watch the movements of the enemy, to keep open the Lafayette road, and to cover the open fields between that point and the position held by Thomas. This brigade remained there the rest of the day. Our skirmishers had not gone far when they came upon Thomas's field-hospital, at Cloud's house, then swarming with the enemy. They came from the same body of Forrest's cavalry that had fired on us from the wood. They were quickly driven out, and our men were warmly welcomed with cheers from dying and wounded men.

"A little farther on we were met by a staff-officer sent by General Thomas to discover whether we were friends or enemies; he did not know whence friends could be coming, and the enemy appeared to be approaching from all directions. All of this shattered Army of the Cumberland left on the field was with Thomas; but not more than one-fourth of the men of the army who went into battle at the opening were there. Thomas's loss in killed and wounded during the two days had been dreadful. As his men dropped out his line was contracted to half its length. Now its flanks were bent back, conforming to ridges shaped like a horse-shoe.

"On the part of Thomas and his men there was no thought but that of fighting. He was a soldier who had never retreated, who had never been defeated. He stood immovable, the 'Rock of Chickamauga.' Never had soldiers greater love for a commander. He imbued them with his spirit, and their confidence in him was sublime.

"To the right of Thomas's line was a gorge, then a high ridge, nearly at right angles thereto, running east and west. Confederates under Kershaw (McLaws's division of Hood's corps) were passing through the gorge, together with Bushrod Johnson's division, which Longstreet was strengthening with Hindman's division; divisions were forming on this ridge for an assault; to their left the guns of a battery were being unlimbered for an enfilading fire. There was not a man to send against the force on the ridge, none to oppose this impending assault. The enemy saw the approaching colors of the Reserve Corps and hesitated.

"At 1 o'clock Granger shook hands with Thomas. Something was said about forming to fight to the right and rear.

" 'Those men must be driven back,' said Granger, pointing to the gorge and ridge. 'Can you do it?' asked Thomas.

" 'Yes. My men are fresh, and they are just the fellows for that work. They are raw troops, and they don't know any better than to charge up there.'

"Granger quickly sent Aleshire's battery of 3-inch rifle guns which he brought up to Thomas's left to assist in repelling another assault about to be made on the Kelly farm front. Whitaker's and Mitchell's brigades under Steedman were wheeled into position and projected against the enemy in the gorge and on the ridge. With ringing cheers they advanced in two lines by double-quick—over open fields, through weeds waist-high, through a little valley, then up the ridge. The enemy opened on them first with artillery, then with a murderous musketry fire. When well up the ridge the men, almost exhausted, were halted for breath. They lay on the ground two or three minutes, then came the command, 'Forward!' Brave, bluff old Steedman, with a regimental flag in his hand, led the way. On went the lines, firing as they ran and bravely receiving a deadly and continuous fire from the enemy on the summit. The Confederates began to break and in another minute were flying down the southern slope of the ridge. In twenty minutes from the beginning of the charge the ridge had been carried.

"Granger's hat had been torn by a fragment of shell; Steedman had been wounded; Whitaker had been wounded, and four of his five staff-officers killed or mortally wounded. Of Steedman's two brigades, numbering 3,500, twenty per cent had been killed and wounded in that twenty minutes; and the end was not yet.

"The enemy massed a force to retake the ridge. They came before our men had rested; twice they assaulted and were driven back. During one assault, as the first line came within range of our muskets, it halted, apparently hesitating, when we saw a colonel seize a flag, wave it over his head, and rush forward. The whole line instantly caught his enthusiasm, and with a wild cheer followed, only to be hurled back again. Our men ran down the ridge in pursuit. In the midst of a group of Confederate dead and wounded they found the brave colonel dead, the flag he carried spread over him where he fell.

"Soon after 5 o'clock Thomas rode to the left of his line, leaving Granger the ranking officer at the center. The ammunition of both Thomas's and Granger's commands was now about exhausted. When Granger had come up he had given ammunition to Brannan and Wood, and that had exhausted his supply. The cartridge-boxes of both our own and the enemy's dead within reach had been emptied by our men. When it was not yet 6 o'clock, and Thomas was still on the left of his line, Brannan rushed up to Granger, saying, 'The enemy are forming for another assault; we have not another round of ammunition—what shall we do?' 'Fix bayonets and go for them,' was the reply. Along the whole line ran the order, 'Fix bayonets.' On came the enemy—our men were lying down. 'Forward,' was sounded. In one instant they were on their feet. Forward they went to meet the charge. The enemy fled. So impetuous was this counter-charge that one regiment, with empty muskets and empty cartridge-boxes, broke through the enemy's line, which, closing in their rear, carried them off as in the undertow."

Late that evening Thomas collected his battered forces and retreated into Chattanooga. As Catton says, Bragg "had fought to the limit of his army's capacity for two days in an attempt to drive Rosecrans away from Chattanooga, and he had at last driven him straight into it. He had won a victory he could not use."*

Bragg now occupied Missionary Ridge overlooking Chattanooga, as well as Lookout Mountain to the west. The Federals had Chattanooga but they were in trouble. As Grant wrote, "Halleck . . . directed all the forces that could be spared from my department to be sent to Rosecrans, suggesting that a good commander like Sherman or McPherson should go with the troops; also that I should go in person to Nashville to superintend the movement. Long before this dispatch was received Sherman was already on his way, and McPherson also was moving east with most of the garrison of Vicksburg.

"All supplies for Rosecrans had to be brought from Nashville. The railroad between this base and the army was in possession of the Government up to Bridgeport, the point at which the road crosses to the south side of the Tennessee River; but Bragg, holding Lookout and Raccoon mountains west of Chattanooga, commanded the railroad, the river, and the shortest and best wagon roads both south and north of the Tennessee, between Chattanooga and Bridgeport. The distance between these two places is but twenty-six miles by rail; but owing to this position of Bragg all supplies for Rosecrans had to be hauled by a circuitous route, north of the river, and over a mountainous country, increasing the distance to over sixty miles. This country afforded but little food for his animals, nearly ten thousand of which had already starved, and none was left to draw a single piece of artillery or even the ambulances to convey the sick. The men had been on half rations of hard bread for a considerable time, with but few other supplies, except beef driven from Nashville across the country. The region along the road became so exhausted of food for the cattle that by the time they reached Chattanooga they were much in the condition of the few animals left alive there, 'on the lift.' Indeed, the beef was so poor that the soldiers were in the habit of saying, with a faint facetiousness, that they were living on half rations of hard bread and 'beef dried on the hoof.' Nothing could be transported but food, and the troops were without sufficient shoes or other clothing suitable for the advancing season. What they had was well worn. The fuel within the Federal lines was exhausted, even to the stumps of trees.

* Bruce Catton, *Never Call Retreat*, p. 250.

There were no teams to draw it from the opposite bank, where it was abundant. The only means for supplying fuel, for some time before my arrival, had been to cut trees from the north bank of the river, at a considerable distance up the stream, form rafts of it, and float it down with the current, effecting a landing on the south side, within our lines, by the use of paddles or poles. It would then be carried on the shoulders of the men to their camps. If a retreat had occurred at this time it is not probable that any of the army would have reached the railroad as an organized body, if followed by the enemy.

"On the morning of the 20th of October I started by train with my staff, and proceeded as far as Nashville. . . . On the morning of the 21st we took the train for the front, reaching Stevenson, Alabama, after dark. Rosecrans was there on his way north.* He came into my car, and we held a brief interview in which he described very clearly the situation at Chattanooga, and made some excellent suggestions as to what should be done. My only wonder was that he had not carried them out. We then proceeded to Bridgeport, where we stopped for the night. From here we took horses and made our way by Jasper and over Waldron's Ridge to Chattanooga. There had been much rain and the roads were almost impassable from mud knee-deep in places, and from washouts on the mountain-sides. The roads were strewn with the debris of broken wagons and the carcasses of thousands of starved mules and horses. I went directly to Thomas's headquarters, and remained there a few days until I could establish my own.

"During the evening most of the general officers called in to pay their respects and to talk about the condition of affairs. They pointed out on the maps the line marked with a red or blue pencil which Rosecrans had contemplated falling back upon. If any of them had approved the move, they did not say so to me. I found General W. F. Smith occupying the position of chief engineer of the Army of the Cumberland. I had known Smith as a cadet at West Point, but had no recollection of having met him after my graduation, in 1843, up to this time. He explained the situation of the two armies and the topography of the country so plainly that I could see it without an inspection. I found that he had established a sawmill on the banks of the river, by utilizing

* Rosecrans had been relieved, and General Thomas was now in command at Chattanooga.

an old engine found in the neighborhood; and by rafting logs from the north side of the river above had got out the lumber and completed pontoons and roadway plank for a second bridge, one flying-bridge being there already. He was also rapidly getting out the materials for constructing the boats for a third bridge. In addition to this he had far under way a steamer for plying between Chattanooga and Bridgeport whenever he might get possession of the river. This boat consisted of a scow made of the plank sawed out at the mill, housed in, with a stern-wheel attached which was propelled by a second engine taken from some shop or factory.

"I telegraphed to Washington this night, notifying Halleck of my arrival, and asking to have Sherman assigned to the command of the Army of the Tennessee, headquarters in the field. The request was at once complied with.

"The next day, the 24th, I started out to make a personal inspection, taking Thomas and Smith with me, besides most of the members of my personal staff. We crossed to the north side of the river, and, moving to the north of detached spurs of hills, reached the Tennessee, at Brown's Ferry, some three miles below Lookout Mountain, unobserved by the enemy. Here we left our horses back from the river and approached the water on foot. There was a picket station of the enemy, on the opposite side, of about twenty men, in full view, and we were within easy range. They did not fire upon us nor seem to be disturbed by our presence. They must have seen that we were all commissioned officers. But, I suppose, they looked upon the garrison of Chattanooga as prisoners of war, feeding or starving themselves, and thought it would be inhuman to kill any of them except in self-defense. That night I issued orders for opening the route to Bridgeport—a 'cracker line,' as the soldiers appropriately termed it. They had been so long on short rations that my first thought was the establishment of a line over which food might reach them."*

* U. S. Grant, "Chattanooga," *Battles and Leaders*, Vol. III.

Lifting the Siege of Chattanooga†

BY GENERAL U. S. GRANT

CHATTANOOGA IS ON THE SOUTH BANK OF THE TENNESSEE, where that river runs nearly due west. It is at the northern end of a valley five or six miles in width through which runs Chattanooga Creek. To the east of the valley is Missionary Ridge, rising from five to eight hundred feet above the creek, and terminating somewhat abruptly a half-mile or more before reaching the Tennessee. On the west of the valley is Lookout Mountain, 2,200 feet above tide-water. Just below the town, the Tennessee makes a turn to the south and runs to the base of Lookout Mountain, leaving no level ground between the mountain and river. The Memphis and Charleston railroad passes this point, where the mountain stands nearly perpendicular. East of Missionary Ridge flows the South Chickamauga River; west of Lookout Mountain is Lookout Creek; and west of that, the Raccoon Mountain. Lookout Mountain at its northern end rises almost perpendicularly for some distance, then breaks off in a gentle slope of cultivated fields to near the summit, where it ends in a palisade thirty or more feet in height. The intrenched line of the enemy commenced on the north end of Missionary Ridge and extended along the crest for some distance south, thence across Chattanooga Valley to Lookout Mountain. Lookout Mountain was also fortified and held by the enemy, who also kept troops in Lookout Valley and on Raccoon Mountain, with pickets extending down the river so as to command the road on the north bank and render it useless to us. In addition to this there was an intrenched line in Chattanooga Valley extending from the river east of the town to Lookout Mountain, to make the investment complete.

Thus the enemy, with a vastly superior force, was strongly fortified to the east, south, and west, and commanded the river below. Practically the Army of the Cumberland was besieged. The enemy, with his cavalry north of the river, had stopped the passing of a train loaded with ammunition

† *Ibid.*

and medical supplies. The Union army was short of both, not having ammunition enough for a day's fighting.

Long before my coming into this new field, General Halleck had ordered parts of the Eleventh and Twelfth corps, commanded respectively by Generals Howard and Slocum, Hooker in command of the whole, from the Army of the Potomac, to reënforce Rosecrans. It would have been folly to have sent them to Chattanooga to help eat up the few rations left there. They were consequently left on the railroad, where supplies could be brought them. Before my arrival Thomas ordered their concentration at Bridgeport.

General W. F. Smith had been so instrumental in preparing for the move which I was now about to make, and so clear in his judgment about the manner of making it, that I deemed it but just to him that he should have command of the troops detailed to execute the design, although he was then acting as a staff-officer, and was not in command of troops.

On the 24th of October, after my return to Chattanooga, the following details were made: General Hooker, who was now at Bridgeport, was ordered to cross to the south side of the Tennessee and march up by Whiteside's and Wauhatchie to Brown's Ferry. General Palmer, with a division of the Fourteenth Corps, Army of the Cumberland, was ordered to move down the river on the north side, by a back road, until opposite Whiteside's, then cross and hold the road in Hooker's rear after he had passed. Four thousand men were at the same time detailed to act under General Smith directly from Chattanooga. Eighteen hundred of them, under General Hazen, were to take sixty pontoon-boats and, under cover of night, float by the pickets of the enemy at the north base of Lookout, down to Brown's Ferry, then land on the south side and capture or drive away the pickets at that point. Smith was to march with the remainder of the detail, also under cover of night, by the north bank of the river, to Brown's Ferry, taking with him all the material for laying the bridge, as soon as the crossing was secured.

On the 26th Hooker crossed the river at Bridgeport and commenced his eastward march. At three o'clock on the morning of the 27th Hazen moved into the stream with his sixty pontoons and eighteen hundred brave and well-equipped men. Smith started enough in advance to be near the river when Hazen should arrive. There are a number of detached spurs of hills north of the river at Chattanooga,

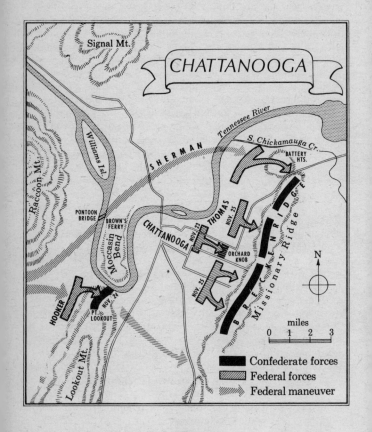

back of which is a good road parallel to the stream, sheltered
from view from the top of Lookout. It was over this road
Smith marched. At five o'clock Hazen landed at Brown's
Ferry, surprised the picket-guard and captured most of it.
By seven o'clock the whole of Smith's force was ferried over
and in possession of a height commanding the ferry. This
was speedily fortified while a detail was laying the pontoon-
bridge. By ten o'clock the bridge was laid, and our extreme
right, now in Lookout Valley, was fortified and connected
with the rest of the army. The two bridges over the Tennessee River—a flying one at Chattanooga and the new one at
Brown's Ferry—with the road north of the river, covered
from both the fire and the view of the enemy, made the connection complete. Hooker found but slight obstacles in his
way, and on the afternoon of the 28th emerged into Lookout
Valley at Wauhatchie. Howard marched on to Brown's
Ferry, while Geary, who commanded a division in the
Twelfth Corps, stopped three miles south. The pickets of the
enemy on the river below were cut off and soon came in and
surrendered.

The river was now open to us from Lookout Valley to
Bridgeport. Between Brown's Ferry and Kelley's Ferry the
Tennessee runs through a narrow gorge in the mountains,
which contracts the stream so much as to increase the current beyond the capacity of an ordinary steamer to stem. To
get up these rapids, steamers must be cordelled, that is,
pulled up by ropes from the shore. But there is no difficulty
in navigating the stream from Bridgeport to Kelley's
Ferry. The latter point is only eight miles from Chattanooga,
and connected with it by a good wagon road, which runs
through a low pass in the Raccoon Mountain on the south
side of the river to Brown's Ferry, thence on the north side to
the river opposite Chattanooga. There were several steamers
at Bridgeport, and abundance of forage, clothing, and provisions.

On the way to Chattanooga I had telegraphed back to
Nashville for a good supply of vegetables and small rations,
which the troops had been so long deprived of. Hooker had
brought with him from the east a full supply of land
transportation. His animals had not been subjected to hard
work on bad roads without forage, but were in good condition. In five days from my arrival at Chattanooga the way
was open to Bridgeport, and, with the aid of steamers and
Hooker's teams, in a week the troops were receiving full ra-

tions. It is hard for any one not an eye-witness to realize the relief this brought. The men were soon reclothed and well fed; an abundance of ammunition was brought up, and a cheerfulness prevailed not before enjoyed in many weeks. Neither officers nor men looked upon themselves any longer as doomed. The weak and languid appearance of the troops, so visible before, disappeared at once.

The enemy was surprised by the movement which secured to us a line of supplies. He appreciated its importance, and hastened to try to recover the line from us. His strength on Lookout Mountain was not equal to Hooker's command in the valley below. From Missionary Ridge he had to march twice the distance we had from Chattanooga, in order to reach Lookout Valley. But on the night of the 28th—29th [of October] an attack was made on Geary, at Wauhatchie, by Longstreet's corps. When the battle commenced, Hooker ordered Howard up from Brown's Ferry. He had three miles to march to reach Geary. On his way he was fired upon by rebel troops from a foot-hill to the left of the road, and from which the road was commanded. Howard turned to the left, and charged up the hill, and captured it before the enemy had time to intrench, taking many prisoners. Leaving sufficient men to hold this height, he pushed on to rëenforce Geary. Before he got up. Geary had been engaged for about three hours against a vastly superior force. The night was dark that the men could not distinguish one another except by the light of the flashes of their muskets. In the darkness and uproar Hooker's teamsters became frightened, and deserted their teams. The mules also became frightened, and, breaking loose from their fastenings, stampeded directly toward the enemy. The latter no doubt took this for a charge, and stampeded in turn. By four o'clock in the morning the battle had entirely ceased, and our "cracker line" was never afterward disturbed.

In securing possession of Lookout Valley, Smith lost one man killed and four or five wounded. The enemy lost most of his pickets at the ferry by capture. In the night engagement of the 28th-29th Hooker lost 416 killed and wounded. I never knew the loss of the enemy, but our troops buried over 150 of his dead, and captured more than 100.

Having got the Army of the Cumberland in a comfortable position, I now began to look after the remainder of my new command. Burnside was in about as desperate a condition as the Army of the Cumberland had been, only he was not yet besieged. He was a hundred miles from the nearest possible base, Big South Fork of the Cumberland River, and much farther from any railroad we had possession of. The roads back were over mountains, and all supplies along the line had since been exhausted. His animals, too, had been staved, and their carcasses lined the road from Cumberland Gap, and far back toward Lexington, Kentucky. East Tennessee still furnished supplies of beef, bread, and forage, but it did not supply ammunition, clothing, medical supplies, or small rations, such as coffee, sugar, salt, and rice.

Stopping to organize his new command, Sherman had started from Memphis for Corinth on the 11th of October. His instructions required him to repair the road in his rear in order to bring up supplies. The distance was about 300 miles through a hostile country. His entire command could not have maintained the road if it had been completed. The bridges had all been destroyed by the enemy and much other damage done; a hostile community lived along the road; guerrilla bands infested the country, and more or less of the cavalry of the enemy was still in the west. Often Sherman's work was destroyed as soon as completed, though he was only a short distance away.

The Memphis and Charleston road strikes the Tennessee River at Eastport, Mississippi. Knowing the difficulty Sherman would have to supply himself from Memphis, I had previously ordered supplies sent from St. Louis on small steamers, to be convoyed by the navy, to meet him at Eastport. These he got. I now ordered him to discontinue his work of repairing roads, and to move on with his whole force to Stevenson, Alabama, without delay. This order was borne to Sherman by a messenger who paddled down the Tennessee in a canoe, and floated over Muscle Shoals; it was delivered at Iuka on the 27th. In this Sherman was notified that the rebels were moving a force toward Cleveland, east Tennessee, and might be going to Nashville, in which event his troops were in the best position to beat them there. Sherman, with his characteristic promptness, abandoned the work he was engaged upon and pushed on at once. On the 1st of November he crossed the Tennessee at Eastport, and that day was in Florence, Alabama, with the head of column, while his troops were crossing at Eastport, with Blair bringing up the rear.

Sherman's force made an additional army, with cavalry, artillery, and trains, all to be supplied by the single-track road from Nashville. All indications pointed also to the probable necessity of supplying Burnside's command, in east Tennessee, 25,000 more, by the same road. A single track could not do this. I therefore gave an order to Sherman to halt General G. M. Dodge's command of eight thousand men at Athens, and subsequently directed the latter to arrange his troops along the railroad from Decatur, north toward Nashville, and to rebuild the road. The road from Nashville to Decatur passes over a broken country, cut up with innumerable streams, many of them of considerable width, and with valleys for below the road-bed. All the bridges over these had been destroyed and the rails taken up and twisted by the enemy. All the locomotives and cars not carried off had been destroyed as effectually as they knew how to destroy them. All bridges and culverts had been destroyed between Nashville and Charleston an the Nashville and Chattanooga roads unite. The rebuilding of this road would give us two roads as far as Stevenson over which to supply the army. From Bridgeport, a short distance farther east, the river supplements the road.

General Dodge, besides being a most capable soldier, was an experienced railroad builder. He had no tools to work with except those of the pioneers—axes, picks, and spades. With these he was able to intrench his men and protect them against surprises by small parties of the enemy. As he had no base of supplies until the road could be completed back to Nashville, the first matter to consider, after protecting his men, was the getting in of food and forage from the surrounding country. He had his men and teams bring in all the grain they could find, or all they needed, and all the cattle for beef, and such other food as could be found. Millers were detailed from the ranks to run the mills along the line of the army; when these were not near enough to the troops for protection, they were taken down and moved up to the line of the road. Blacksmith shops, with all the iron and steel found in them, were moved up in like manner. Blacksmiths were detailed and set to work making the tools necessary in railroad and bridge building. Axemen were put to work getting out timber for bridges, and cutting fuel for the locomotives when the road should be completed; car-builders were set to work repairing the locomotives and cars. Thus every branch of railroad-building, making tools to work with, and supplying the workingmen with food, was all

going on at once, and without the aid of a mechanic or
laborer except what the command itself furnished. But rails
and cars the men could not make without material, and
there was not enough rolling stock to keep the road we
already had worked to its full capacity. There were no rails
except those in use. To supply these deficiencies I ordered
eight of the ten engineers General McPherson had at
Vicksburg to be sent to Nashville, and all the cars he had,
except ten. I also ordered the troops in west Tennessee to
points on the river and on the Memphis and Charleston
road, and ordered the cars, locomotives, and rails from all
the railroads, except the Memphis and Charleston, to
Nashville. The military manager of railroads, also, was
directed to furnish more rolling stock, and, as far as he
could, bridge material. General Dodge had the work
assigned him finished within forty days after receiving his
orders. The number of bridges to rebuild was 182, many of
them over deep and wide chasms. The length of road
repaired was 182 miles.

My orders for the battle were all prepared in advance of
Sherman's arrival, except the dates, which could not be fixed
while troops to be engaged were so far away. The possession
of Lookout Mountain was of no special advantage to us now.
Hooker was instructed to send Howard's corps to the north
side of the Tennessee, thence up behind the hills on the
north side, and to go into camp opposite Chattanooga; with
the remainder of the command Hooker was, at a time to be
afterward appointed, to ascend the western slope between
the upper and lower palisades, and so get into Chattanooga
Valley.

The plan of battle was for Sherman to attack the enemy's
right flank, form a line across it, extend our left over South
Chickamauga River, so as to threaten or hold the railroad in
Bragg's rear, and thus force him either to weaken his lines
elsewhere or lose his connection with his base at Chickamauga Station. Hooker was to perform like service on our right.
His problem was to get from Lookout Valley to Chattanooga
Valley in the most expeditious way possible; cross the latter
valley rapidly to Rossville, south of Bragg's line on Missionary Ridge, form line there across the ridge, facing north,
with his right flank extended to Chickamauga Valley east of
the ridge, thus threatening the enemy's rear on that flank
and compelling him to reënforce this also. Thomas, with the

Army of the Cumberland, occupied the center, and was to assault while the enemy was engaged with most of his forces on his two flanks.

To carry out this plan, Sherman was to cross the Tennessee at Brown's Ferry and move east of Chattanooga to a point opposite the north end of Missionary Ridge, and to place his command back of the foot-hills out of sight of the enemy on the ridge. There are two streams called Chickamauga emptying into the Tennessee River east of Chattanooga: North Chickamauga, taking its rise in Tennessee, flowing south and emptying into the river some seven or eight miles east; while the South Chickamauga, which takes its rise in Georgia, flows northward, and empties into the Tennessee some three or four miles above the town. There were now 116 pontoons in the North Chickamauga River, their presence there being unkown to the enemy.

At night a division was to be marched up to that point, and at two o'clock in the morning moved down with the current, thirty men in each boat. A few were to land east of the mouth of the South Chickamauga, capture the pickets there, and then lay a bridge connecting the two banks of the river. The rest were to land on the south side of the Tennessee, where Missionary Ridge would strike it if prolonged, and a sufficient number of men to man the boats were to push to the north side to ferry over the main body of Sherman's command, while those left on the south side intrenched themselves. Thomas was to move out from his lines facing the ridge, leaving enough of Palmer's corps to guard against an attack down the valley. Lookout Valley being of no present value to us, and being untenable by the enemy if we should secure Missionary Ridge, Hooker's orders were changed. His revised orders brought him to Chattanooga by the established route north of the Tennessee. He was then to move out to the right to Rossville.

The next day after Sherman's arrival I took him, with Generals Thomas and Smith and other officers, to the north side of the river and showed them the ground over which Sherman had to march, and pointed out generally what he was expected to do. As soon as the inspection was over, Sherman started for Bridgeport to hasten matters, rowing a boat himself, I believe, from Kelley's Ferry. Sherman had left Bridgeport the night of the 14th, reached Chattanooga the evening of the 15th, made the above-described inspection the morning of the 16th, and started back the same evening to hurry up his command, fully appreciating the importance of time.

His march was conducted with as much expedition as the roads and season would admit of. By the 20th he was himself at Brown's Ferry with head of column, but many of his troops were far behind, and one division, Ewing's, was at Trenton, sent that way to create the impression that Lookout was to be taken from the south. Sherman received his orders at the ferry, and was asked if he could not be ready for the assult the following morning. It was impossible to get Sherman's troops up for the next day. I then asked him if they could not be got up to make the assault on the morning of the 22d, and ordered Thomas to move on that date. But the elements were against us. It rained all the 20th and 21st. The river rose so rapidly that it was difficult to keep the pontoons in place.

Meantime Sherman continued his crossing, without intermission, as fast as his troops could get up. The crossing had to be effected in full view of the enemy on the top of Lookout Mountain. Once over, the troops soon disappeared behind the detached hills on the north side, and would not come to view again, either to watchmen on Lookout Mountain or Missionary Ridge, until they emerged between the hills to strike the bank of the river. But when Sherman's advance reached a point opposite the town of Chattanooga, Howard, who, it will be remembered, had been concealed behind the hills on the north side, took up his line of march to join the troops on the south side. His crossing was in full view both from Missionary Ridge and the top of Lookout, and the enemy, of course, supposed these troops to be Sherman's. This enabled Sherman to get to his assigned position without discovery.

During the night of the 21st the rest of the pontoon-boats, completed, one hundred and sixteen in all, were carried up to and placed in North Chickamauga. The material for the roadway over these was deposited out of view of the enemy within a few hundred yards of the bank of the Tennessee where the north end of the bridge was to rest.

Lookout Mountain*

BY GENERAL J. S. FULLERTON

GENERAL GRANT'S PLAN, IN BRIEF, now was to turn Bragg's right. He selected his old army—the Army of the Tennessee, under Sherman—to open the battle, to make the grand attack, and to carry Missionary Ridge as far as Tunnel Hill. The Army of the Cumberland was simply to get into position and coöperate.

No battle-field in our war, probably none in history, where large armies were engaged, was so spectacular or so well fitted for a display of soldierly courage and daring as the amphitheater of Chattanooga. Late on the night of November 22d a sentinel who had deserted from the enemy was brought to General Sheridan, and informed him that Bragg's baggage was being reduced and that he was about to fall back. On account of these indications and reports, General Grant decided not to wait longer for General Sherman's troops to come up, but to find out whether Bragg was in fact withdrawing, and, if so, to attack him at once. Therefore, at eleven o'clock on the morning of the 23rd, he directed General Thomas to "drive in the enemy's pickets," and feel his lines for the purpose of finding out whether he still held in force. Thus Grant was about to change his plans. He was compelled to depart from his original purpose, and was obliged to call on troops of the Army of the Cumberland to make the first offensive movement.

General Thomas ordered General Granger, commanding the Fourth Corps, to throw one division forward in the direction of Orchard Knob, with a second division in support, to discover if the enemy still remained near his old camp.

Orchard Knob is a rough, steep hill, one hundred feet high, covered with a growth of small timber, rising abruptly from the Chattanooga Valley, and lying about half-way between our outer pits and the breastworks of logs and stones. At its western base, and extending for a mile beyond, both north and south of the hill, were other rifle-pits, hid in part

* From "The Army of the Cumberland at Chattanooga," *Battles and Leaders*, Vol. III.

by a heavy belt of timber that extended about a quarter of a mile from the foot of the hill into the plain. Between this belt of timber and our lines were open fields, in which there was not a tree, fence, or other obstruction, save the bed of the East Tennessee Railroad. On the plain were hundreds of little mounds, thrown up by our own and the enemy's pickets, giving it the appearance of an overgrown prairie-dog village.

At noon General Grant, Assistant Secretary of War Dana, General Thomas, Generals Hooker, Granger, Howard, and other distinguished officers stood on the parapet of Fort Wood facing Orchard Knob, waiting to see this initial movement—the overture to the battle of Chattanooga. At half-past twelve, Wood's division, supported by Sheridan, marched out on the plain in front of the fort. It was an inspiriting sight. Flags were flying; the quick, earnest steps of thousands beat equal time. The sharp commands of hundreds of company officers, the sound of the drums, the ringing notes of the bugle, companies wheeling and countermarching and regiments getting into line, the bright sun lighting up ten thousand polished bayonets till they glistened and flashed like a flying shower of electric sparks—all looked like preparations for a peaceful pageant, rather than for the bloody work of death.

Groups of officers on Missionary Ridge looked down through their glasses, and the enemy's pickets, but a few hundred yards away, came out of their pits and stood idly looking on, unconcernedly viewing what they supposed to be preparations for a grand review. But at half-past one o'clock the advance was sounded. Instantly Wood's division, moving with the steadiness of a machine, started forward. Not a straggler or laggard was on the field, and, what was probably hardly ever before seen, drummers were marching with their companies, beating the charge. Now the enemy realized, for the first time, that it was not a review. His pickets fell back to their reserves. The reserves were quickly driven back to the main line. Firing opened from the enemy's advanced rifle-pits, followed by a tremendous roll of musketry and roar of artillery. Men were seen on the ground, dotting the field over which the line of battle had passed. Ambulances came hurrying back with the first of the wounded. Columns of puffy smoke arose from the Orchard Knob woods. A cheer, faint to those on the parapet of Fort Wood, indicated that the boys in blue were carrying the

Lookout Mountain: *The battle above the clouds*

breastworks on the Knob! A sharp, short struggle, and the hill was ours.

About four o'clock in the afternoon of November 23d, when it became certain that Osterhaus, cut off by the breaking of the pontoon-bridge at Brown's Ferry, would be attached to Hooker's command, General Thomas directed Hooker to make a demonstration against Lookout Mountain the next morning, and, if the demonstration showed it could be carried, to proceed to take it. Later in the day, orders to the same effect came to General Hooker from General Grant. The success at Orchard Knob, and the breaking of the bridge, caused this radical change to be made in Grant's plans. Yet he still held to the chief feature, which was to turn Bragg's right.

The morning of November 24th opened with a cold, drizzling rain. Thick clouds of mist were settling on Lookout Mountain. At daybreak Geary's division, and Whitaker's brigade of Cruft's division, marched up to Wauhatchie, the nearest point at which Lookout Creek, swelled by recent rains, could be forded, and at eight o'clock they crossed. The heavy clouds of mist reaching down the mountain-side hid the movement from the enemy, who was expecting and was well prepared to resist a crossing at the Chattanooga road below. As soon as this movement was discovered, the enemy withdrew his troops from the summit of the mountain, changed front, and formed a new line to meet our advance, his left resting at the palisade, and his right at the heavy works in the valley, where the road crossed the creek. Having crossed at Wauhatchie, Whitaker's brigade, being in the advance, drove back the enemy's pickets, and quickly ascended the mountain till it reached the foot of the palisade. Here, firmly attaching its right, the brigade faced left in front, with its left joined to Geary's division. Geary now moved along the side of the mountain, and through the valley, thus covering the crossing of the rest of Hooker's command. In the meantime Grose's brigade was engaging the enemy at the lower road crossing, and Woods' brigade of Osterhaus's division was building a bridge rather more than half a mile farther up the creek. Geary, moving down the valley, reached this point at eleven o'clock, just after the bridge was finished, and as Osterhaus's division and Grose's brigade were crossing. Hooker's command, now united in the enemy's field, was ready to advance and sweep around the mountain. His line, hanging at the base of the palisades like a great pendulum, reached down the side of the mountain to the valley, where the force that had just crossed the creek was attached as its weight. Now, as, at the command of Hooker, it swung forward in its upward movement, the artillery of the Army of the Cumberland, on Moccasin Point, opened fire, throwing a stream of shot and shell into the enemy's rifle-pits at the foot of the mountain, and into the works thickly planted on the "White House" plateau. At the same time the guns planted by Hooker on the west side of the creek opened on the works which covered the enemy's right. Then followed a gallant assault by Osterhaus and Grose. After fighting for nearly two hours, step by step up the steep mountain-side, over and through deep gullies and ravines, over great rocks and fallen trees, the earth-works on the plateau were assaulted and carried, and the enemy was driven out and forced to fall back. He did so slowly and reluctantly, taking advantage of the rough ground to continue the fight. It was now two o'clock. A halt all along the line was ordered by General Hooker, as the clouds had grown so thick that further advance was impracticable, and as his ammunition was almost exhausted and more could not well be brought up the mountain. But all the enemy's works had been taken. Hooker had carried the mountain on the east side, had opened communication with Chattanooga, and he commanded the enemy's line of defensive works in Chattanooga Valley.

At two o'clock Hooker reported to General Thomas and informed him that he was out of ammunition. Thomas at once sent Carlin's brigade from the valley, each soldier taking with him all the small ammunition he could carry. At five o'clock Carlin was on the mountain, and Hooker's skirmishers were quickly supplied with the means of carrying on their work.

In the morning it had not been known in Chattanooga, in Sherman's army, or in Bragg's camp, that a battle was to be fought. Indeed, it was not definitely known even to General Grant; for Hooker was only ordered to make a demonstration, and, if this showed a good chance for success, then to make and attack. Soon after breakfast, Sherman's men at the other end of the line, intent on the north end of Missionary Ridge, and Thomas's men in the center, fretting to be let loose from their intrenchments, were startled by the sound of artillery and musketry firing in Lookout Valley. Surprise possessed the thousands who turned their anxious eyes toward the mountain. The hours slowly wore away; the roar of battle increased, as it came rolling around the point of the mountain, and the anxiety grew. A battle was being fought just before and above them. They could hear, but could not see how it was going. Finally, the wind, tossing about the clouds and mist, made a rift that for a few minutes opened a view of White House plateau. The enemy was seen to be in flight, and Hooker's men were in pursuit! Then went up a mighty cheer from the thirty thousand in the valley that was heard above the battle by their comrades on the mountain.

As the sun went down, the clouds rolled away, and the night came on clear and cool. A grand sight was old Lookout that night. Not two miles apart were the parallel camp-fires of the two armies, extending from the summit of the mountain to its base, looking like streams of burning lava, while in between, the flashes from the skirmishers' muskets glowed like giant fire-flies.

The next morning there was silence in Hooker's front. Before daylight eight adventurous, active volunteers from the 8th Kentucky Infantry scaled the palisades and ran up the Stars and Stripes. The enemy had stolen away in the night.

Although General Grant had twice changed his original plan, first in the movement from the center, then in the reconnoissance and resulting attack on Lookout Mountain, he still adhered to his purpose of turning Bragg's right, and made no change in the instructions given to General Sherman, except as to the time of attack. Every necessary preparation for crossing Sherman's troops had been made secretly, under direction of General W. F. Smith; 116 pontoons had been placed in North Chickamauga Creek, and in ravines near its mouth, and many wagon-loads of "balks" (stringers) and chess (flooring) had been hid near by. Sherman had his troops well massed on the north side of the river. After dark, November 23d, Colonel James Barnett, the gallant and skillful Chief of Artillery, of the Army of the Cumberland under Rosecrans, to whom was assigned the duty of covering Sherman's crossing, and protecting the pontoon bridge, planted the guns of six six-gun batteries on the low foot-hills, and a battery of siege guns on the higher ground on the north side of the river. At midnight General Giles A. Smith's brigade entered the pontoons, floated out of North Chickamauga Creek, and was rowed to the south bank of the river. Landing quietly, he surprised and captured the enemy's pickets, and secured a firm foothold. The pontoons were sent across the river, and with these and the small steamboat brought up from Chattanooga General Morgan L. Smith's and General John E. Smith's divisions were ferried over the river. As soon as these troops had been landed, work was commenced on the pontoon-bridge, which was skillfully laid under the supervision of General W. F. Smith. The bridge was 1,350 feet in length, and was completed by eleven o'clock in the morning, when General Ewing's division and Sherman's artillery crossed. At one o'clock, just as Hooker was rounding the front of Lookout Mountain, the roar of his battle stirring the blood of the veterans of the Army of the Tennessee, General Sherman gave the command, "Forward!" At three thirty General Sherman took the hill which was supposed to be the north end of the ridge, and soon afterward took another hill a little in advance, both separated by a deep depression from the heavily fortified Tunnel Hill, on which Bragg's right flank rested and which was Sherman's objective point.

None of the men of the Army of the Cumberland, who for nine weeks were buried in the trenches at Chattanooga, can ever forget the glorious night of the 24th of November. As the sun went down, the clouds rolled up the mountain, and the mist was blown out of the valley. Night came on clear, with the stars lighting up the heavens. But there followed a sight to cheer their hearts and thrill their souls. Away off to their right, and reaching skyward, Lookout Mountain was ablaze with the fires of Hooker's men, while off to their left, and reaching far above the valley, the north end of Missionary Ridge was aflame with the lights of Sherman's army. The great iron crescent that had, with threatening aspect, so long hung over them, was disappearing. The only thought that dampened their enthusiasm was that the enemy was being destroyed on the flanks, while they were tied down in the center, without a part in the victories. But late that night General Grant, thinking that General Sherman had carried Tunnel Hill, and acting in that belief, gave orders for the next day's battle. General Sherman was directed to attack the enemy at early dawn, Thomas to co-operate with him, and Hooker, to be ready to advance into Chattanooga Valley, to hold the road that zigzagged from the valley to the summit. Early the next morning, when General Grant learned that the ridge had not been carried as far as Tunnel

Missionary Ridge: *Thomas's Union troops charging uphill*

Hill, and that Lookout Mountain had been evacuated by the enemy, he suspended his orders, except those to Sherman, and directed Hooker to come down from the mountain, to carry the pass at Rossville, and then operate on Bragg's left and rear. Bragg's army was now concentrated on Missionary Ridge, and in the valley at the east foot. Cheatham's and Stevenson's divisions had been withdrawn from Lookout Mountain on the night of the 24th, and, marching all night, were seen at dawn the next morning moving along the summit of Missionary Ridge, on the way to reënforce Bragg's right. For several hours after daylight the flowing of this steady stream of troops continued.

Early in the morning of the 25th General Grant and General Thomas established their headquarters on Orchard Knob, a point from which the best view of the movements of the whole army could be had. At sunrise General Sherman commenced his attack, but after repeated assaults and severe fighting, it appearing to be impossible for General Sherman to take the enemy's works, operations ceased early in the afternoon.

Meanwhile Hooker was detained three hours at Chattanooga Creek, while a bridge that the retreating enemy had burned was being rebuilt. As soon as he had taken Rossville, he moved against the south end of Missionary Ridge. The ridge was quickly carried, and, sweeping northward, Hooker soon came upon Stewart's division, posted on the summit, and behind the earth-works which the Army of the Cumberland had thrown up the day after Chickamauga. Cruft's division assaulted and carried the works, thus having the good fortune of retaking the works they themselves had constructed. It was by this time nearly sundown. Hooker reached the south end of the ridge too late in the day to relieve the pressure on Sherman, who was at the north end six miles off. Bragg's right had not been turned. Success had not followed Sherman's movement. The battle as planned had not been won.

Late on this memorable afternoon there was an accident—an accident like the charge at Balaklava; though, unlike this theme for poetry, it called for greater daring, and was attended by complete success, and yielded most important results, for it led to the complete shattering of the enemy's army, and drove him from the field. On Orchard Knob, and opposite the center of Missionary Ridge, were four divisions of the Army of the Cumberland. On the left was Baird's division; then Wood's and Sheridan's divisions occupying the lines which, two days before, they had taken in their magnificent advance; on the right was R. W. Johnson's division—all under the personal command of Thomas. It was past three o'clock. General Sherman had ceased operations. General Hooker's advance had not yet been felt. The day was dying, and Bragg still held the ridge. If any movement to dislodge him was to be made that day it must be made at once. At half-past three o'clock an attack was ordered by General Grant. He had changed his plan of battle. At once orders were issued that at the firing, in rapid succession, of six guns on Orchard Knob, Thomas's whole line should instantaneously move forward. Sheridan's and Wood's divisions in the center, Sheridan to be supported on the right by Johnson, and Wood on the left by Baird. This demonstration was to be made to relieve the pressure on Sherman. The only order given was to move forward and take the rifle-pits at the foot of the ridge. In Sheridan's division the order was, "As soon as the signal is given, the whole line will advance, and you will take what is before you."

Between Orchard Knob and Missionary Ridge was a valley, partly covered with a small growth of timber. It was wooded in front of the right of Baird's and of the whole of Wood's division. In front of Sheridan's and Johnson's it had been almost entirely cleared. At the foot of the ridge were heavy rifle-pits, which could be seen from Orchard Knob, and extending in front of them, for four and five hundred yards, the ground was covered with felled trees. There was a good plain for both direct and enfilading fire from the rifle-pits, and the approaches were commanded by the enemy's artillery. At this point the ridge is five or six hundred feet high. Its side, scored with gullies and showing but little timber, had a rough and bare appearance. Half-way up was another line of rifle-pits, and the summit was furrowed with additional lines and dotted over with epaulements, in which were placed fifty pieces of artillery. Directly in front of Orchard Knob, and on the summit of the ridge, in a small house was Bragg's headquarters.

At twenty minutes before four the signal guns were fired. Suddenly twenty thousand men rushed forward, moving in line of battle by brigades, with a double line of skirmishers in front, and closely followed by the reserves in mass. The big siege-guns in the Chattanooga forts roared above the light artillery and musketry in the valley. The enemy's rifle-pits were ablaze, and the whole ridge in our front had broken out like another Aetna. Not many minutes afterward our men were seen working through the felled trees and other obstructions. Though exposed to such a terrific fire, they neither fell back nor halted. By a bold and desperate push they broke through the works in several places and opened flank and reverse fires. The enemy was thrown into confusion, and took precipitate flight up the ridge. Many prisoners and a large number of small-arms were captured. The order of the commanding general had now been fully and most successfully carried out. But it did not go far enough to satisfy these brave men, who thought the time had come to finish the battle of Chickamauga. There was a halt of but a few minutes, to take breath and to re-form lines; then, with a sudden impulse, and without orders, all started up the ridge. Officers, catching their spirit, first followed, then led. There was no thought of supports or of protecting flanks, though the enemy's line could be seen, stretching on either side.

As soon as this movement was seen from Orchard Knob, Grant quickly turned to Thomas, who stood by his side, and I heard him say angrily: "Thomas, who ordered those men up the ridge?" Thomas replied, in his usual slow, quiet manner: "I don't know; I did not." Then, addressing General Gordon Granger, he said, "Did you order them up, Granger?" "No," said Granger; "they started up without orders. When those fellows get started all hell can't stop them." General Grant said something to the effect that somebody would suffer if it did not turn out well, and then, turning, stoically watched the ridge. He gave no further orders.

As soon as Granger had replied to Thomas, he turned to me, his chief-of-staff, and said: "Ride at once to Wood, and then to Sheridan, and ask them if they ordered their men up the ridge, and tell them, if they can take it, to push ahead." As I was mounting, Granger added: "It is hot over there, and you may not get through. I shall send Captain Avery to Sheridan; and other officers after both of you." As fast as my horse could carry me, I rode first to General Wood, and delivered the message. "I didn't order them up," said Wood; "they started up on their own account, and they are going up, too! Tell Granger, if we are supported, we will take and hold the ridge!" As soon as I reached General Wood, Captain Avery got to General Sheridan, and delivered his message. "I didn't order them up," said Sheridan; "but we are going to take the ridge!" He then asked Avery for his flask and waved it at a group of Confederate officers, standing just in front of Bragg's headquarters, with the salutation, "Here's at you!" At once two guns—the "Lady Breckinridge" and the "Lady Buckner"—in front of Bragg's headquarters were fired at Sheridan and the group of officers about him. One shell struck so near as to throw dirt over Sheridan and Avery. "Ah!" said the general, "that is ungenerous; I shall take those guns for that!" Before Sheridan received the message taken by Captain Avery, he had sent a staff-officer to Granger, to inquire whether "the order given to take the rifle-pits meant the rifle-pits at the base, or those on the top of the ridge." Granger told this officer that "the order given was to take those at the base." Conceiving this to be an order to fall back, the officer, on his way to Sheridan, gave it to General Wagner, commanding the Second Brigade of the division, which was then nearly half-way up the ridge. Wagner ordered his brigade back to the rifle-pits at the base, but only remained there till Sheridan, seeing the mistake, ordered it forward. It again advanced under a terrific fire.

The men, fighting and climbing up the steep hill, sought the roads, ravines, and less rugged parts. The ground was so broken that it was impossible to keep a regular line of battle. At times their movements were in shape like the flight of migratory birds—sometimes in line, sometimes in mass, mostly in V-shaped groups, with the points toward the enemy. At these points regimental flags were flying, sometimes drooping as the bearers were shot, but never reaching the ground, for other brave hands were there to seize them. Sixty flags were advancing up the hill. Bragg was hurrying large bodies of men from his right to the center. They could be seen hastening along the ridge. Cheatham's division was being withdrawn from Sherman's front. Bragg and Hardee were at the center, urging their men to stand firm and drive back the advancing enemy, now so near the summit—indeed, so near that the guns, which would not be sufficiently depressed to reach them, became useless. Artillerymen were lighting the fuses of shells, and bowling them by hundreds down the hill. The critical moment arrived when the summit was just within reach. At six different points, and almost simultaneously, Sheridan's and Wood's divisions broke over the crest—Sheridan's first, near Bragg's headquarters; and in a few minutes Sheridan was beside the guns that had been fired at him, and claiming them as captures of his division. Baird's division took the works on Wood's left almost immediately afterward; and then Johnson came up on Sheridan's right. The enemy's guns were turned upon those who still remained in the works, and soon all were in flight down the eastern slope. Baird got on the ridge just in time to change front and oppose a large body of the enemy moving down from Bragg's right to attack our left. After a sharp engagement, that lasted till dark, he drove the enemy back beyond a high point on the north, which he at once occupied.

The sun had not yet gone down, Missionary Ridge was ours, and Bragg's army was broken and in flight! Dead and wounded comrades lay thickly strewn on the ground: but thicker yet were the dead and wounded men in gray. Then followed the wildest confusion, as the victors gave vent to their joy. Some madly shouted; some wept from very excess of joy; some grotesquely danced out their delight—even our wounded forgot their pain, to join in the general hurrah. But Sheridan did not long stop to receive praise and congratulations. With two brigades he started down the Mission Mills road, and found, strongly posted on a second hill, the enemy's rear. They made a stout resistance, but by a sudden flank movement he drove them from the heights and captured two guns and many prisoners. The day was succeeded by a clear moonlight night. At seven o'clock General Granger sent word to General Thomas that by a bold dash at Chickamauga Crossing he might cut off a large number of the enemy now supposed to be leaving Sherman's front, and that he proposed to move in that direction. It was midnight before guides could be found, and then General Sheridan again put his tired and well-worn men in motion. He reached the creek just as the rear-guard of the enemy was crossing, and pressed it so closely that it burned the pontoon-bridge before all its troops were over. Here Sheridan captured several hundred prisoners, a large number of quartermasters' wagons, together with caissons, artillery, ammunition, and many small-arms.

In this battle Sheridan's and Wood's divisions—the two center assulting divisions—took 31 pieces of artillery, several thousand small-arms, and 3,800 prisoners. In that one hour of assault they lost 2,337 men in killed and wounded—over 20 per cent of their whole force! On the northern end of the ridge General Sherman lost in his two days' fighting 1,697 in killed and wounded. Of these, 1,268 were in his own three divisions. During the night the last of Bragg's army was withdrawn from Missionary Ridge, and Chattanooga from that time remained in undisputed possession of the Union forces.

THE BLOCKADE-RUNNERS

AFTER ADMIRAL FARRAGUT TOOK ORLEANS he wanted to move immediately against the forts in Mobile Bay, either to occupy the city of Mobile or seal off the harbor from use by blockade-runners. President Lincoln had other plans; he ordered Farragut to proceed up the Mississippi River to attack Vicksburg. There, in 1862, Farragut's fleet took a hammering from shore batteries. He returned to the Gulf, but it was then too late to risk an attack solely with his wooden ships. The forts defending the entrance to the Bay had been strengthened, and it was rumored that the Confederates were building rams. Farragut would need ironclads to get past the forts, but he wouldn't receive any until 1864. In the meantime, he blockaded the Gulf coast.

"To guard the ordinary entrances to these ports was comparatively a simple task. There was, however, a greater difficulty to be met; for the outer coast-line is only the exterior edge of a series of islands between which and the mainland there is an elaborate network of navigable sounds and passages, having numerous inlets communicating with the sea. These inlets were frequently changing under the influence of the great storm; new channels would be opened and old ones filled up. As soon as we closed a port, by stationing vessels at the main entrance thereto, the blockade-runners would slip in at some of the numerous remote inlets, reaching their destination by the inside passages; so that blockade-running flourished until we were able to procure as many blockaders as there were channels and inlets to be guarded. The extreme diversity of the services required of these blockading vessels made it difficult to obtain ships that could meet the varying necessities. They must be heavy enough to contend with the enemy's rams, or they would be driven away from the principal ports. They must be light enough to chase and capture the swift blockade-runners. They must be deep enough in the water to ride out in safety the violent winter gales, and they must be of such light draft as to be able to go near enough to the shallow inlets to blockade them efficiently.

"The blockading fleets of all the important harbors were composed of several very heavy ships, with a few vessels of the lighter class, the rest of the fleet represented some of the other classes needed. But it was impossible to do this along the entire coast, and it sometimes happened that the Confederate ironclads perversely attacked the lighter vessels, as in the case of the rams at Charleston selecting for their victims the *Mercedita* and the *Keystone State,* instead of the heavier ships; while, on the other hand, the swift blockade-runners disclosed themselves most frequently to the ponderous and slow-moving ships that were least able to catch them. . . ."*

The struggle to make the blockade work was naturally countered by Confederate evasive measures. "Four categories of ships engaged in blockade-running: those owned by the Confederate government; those owned by the state governments; those owned by private individuals or groups of speculators; and foreign ships. Of these the third and fourth categories were the most important, though government-owned blockade-runners gave a good account of themselves. It has been estimated that altogether some 600 ships were engaged, at one time or another, in the lucrative and exciting business of blockade-running, but this estimate is palpably too low; that there were, altogether, some 8,000 violations of the blockade; and that blockade-runners brought in altogether over 600,000 small arms, 550,000 pair of shoes, and large quantities of meat, coffee, saltpeter, lead, and other items. At the same time substantial quantities of supplies were brought in from Mexico, across the Rio Grande, and there was at all times a lively trade with the North: General Sherman said that Cincinnati furnished more goods to the Confederacy than Charleston!

"All this would indicate that the blockade was but loosely enforced, and it cannot be denied that it was pretty ineffective in 1861 and even in 1862. Thereafter, however—what with the fall of New Orleans and of Fort Royal and the sealing up of other harbors—it became increasingly effective, and the South felt the pinch seriously. It is estimated that the chances of capture were one in ten in 1861, but one

* From Horace Wait, *The Blockade of the Confederacy.*

in three by 1864, and with the capture of Wilmington in January 1865 blockade-running practically ceased."†

But in 1863, when blockade-runners were most successful, Horace Wait says, "the arrivals and departures were equal to one steamer a day, taking all of the Confederate ports together. Prior to this no such attempts had ever been made to violate a blockade. The industrial necessities of the principal maritime nations stimulated them to unusual efforts, in return for which they looked forward to a rich harvest. The British especially had abundant capital, the finest and swiftest ships ever built, manned by the most energetic seamen. They felt confident that they could monopolize the Southern cotton and the markets of the Confederacy; but when it was found that neither swift steamers, skilled officers, nor desperate efforts could give security to their best investments of capital, and that the perils to their beautiful vessels and precious cargoes increased as fast as their efforts to surmount them, ultimately becoming even greater in proportion than the enormous gains of the traffic when successful, they were at last driven off from our coast entirely, and kept at bay, though armed and supported by the greatest of foreign powers. They finally gave up the business, admitting that the blockade was a success. A Confederate officer stated that when Fort Fisher fell their last port was gone, and blockade-running was at an end.

"This signal defeat of that extraordinary development of our Civil War has been spoken of as one of the great moral lessons of our struggle. After the war British officers frankly stated to our naval officers that they considered the blockade and its enforcement the great fact of the war. This was the first time in the history of naval warfare that a steam navy had been kept at sea for so long a period. The Confederates menaced the blockading fleets with nine ironclads which would have been a match for any ironclads in the French or English navy afloat at that time; therefore it becomes manifest that a fleet which could hold in check ironclads, as well as shut out blockade-runners that were the swiftest steamers built at that time, must have combined speed and power to an extent never before displayed in naval warfare. . . ."*

Meanwhile, in August, 1864, Admiral Farragut got his ironclad monitors. Several months before, the Confederate

† Henry Steele Commager, *The Blue and the Gray,* pp. 846–47.
* Wait, *op. cit.*

ram *Tennessee* had been observed in the Bay. She was considered "the strongest and most powerful iron-clad ever put afloat. She looked like a great turtle; her sloping sides were covered with iron plates six inches in thickness, thoroughly riveted together, and she had a formidable iron beak projecting under the water. Her armament consisted of six heavy Brooke rifles, each sending a solid shot weighing from 95 to 110 pounds—a small affair compared with the heavy guns of the present time, but irresistible then against everything but the turrets of the monitors. In addition to these means of resistance, the narrow channel to within a few hundred yards of the shore had been lined with torpedoes. These were under the water, anchored to the bottom. Some of them were beer-kegs filled with powder, from the sides of which projected numerous little tubes containing fulminate, which it was expected would be exploded by contact with the passing vessels, but the greater part were tin cones fitted with caps.

"Except for what Farragut had already accomplished on the Mississippi, it would have been considered a foolhardy experiment for wooden vessels to attempt to pass so close to one of the strongest forts on the coast."†

Farragut planned his attack for August 5. Lieutenant Kinney described the situation in Mobile Bay. The Bay "gradually widens from the city to the gulf, a distance of thirty miles. The entrance is protected by a long narrow arm of sand, with Fort Morgan on the extreme western point. Across the channel from Fort Morgan, and perhaps three miles distant, is Dauphine Island, a narrow strip of sand with Fort Gaines at its eastern end. Further to the west is little Fort Powell, commanding a narrow channel through which light-draught vessels could enter the bay. Between Dauphine Island and Fort Morgan, and in front of the main entrance to the bay, is Sand Island, a barren spot, under the lee of which three of our monitors were lying. The army signal officers were sent on board the fleet, not with any intention of having their services used in passing the forts, but in order to establish communication afterward between the fleet and the army, for the purpose of cooperating in the capture of the forts. The primary objects of Admiral Farragut in entering the bay were to close Mobile to the outside world, to capture or destroy the *Tennessee,* and to cut

† From John C. Kinney, "Farragut at Mobile Bay," *Battles and Leaders,* IV, 382.

off all possible means of escape from the garrisons of the forts. . . . There was no immediate expectation of capturing the city of Mobile, which was safe by reason of a solid row of piles and torpedoes across the river, three miles below the city. Moreover, the larger vessels of the fleet could not approach within a dozen miles of the city, on account of shallow water."*

Farragut at Mobile Bay†

BY LIEUTENANT JOHN C. KINNEY

At sunset the last orders had been issued, every commander knew his duty, and unusual quiet prevailed in the fleet. The sea was smooth, a gentle breeze relieved the mid-summer heat, and the night came on serenely and peacefully, and far more quietly than to a yachting fleet at Newport. For the first hour after the candles were lighted below, the stillness was almost oppressive. The officers of the *Hartford* gathered around the ward-room table, writing letters to loved ones far away, or giving instructions in case of death. As brave and thoughtful men, they recognized the dangers that they did not fear, and made provision for the possibilities of the morrow. But this occupied little time, and then, business over, there followed an hour of unrestrained jollity. Many an old story was retold and ancient conundrum repeated. Old officers forgot, for the moment, their customary dignity, and it was evident that all were exhilarated and stimulated by the knowledge of the coming struggle. There was no other "stimulation," for the strict naval rules prevented. Finally, after a half-hour's smoke under the forecastle, all hands turned in. The scene on the flag-ship was representative of the night before the battle throughout the fleet.

It was the admiral's desire and intention to get under way by daylight, to take advantage of the inflowing tide; but a dense fog came on after midnight and delayed the work of forming line.

* Kinney, *op. cit.*, p. 385.
† *Ibid.*, pp. 385–400.

It was a weird sight as the big ships "balanced to partners," the dim outlines slowly emerging like phantoms in the fog. The vessels were lashed together in pairs, fastened side by side by huge cables. All the vessels had been stripped for the fight, the top-hamper being left at Pensacola, and the starboard boats being either left behind or towed on the port side. The admiral's steam-launch, the *Loyall,* named after his son, steamed alongside the flag-ship on the port side.

It was a quarter of six o'clock before the fleet was in motion. Meantime a light breeze had scattered the fog and left a clear, sunny August day. The line moved slowly, and it was an hour after starting before the opening gun was fired. This was a 15-inch shell from the *Tecumseh,* and it exploded over Fort Morgan. Half an hour afterward the fleet came within range and the firing from the starboard vessels became general, the fort and the Confederate fleet replying. The fleet took position across the entrance to the bay and raked the advance vessels fore and aft, doing great damage, to which it was for a time impossible to make effective reply. Gradually the fleet came into close quarters with Fort Morgan, and the firing on both sides became terrific. The wooden vessels moved more rapidly than the monitors, and as the *Brooklyn* came opposite the fort, and approached the torpedo line, she came nearly alongside the rear monitor. To have kept on would have been to take the lead, with the ram *Tennessee* approaching and with the unknown danger of the torpedoes underneath. At this critical moment the *Brooklyn* halted and began backing and signaling with the army signals. The *Hartford* was immediately behind and the following vessels were in close proximity, and the sudden stopping of the *Brooklyn* threatened to bring the whole fleet into collision, while the strong inflowing tide was likely to carry some of the vessels to the shore under the guns of the fort.

On the previous night the admiral had issued orders that the army signal officers were not to be allowed on deck during the fight, but were to go into the cockpit, on the lower deck, and assist the surgeons. The reason assigned was that these officers would not be needed during the passage of the forts, but would be wanted afterward to open communication with the army, and that therefore it would be a misfortune to have any of them disabled. The two army signal officers on the *Hartford* disrelished this order exceedingly, and, after consulting together, decided that in the confusion of the occasion their presence on deck would probably not be noticed, and that they would evade the command if possible. In this they were successful until shortly before passing Sand Island and coming within range of Fort Morgan. Then the executive officer, Lieutenant Commander Lewis A. Kimberly, who never allowed anything to escape his attention, came to them very quietly and politely, and told them the admiral's order must be obeyed. We were satisfied from his manner that the surgeons had need of us, and, without endeavoring to argue the matter, made our way to the stifling hold, where Surgeon Lansdale and Assistant-Surgeon Commons, with their helpers, were sitting, with their paraphernalia spread out ready for use.

Nearly every man had his watch in his hand awaiting the first shot. To us, ignorant of everything going on above, every minute seemed an hour, and there was a feeling of great relief when the boom of the Tecumseh's first gun was heard. Presently one or two of our forward guns opened, and we could hear the distant sound of the guns of the fort in reply. Soon the cannon-balls began to crash through the deck above us, and then the thunder of our whole broadside of nine Dahlgren guns kept the vessel in a quiver. But as yet no wounded were sent down, and we knew we were still at comparatively long range. In the intense excitement of the occasion it seemed that hours had passed, but it was just twenty minutes from the time we went below, when an officer shouted down the hatchway: "Send up an army signal officer immediately: the Brooklyn is signaling." In a moment the writer was on deck, where he found the situation as already described. Running on to the forecastle, he hastily took the Brooklyn's message, which imparted the unnecessary information, "The monitors are right ahead; we cannot go on without passing them." The reply was sent at once from the admiral, "Order the monitors ahead and go on." But still the Brooklyn halted, while, to add to the horror of the situation, the monitor Tecumseh, a few hundred yards in the advance, suddenly careened to one side and almost instantly sank to the bottom, carrying with her Captain Tunis A. M. Craven and the greater part of his crew, numbering in all 114 officers and men. The pilot, John Collins, and a few men who were in the turret jumped into the water and were rescued by a boat from the Metacomet, which, under charge of Acting Ensign Henry C. Nields, rowed up un-

der the guns of the fort and through a deadly storm of shot
and shell and picked them up. Meantime the *Brooklyn*
failed to go ahead, and the whole fleet became a stationary
point-blank target for the guns of Fort Morgan and of the
rebel vessels. It was during these few perilous moments that
the most fatal work of the day was done to the fleet.

Owing to the *Hartford's* position, only her few bow guns
could be used, while a deadly rain of shot and shell was
falling on her, and her men were being cut down by scores,
unable to make reply. The sight on deck was sickening
beyond the power of words to portray. Shot after shot came
through the side, mowing down the men, deluging the decks
with blood, and scattering mangled fragments of humanity
so thickly that it was difficult to stand on the deck, so slippery was it. The old expression of the "scuppers running
blood," "the slippery deck," etc., give but the faintest idea of
the spectacle on the *Hartford*. The bodies of the dead were
placed in a long row on the port side, while the wounded
were sent below until the surgeons' quarters would hold no
more. A solid shot coming through the bow struck a gunner
on the neck, completely severing head from body. One poor
fellow (afterward an object of interest at the great Sanitary
Commission Fair in New York) lost both legs by a cannon-
ball; as he fell he threw up both arms, just in time to have
them also carried away by another shot. At one gun, all the
crew on one side were swept down by a shot which came
crashing through the bulwarks. A shell burst between the
two forward guns in charge of Lieutenant Tyson, killing and
wounding fifteen men. The mast upon which the writer was
perched was twice struck, once slightly, and again just
below the foretop by a heavy shell, from a rifle on the Con-
federal gun-boat *Selma*. Fortunately the shell came
tumbling end over end, and buried itself in the mast, butt-
end first, leaving the percussion-cap protruding. Had it
come point first, or had it struck at any other part of the mast
than in the reënforced portion where the heel of the topmast
laps the top of the lower mast, this contribution to the
literature of the war would probably have been lost to the
world, as the distance to the deck was about a hundred feet.
As it was, the sudden jar would have dislodged any one from
the crosstrees had not the shell been visible from the time it
left the *Selma,* thus giving time to prepare for it by an extra
grip around the top of the mast. Looking out over the water,
it was easy to trace the course of every shot, both from the

guns of the *Hartford* and from the Confederate fleet. Another signal message from the *Brooklyn* told of the sinking of the *Tecumseh,* a fact known already, and another order to "go on" was given and was not obeyed.

Soon after the fight began, Admiral Farragut, finding that the lowhanging smoke from the guns interfered with his view from the deck, went up the rigging of the mainmast as far as the futtock-shrouds, immediately below the maintop. The pilot, Martin Freeman, was in the top directly overhead, and the fleet-captain was on the deck below. Seeing the admiral in this exposed position, where, if wounded, he would be killed by falling to the deck, Fleet-Captain Drayton ordered Knowles, the signal-quartermaster, to fasten a rope around him so that he would be prevented from falling.

Finding that the *Brooklyn* failed to obey his orders, the admiral hurriedly inquired of the pilot if there was sufficient depth of water for the *Hartford* to pass to the left of the *Brooklyn*. Receiving an affirmative reply, he said: "I will take the lead," and immediately ordered the *Hartford* ahead at full speed. As he passed the *Brooklyn* a voice warned him of the torpedoes, to which he returned the contemptuous answer, "Damn the torpedoes." This is the current story, and may have some basis of truth. But as a matter of fact, there was never a moment when the din of the battle would not have drowned any attempt at a conversation between the two ships, and while it is quite probable that the admiral made the remark it is doubtful if he shouted it to the *Brooklyn*.

Then was witnessed the remarkable sight of the *Hartford* and her consort, the *Metacomet,* passing over the dreaded torpedo ground and rushing ahead far in advance of the rest of the fleet, the extrication of which from the confusion caused by the *Brooklyn*'s halt required many minutes of valuable time. The *Hartford* was now moving over what is called the "middle ground," with shallow water on either side, so that it was impossible to move except as the channel permitted. Taking advantage of the situation, the Confederate gun-boat *Selma* kept directly in front of the flag-ship and raked her fore and aft, doing more damage in reality than all the rest of the enemy's fleet. The other gun-boats, the *Gaines* and the *Morgan*, were in shallow water on our starboard bow, but they received more damage from the *Hartford*'s broadsides than they were able to inflict. Meanwhile the ram *Tennessee,* which up to this time had contented herself with simply firing at the approaching fleet, started for the *Hartford,* apparently with the intention of striking her amidships. She came on perhaps for half a mile, never approaching nearer than a hundred yards, and then suddenly turned and made for the fleet, which, still in front of the fort, was gradually getting straightened out and following the *Hartford.* This change of course on the part of the ram has always been a mystery. The captain of the ram, in papers published since the war, denies that any such move was made, but it was witnessed by the entire fleet, and is mentioned by both Admiral Farragut and Fleet-Captain Drayton in their official reports.

The *Hartford* had now run a mile inside the bay, and was suffering chiefly from the raking fire of the *Selma,* which was unquestionably managed more skillfully than any other Confederate vessel. Captain (now Admiral) Jouett, commanding the *Hartford*'s escort, the *Metacomet,* repeatedly asked permission of the admiral to cut loose and take care of the *Selma,* and finally, at five minutes past eight, consent was given. In an instant the cables binding the two vessels were cut, and the *Metacomet,* the fastest vessel in the fleet, bounded ahead. The *Selma* was no match for her, and, recognizing her danger, endeavored to retreat up the bay. But she was speedily overhauled, and when a shot had wounded her captain and killed her first lieutenant she surrendered. Before this the *Gaines* had been crippled by the splendid marksmanship of the *Hartford*'s gunners, and had run aground under the guns of the fort, where she was shortly afterward set on fire, the crew escaping to the shore. The gunboat *Morgan,* after grounding for a few moments on the shoals to the east of Navy Cove, retreated to the shallow water near the fort, whence she escaped the following night to Mobile. The *Hartford,* having reached the deep water of the bay, about three miles north of Dauphine Island, came to anchor.

Let us now return to the other vessels of the fleet, which we left massed in front of Fort Morgan by the remarkable action of the *Brooklyn* in stopping and refusing to move ahead. When the ram *Tennessee* turned away from the *Hartford,* as narrated, she made for the fleet, and in their crowded and confused condition it seemed to be a matter of no difficulty to pick out whatever victims the Confederate commander (Admiral Franklin Buchanan) might desire, as

he had done in 1861 when commanding the *Merrimac* in
Hampton Roads. Before he could reach them the line had
become straightened, and the leading vessels had passed the
fort. Admiral Jenkins, who commanded the *Richmond* during the fight, writing of this part of the fight, for the use of
the present writer, says:

> During the delay under the guns of Fort Morgan and
> the waterbattery by the backing of the *Brooklyn,* the
> vessels astern had remained apparently stationary, so that
> the nearest one to the *Richmond* was about half a mile
> off, and some of them paid very dearly, for the men of the
> water-battery, who had been driven away from their guns
> and up the sand hills by the fire of the *Richmond* and
> *Chickasaw,* had time to return and attack them. When
> the *Hartford* "cut adrift" from the *Brooklyn* and
> *Richmond*—the only safe thing possible to do—the *Ten-
> nessee* and the three gun-boats pursued her. That is, the
> *Tennessee,* after getting above the lines of torpedoes,
> turned into the main ship-channel and followed the
> *Hartford,* while the gun-boats were in shallow water to
> the northward, where our heavy vessels could not go after
> them. When the *Tennessee* was within probably half a
> mile of the *Hartford,* she suddenly turned her head
> toward the *Brooklyn* and *Richmond* (both close
> together). As she approached, every one on board the
> *Richmond* supposed that she would ram the *Brooklyn;*
> that, we thought, would be our opportunity, for if she
> struck the *Brooklyn* the concussion would throw her port
> side across our path, and being so near to us, she would
> not have time to "straighten up," and we would strike her
> fairly and squarely, and most likely sink her.
> The guns were loaded with solid shot and heaviest
> powder charge; the forecastle gun's crew were ordered to
> get their small-arms and fire into her gun-ports; and as
> previously determined, if we came in collision at any time,
> the orders were to throw gun charges of powder in bags
> from the fore and main yard-arms down her smoke-stack
> (or at least try to do so). To our great surprise, she
> sheered off from the *Brooklyn,* and at about one hundred
> yards put two shot or shells through and through the
> *Brooklyn*'s sides (as reported), doing much damage.
> Approaching, passing, and getting away from the
> *Richmond,* the ram received from us three full broadsides

of 9-inch solid shot, each broadside being eleven guns. They were well aimed and all struck, but when she was examined next day, no other indications were seen than scratches. The musketry fire into the two ports prevented the leveling of her guns, and therefore two of her shot or shell passed harmlessly over the *Richmond*, except the cutting of a ratline in the port main-shroud, just under the feet of the pilot, while the other whistled unpleasantly close to Lieutenant Terry's head. The *Tennessee* passed toward the *Lackawanna,* the next vessel astern, and avoided her—wishing either to ram Captain Strong's vessel (the *Monongahela*), or cross his bow and attack McCann's vessel (the *Kennebec,* Strong's consort). Strong was ready for her, and, anticipating her object, made at her, but the blow (by the quick manœuvering of the *Tennessee*) was a glancing one, doing very little damage to either Strong's or McCann's vessel. Thence the *Tennessee,* after firing two broadsides into the *Oneida,* proceeded toward the fort, and for a time entirely disappeared from our sight. During this time the three gunboats were proceeding, apparently, up the bay, to escape. The *Hartford* was closely watched with our glasses, and soon after the *Tennessee* had left Strong, the *Metacomet* (Jouett) was seen to cast off; and divining the purpose, the *Port Royal* (Gherardi) was ordered to cast off from the *Richmond* and go in chase of the enemy, pointing in the direction of the three gun-boats of the enemy. George Brown (in the *Itasca*) cast off from the *Ossipee* and (I believe) McCann did also, and steered for the enemy. By this time Jouett had come up with the *Selma,* and the fight commenced. A very few minutes after Gherardi had left the side of the *Richmond,* and the other small vessels had left their consorts, a thick mist, with light rain (just enough to wet the deck), passed over the *Richmond,* obscuring from sight every object outside the vessel; indeed, for a few minutes the bowsprit of the *Richmond* could not be seen from the poop-deck. This mist and rain, in a cloudless sunshiny day, were slowly wafted over the waters toward the fort and pilot town, enabling John W. Bennett, commanding one of the enemy's gun-boats, and George W. Harrison, commanding the other, to shape their courses for safety, in shoal water, and finally under Fort Morgan. Gherardi in the *Port Royal* (as soon as he could see) saw only the *Selma* and *Metacomet,* and continued his course for them.

Whatever damage was done by the *Tennessee* to the fleet in passing the fort was by the occasional discharge of her guns. She failed to strike a single one of the Union vessels, but was herself run into by the *Monongahela,* Captain Strong, at full speed. The captain says in his report:

> After passing the forts I saw the rebel ram *Tennessee* head on for our line. I then sheered out of the line to run into her, at the same time ordering full speed as fast as possible. I struck her fair, and swinging around poured in a broadside of solid 11-inch shot, which apparently had little if any effect upon her.

This modest statement is characteristic of the gallant writer, now dead, as are so many others of the conspicuous actors in that day's work. The *Monongahela* was no match for the *Tennessee,* but she had been strengthened by an artificial iron prow, and being one of the fastest—or rather, *least slow*—of the fleet, was expected to act as a ram if opportunity offered. Captain Strong waited for no orders, but seeing the huge ram coming for the fleet left his place in the line and attacked her, as narrated. It was at this time that the *Monongahela*'s first lieutenant, Roderick Prentiss, a brave and gifted young officer, received his death wound, both legs being shattered.

At last all the fleet passed the fort, and while the ram ran under its guns the vessels made their way to the *Hartford* and dropped their anchors, except the *Metacomet, Port Royal, Kennebec,* and *Itasca.* After the forts were passed, the three last named had cut loose from their escorts and gone to aid the *Metacomet* in her struggle with the *Selma* and *Morgan.*

The thunder of heavy artillery now ceased. The crews of the various vessels had begun to efface the marks of the terrible contest by washing the decks and clearing up the splinters. The cooks were preparing breakfast, the surgeons were busily engaged in making amputations and binding arteries, and under canvas, on the port side of each vessel, lay the ghastly line of dead waiting the sailor's burial. As if by mutual understanding, officers who were relieved for immediate duty gathered in the ward-rooms to ascertain who of their mates were missing, and the reaction from such a season of tense nerves and excitement was just setting in when the hurried call to quarters came and the word passed around, "The ram is coming."

The *Tennessee,* after remaining near Fort Morgan while the fleet had made its way four miles above to its anchorage—certainly as much as half an hour—had suddenly decided to settle at once the question of the control of the bay. Single-handed she came on to meet the whole fleet, consisting now of ten wooden vessels and the three monitors. At that time the *Tennessee* was believed to be the strongest vessel afloat, and the safety with which she carried her crew during the battle proved that she was virtually invulnerable. Fortunately for the Union fleet she was weakly handled, and at the end fell a victim to a stupendous blunder in her construction—the failure to protect her rudder-chains. The spectacle afforded the Confederate soldiers, who crowded the ramparts of the two forts—the fleet now being out of range—was such as has very rarely been furnished in the history of the world. To the looker-on it seemed as if the fleet was at the mercy of the ram, for the monitors, which were expected to be the chief defense, were so destitute of speed and so difficult to manœuvre that it seemed an easy task for the *Tennessee* to avoid them and sink the wooden vessels in detail. Because of the slowness of the monitors, Admiral Farragut selected the fastest of the wooden vessels to begin the attack. While the navy signals for a general attack of the enemy were being prepared, the *Monongahela* (Captain Strong) and the *Lackawanna* (Captain Marchand) were ordered by the more rapid signal system of the army to "run down the ram," the order being immediately repeated to the monitors.

The *Monongahela,* with her prow already somewhat weakened by the previous attempt to ram, at once took the lead, as she had not yet come to anchor. The ram from the first headed for the *Hartford,* and paid no attention to her assailants, except with her guns. The *Monongahela,* going at full speed, struck the *Tennessee* amidships—a blow that would have sunk almost any vessel of the Union navy, but which inflicted not the slightest damage on the solid iron hull of the ram. (After the surrender it was almost impossible to tell where the attacking vessel had struck.) Her own iron prow and cutwater were carried away, and she was otherwise badly damaged about the stern by the collision.

The *Lackawanna* was close behind and delivered a smiliar blow with her wooden bow, simply causing the ram to lurch slightly to one side. As the vessels separated the *Lackawanna* swung alongside the ram, which sent two shots through her and kept on her course for the *Hartford,* which was now the next vessel in the attack. The two flag-ships approached each other, bow to bow, iron against oak. It was impossible for the *Hartford,* with her lack of speed, to circle around and strike the ram on the side; her only safety was in keeping pointed directly for the bow of her assailant. The other vessels of the fleet were unable to do anything for the defense of the admiral except to train their guns on the ram, on which as yet they had not the slightest effect.

It was a thrilling moment for the fleet, for it was evident that if the ram could strike the *Hartford* the latter must sink. But for the two vessels to strike fairly, bows on, would probably have involved the destruction of both, for the ram must have penetrated so far into the wooden ship that as the *Hartford* filled and sank she would have carried the ram under water. Whether for this reason or for some other, as the two vessels came together the *Tennessee* slightly changed her course, the port bow of the *Hartford* met the port bow of the ram, and the ships grated against each other as they passed. The *Hartford* poured her whole port broadside against the ram, but the solid shot merely dented the side and bounded into the air. The ram tried to return the salute, but owing to defective primers only one gun was discharged. This sent a shell through the berthdeck, killing five men and wounding eight. The muzzle of the gun was so close to the *Hartford* that the powder blackened her side.

The admiral stood on the quarter-deck when the vessels came together, and as he saw the result he jumped on to the port-quarter rail, holding to the mizzen-rigging, a position from which he might have jumped to the deck of the ram as she passed. Seeing him in this position, and fearing for his safety, Flag-Lieutenant Watson slipped a rope around him and secured it to the rigging, so that during the fight the admiral was twice "lashed to the rigging," each time by devoted officers who knew better than to consult him before acting. Fleet-Captain Drayton had hurried to the bow of the *Hartford* as the collision was seen to be inevitable, and expressed keen satisfaction when the ram avoided a direct blow.

The *Tennessee* now became the target for the whole fleet, all the vessels of which were making toward her, pounding her with shot, and trying to run her down. As the *Hartford* turned to make for her again, we ran in front of the *Lackawanna,* which had already turned and was moving under full headway with the same object. She struck us on our starboard side, amidships, crushing halfway through, knocking two portholes into one, upsetting one of the Dahlgren guns, and creating general consternation. For a time it was thought that we must sink, and the cry rang out over the deck: "Save the admiral! Save the admiral!" The port boats were ordered lowered, and in their haste some of the sailors cut the "falls," and two of the cutters dropped into the water wrong side up, and floated astern. But the admiral sprang into the starboard mizzen-rigging, looked over the side of the ship, and, finding there were still a few inches to spare above the water's edge instantly ordered the ship ahead again at full speed, after the ram. The unfortunate *Lackawanna,* which had struck the ram a second blow, was making for her once more, and, singularly enough, again came up on our starboard side, and another collision seemed imminent. And now the admiral became a trifle excited. He had no idea of whipping the rebels to be himself sunk by a friend, nor did he realize at the moment that the *Hartford* was as much to blame as the *Lackawanna.* Turning to the writer he inquired. "Can you say 'For God's sake' by signal?" "Yes, sir," was the reply. "Then say to the *Lackawanna,* 'For God's sake get out of our way and anchor!'" In my haste to send the message, I brought the end of my signal flag-staff down with considerable violence upon the head of the admiral, who was standing nearer than I thought, causing him to wince perceptibly. It was a hasty message, for the fault was equally divided, each ship being too eager to reach the enemy, and it turned out all right by a fortunate accident, that Captain Marchand never received it. The army signal officer on the *Lackawanna,* Lieutenant Myron Adams (now pastor of Plymouth Congregational Church in Rochester, N. Y.), had taken his station in the foretop, and just as he received the first five words—"For God's sake get out"—the wind flirted the large United States flag at the mast-head around him, so that he was unable to read the conclusion of the message.

The remainder of the story is soon told. As the *Tennessee* left the *Hartford* she became the target of the entire fleet, and at last the concentration of solid shot from so many guns began to tell. The flag-staff was shot away, the smoke-stack

Capture of the Confederate ram Tennessee

was riddled with holes, and finally disappeared. The monitor *Chickasaw,* Lientenant-Commander Perkins, succeeded in coming up astern and began pounding away with 11-inch solid shot, and one shot from a 15-inch gun of the *Manhattan* crushed into the side sufficiently to prove that a few more such shots would have made the casemate untenable. Finally, one of the *Chickasaw*'s shots cut the rudder-chain of the ram and she would no longer mind her helm. At this time, as Admiral Farragut says in his report, "she was sore beset. The *Chickasaw* was pounding away at her stern, the *Ossipee* was approaching her at full speed, and the *Monongahela, Lackawanna,* and this ship were bearing down upon her, determined upon her destruction." From the time the *Hartford* struck her she did not fire a gun. Finally the Confederate admiral, Buchanan, was severely wounded by an iron splinter or a piece of a shell, and just as the *Ossipee* was about to strike her the *Tennessee* displayed a white flag, hoisted on an improvised staff through the grating over her deck. The *Ossipee* (Captain Le Roy) reversed her engine, but was so near that a harmless collision was inevitable. Suddenly the terrific cannonading ceased, and from every ship rang out cheer after cheer, as the weary men realized that at last the ram was conquered and the day won. The *Chickasaw* took the *Tennessee* in tow and brought her to anchor near the *Hartford.* The impression prevailed at first that the *Tennessee* had been seriously injured by the ramming she had received and was sinking, and orders were signaled to send boats to assist her crew, but it was soon discovered that this was unnecessary.

Fort Powell, was evacuated about 10 P.M. that night, the officers and men escaping to the mainland. The *Chickasaw* also tackled Fort Gaines on the 6th, and speedily convinced the commanding officer that it would be folly to attempt to withstand a siege. The result was a surrender to the army and navy the next morning.

Fort Morgan was at once invested, and surrendered on the 23d of August.

ON TO ATLANTA

THE CAMPAIGNS WAGED BY THE UNION GENERALS in the West had been strikingly more successful than those in the East. Abraham Lincoln, a midwesterner himself, asked U. S. Grant to come East and run the whole war. He made Grant a Lieutenant General, the first officer in the U. S. Army to hold so high a rank since George Washington. This meant that Grant was commander-in-chief of all Union forces. Since Grant chose not to operate from a desk in Washington, Halleck was appointed chief of staff. Grant would take to the field and lead the Army of the Potomac against Lee.

But first Grant wanted to see General Sherman, his successor in the West, to confer on broad, basic strategy. In Cincinnati, the two generals agreed on the essentials necessary to defeat the Confederacy. As Lloyd Lewis says, Sherman marveled "that Grant should decide to 'go East, a stranger almost among strange troops; . . . a more daring thing was never done by man on earth.' But at any rate he and his friend had the war in their own hands. Each believing that 'in war a town is a military weakness,' they did not need to reassure each other that from now on there would be no more scattering of troops to hold citadels. Grant, with the simplicity of genius, said that there were but two objectives: one, Lee's army in Virginia, the other (army), mobilized at Dalton, thirty miles south of Chattanooga, under J. E. Johnston, now restored to command. The Confederacy would have its best leaders against them. Every effort must now be bent toward endless, relentless fighting, summer, winter, all the time—the kind of warfare both Grant and Sherman had preached, 'blows, thick and fast.' It would be hideous carnage, but the most merciful in the end if it could halt these years of wastage."* Or as General Sherman said after the war, "He was to go for Lee and I was to go for Joe

* *Sherman: Fighting Prophet*, p. 345.

Johnston." Sherman's first job was to reorganize the western armies, and he set about doing it.

By May 6, he had 98,000 troops and 254 cannon ready to move against the Confederates at Dalton, Georgia. There would be no frontal assault on the Confederate positions in the mountains before Dalton; instead, General McPherson's corps was sent around Johnston's rear to cut his supply lines at the railroad center of Resaca. Sherman's attack, according to Lewis, made the best use of his generals—"slow, unconquerable Thomas in the center as a bulwark against counterattack; McPherson and Schofield, younger, more aggressive men, on the flanks with smaller, fleeter armies marching in swiftly traveled arcs, feinting, swerving, feinting again, then suddenly striking like hammers into Johnston's ribs. If McPherson should seize the railroad in Johnston's rear, the latter would be driven into the less hilly country to the east, where Sherman felt certain he would destroy half the Confederate army and capture its cannon."*

McPherson failed to take Resaca before Johnston supplied reinforcements. Sherman then sent both Thomas and Schofield around Johnston's flank, which forced Johnston to pull his army out of Dalton. Wherever possible, Sherman resorted to artful flanking movements and Johnston continued to retreat rather than contest Sherman. Johnston's failure to cope with end runs may be better understood when one considers that he had only 65,000 troops, while Sherman had 110,000. The extra men gave Sherman greater mobility.

At Kennesaw Mountain Sherman varied his tactics. Again the Confederates were strongly entrenched, and they had weakened their center in order to strengthen their flanks. Sherman tried to break through the center but met with little success. Then, to avoid stalling his drive, Sherman resumed his flanking tactics—and once more Johnston was forced to retreat.

By the middle of July Sherman's armies had crossed the Chattahoochee River a few miles from Atlanta. The Georgia city was second only to Richmond in industrial importance. Its capture would deprive the Confederacy of sorely needed arms and munitions and an important rail center.

Because Johnston had failed to mount a major counterattack to stop Sherman's drive, President Davis was under pressure to install a more aggressive general. On July 17

* *Ibid.*, p. 357.

General John Bell Hood was given command of the Confederate troops in Atlanta.

A fiery Texan, Hood wasted little time. On July 20 he struck the Union armies first at Peachtree creek north of the city, and on July 22 he attacked a Union flanking force east of Atlanta. Here he almost succeeded in destroying McPherson's corps. But the attacks were not coordinated and both were repelled. Hood them turned to preparing Atlanta for siege. But he reckoned without Sherman, who had already sent a strong force to outflank the city, this time to the west.

The Fall of Atlanta*

BY CAPTAIN W. F. HINMAN

THE SOUTHERN PEOPLE WANTED A GENERAL who would fight rather than run. Such a one they found in Hood. He was a brave man, but rash and not properly equipped to handle a large army and conduct a great campaign. He had served two years in Lee's Virginia army, and was wounded at Gettysburg. Going west with Longstreet, in command of a division he lost a leg at Chickamauga. In the spring of 1864 he was assigned to the command of a corps in the army of Johnston at Dalton. General Schofield and General McPherson were classmates of Hood at West Point. General Sherman inquired of them as to his characteristics and at once made up his mind that the change "meant fight." He immediately issued orders to his corps, division, brigade and regimental commanders to hold themselves and their commands at all times in readiness for instant action. Events soon proved that these cautionary words were timely and judicious.

On the 19th the Sixty-fourth Ohio and Twenty-seventh Illinois, under the command of Colonel Robert C. Brown, were ordered to make a reconnoisance along the Decatur road, if possible as far as Peachtree creek. About three miles out, the column reached the creek and found the enemy's pickets in strong rifle-pits on the opposite bank, and the bridge burned. The situation was reported back to head-

* From *The Story of the Sherman Brigade.*

quarters, and in a short time Colonel Brown's command was relieved by Stanley's division.

Hood did not wait long before showing his purpose to fight. He made the 20th of July an exciting day for us and many others of Sherman's army. On that day was fought the battle of Peachtree creek. The stress of the fighting fell upon the Twentieth corps, but we got enough of it to make it decidedly interesting. During the early part of the day we did a good deal of wild maneuvering, evidently in search of a place where we would be expected to do something. At length we seemed to have found it, and our brigade was formed in mass for a charge upon the Confederate works, which were on high ground some four hundred yards distant, the intervening space being open, with no cover. With a vivid recollection of our experience at Kennesaw, we did not relish the prospect before us, and no regrets were expressed when, after a more careful survey of the ground, the plan was changed and the order to assault was revoked.

At this time Hooker's Twentieth corps became heavily engaged at some distance to our right. Sherman's line was much attenuated and broken, McPherson and Schofield being six or eight miles to the left. It was Hood's evident purpose to burst through the Union center and disrupt the line. The roar of musketry and artillery upon our right indicated fierce fighting. Our division was advanced to support Hooker's left and foil any attempt to turn his flank. The first and second brigades were in the advance; ours, in reserve. The former halted and began to throw up intrenchments. They had not half finished their work, when a large mass of the enemy, in three successive lines, emerged from the woods and charged them, with blood-curdling yells. The Union soldiers withheld their fire until the rebels were within fifty yards and then delivered a volley so destructive that the assailants recoiled and fled in disorder.

At the left of the Second brigade was a deep ravine which was not occupied by our troops. It was soon discovered that a column of the enemy was moving through this ravine for the apparent purpose of gaining our rear. Our brigade was instantly dispatched to check this movement. We formed line of battle to the left of the road and parallel to it, and advanced. Reaching the crest of a low ridge our skirmishers came upon those of the enemy, not more than thirty yards distant. In their rear we could see a heavy line advancing upon us. Our position was not advantageous for defence, and our single brigade was evidently greatly inferior in strength to the force we must encounter. We were instantly ordered to "about face" and move back to the road, which was upon high ground and a good place to fight. We made our change of base at double-quick, and the rebels, supposing us to be in full retreat, followed swiftly, with loud cheers. Our officers were cautioned not to permit their men to keep on running after regaining the road, but to halt them there face about and confront the enemy.

There was little need for the caution; our soldiers were too well schooled in war. There seemed to be scarcely a man in the ranks who did not comprehend, as well as those who wore shoulder straps, the situation of affairs and the need of the moment. At the road the men turned by a common impulse, and, partly covered by a fence, faced the foe. The rebel skirmishers were almost at our heels and the main body was not more than two hundred yards away. Our men poured into them a staggering volley and immediately began to "load and fire at will," each man working with the energy of desperation. Never did soldiers stand more bravely to their work. There was scarcely a laggard or a skulker. The rebels halted and delivered a volley, but they were upon much lower ground than ourselves and most of their shots passed harmlessly over our heads.

In the meantime two or three batteries had been brought up, on the other side of Peachtree creek, and so posted as to completely enfilade the rebel line. The guns opened with canister, and scarely a dozen shots had been fired, when the Confederates broke and fled in dismay to the cover of the ravine, from which they had debouched before forming for the charge. They seemed to be satisfied for that day, as they did not reappear to renew the attack. Our loss was singularly small, the killed and wounded in our brigade numbering less than thirty, while that of the rebels in our front, judging from the dead and severely wounded left upon the field, was more than ten times that number.

As we did not move immediately, details were sent out to care for the rebel wounded. Sixty or more were brought in and received the attention of our surgeons. I have never forgotten a mere boy, belonging to a Georgia regiment, whom we brought in and laid upon a blanket under a tree. He was helpless, a bullet having crushed his thigh. We gave him food and water, and did what else we could to mitigate his suffering. The tears gathered in his eyes as he said:

"They told us that you-all would kill us if you took us prisoners. I didn't think you'd be so kind to me!"

To the right Hooker repelled every assault. He lost near two thousand men, but inflicted upon the enemy a loss of twice his own.

During the night of the 21st, the rebels retired within the defences of Atlanta. The forts and earthworks of all kinds were exceedingly strong. Thousands of Negroes had been employed for weeks in their construction. On the 22nd we advanced until we were within half a mile of the fortifications and could go no farther. We were fired upon by a rebel battery with fatal effect. "Pony" Seavolt, a young musician of Company C, Sixty-fifth, was instantly killed by a solid shot. Several were wounded by fragments of shell. On this day occurred, upon the left, the most severe distinct engagement of the entire campaign, in which the much-lamented General McPherson was killed.

That day Captain Alfred A. Reed, of the Sixty-fourth, had an exceedingly close call. A cannon shot knocked into flinders a barricade of rails behind which he was lying. A large splinter struck him upon the head, tearing away a portion of the scalp and laying bare the skull. The doctors patched him up in pretty fair shape, but for a good while he was literally a "sore-head."

From this point dates the "siege of Atlanta," which continued five weeks. General Sherman disposed his army in a semi-circular line extending about half way around the town, and as near to the Confederate fortifications as possible. Orders were promulgated to build works that would be impregnable to assault. For a week the men toiled day and night, strengthening their position and protecting it by all the devices known to military art. For a time the rebels caused us constant annoyance by shelling our lines with the greatest industry. Every day men engaged upon the intrenchments were killed or wounded, but the work went right on. Forts were built and heavy siege guns were brought up and mounted in them. Within a few days after his arrival, Sherman began to throw shells into Atlanta and kept it up at frequent intervals during the siege. Many of the citizens dug caves in the earth, where they slept to escape the unwelcome visitors.

Day and night the Union army lay in the trenches, with muskets constantly loaded and at hand, ready for use. About once a week each regiment was permitted to go to the rear for a day and a night, to rest and "clean up." Here and there was a man who lived in utter disregard of cleanliness. A person directly from home might have thought this of all of us, judging from our appearance, but nine-tenths of the soldiers kept their bodies and their clothing in the best condition possible under the circumstances. In more than one case an incorrigible was taken to a stream by his comrades, who stripped him by main force and scrubbed him from head to foot. If he got mad about it, they only scrubbed the harder.

The enemy made frequent bluffs with both musketry and artillery, and at all times we were called to stand at the works, often for hours together. We changed our location several times as the line was now and then readjusted. Every possible chance was improved to gain an advantage of position. Tents were pitched close to the works, and during the quiet hours the men lay in their little shelters, sleeping, reading, writing or playing with the "pasteboards." The latter was the most popular method of whiling away the time. If a few shots were heard every man seized his musket and in ten seconds was in his place at the intrenchments. Whenever the rebel artillery opened there was a scramble for the shelter of the works. At the more exposed points many of the soldiers dug "gopher holes" into which they dodged like prairie dogs to avoid the missiles. A very strong line of outposts was maintained and picket duty was frequent and arduous. All the posts were protected by works impervious to bullets. In many cases the changing of pickets, once in twenty-four hours, had to be done at night, as the exposure by day was certain to provoke the enemy's fire.

The men of the Sixth battery constructed a furnace for heating shot, the material therefor being supplied by an old brick chimney. One afternoon in the early part of August, they put a lot of twelve-pound solid shot into the furnace, brought them to a red heat, and in the evening threw them over into Atlanta. A large fire was soon seen, which, according to statements of rebel pickets the next morning, was caused by the shot. It is scarcely necessary to say that the battery boys did not undertake the experiment of heating shells.

At this time some changes were made in the composition of our brigade and the number of its regiments was reduced from nine to seven. The term of the Twenty-second and Twenty-seventh Illinois, which were non-veteran regiments, expired, and they went to the rear to be mustered out of service. Colonel Opdycke was wanted to command the First brigade of the division, and he took the One Hundred and Twenty-fifth Ohio with him. In its place we received the Fifteenth Missouri, Colonel Joseph Conrad. This was a St. Louis regiment, composed almost entirely of Germans. The men talked "Dutch" among themselves and the officers gave their commands in that language. But it was a most excellent regiment. One of its distinctive features was its splended corps of trained buglers. After the death of McPherson, General Howard was taken to command the Army of the Tennessee, and General David S. Stanley succeeded to the command of the Fourth corps.

Two or three times we engaged in making those riotous demonstrations against the rebels, the purpose of which was to amuse them and divert their attention from some movement that was being executed at another point on our line. One of these, in the early part of August, was particularly protracted and noisy. The Army of the Tennessee was to undertake some important operation, and the men upon the outposts along the front of the Fourth corps were ordered to fire incessantly, yell, and in every way raise all the racket possible, to lead the Johnnies to believe we were going to assault. In the ordinary conditions of life deception is not classed among the Christian virtues, but "everything is fair in love and war," and it "went" in the army. In order to make the affair more impressive, an extra regiment from each brigade was sent to the outpost to swell the volume of noise. We happened to be on picket that day, and the boys had great sport. The rebel pickets were so near us that voices could be easily heard.

When the hour fixed for the demonstration arrived, the officers shouted with all the lung power at their command: "Forward! Double-quick! March!" and the buglers almost blew their heads off in sounding the advance. Then the fusillade began. From their well-intrenched posts the men fired a withering volley, shouting and yelling like savages. Then they kept loading and firing, each on his own account, with furious energy. The rebels returned the fire with equal vigor, and for two hours the woods fairly blazed with burning powder. It was hard on the trees and bushes, which were the only sufferers. When it was "all over" they looked as if they had been swept by a mowing machine. In front of one post—the garrison of which had been reinforced for the occasion and numbered twelve or fifteen men—was an oak tree, six or eight inches in diameter. The men concentrated their fire upon that tree and within an hour the bullets cut it down. Its fall was greeted with prodigious yells. During those two hours the men fired from eighty to a hundred rounds each. When the riot ceased, we were relieved and went to the rear to refill our empty cartridge boxes. We do not know whether we scared anybody or not, but if we didn't it certainly was not our fault, for we tried hard and made noise enough. After the order was given to cease firing this colloquy occurred:

"I say, Yank!"

"Hello, Johnny!"

"Think ye'r' raisin' Cain, don't ye?"

"Oh, that's all right, Johnny; jest havin' a little fun with ye! We've got more bullets 'n we know what ter do with 'n' we thought you rebs 'd like ter have a few of 'em. Ye better gather 'em up, ye may need 'em!

"Oh, come off! We'un's got 'nough ter make you-all mighty sick! Hood's a fighter, *he* is! But say, when ye goin' ter take Atlanta."

"We'll git thar, Eli, one o' these fine mornin's! Goin' after some more catridges now; watch out when we come back. Good bye, Johnny!"

"Good bye, Yank!"

The weather during August was extremely hot. The men literally sweltered in the trenches and under their "pup" tents. At night myriads of mosquitoes swarmed about the picket posts and gave us as much annoyance as did the rebels. Mails were as regular as could be expected, usually three or four each week. Most of the time we had full rations of the three essentials, hardtack, bacon and coffee, but the daily bill of fare became painfully monotonous. There was no possible chance to do any foraging, and the soldiers would have given a week's pay for a supply of vegetables.

At long intervals fresh beef was issued, cattle being driven on the hoof all the way from Chattanooga. They didn't find much to eat on the way, and by the time they reached the army they were little more than a structural framework of bones. The boys used to say as they picked their bones— that is, the beef bones—that the commissary people killed each night the animals which were so nearly played out that they could not endure another day's march, and this seemed to be very near the truth. The hind quarters furnished about all the meat that was edible, and even that is not saying much. But the fact that the animals were not all hind quarters caused a great deal of friction in the matter of distribution. Each company always insisted that it was its turn to have steak, and there were many heated arguments between the commissary-sergeants and the orderlies. "Jim" Mills, the purveyor of the Sixty-fifth, was not a profane man; it is a wonder that he did not become so while issuing fresh beef during the Atlanta campaign. Three-quarters of the men only got skinny ribs and lean soup-shanks, and they did swearing enough to go around.

All the commissary sergeants had this cross to bear, for human nature was much alike in all regiments and there was everywhere the same disturbance over the apportionment of fresh beef. It will be appropriate to narrate here a beef incident that occurred in the Sixty-fourth, although its chronological place would be a year earlier. One day, while we were in camp at Hillsboro, Tennessee, Commissary-sergeant William H. Farber had one of his periodical struggles with a beef carcass. He carefully superintended the carving and brought all the energies of his intellect to bear upon the matter of its equitable division. He arranged the pieces in ten piles, referring to a memorandum, which he kept to see which companies were due for steak, and which must this time be content with neck, shank or rib. When he had finished his task he surveyed the heaps with calm satisfaction and then yelled:

"Orderlies, fer yer fresh beef!"

The orderlies were promptly on hand and kicking began at once, with even greater violence than usual, for the "critter" had been a lean one and the spread was not tempting. Two or three of the orderlies, who found steak in their portions, were estopped from joining in the insurrection, but all the others jumped on Farber, vehemently declaring in chorus, that they had neck and shank *all* the time, and nothing else. Conscious of his rectitude, Farber assured them that he had endeavored to divide the beef with perfect fairness. He showed them his record of previous issues, but they pronounced it a fraud. Their memories were short, and none of them could remember ever having had any of the choice cuts. They charged him with always providing a good supply of porterhouse or sirloin for his own mess—the non-commissioned staff. At length Farber got hot under the collar and declared his ultimatum, that each of them could take his assigned portion or go without.

Several of the orderlies, knowing that they would catch "Hail Columbia" from the men, refused to do so. They went at once to their respective company commanders and entered formal complaint against the commissary-sergeant, and this was promptly carried up to Colonel McIlvaine. The latter, in his brusque, excited way, determined to settle the matter once for all. Summoning the company commanders he bore down upon Farber with fire in his eye. In words that scorched, he told Farber, who stood quaking in his shoes, of the complaints that had come to his ears, and of his purpose to go to the bottom of the difficulty, then and there. The officers all stood around those piles of meat and held an inquest over the remains, McIlvaine acting as coroner. The colonel examined Farber's list showing the number of men in each company, and, with a critical eye, scanned the various portions. Farber half expected to be sentenced to have his head shaved and be drummed out of camp to the tune of the "Rogue's March," but he began to breathe freely when Colonel McIlvaine said, addressing the officers:

"If there is one of you who thinks he can make a fairer division than that, I will have the meat thrown into a pile and he can try it."

To this there was no response, and after a pause the colonel added, with a good deal of asperity;

"Go to your quarters, and any officer or man who grumbles hereafter about the division of beef will be at once put under arrest. This thing has got to stop right here!"

And that was the end of the great beef riot in the Sixty-fourth.

When the army left Chattanooga it had with it a herd of three or four thousand cattle, convoyed by an entire brigade of soldiers. One night, near Resaca, a furious thunder-storm stampeded the cattle and several hundred of them galloped directly into the enemy's lines.

Occasionally we received small portions of desiccated vegetables—the result of a scheme evolved by some genius to supply the soldiers with vegetable food. The stuff came in slabs about a foot square and an inch thick. It was composed of a mixture containing pretty nearly everything known to the vegetable kingdom. By hydraulic or some other pressure all the juices were squeezed out, leaving only the fiber, and this would "keep" for an indefinite period. The boys made great sport of it at first, but they found it good and wholesome. It was used in the form of soup, of which a cubic inch would make a quart. Of course its scientific name, "desiccated" was speedily changed to "desecrated" or "consecrated," and the boys never called it anything else. The great Sanitary Commission—a noble organization extending thoughout the entire north—undertook to send supplies of fresh vegetables, such as potatoes and onions, to the soldiers in the field. Most of them were, however, side-tracked at points in the rear, and only a small portion ever reached us. The tear-starting onion, drastic and malodorous, was always warmly welcomed. It was eaten raw, with the keenest relish. Three or four times onions were passed around, at the rate of about a bushel to a regiment. The onion is well known to the medical profession as an anti-scorbutic, and was often used in the hospitals as a remedy for scurvy, or as a preventive. The soldiers would gladly have devoured thousands of bushels if they could have had them.

Many will remember one beautiful Sunday evening toward the end of August, when the sound of strife was hushed and quiet reigned along the lines. One of our bands took position just behind the works and played "The Star-spangled Banner," eliciting loud cheers from the soldiers. A Confederate band responded with "The Bonnie Blue Flag," and it was the turn of the rebels to cheer. For an hour the bands played alternately—"Hail Columbia" and "Dixie"; "Red, White and Blue" and "My Maryland"; Rally Round the Flag" and "The Palmetto Tree"; "John Brown's Body" and "Ole Virginny"; followed by sentimental selections, such as "Annie Laurie," "Bowld Soger Boy," "The Girl I Left Behind Me," "Old Kentucky Home," "Suwanee River," and "Home, Sweet Home." No shot vexed the ear. The softening strains of music cast their spell over Union and Confederate. For the time the fierce passions of war were hushed, tender thoughts of home and loved ones filled every heart, and a spirit of gentleness and peace brooded over the hostile armies.

Captain Thomas E. Tillotson, of the Sixty-fourth—his comrades usually addressed him by his middle name, Eugene—was at this time serving on the staff of General John Newton commanding the division, his position being that of acting assistant inspector general. While the army was lying in the trenches before Atlanta, Tillotson had an experience that was enough to bleach the hair of the average man. One of his functions was to have supervision of the picket line. Whenever the troops halted in a new position, it was his duty to post the pickets. One day General Newton, who was sometimes a little querulous, asked the captain how many men he had on the picket line covering the front of the division.

"I cannot say exactly, sir," answered Tillotson, saluting, "but we have the usual force out there."

"You don't know!" exclaimed the general, fiercely. "A fine inspector you are, not to know how many men you have on post. It's your business to know, and I want you to find out, and be quick about it, too!"

Now everyone who remembers Tillotson as a soldier, knows that he never flinched in the face of danger, and that he was conspicuously faithful and conscientious in the performance of duty. So marked were his courage and efficiency that at the close of the war he was brevetted major, for "gallant and meritorious services."

Stung by the sharp and ungracious words of his chief, his face flushed as he touched his hat and replied: "All right, General, I'll find out at once and let you know." Then he put spurs to his horse and dashed away.

Tillotson decided that the way to obtain the desired information was to go and see. He determined not to go on foot, either, although that would have been far less dangerous. So he picked his way on horseback through the opening in the abatis and brush in front of the breastworks, and rode out so near to the picket line that he could see the piles of fresh earth which indicated the location of the picket posts; for all the videttes were protected by small intrenchments. So close were the hostile lines that the change of pickets could only be made at night. He began at the left and counted the dirt piles, multiplying the total by three, that being the number of men on each post. They were stationed in this way so that if one or two should be killed or wounded, the post would not be left unguarded.

Soon after the captain started on his perilous ride, he was discovered by the sharp eyes of the rebel pickets, who promptly opened fire upon him. The firing rapidly increased until it seemed that an attack upon the Union line was about to be made. The bullets flew thickly above and around him, but Tillotson heeded them not until his task was fully accomplished. Then he galloped back within the works as fast as his horse could carry him. That he was not struck by the flying missiles was to him as strange as it was gratifying.

Meanwhile, the rebel fusillade had been attended with the

usual result. The entire division was formed in line of battle at the works, to await the onslaught by the foe. But our pickets did not come in, as they would have done had the enemy advanced, and the scare soon wore itself out. After Tillotson disappeared the firing ceased.

Captain Tillotson rode directly to the spot where he had left General Newton, whom he supposed to be impatiently awaiting the report for which he had made such a peppery demand. But the general had returned to his headquarters as soon as he discovered that the noise on the picket line did not mean business. Tillotson found him and reported the exact number of men on the line of outposts. The general had evidently forgotten the errand upon which he had sent him, for as he looked at man and horse, both dripping with perspiration, he asked:

"How do you know?"

"I counted them sir!" said Tillotson.

"Was that you out there in front drawing the fire of the rebels, which alarmed the army and caused that rush to the works?"

"Yes, General, it was!"

"Well, sir," replied Newton, "all I have to say is that you were a fool!" prefacing the last word with the usual sheolic adjective.

"Yes, General Newton, I believe I was!" said Tillotson, dumbfounded to find that his dangerous ride had been worse than useless.

During all these weeks General Sherman had been seeking a solution of the perplexing problem—how to take Atlanta. To carry its formidable defences by assault was out of the question; no weak spot could be found which offered promise of success. Nothing could be gained by lying idly where we were. It only remained to try the effect of another great turning movement, and this Sherman decided to do, by throwing the body of his army upon the railroads to the southward of Atlanta. Orders were issued on the 24th of August to march that night. The Twentieth corps was directed to take post at the Chattahoochee River, to protect the railroad bridge. The movement began soon after nightfall. At the usual hour all the buglers blew the customary calls, "retreat" and "tattoo," and fires were replenished. All this was to inform the enemy that there was nothing going on out of the ordinary within the Union lines. The movement was by the right, to the west and south of the town, by a wide detour, to avoid detection as long as possible. Beginning at the extreme left of the long line, one regiment and brigade after another broke off, silently left the trenches, and marched swiftly to the right, in rear of the intrenchments.

At dark we struck tents and put ourselves in order for traveling. We were directed to be ready to march at ten o'clock, but it was much later when we got off. Hour after hour the troops from the left streamed past in continuous procession. Soon after midnight our brigade moved out into the darkness. Silence was enjoined upon all. The wheels of the artillery were muffled to deaden their noise. For two hours our journey was exceedingly wearisome. We halted and marched alternately, five minutes at a time, and by two o'clock we had made but a couple of miles. By that time they got the kinks out of the long column and we marched very rapidly until daylight. We halted in rear of the Seventeenth corps, and, after an hour for breakfast, began, from sheer force of habit, to throw up intrenchments. Before the work was fairly under way we were ordered to fall in, and off we went, making but a few brief halts until four o'clock in the aftenoon when we pitched tents on the bank of Utoy creek. After two hours of hard labor, building breastworks, we ate our suppers and threw ourselves upon the ground to sleep. The men had not closed their eyes since morning of the previous day. Many were prostrated by heat and exertion and all were greatly exhausted.

The peering eyes and listening ears of the Confederate pickets around Atlanta did not until dawn discover the evacuation. When morning broke they missed the familiar crack of muskets. Venturing to reconnoiter, they found the Union works deserted. Sherman's army had disappeared as completely as if it had been swallowed by an earthquake. The rebels at once jumped to the conclusion that Sherman had given it up as a bad job. General Hood gleefully telegraphed to Richmond and other points in the south that the siege was raised and the Yankees were in full retreat. The south was thrown into a paroxysm of rejoicing. Congratulations poured in upon General Hood, while his soldiers indulged in frantic demonstrations of delight. But this did not last long. Before twenty-four hours had passed, Hood knew that Sherman was flanking again, and bestirred himself to meet the menace to his rear.

In the afternoon of the 27th we resumed the march, advancing about six miles. We traveled slowly and it was near-ly dark when we halted for the night. The Sixty-fifth was or-dered to occupy a hill a short distance in front of the line, and there we worked till midnight, fortifying our position. Since leaving Atlanta we had passed through a country abounding in forage of all kinds, and supplied ourselves plenteously with green corn and vegetables, and an occa-sional pig or chicken.

During the ensuing three days we hitched along slowly, a few miles at a time, building half a dozen lines of breastworks and skirmishing with rebel cavalry that hovered around us. We reached the Montgomery railroad and followed it some distance toward Atlanta. The track had been totally destroyed by troops in advance of us, all the ties having been burned and the rails bent and twisted. We learned that a picnic train had passed toward Atlanta half an hour before the troops reached the road. However, the left of the line captured the train—seven cars with their load of fried chicken, etc., as well as the fair damsels who ex-pected a good time in celebrating the raising of the siege of Atlanta. The ladies were allowed to make their way homeward on foot.

During the night of the 30th, being on picket, we ob-served and reported the southward movement of a large body of Confederate troops, by a road half a mile in our front. This was the force sent by Hood, under Hardee, to Jonesboro, where it was soundly whipped by the Fourteenth corps. On the 31st we were kept constantly dodging about from one point to another. We built that day four different lines of intrenchments, and didn't fire a shot from either of them. At night we came to a pause within a mile of the railroad to Macon. Wood's division had already reached this road, and a long stretch of smoke told that it was engaged in the work of destruction. Every man in Sherman's army knew that the success of the movement was already assured, and the night was vocal with shouts and cheers.

On the morning of September 1st we took an early start and marched to the Macon railroad. Our division stacked arms and the men were told to "go in." They went, with a glad alacrity that cannot be described. We had suffered a good many times from the cutting of our cracker-line, and this was the first time our boys had found an opportunity to administer to the rebels a dose of their own medicine. It was a novel experience, and officers and men sprang to the work

with the greatest zeal and vigor, not forgetting to give vent
to their satisfaction in loud and repeated yells. A long row of
men ranged themselves, as close together as they could
stand, at one side of the track. Seizing the rails and ties they
just tipped over the track, bottom side up. The ties were
then disengaged, laid in piles, and the torch was applied.
Across these piles the rails were laid. The flames were
stimulated by brush and dry logs that were heaped upon
them. When the rails were at a red heat in the middle, for a
distance of three or four feet, they were bent around trees
and stumps, twisted and distorted into all imaginable
shapes, and left to cool. Railroad iron worn out or destroyed
in the south could not be replaced, and we knew that it would
be many a day before *that* road would be used again, for the
job was well and thoroughly done.

About the middle of the afternoon we rested from our
labors, having finished the task assigned us. After an interview with our haversacks, we fell in and marched to a point
near Jonesboro, where severe fighting was in progress. The
Fourteenth corps captured an entire brigade and ten pieces
of artillery. The Fourth was scheduled to get in the rear and
cut off the retreat of the enemy. We tried hard to reach the
right spot on time, but the distance was too great, and the
rebels got away. We captured a large field hospital, in which
were several hundred Confederate wounded. We do not
claim any glory for that achievement, but it lay directly in
our path and we took possession. One of the most unpleasant sights I ever looked upon was a heap of eight or ten legs
and arms that had been amputated.

During the night of September 1st we were startled by
heavy and continuous explosions in the direction of Atlanta.
At times it sounded like the roar of artillery, as though a
battle were in progress. Later the sky was illumined by the
glare of a conflagration. We did not *know* what caused the
disturbance but we guessed, and correctly, that Hood was
evacuating Atlanta. Early in the morning of the 2nd, a re-
connoitering force from the Twentieth corps, at the crossing
of the Chattahoochee, entered Atlanta unopposed, and soon
afterward the city was formally surrendered by the mayor to
General Slocum. Before noon of that day a courier reached
General Sherman with a message from Slocum informing
him of the event, and it was immediately published to the
army. *Such* yelling! "Atlanta is ours, and fairly won," was
the dispatch sent by Sherman to Washington. It electrified

the people of the north, being everywhere greeted with the liveliest rejoicing and patriotic enthusiasm.

About ten o'clock on the 2nd, the Fourth corps started in pursuit of the rebel force which had retreated after the battle of the previous day. Passing through Jonesboro, we continued southward to Lovejoy's station, where, in the afternoon, we found the enemy occupying a strong position and hard at work throwing up intrenchments. Bradley's brigade was in the advance and it was ordered to storm the rebel works, which were upon the crest of a ridge, the intervening space being an open field, without cover of any kind. It had an ugly look, and pulses quickened and hearts throbbed as we lay in momentary expectation of the word to go forward. After a careful inspection of the position and a consultation of the generals, it was decided that an assault would be extra-hazardous, inevitably entailing great loss of life, and the enterprise was abandoned. The brigade was ready to go at command, but there was not a man in it who did not experience a sense of relief when word was passed along the line that the order to charge had been countermanded.

The Sixty-fourth had a very warm encounter with the enemy's skirmishers at Lovejoy's. Sergeant Andrew Towsley, of Company G, a most excellent soldier, was killed, and a number were wounded.

Here ended the Atlanta campaign, which, for continuous marching, fighting and intrenching, tenacity of purpose on the part of the commanding general, and the courage and endurance of the officers and soldiers composing his army, has no parallel in the record of the war except in the contemporaneous campaign of General Grant against Lee. The losses of the Sixty-fourth, from Rocky Face ridge to Lovejoy's were: officers, three killed, six wounded; enlisted men, twenty-five killed, one hundred wounded, three captured—total, one hundred and thirty-seven. The Sixty-fifth lost: officers, two killed (besides General Harker), four wounded; enlisted men, nine killed, fifty-five wounded, two missing—total, seventy-two. The loss of the Sixth battery was: killed or mortally wounded, one officer, four enlisted men; wounded, seven. Harker's brigade entered the campaign in May with about twenty-six hundred men. Its losses in killed and wounded were ten hundred and forty-one—40 per cent.

At Lovejoy's we bade good-bye to our "esteemed contemporary," the Third Kentucky. Its time having expired, it was ordered to the rear to be mustered out. For eighteen months this excellent regiment had been a member of our brigade family, and we had formed many warm attachments among its members. Hearty cheers were exchanged as the brave, warm-hearted Kentuckians turned their steps homeward. Just before it started, it was visited by many officers and men of the Sixty-fourth and Sixty-fifth, who mingled with their comrades, congratulated them that their long and faithful service was ended, and gave them friendly farewells. We always liked the Third Kentucky. It was composed of excellent material and its record was without a stain. Whenever we were in a tight place, if that regiment was at hand we knew it could be depended upon to stay by to the last extremity. In one of its companies the last of five brothers was killed at Kennesaw.

After lying two days at Lovejoy's, we marched leisurely back to Atlanta, the prize of the four months' campaign. We pitched our camp a mile and a half east of the town, near the battle ground of July 22nd, where General McPherson was killed. It was understood that we would remain there a considerable time, for a season of rest after the arduous service since leaving Chattanooga in May. It is likely that this program would have been carried out had not General Hood perversely spoiled our calculations. As it was we stayed at Atlanta just sixteen days.

MAKING GEORGIA HOWL

On September 2, Sherman's footsore riflemen marched into Atlanta. Hood retreated southeast to Lovejoy's Station. For a month "Uncle Billy" Sherman rested his troops. They had marched steadily for almost four months. Now, three-year enlistments were up for many of them. Sherman waited for new recruits to fill up the ranks, and calmly calculated his next move.

Because of Atlanta's industrial importance to the South, he considered leaving an occupation force, but this would immobilize 30,000 troops. Next he considered reducing the manpower of the city by shifting a quarter of it elsewhere—many citizens were highly skilled in the making of arms and munitions—but this proposal provoked howls of protest. Eventually Sherman decided to put the torch to the foundries and munition factories and evacuate the city. After that, he would lead his army on through Georgia, cutting a swath through the heart of the South which, so far, had been untouched by the war. His troops would have to live off the country, because supply lines to depots in the North could not be maintained.

Meanwhile Hood decided to shift his army to the southwest, outflank Sherman, and then drive north for Tennessee; on the way he would attack and destroy Sherman's already overextended supply lines. Sherman had been concerned with just such a move. He had telegraphed General Grant to explain how he would deal with this threat: "It will be a physical impossibility to protect the roads, now that Hood, Forrest and Wheeler, and the whole batch of devils are turned loose without home or habitation. . . . I propose we break up the railroad from Chattanooga, and strike out with wagons to Milledgeville, Millen and Savannah. Until we can repopulate Georgia, it is useless to occupy it, but the utter destruction of its roads, houses and people will cripple their military resources. By attempting to hold the roads we will lose 1,000 men monthly, and will gain no result. I can make the march, and make Georgia howl."

The telegram had hardly been sent before Hood headed north. Sherman wired Grant again: "I would infinitely prefer to make a wreck of the road and of the country from Chattanooga to Atlanta . . . and, with my effective army, move through Georgia, smashing things to the sea. Hood may turn into Tennessee and Kentucky, but I believe he will be forced to follow me. Instead of being on the defensive, I would be on the offensive; instead of guessing at what he means to do, he would have to guess at my plans. The difference in war is full 25 per cent. I can make Savannah, Charleston or the mouth of the Chattahoochee."

Grant replied: "If you were to cut loose, I do not believe you would meet Hood's army, but would be bushwacked by all the old men, little boys and such railroad guards as are still left at home. . . . If there is any way of getting at Hood's army, I would prefer that, but I must trust to your own judgment. I find I shall not be able to send a force from here to act with you at Savannah. Your movements, therefore, will be independent of mine, at least until the fall of Richmond takes place."

Sherman sent George Thomas back to Nashville to organize an army to deal with Hood and released two corps from Atlanta to follow Thomas north. Thomas would keep his troops concentrated at Nashville and Chattanooga so that Hood's cavalry could not cut them up.

Of Sherman's decision, B. H. Liddell Hart says, "It was a supreme act of moral courage. To leave the enemy in his rear, to divide his army, to cut himself adrift from railroad and telegraph, from supplies and reinforcements, and launch not a mere raiding force of cavalry but a great army into the heart of a hostile country—pinning his faith and his fortune on a principle which he had deduced by reasoning contrary to orthodoxy. And with nothing to fortify his spirit beyond that reasoning, for his venture was to be made under the cloud of the dubious permission of his military superior, the anxious fears of his President, and the positive objections of their advisors. If it requires great moral courage under such gloomy conditions to launch an army to an attack from a secure base, how much greater the effort and strength of will required to launch an army 'into the blue.' "*

* B. H. Liddell Hart, *Sherman*, p. 330.

The March to the Sea†

BY MAJOR GEORGE W. NICHOLS

BEFORE FAIRLY ENTERING UPON A RECITAL of the incidents attending the great march seaward, it is important to glance at the organization of the army, and to gain at least a general idea of its main features.

The grand army under the supreme command of General Sherman is divided into two armies, called the Right and Left Wings, each of which has a separate army commander—General Howard, of the right wing, and General Slocum, of the left.

The right wing of the army is called the Army of Tennessee, and is commanded by General Howard. It is composed of two corps, the 15th and the 17th.

The left wing of the army is called the Army of Georgia, and is commanded by General Slocum. It also contains two corps, the 14th and the 20th.

The order of march is issued by the army commanders the preceding night, from them to the corps commanders, and then passed along until every soldier, teamster, and camp-follower knows that an early start is to be made. "The second division will be on the Milledgeville road promptly at five o'clock" reads an order, by way of instance.

At three o'clock the watch-fires are burning dimly, and, but for the occasional neighing of horses, all is so silent that it is difficult to imagine that twenty thousand men are within a radius of a few miles. The ripple of the brook can be distinctly heard as it breaks over the pebbles, or winds petulantly about the gnarled roots. The wind sweeping gently through the tall pines overhead only serves to lull to deeper repose the slumbering soldier, who in his tent is dreaming of his far-off Northern home.

But in an instant all is changed. From some commanding elevation the clear-toned bugle sounds out the *reveille,* and another and another responds, until the startled echoes double and treble, the clarion calls. Intermingled with this comes

† Condensed from *Story of the Great March.*

the beating of drums, often rattling and jarring on unwilling ears. In a few moments the peaceful quiet is replaced by noise and tumult, arising from hill and dale, from field and forest. Camp-fires, hitherto extinct or smouldering in dull gray ashes, awaken to new life and brilliancy, and send forth their sparks high into the morning air. Although no gleam of sunrise blushes in the east, the harmless flames on every side light up the scene, so that there is no disorder or confusion.

The aesthetic aspects of this sudden change do not, however, occupy much of the soldier's time. He is more practically engaged in getting his breakfast ready. The potatoes are frying nicely in the well-larded pan; the chicken is roasting delicately on the red-hot coals, and grateful fumes from steaming coffee-pots delight the nostrils. The animals are not less busy. An ample supply of corn and huge piles of fodder are greedily devoured by these faithful friends of the boys in blue, and any neglect is quickly made known by the pawing of neighing horses and the fearful braying of the mules. Amid all this the busy clatter of tongues and tools—a Babel of sound, forming a contrast to the quiet of the previous hour as marked as that between peace and war.

Then the animals are hitched into the traces, and the droves of cattle relieved from the night's confinement in the corral. Knapsacks are strapped, men seize their trusty weapons, and as again the bugles sound the note of command, the soldiers fall into line and file out upon the road.

A day's march varies according to the country to be traversed or the opposition encountered. If the map indicates a stream crossing the path, probably the strong party of mounted infantry or of cavalry which has been sent forward the day before has found the bridges burned, and then the pontoons are pushed on to the front. If a battle is anticipated, the trains are shifted to the rear of the centre. Under any circumstances, the divisions having the lead move unencumbered by wagons, and in close fighting trim. The ambulances following in the rear of the division are in such close proximity as to be available if needed. In the rear of each regiment follow the pack-mules, laden with every kind of camp baggage, including blankets, pots, pans, kettles, and all the kitchen-ware needed for cooking. Here will be found the led horses, and with them the Negro servants, who form an important feature of the *menage*.

Having placed the column upon the road, let us now

Marching through Georgia

follow that long line of muskets gleaming in the rays of the morning sunlight, and ride, heedless of the crack of the rifles, to the head of the column. The advance are driving a squad of Rebel cavalry before them so fast that the march is not in the least impeded. The flankers spread out, on a line parallel to the leading troops, for several hundred yards, more or less, as the occasion may require. They search through the swamps and forests, ready for any concealed foe, and anxiously looking out for any line of works which may have been thrown up by the enemy to check our progress. Here the General of the division, if a fighting man, is most likely to be found; his experienced eye noting that there is no serious opposition, he orders up a brigade or another regiment, who, in soldier's phraseology, send the Rebel rascals "kiting," and the column moves on. A large plantation appears by the road-side. If the "bummers" have been ahead, the chances are that it has been visited, in which event the interior is apt to show evidences of confusion; but the barns are full of corn and fodder, and parties are at once detailed to secure and convey the prize to the road-side. As the wagons pass along they are not allowed to halt, but the gain or fodder is stuffed into the front and rear of the vehicles as they pass, the unhandy operation affording much amusement to the soldiers, and not unfrequently giving them a poor excuse for swearing as well as laughing.

When the treasure-trove of grain, and poultry, and vegetables has been secured, one man is detailed to guard it until the proper wagon comes along. Numbers of these details will be met, who, with proper authority, have started off early in the morning, and have struck out miles away from the flank of the column. They sit upon some cross-road, surrounded with their spoils—chickens, turkeys, geese, ducks, pigs, hogs, sheep, calves, nicely-dressed hams, buckets full of honey, and pots of fresh white lard.

A Roman consul returning with victorious eagles would not wear a more triumphant air than this solitary guard. The soldiers see it, and gibe him as they pass:

"Say, you thar! where did you steal them pigs?"

"Steal!" is the indignant response; "steal!—perhaps you would like to have one of '*them*' pigs yourself."

An officer who is riding along gazes upon the appetizing show. He has recently joined, never has been on one of Sherman's raids, and does not know that a soldier will not sell his chickens for any price.

"Ah! a nice pair of ducks you have there, soldier; what will you take for them?"

Firmly, but respectfully, the forager makes answer, touching his cap the while, "They are not in the market. We *never* sell our stuff, sir—couldn't think of it."

The officer rides away through a battery of wide grins from the bystanders, and never again offers to buy the spoils of a forager.

As rumors of the approach of our army reached the frightened inhabitants, frantic efforts were made to conceal not only their valuable personal effects, plate, jewelry, and other rich goods, but also articles of food, such as hams, sugar, flour, etc. A large part of these supplies were carried to the neighboring swamps; but the favorite method of concealment was the burial of the treasures in the pathways and gardens adjoining the dwelling-houses. Sometimes, also, the grave-yards were selected as the best place of security from the "vandal hands of the invaders." Unfortunately for these people, the Negroes betrayed them, and in the early part of the march the soldiers learned the secret. It is possible that supplies thus hidden may have escaped the search of our men; but, if so, it was not for want of diligent exploration. With untiring zeal the soldiers hunted for concealed treasures. Wherever the army halted, almost every inch of ground in the vicinity of the dwellings was poked by ramrods, pierced with sabres, or upturned with spades. The universal digging was good for the garden land, but its results were distressing to the Rebel owners of exhumed property, who saw it rapidly and irretrievably "confiscated." It was comical to see a group of these red-bearded, barefooted, ragged veterans punching the unoffending earth in an apparently idiotic, but certainly most energetic way. If they "struck a vein" a spade was instantly put in requisition, and the coveted wealth was speedily unearthed. A woman standing upon the porch of a house, apparently watching their proceedings, instantly became an object of suspicion, and she was watched until some movement betrayed a place of concealment. The fresh earth recently thrown up, a bed of flowers just set out, the slightest indication of a change in appearance or position, all attracted the gaze of these military agriculturists. It was all fair spoil of war, and the search made one of the excitements of the march.

There is a halt in the column. The officer in charge of the

pioneer corps, which follows the advance guard, has discovered an ugly place in the road, which must be "corduroyed" at once, before the wagons can pass. The pioneers quickly tear down the fence near by and bridge over the treacherous place, perhaps at the rate of a quarter of a mile in fifteen minutes. If rails are not near, pine saplings and split logs supply their place. Meanwhile the bugles have sounded, and the column has halted. The soldiers, during the temporary halt, drop out of line on the road-side, lying upon their backs, supported by their still unstrapped knapsacks. If the halt is a long one, the different regiments march by file right, one behind the other, into the fields, stacking their muskets, and taking their rest at ease, released from their knapsack.

These short halts are of great benefit to the soldier. He gains a breathing-spell, has a chance to wipe the perspiration from his brow and the dust out of his eyes, or pulls off his shoes and stockings to cool his swollen, heated feet, though old campaigners do not feel the need of this. He munches his bit of hard bread, or pulls out a book from his pocket, or oftener a pipe, to indulge in that greatest of luxuries to the soldier, a soothing, refreshing smoke. Here may be seen one group at a brook-side, bathing their heads and drinking; and another, crowded round an old song-book, are making very fair music. One venturesome fellow has kindled a fire, and is brewing a cup of coffee. All are happy and jolly; but when the bugle sounds "fall in," "attention," and "forward," in an instant every temporary occupation is dropped, and they are on the road again.

This massing of brigades and wagons during a halt is a proper and most admirable arrangement. It keeps the column well closed up; and if a brigade or division has by some means been delayed, it has the opportunity to overtake the others. The 20th Corps manage this thing to perfection.

A great many of the mounted officers ride through the fields, on either side of the line of march, so as not to interfere with the troops. General Sherman always takes to the fields, dashing through thickets or plunging into the swamps, and, when forced to take the road, never breaks into a regiment or brigade, but waits until it passes, and then falls in. He says that they, and not he, have the right to the road.

Sometimes a little creek crosses the path, and at once a foot-bridge is made upon one side of the way for those who wish to keep dry-shod; many, however, with a shout of derision, will dash through the water at a run, and then they all shout the more when some unsteady comrade misses his footing and tumbles in at full length. The unlucky wight, however, takes the fun at his expense in the best of humor. Indeed, as a general rule, soldiers are good-humored and kind-hearted to the last degree. I have seen a soldier stand at a spring of water for ten minutes, giving thirsty comers cool draughts, although it would delay him so that he would have to run a quarter of a mile or more to overtake his company. The troops, by the way, kept their ranks admirably during this Georgia campaign. Occasionally, however, they would rush for a drink of water, or for a beehive which they would despoil of its sweets with a total disregard of the swarm of bees buzzing about their ears but which, strange to say, rarely stung.

But the sun has long since passed the zenith, the droves of cattle which have been driven through the swamps and fields are lowing and wandering in search of a corral, the soldiers are beginning to lag a little, the teamsters are obliged to apply the whip oftener, ten or fifteen miles have been traversed, and the designated halting-place for the night is near. The column must now be got into camp.

Officers ride on in advance to select the ground for each brigade, giving the preference to slopes in the vicinity of wood and water. Soon the troops file out into the woods and fields, the leading division pitching tents first, those in the rear marching on yet farther, ready to take their turn in the advance the next day.

As soon as the arms are stacked, the boys attack the fences and rail-piles, and with incredible swiftness their little shelter-tents spring up all over the ground. The fires are kindled with equal celerity, and the luxurious repast prepared, while "good digestion waits on appetite, and health on both." After this is heard the music of dancing or singing, the pleasant buzz of conversation, and the measured sound of reading. The wagons are meanwhile parked and the animals fed. If there has been a fight during the day, the incidents of success or failure are recounted; the poor fellow who lies wounded in "the anguish-laden ambulance" is not forgotten, and the brave comrade who fell in the strife is remembered with words of loving praise.

By-and-by the tattoo rings out on the night air. Its familiar sound is understood. "Go to rest, go to rest," it says, plainly as organs of human speech.

Shortly after follows the peremptory command of "Taps." "Out lights, out lights, out lights!" The soldier gradually disappears from the campfire. Rolled snugly in his blanket, the soldier dreams again of home, or revisits in imagination the battle-fields he has trod. The animals, with dull instinct, lie down to rest, and with dim gropings of consciousness ruminate over "fresh fields and pastures new." The fires, neglected by the sleeping men, go out, gradually flickering and smouldering, as if unwilling to die.

MILLEDGEVILLE, NOVEMBER 24TH

We are in full possession of the capital of the State of Georgia, and without firing a gun in its conquest. A few days ago, the Legislature, which had been in session, hearing of our approach, hastily decamped without any adjournment. The legislative panic spread among the citizens to such an extent as to depopulate the place, except a few old gentlemen and ladies and the Negroes.

General Slocum, with the 20th Corps, first entered the city, arriving by way of Madison, having accomplished his work of destroying the railroads and valuable bridges at that place. The fright of the legislators, as described by witnesses, must have been comical in the extreme. They little imagined the movement of our left wing, hearing first of the advance of Kilpatrick on the extreme right toward Macon, and supposing that to be another raid. What their opinion was when Howard's army appeared at M'Donough it would be difficult to say and their astonishment must have approached insanity when the other two columns were heard from—one directed toward Augusta, and the other swiftly marching straight upon their devoted city.

It seemed as if they were surrounded upon all sides except toward the east, and that their doom was sealed. With the certain punishment for their crimes looming up before them, they sought every possible means of escape. Private effects, household furniture, books, pictures, were conveyed to the depot, and loaded into the cars until they were filled and heaped, and the flying people could not find standing-room.

Any and every price was obtained for a vehicle. A thousand dollars was cheap for a common buggy, and men rushed about the streets in an agony of fear lest they should "fall victims to the ferocity of the Yankees."

Several days of perfect quiet passed after this exodus,

when, on a bright sunshiny morning, a regiment entered the city, with a band playing national airs, which music had long been hushed in the capital of Georgia.

But few of the troops were marched through the city. Two or three regiments were detailed, under the orders of the engineers, to destroy certain property designated by the General Commanding. The magazines, arsenals, depot buildings, factories of various kinds, with store-houses containing large amounts of government property, and about seventeen hundred bales of cotton, were burned. Private houses were respected every where, even those of noted Rebels, and I heard of no instance of pillage or insult to the inhabitants. One or two of the latter, known as having been in the Rebel army, were made prisoners of war, but the surgeons at the hospitals, the principal of the Insane Asylum, and others, expressed their gratitude that such perfect order was maintained throughout the city.

General Sherman is at the executive mansion, its former occupant having, with extremely bad grace fled from his distinguished visitor, taking with him the entire furniture of the building. As General Sherman travels with a *menage* (a roll of blankets and a haversack full of "hardtack"), which is as complete for a life in the open air as in a palace, this discourtesy of Governor Brown was not a serious inconvenience.

Just before his entrance into Milledgeville, General Sherman camped on one of the plantations of Howell Cobb. It was a coincidence that a Macon paper, containing Cobb's address to the Georgians as General Commanding, was received the same day. This plantation was the property of Cobb's wife, who was a Lamar. I do not know that Cobb ever claimed any great reputation as a man of piety or singular virtues, but I could not help contrasting the call upon his fellow-citizens to "rise and defend their liberties, homes, etc., from the step of the invader, to burn and destroy every thing in his front, and assail him on all sides," and all that, with his own conduct here, and the wretched condition of his Negroes and their quarters.

We found his granaries well filled with corn and wheat, part of which was distributed and eaten by our animals and men. A large supply of sirup made from sorghum (which we have found at nearly every plantation on our march) was stored in an out-house. This was also disposed of to the soldiers and the poor decrepit Negroes which this humane,

liberty-loving major general left to die in this place a few days
ago. Becoming alarmed, Cobb sent for and removed all the
able-bodied mules, horses, cows, and slaves. He left here
some fifty old men—cripples—and women and children,
with nothing scarcely covering their nakedness, with little or
no food, and without means of procuring it. We found them
cowering over the fireplaces of their miserable huts, where
the wind whirled through the crevices between the logs,
frightened at the approach of the Yankees, who, they had
been told, would kill them. A more forlorn, neglected set of
human beings I never saw.

General Sherman distributed to the Negroes with his own
hands the provisions left here, and assured them that we
were their friends, and they need not be afraid that we were
foes. An old man answered him: "I spose dat you'se true;
but, massa, you'se 'll go way to-morrow, and anudder white
man'll come." He had never known any thing but persecu-
tions and injury from the white man, and had been kept in
such ignorance of us that he did not dare to put faith in any
white man.

General Sherman invites all able-bodied Negroes (others
could not make the march) to join the column, and he takes
especial pleasure on some occasions, when they join the procession, in telling them they are free; that Massa Lincoln
has given them their liberty, and that they can go where
they please; that if they earn their freedom they should
have it, but that Massa Lincoln had given it to them any
how. They seem to understand that the proclamation of
freedom had made them free; and I have met but few instances where they did not say they expected the Yankees
were coming down some time or other, and very generally
they are possessed with the idea that we are fighting for
them, and that their fredom is the object of the war.

General Sherman's opening move in the present campaign has been successful in the highest degree. First marching his army in three columns, with a column of cavalry on
his extreme right, upon eccentric lines, he diverted the attention of the enemy, so that the Rebels concentrated their
forces at extreme points, Macon and Augusta, leaving
unimpeded the progress of the central columns.

The roads each column was to follow were carefully
designated, the number of miles each day to be traveled,
and the points of rendezvous were given at a certain date.
All of these conditions were fulfilled to the letter. Slocum,

with the 20th Corps, arrived at Milledgeville on the 22d instant, preceding Davis, with the 14th Corps, one day. On the same day Kilpatrick struck the Macon and Western road, destroying the bridge at Walnut Creek. The day following, Howard, with the 15th and 17th Corps, arrived at Gordon, and began the destruction of the Georgia Central Railroad.

It was near here that the most serious fight of the campaign has occurred up to this date. General Walcott, in command of a detachment of cavalry and a brigade of infantry, was thrown forward to Griswoldville, toward Macon, for demonstrative purposes merely. The enemy, about five thousand strong, advanced upon our troops, who had thrown up temporary breastworks, with a section of battery in position. The cavalry fell slowly back on either flank of the brigade, protecting them from attack in flank and rear. The Rebels were chiefly composed of militia, although a portion of Hardee's old corps was present, having been brought up from Savannah.

With the ignorance of danger common to new troops, the Rebels rushed upon our veterans with the greatest fury. They were received with grape-shot and musketry at point-blank range, our soldiers firing coolly, while shouting derisively to the quivering columns to come on, as if they thought the whole thing a nice joke. The Rebels resumed the attack, but with the same fatal results, and were soon in full flight, leaving more than three hundred dead on the field. Our loss was some forty killed and wounded, while their killed, wounded, and prisoners are estimated to exceed two thousand five hundred. A pretty severe lesson they have received.

NEAR TENNILLE STATION, ON THE
GEORGIA CENTRAL RAILROAD, NOVEMBER 27TH

Since writing the above the army has moved forward all along the line. The Rebels seem to have understood, but too late, that it was not Sherman's intention to make a serious attack upon Macon. They have, however, succeeded in getting Wheeler across the Oconee at a point below the railroad bridge. We first became aware of their presence in our front by the destruction of several small bridges across Buffalo Creek, on the two roads leading to Sandersville, over which were advancing the 20th and 14th Corps.

We were delayed but a few hours. The passage was also contested by the Rebel cavalry under Wheeler, and they fought our front all the way, and into the streets of Sandersville. The 20th Corps had the advance, deploying a regiment as skirmishers, and forming the remainder of a brigade in line of battle on either side of the road. The movement was executed in the handsomest manner, and was so effectual as not to impede the march of the column in the slightest degree, although the roll of musketry was unceasing. Our loss was not serious—about twenty killed and wounded.

As the 20th Corps entered the town they were met by the 14th, whose head of column arrived at the same moment. While these two corps had found the obstructions above mentioned, the army under General Howard was attempting to throw a pontoon across the Oconee at the Georgia Central Railroad bridge. Here they met a force under the command of General Wayne, which was composed of a portion of Wheeler's cavalry, militia, and a band of convicts who had been liberated from the penitentiary upon the condition that they would join the army.

The most of these desperadoes have been taken prisoners, dressed in their state prison clothing. General Sherman has turned them loose, believing that Governor Brown had not got the full benefits of his liberality. The Rebels did not make a remarkably stern defense of the bridge, for Howard was able to cross his army yesterday, and began breaking railroad again to-day. In fact, all the army, except one corps, is engaged in this same work. Wayne, with his army, was hardly able to reach this point, where he met General Hardee, who had managed to get around here from Macon. Our troops struck the railroad at this station a few hours after the frightened band escaped.

We had been told that the country was very poor east of the Oconee, but our experience has been a delightful gastronomic contradiction of the statement. The cattle trains are getting so large that we find difficulty in driving them along. Thanksgiving-day was very generally observed in the army, the troops scorning chickens in the plenitude of turkeys with which they had supplied themselves.

Vegetables of all kinds, and in unlimited quantities, were at hand, and the soldiers gave thanks as soldiers may, and were merry as only soldiers can be. In truth, so far as the

gratification of the stomach goes, the troops are pursuing a
continuous thanksgiving.

In addition to fowls, vegetables, and meats, many obtain
a delicious sirup made from sorghum, which is cultivated on
all the plantations, and stored away in large troughs and
hogsheads. The mills here and there furnish fresh supplies
of flour and meal, and we hear little or nothing of
"hardtack"—that terror to weak mastication. Over the sections of country lately traversed I find very little cultivation
of cotton. The commands of Davis appear to have been
obeyed; and our large droves of cattle are turned nightly into the immense fields of ungathered corn to eat their fill,
while the granaries are crowded to overflowing with both
oats and corn.

We have also reached the sand regions, so that the fall of
rain has no terrors; the roads are excellent, and would become firmer from a liberal wetting. The rise of the rivers will
not trouble us much, for each army corps has its pontoon,
and the launching of its boats is a matter of an hour.

TENNILLE STATION, NOVEMBER 28TH

The destruction of railroads in this campaign has been
most thorough. The work of demolition on such long lines of
road necessarily requires time, but the process is performed
as expeditiously as possible, in order to prevent any serious
delay of the movement of the army. The method of destruction is simple, but very effective. Two ingenious instruments
have been made for this purpose. One of them is a clasp,
which locks under the rail. It has a ring in the top, into
which is inserted a long lever, and the rail is thus ripped
from the sleepers. The sleepers are then piled in a heap and
set on fire, the rails roasting in the flames until they bend by
their own weight. When sufficiently heated, each rail is
taken off by wrenches fitting closely over the ends, and by
turning in opposite directions, it is so twisted that even a
rolling-machine could not bring it back into shape. In this
manner we have destroyed thirty miles of rails which lay in
the city of Atlanta, and all on the Augusta and Atlanta Road
from the last-named place to Madison, besides the entire
track of the Central Georgia line, from a point a few miles
east of Macon to the station where I am now writing.

NEAR JOHNSTON, SOUTH SIDE OF THE GEORGIA RAILROAD, NOVEMBER 29TH

All day long the army has been moving through magnificent pinewoods—the savannas of the South, as they are termed. I have never seen, and I can not conceive a more picturesque sight than the army winding along through these grand old woods. The pines, destitute of branches, rise to a height of eighty or ninety feet, their tops being crowned with tufts of pure green. They are widely apart, so that frequently two trains of wagons and troops in double column are marching abreast. In the distance may be seen a troop of horsemen—some General and his staff—turning about here and there, their gray uniforms and red and white flags contrasting harmoniously with the bright yellow grass underneath and the deep evergreen.

The most pathetic scenes occur upon our line of march daily and hourly. Thousands of Negro women join the column, some carrying household goods, and many of them carrying children in their arms, while older boys and girls plod by their side. All these women and children are ordered back, heartrending though it may be to refuse them liberty. One begs that she may go to see her husband and children at Savannah. Long years ago she was forced from them and sold. Another has heard that her boy was in Macon, and she is "done gone with grief goin' on four years."

But the majority accept the advent of the Yankees as the fulfillment of the millennial prophecies. The "day of jubilee," the hope and prayer of a lifetime, has come. They can not be made to understand that they must remain behind, and they are satisfied only when General Sherman tells them, as he does every day, that we shall come back for them some time, and that they must be patient until the proper hour of deliverance arrives.

The other day a woman with a child in her arms was working her way along among the teams and crowds of cattle and horsemen. An officer called to her kindly:"Where are you going, aunty?"

She looked up into his face with a hopeful, beseeching look, and replied:

"I'se gwine whar you'se gwine, massa."

NOVEMBER 30TH

With the exception of the 15th Corps, our army is across the Ogeechee without fighting a battle. This river is a line of great strength to the Rebels, who might have made its passage a costly effort for us, but they have been outwitted and outmanœuvred. I am more than ever convinced that, if General Sherman intends to take his army to the sea-board, it is his policy to avoid any contest which will delay him in the establishment of a new base of operations and supplies; if he is able to establish this new base, and at the same time destroy all lines of communication from the Rebel armies with the great cities, so that they will be as much isolated as if those strong-holds were in our hands, he will have accomplished the greatest strategic victory in the war, and all the more welcome because bloodless. Macon, Augusta, Savannah, or Charleston are of no strategic value to us, except that they are filled with munitions of war, and that the two latter might be useful to us as a base of supplies, with the additional moral advantage which would result from their capture. All these places, however, are vitally important to the enemy, as the source of a large part of their supplies of ammunition and commissary stores.

We have heard to-day from Kilpatrick and from Millen. Kilpatrick has made a splendid march, fighting Wheeler all the way to Waynesboro, destroying the railroad bridge across Brier Creek, between Augusta and Millen. It is with real grief that we hear he was unable to accomplish the release of our prisoners in the prison-pen at Millen. It appears that for some time past the Rebels have been removing our soldiers from Millen; the officers have been sent to Columbia, South Carolina, and the privates farther south, somewhere on the Gulf Railroad.

We have had very little difficulty in crossing the Ogeechee. The 20th Corps moved down the railroad, destroying it as far as the bridge. The 17th Corps covered the river at that point, where a light brigade was only partially destroyed. It was easily repaired, so that the infantry and cavalry could pass over it, while the wagons and artillery used the pontoons. The Ogeechee is about sixty yards in width at this point. It is approached on the northern or western side through swamps, which would be impassable but for the sandy soil, which packs solidly when the water covers the roads, although in places there are treacherous quicksands which we are obliged to corduroy.

This evening I walked down to the river, where a striking and novel spectacle was visible. The fires of pitch pine were flaring up into the mist and darkness; figures of men and horses loomed out of the dense shadows in gigantic proportions; torch-lights were blinking and flashing away off in the forests; and the still air echoed and re-echoed with the cries of teamsters and the wild shouts of the soldiers. A long line of the troops marched across the foot-bridge, each soldier bearing a torch, and, as the column marched, the vivid light was reflected in quivering lines in the swift-running stream.

Soon the fog, which here settles like a blanket over the swamps and forests of the river-bottoms, shut down upon the scene; and so dense and dark was it that torches were of but little use, and our men were directed here and there by the voice.

"Jim, are you there?" shouted one.

"Yes, I *am* here," was the impatient answer.

"Well, then, go straight ahead."

"Straight ahead! where in thunder is 'straight ahead?'"

And so the troops shuffled upon and over each other, and finally blundered into their quarters for the night.

As we journey on from day to day, it is curious to observe the attentions bestowed by our soldiers upon camp pets. With a care which almost deserves the name of tenderness, the men gather helpless, dumb animals around them; sometimes an innocent kid whose mother has been served up as an extra ration, and again a raccoon, a little donkey, a dog, or a cat. One regiment has adopted a fine Newfoundland dog, which soon became so attached to its new home that it never strayed, but became a part of the body, recognizing the face of every man in it. These pets are watched, fed, protected, and carried along with a faithfulness and affection which constantly suggest the most interesting psychological queries.

The favorite pet of the camp, however, is the hero of the barn-yard. There is not a regiment nor a company, not a teamster nor a Negro at head-quarters, nor an orderly, but has a "rooster" of one kind or another. When the column is moving, these haughty game-cocks are seen mounted upon the breech of a cannon, tied to the pack-saddle of a mule, among pots and pans, or carried lovingly in the arms of a mounted orderly; crowing with all his might from the interior of a wagon, or making the woods re-echo with his triumphant notes as he rides perched upon the knapsack of a soldier. These cocks represent every known breed, Polish and Spanish, Dorkings, Shanghais and Bantams—high-blooded specimens travelling with those of their species who may not boast of noble lineage. They must all fight, however, or be killed and eaten. Hardly has the army gone into camp before these feathery combats begin. The cocks use only the spurs with which Nature furnishes them; for the soldiers have not yet reached the refinement of applying artificial gaffs, and so but little harm is done. The game-cocks which have come out of repeated conflicts victorious are honored with such names as "Bill Sherman," "Johnny Logan," etc.; while the defeated and bepecked victim is saluted with derisive appellations, such as "Jeff. Davis," "Beauregard," or "Bob Lee."

Cock-fighting is not, perhaps, one of the most refined or elevating of pastimes, but it furnishes food for a certain kind of fun in camp; and as it is not carried to the point of cruelty, the soldiers can not be blamed for liking it.

MILLEN, DECEMBER 3D

Pivoted upon Millen, the army has swung slowly round from its eastern course, and is now moving in six columns upon parallel roads southward. Until yesterday it was impossible for the Rebels to decide whether or not it was General Sherman's intention to march upon Augusta. Kilpatrick had destroyed the bridge above Waynesboro, and, after falling back, had again advanced, supported by the 14th Army Corps, under General Davis. South of this column, moving eastward through Birdsville, was the 20th Corps, commanded by General Slocum. Yet farther south, the 17th Corps, General Blair in command, followed the railroad, destroying the track as it advanced. West and south of the Ogeechee, the 15th Corps, General Osterhaus in immediate command, but under the eye of General Howard, has moved in two columns.

Until now, Davis and Kilpatrick have been a cover and shield to the real movement of the army. At no time has it been possible for Hardee to interpose any serious obstacle to the advance of our main body, for our left wing has always been a strong arm thrust out in advance, ready to encounter any force which might attempt to bar the way.

The Rebel councils of war appear to have been completely deceived, for we hear it reported that Bragg and Longstreet are at Augusta, with ten thousand men made up of militia, two or three South Carolina regiments, and a portion of Hampton's Legion, sent there for remount. It is possible, now that the curtain has been withdrawn, and as it may appear their ten thousand men, may attempt to harass our rear, but they can accomplish nothing more than the loss of a few lives. They can not check our progress.

The work so admirably performed by our left wing, so far as it obliged the Rebels in our front constantly to retreat, by threatening their rear, now becomes the office of the 15th Corps, which is divided, and will operate on the right and left banks of the river. These two columns are marching, one day in advance of the main body, down the peninsula formed by the Savannah and Ogeechee rivers, with a detachment thrown over to the south side of the latter stream.

These flank movements are of the greatest necessity and value. They have taken place in the following order: first, the right wing, with Kilpatrick's cavalry, moved upon Macon, in the early part of the campaign; next, after disappearing from that flank, to the great amazement of the Rebels, the same troops marched across our rear and suddenly appeared upon our left flank, supported by Davis, and demonstrating savagely upon Augusta; and now Howard is performing the same office on our right. This style of manœuvring has not been practiced on account of any apprehension that we can not run over and demolish any Rebel force in Georgia, for all the troops of the enemy in the state could not stand for a moment against this army on any battle-field; but because General Sherman neither wishes to sacrifice life needlessly nor be detained. A very small force of infantry or cavalry in position at a river-crossing could delay a marching column half a day, or longer; our flanking column prevents this. Besides, our soldiers have tired of chickens, sweet potatoes, sorghum, etc., and have been promised oysters at the sea-side—oysters roasted, oysters fried, oysters stewed, oysters on the half shell, oysters in abundance, without money and without price. In short, the soldiers themselves don't wish to be delayed!

The railroad, which has received our immediate attention within the last week, is altogether the best I have seen in the state, though the rail itself is not so heavy as the T rail on the

Augusta and Atlanta road. The rail on the Georgia Central is partially laid with the **U**, and partly with light **T** rail, but it is all fastened to parallel string-pieces, which are again fixed to the ties. The station-houses are generally built of brick, in the most substantial manner, and are placed at distances of fifteen or twenty miles apart. They have been destroyed by our army all the way along from Macon. The extensive depot at Millen was a wooden structure of exceedingly graceful proportions. It was ignited in three places simultaneously, and its destruction was a brilliant spectacle; the building burning slowly, although there was sufficient wind to lift the vast volume of smoke and exhibit the exquisite architecture traced in lines of fire. This scene was so striking that even the rank and file observed and made comments upon it among themselves—a circumstance which may be counted as unusual, for the taste for conflagrations has been so cultivated of late in the army that any small affair of that kind attracts very little attention.

We daily traverse immense corn-fields, each of which covers from one hundred to one thousand acres. These fields were once devoted to the cultivation of cotton, and it is surprising to see how the planters have carried out the wishes or orders of the Rebel Government; for cotton has given way to corn. A large amount of cotton has been destroyed by our army in this campaign, but it must have been a small portion even of the limited crop raised, as our destruction has chiefly been upon the line of the railroads. As nearly as I can learn, two thirds of this cotton has been sent over the Georgia Central Railroad to Augusta by way of Millen; thence a limited amount has been transported to Wilmington for trans-Atlantic shipment; the remainder is at Columbia, South Carolina, at Columbus, Georgia, and at Montgomery, Alabama. I think it will be found, however, when the facts are known, that no large amounts of cotton are stored in any one place. The policy of scattering the crop is probably the wisest the Rebels could have adopted.

It is well ascertained that the country west of the Savannah River is expected to furnish supplies for the Rebel armies in the West; for although corn and beef are sent from this district to Lee's army, he draws the bulk of his supplies from the states east of the Savannah, and there is no region so prolific as that about Columbia. I note this fact because I wish to correct the impression, so general at the North, that the Eastern armies are fed from the Southwest. One thing is certain, that neither the West nor the East will draw any supplies from the counties in this state traversed by our army for a long time to come. Our work has been the next thing to annihilation.

OGEECHEE CHURCH, DECEMBER 6TH

For two days past the army has been concentrated at this point, which is the narrowest part of the peninsula. General Howard is still on the west side of the Ogeechee, but he is within supporting distance, and has ample means of crossing the river, should it be necessary, which is not at all probable.

Kilpatrick has again done noble work. On Sunday last, while marching toward Alexander for the purpose of more thoroughly completing the destruction of the railroad bridge crossing Brier Creek, he found Wheeler near Waynesboro and fought him several times, punishing him severely in each instance, driving his infantry and cavalry before him through Waynesboro and beyond the bridge, which was completely destroyed. Kilpatrick, having performed this feat, rejoined the main body of our army, then marching southward.

One important object of this eccentric movement of Kilpatrick is to impress the Rebel leaders with the conviction that we intend to march upon Augusta. To divide and scatter their force is our main purpose. Let them keep a large army in Augusta until we reach the sea, and then they can go where they please!

DECEMBER 8TH

The army has been advancing slowly and surely, but as cautiously as if a strong army were in our front. The relative position of the troops has not materially changed during the past few days, except that we are all farther south. From fifteen to twenty miles distant lies Savannah, a city which is probably in some perturbation at the certainty of our approach. If the Rebels intend fighting in defense of the city, the battle will be an assault of fortifications; for as yet we have only skirmished with parties of cavalry.

DECEMBER 10TH

The army has advanced some six miles to-day, and has met everywhere a strong line of works, which appear to be held by a large force, with heavy guns in position. Their line, although extended, is more easily defended because of a succession of impassable swamps which stretch across the peninsula. All the openings between these morasses and the roads which lead through them are strongly fortified, and the approaches have been contested vigorously, but with little loss to us. General Sherman seems to avoid the sacrifices of life, and I doubt his making any serious attack until he has communicated with the fleet.

We have now connected our lines, so that the corps are within supporting distance of each other. The soldiers are meanwhile in most cheerful spirits, displaying the unconcern which is the most characteristic feature of our troops.

The necessity of an open communication with the fleet is becoming apparent, for the army is rapidly consuming its supplies, and replenishment is vitally important. Away in the distance, across the rice-fields, as far as the banks of the Ogeechee, our signal-officers are stationed, scanning the seaward horizon in search of indications of the presence of the fleet, but thus far unsuccessfully. On the other side of the river, within cannon range, stand the frowning parapets of Fort McAllister, its ponderous guns and rebel garrison guard the only avenue open to our approach.

This evening a movement of the greatest importance has begun. Hazen's division of the 15th Corps is marching to the other side of the river. Fort McAllister must be taken. To-morrow's sun will see the veterans whom Sherman led upon the heights of Missionary Ridge within striking distance of its walls.

FORT McALLISTER, DECEMBER 13TH

Fort McAllister is ours. I saw the heroic assuault from the point of observation selected by General Sherman at the adjacent rice-mill.

During the greater part of to-day the General gazed anxiously toward the sea, watching for the appearance of the fleet. About the middle of the afternoon he descried a light column of smoke creeping lazily along over the flat marshes, and soon the spars of a steamer were visible, and then the flag of our Union floated out.

The sun was now fast going down behind a grove of water-oaks, and as his last rays gilded the earth, all eyes once more turned toward the Rebel fort. Suddenly white puffs of smoke shot out from the thick woods surrounding the line of works. Hazen was closing in, ready for the final rush of his column directly upon the fort. A warning answer came from the enemy in the roar of heavy artillery—and so the battle opened.

General Sherman walked nervously to and fro, turning quickly now and then from viewing the scene of conflict to observe the sun sinking slowly behind the tree-tops. No longer willing to bear the suspense, he said:

"Signal General Hazen that he must carry the fort by assault, to-night if possible."

The little flag waved and fluttered in the evening air, and the answer came:

"I am ready, and will assault at once!"

The words had hardly passed when from out the encircling woods there came a long line of blue coats and bright bayonets, and the dear old flag was there, waving proudly in the breeze. Then the fort seemed alive with flame; quick, thick jets of fire shooting out from all its sides, while the white smoke first covered the place and then rolled away from the glacis. The line of blue moved steadily on; too slowly, as it seemed to us, for we exclaimed, "Why don't they dash forward?" but their measured step was unfaltering. Now the flag goes down, but the line does not halt. A moment longer, and the banner gleams again in the front. Then the enemy's fire redoubled in rapidity and violence. The line of blue entered the enshrouding folds of smoke. The flag was at last dimly seen, and then it went out of sight altogether.

"They have been repulsed!" said one of the group of officers who watched the fight.

The firing ceased. The wind lifted the smoke. Crowds of men were visible on the parapets, fiercely fighting—but our flag was planted there. There were a few scattering musket-shots, and then the sounds of battle ceased. Then the bomb-proofs and parapets were alive with crowding swarms of our men, who fired their pieces in the air as a *feu de joie*. Victory! The fort was won.

This evening we have enjoyed unrestricted opportunities

of examining Fort McAllister. It is a large inclosure, with wide parapets, a deep ditch, a thickly-planted palisades, which latter are broken in several places where our men passed through. The dead and wounded are lying where they fell. Groups of soldiers are gathered here and there, laughing and talking of the proud deed that had been done. One said:

"If they had had embrasures for these guns," pointing to them, "we should have got hurt."

SAVANNAH, DECEMBER 20TH

The fall of Fort McAllister has been quickly followed by the evacuation of this great commercial city, which we gain without a battle.

Two events combined to insure this important result: first, the capture of Fort McAllister by direct assault, a feat which seems to have impressed the Rebels in a manner which can only be appreciated by talking with the deserters who constantly come into our lines in squads, and who assert that the soldiers in Savannah did not hesitate openly to declare that it was a useless sacrifice of life to defend the city. This terror was shared by the citizens in a magnified degree; and now we know for a certainty that the mayor and alderman, with a large body of citizens, waited upon General Hardee and insisted upon the surrender of the city.

The second reason was a flank movement, which was in process of operation. In two days more we should have had a division operating with Foster upon Savannah by way of Broad River, which would have rendered escape impossible. Practically, all avenues to the city were closed up by our army, which stretched from the Savannah to the Ogeechee rivers, and by Foster's troops, which covered the Savannah and Charleston Railroad.

The path by which Hardee finally escaped led through swamps which were previously considered impracticable. The Rebel general obtained knowledge of our movement through his spies, who swarmed in our camp.

It was fortunate that our troops followed so quickly after the evacuation of the city by the enemy, for a mob had gathered in the streets, and were breaking into the stores and houses. They were with difficulty dispersed by the bayonets of our soldiers, and then, once more, order and confidence prevailed throughout the conquered city.

We have won a magnificent prize—the city of Savannah, more than two hundred guns, magazines filled with ammunition, thirty-five thousand bales of cotton, three steamboats, several locomotives, and one hundred and fifty cars, and stores of all kinds. We had not been in occupation forty-eight hours before the transport steamer *Canonicus,* with General Foster on board, lay alongside a pier, and our new line of supplies was formed.

ON THE ROAD TO RICHMOND

When sherman moved south from Chattanooga, Grant had been in Washington only six weeks. But in that time, he had worked hard. According to Catton, "Grant reorganized his cavalry, bringing tough little Phil Sheridan in from the West to turn the cavalry corps into a fighting organization. As April wore away, the effect of all this began to be felt, and the army displayed a quiet new confidence. Lee might be just over the Rapidan, but there was a different feeling in the air; maybe this spring it would be different.

"Maybe it would; what a general could do would be done. But in the last analysis everything would depend on the men in the ranks, and both in the East and in the West the enlisted man was called on that winter to give his conclusive vote of confidence in the conduct of the war. He gave his vote in the most direct way imaginable—by re-enlisting voluntarily for another hitch.

"Union armies in the Civil War did not sign for the duration. They enlisted by regiments, and the top term was three years. This meant—since the hard core of the United States Army was made up of the volunteers who had enlisted in 1861—that as the climactic year of 1864 began the army was on the verge of falling apart. Of 956 volunteer infantry regiments, as 1863 drew to a close 455 were about to go out of existence because their time would very soon be up. Of 158 volunteer batteries, 81 would presently cease to exist.

"There was no way on earth by which these veterans could be made to remain in the army if they did not choose to stay. If they took their discharges and went home—as they were legally and morally entitled to do—the war effort would simply collapse. New recruits were coming in but because Congress in its wisdom had devised the worst possible system for keeping the army up to strength, the war could not be won without the veterans. Enlistments there were, in plenty; and yet—leaving out of consideration the fact that raw recruits could not hope to stand up to the battle-trained old-timers led by Lee and Johnston—they were not doing the army very much good. Heavy cash bounties were offered to men who would enlist; when cities, states, and Federal government offers were added up, a man might get as much as a thousand dollars just for joining the army. This meant that vast numbers of men were enlisting for the money they would get and then were deserting as quickly as possible—which was usually pretty quickly, since the Civil War authorities never really solved the problem of checking desertion—and going off to some other town to enlist all over again under a different name, collecting another bounty, and then deserting again to try the same game in still a third place. The 'bounty man' was notorious as a shirker, and the veterans detested him. Grant once estimated that not 12 per cent of the bounty men ever did any useful service at the front.

"There was a draft act, to be sure, but it contained a flagrant loophole. A man who was drafted could avoid service (unless and until his number was drawn again) by paying a three-hundred-dollar commutation fee; better yet, he could permanently escape military service by hiring a substitute to go to war for him. Clever entrepreneurs eager to make a quick dollar set themselves up in business as substitute brokers, and any drafted man who could afford the price—which often ran up to a thousand dollars or more—could get a broker to find a substitute for him. The substitutes who were thus provided were, if possible, even more worthless as a class than the bounty men. Cripples, diseased men, outright half-wits, epileptics, fugitives from workhouse and poor farm—all were brought forward by the substitute brokers and presented to the harassed recruiting agents as potential cannon fodder. The brokers made such immense profits that they could usually afford any bribery that might be necessary to get their infirm candidates past the medical examination, and the great bulk of the men they sent into the army were of no use whatever.

"Any regiment that contained any substantial percentage of bounty men or substitutes felt itself weakened rather than strengthened by its reinforcements. The 5th New Hampshire—originally one of the stoutest combat units in the Army of the Potomac—got so many of these people that it leaked a steady stream of deserters over to the Confederacy; so many, indeed, that at one time the Rebels opposite this regiment sent over a message asking when they might expect to get the regimental colors, and put up a sign reading: 'Headquarters, 5th New Hampshire Volunteers. Recruits wanted.' It is recorded that a Federal company commander finding some of his bounty men actually under fire, sharply ordered the men to take cover: 'You cost twelve hundred dollars apiece and I'm damned if I am going to have you throw your lives away—you're too expensive!'

"The war could not be won, in other words, unless a substantial percentage of the veterans would consent to re-enlist, and the most searching test the Union cause ever got came early in 1864, when the government—hat in hand, so to speak—went to the veteran regiments and pleaded with the men to join up for another hitch. It offered certain inducements—a four-hundred-dollar bounty (plus whatever sum a man's own city or county might be offering), a thirty-day furlough, the right to call oneself a 'veteran volunteer,' and a neat chevron that could be worn on the sleeve.

"Astoundingly, 136,000 three-year veterans re-enlisted. They were men who had seen the worst of it—men who had eaten bad food, slept in the mud and the rain, made killing marches, and stood up to Rebel fire in battles like Antietam and Stone's River, Chickamauga and Gettysburg—and they had long since lost the fine flush of innocent enthusiasm that had brought them into the army in the first place. They appear to have signed up for a variety of reasons. The furlough was attractive, and an Illinois soldier confessed that the four-hundred-dollar bounty 'seemed to be about the right amount for spending money while on furlough.' Pride in the regiment was also important; to be able to denominate one's regiment veteran volunteers, instead of plain volunteers, meant a good deal. In many cases the men had just got used to soldiering. . . .

"Whatever their reason, the men did re-enlist, and in numbers adequate to carry on the war. It was noteworthy that re-enlistments were hardest to get in the Army of the Potomac; when Meade added up the results at the end of March he found that he had twenty-six thousand re-enlistments, which meant that at least half of the men whose time was expiring had refused to stay with the army. Nevertheless, even this figure was encouraging. It was insurance; the army would not dissolve just when Grant was starting to use it."*

* From Bruce Catton, *This Hallowed Ground,* pp. 317, 318, 319.

U. S. Grant believed the war would be won only if General Lee's army could be defeated.† He would seek battle with Lee wherever possible. He had the guns, the manpower, the supplies—and unlike his prodecessors he meant to apply pressure continuously, ruthlessly, and with full knowledge of his own power.

And so, on May 4, the Army of the Potomac moved out of camp, across the Rapidan, and into the Wilderness, to try again what four previous attempts had failed to do—crush Lee's Army and capture Richmond.

From the Wilderness to Cold Harbor‡

BY PRIVATE FRANK WILKESON

THE ENLISTED MEN OF THE BATTERY I SERVED WITH ate breakfast and struck their camp at Brandy Station before sunrise. It was a beautiful morning, cool and pleasant. The sun arose above an oak forest that stood to the east of us, and its rays caused thousands of distant rifle barrels and steel bayonets to glisten as fire points. In all directions troops were falling into line. The air resounded with the strains of martial music. Standards were unfurled and floated lazily in the light wind. Regiments fell into line on the plain before us. We could see officers sitting on their horses before them, as though making brief speeches to their soldiers, and then the banners would wave, and the lines face to the right into column of fours and march off; and then the sound of exultant cheering would float to us. Short trains of white-capped and dust-raising wagons rolled across the plain. The heavy-artillery regiment of Germans serving as infantry, which had been encamped to our left during the winter, fell into line. We light-artillery men laughed to see the burdens these sturdy men had on their backs. Jellet, the gunner of the piece I served on, joined me as I stood leaning against a cool gun. He smiled, and said, significantly: "They will throw away

† Grant had dispatched 35,000 troops under Butler to the James River, to bring pressure on Richmond from the east. Butler accomplished nothing more than a standoff with Beauregard who was entrenched on a line between the James and Appomattox rivers.
‡ Condensed from *Recollections of a Private Soldier in the Army of the Potomac*.

those loads before they camp to-night." A word of command rang out in front of their regiment. They faced to the right and marched toward Ely's Ford of the Rapidan, and toward the Wilderness that lay beyond. "Boots and saddles!" was cheerily blown. The light-artillery men stood to their guns. The horses were harnessed and hitched in, the drivers mounted, and we moved off to take position in the column directly behind the heavily laden Germans. We were in high spirits; indeed we were frisky, and walked along gayly. The men talked of the coming battle, and they sang songs about the soul of John Brown, alleged to be marching on, songs indicative of a desire to hang Jeff. Davis to a sour apple-tree.

We marched toward Ely's Ford pretty steadily for a couple of hours. As we drew near it, we saw that the troops were beginning to jam around its approaches. They were being massed quicker than they could cross. We halted at a short distance from the ford and impatiently waited for our turn to cross. I noticed that the Germans in our front were sitting on their knapsacks engaged in mopping their faces with red handkerchiefs.

A staff officer rode out of the apparently confused mass of men jammed around the ford, and galloped toward us. As he passed the German soldiers, they slowly arose and, resuming their back-breaking burdens, marched off. The staff officer rode to us, and told our captain to follow the Germans closely.

We crossed the Rapidan on a pontoon bridge, and filled our canteens and drank deeply as we crossed. Then we marched over a narrow strip of valley land; then came a long, steep hill that led up to the comparatively level table-land of the Wilderness. This was the hill that caused the Germans to part with their personal property. Spare knapsacks, bursting with richness, were cast aside near its base. Near the top of the hill we found many well-filled haversacks, and we picked up every one of them and hung them on the limbers and caissons and guns. The mine was rich, and we worked it thoroughly. Now we began to come on stragglers—men who had overloaded themselves, or who were soft and unfit to march in their gross condition.

We felt it a duty to tenderly inquire into the condition of the health of these exhausted men, and did so pleasantly; but they, the ill-conditioned persons, resented our expressions of love and pity as though they had been insulting remarks.

On the upland we marched briskly. I saw no inhabitants in this region. They had fled before our advance, abandoning their homes. The soil was poor and thin, and the fields were covered with last year's dead grass, and this grass was burning as we passed by. We marched steadily until the old Chancellorsville House was in sight. Many of the trees standing around us were bullet-scarred. We stood idly in the road for some time, then we went on for a few hundred yards, and parked in a field by the road, with the Germans in camp ahead of us.

During the day we had occasionally heard the faint report of distant rifles or the heavy, muffled report of a gun, and we suspected that our cavalry was feeling of Lee's men, who were intrenched near Mine Run, but whose pickets were all over the adjacent country. All of the enlisted men hoped that they would get through the Wilderness—a rugged, broken area of upland that extends from the Rapidan River close to Spotsylvania—without fighting. The timber is dense and scrubby, and the whole region is cut up by a labyrinth of roads which lead to clearings of charcoal pits and there end. Deep ravines, thickly clad with brush and trees, furrow the forest. The Confederates knew the region thoroughly. We knew nothing, excepting that the Army of the Potomac, under Hooker, had once encounted a direful disaster on the outskirts of this desolate region.

In the evening, after supper, I walked with a comrade to the spot where General Pleasanton had massed his guns and saved the army under Hooker from destruction, by checking the impetuous onslaught of Stonewall Jackson's Viginian infantry, fresh from the pleasures of the chase of the routed Eleventh Corps. We walked to and fro over the old battlefield, looking at bullet-scarred and canister-riven trees. The men who had fallen in that fierce fight had apparently been buried where they fell, and buried hastily. Many polished skulls lay on the ground. Leg bones, arm bones, and ribs could be found without trouble. Toes of shoes, and bits of faded, weather-worn uniforms, and occasionally a grinning, bony, fleshless face peered through the low mound that had been hastily thrown over these brave warriors. As we wandered to and fro over the battle-ground, looking at the gleaming skulls and whitish bones, and examining the exposed clothing of the dead to see if they had been Union or Confederate soldiers, many infantrymen joined us. It grew dark, and we built a fire at which to light our pipes close to where we thought Jackson's men had formed for the charge, as the graves were thickest there, and then we talked of the battle of the preceding year. One veteran told the story of the burning of some of the Union soldiers who were wounded during Hooker's fight around the Wilderness, as they lay helpless in the woods.

"This region," indicating the woods beyond us with a wave of his arm, "is an awful place to fight in. The utmost extent of vision is about one hundred yards. Artillery cannot be used effectively. The wounded are liable to be burned to death. I am willing to take my chances of getting killed, but I dread to have a leg broken and then to be burned slowly; and these woods will surely be burned if we fight here. I hope we will get through this chaparral without fighting," and he took off his cap and meditatively rubbed the dust off the red clover leaf which indicated the division and corps he belonged to. As we sat silently smoking and listening to the story, an infantry soldier who had, unobserved by us, been prying into the shallow grave he sat on with his bayonet, suddenly rolled a skull on the ground before us, and said in a deep, low voice: "That is what you are all coming to, and some of you will start toward it to-morrow." It was growing late, and this uncanny remark broke up the group, most of the men going to their regimental camps. A few of us still sat by the dying embers and smoked. As we talked we heard picket firing, not brisk, but at short intervals the faint report of a rifle quickly answered. And we reasoned correctly that a confederate skirmish line was in the woods, and that battle would be offered in the timber. The intelligent enlisted men of the Second Corps with whom I talked that night listened attentively to the firing, now rising, now sinking into silence, to again break out in another place. All of them said that Lee was going to face Grant in the Wilderness, and they based their opinion on the presence of the Confederate skirmish line in the woods. And all of them agreed that the advantages of position were with Lee, and that his knowledge of the region would enable him to face our greatly superior army in point of numbers, with a fair prospect of success.

It was past midnight when I crept under the caisson of my gun and pillowed my head on my knapsack. The distant rifle-shots on the picketline grew fainter and fainter, then were lost in the nearer noises of the camps, and I slept.

The next morning I was awakened by a bugle call to find

the battery I belonged to almost ready to march. I hurriedly toasted a bit of pork and ate it, and quickly chewed down a couple of hard tack, and drank deeply from my canteen, and was ready to march when the battery moved. We struck into the road, passed the Chancellorsville House, turned to the right, and marched up a broad turnpike toward the Wilderness forest. After marching on this road for a short distance we turned to the left on an old dirt road, which led obliquely into the woods. The picket firing had increased in volume since the previous evening, and there was no longer any doubt that we were to fight in the Wilderness. The firing was a pretty brisk rattle, and steadily increasing in volume. About ten o'clock in the morning the soft spring air resounded with a fierce yell, the sound of which was instantly drowned by a roar of musketry, and we knew that the battle of the Wilderness had opened. The battery rolled heavily up the road into the woods for a short distance, when we were met by a staff officer, who ordered us out, saying:

"The battle has opened in dense timber. Artillery cannot be used. Go into park in the field just outside of the woods."

We turned the guns and marched back and went into park. Battery after battery joined us, some coming out of the woods and others up the road from the Chancellorsville House, until some hundred guns or more were parked in the field. We were then the reserve artillery.

Ambulances and wagons loaded with medical supplies galloped on the field, and a hospital was established behind our guns. Soon men, singly and in pairs or in groups of four or five, came limping slowly or walking briskly, with arms across their breasts and their hands clutched into their blouses, out of the woods. Some carried their rifles. Others had thrown them away. All of them were bloody. They slowly filtered through the immense artillery park and asked, with bloodless lips, to be directed to a hospital. Powder smoke hung high above the trees in thin clouds. The noise in the woods was terrific. The musketry was a steady roll, and high above is sounded the inspiring charging cheers and yells of the now thoroughly excited combatants.

By noon I was quite wild with curiosity, and, confident that the artillery would remain in park, I decided to go to the battle-line and see what was going on. I neglected to ask my captain for permission to leave the battery, because I feared he would not grant my request, and I did not want to disobey orders by going after he had refused me. I walked out of the camp and up the road. The wounded men were becoming more and more numerous. I saw men, faint from loss of blood, sitting in the shade cast by trees. Other men were lying down. All were pale, and their faces expressed great suffering. As I walked I saw a dead man lying under a tree which stood by the roadside. He had been shot through the chest and had struggled to the rear; then, becoming exhausted or choked with blood, he had laid down on a carpet of leaves and died. His pockets were turned inside out. A little farther on I met a sentinel standing by the roadside.

He eyed me inquiringly, and answered my question as to what he was doing there, saying: "Sending stragglers back to the front." Then he added, in an explanatory tone: "No enlisted man can go past me to the rear unless he can show blood."

I explained to the sentinel that I was a light-artillery man, and that I wanted to see the fight.

"Can I go past you?" I inquired.

"Yes," he replied, "you can go up. But you had better not go," he added. "You have no distinctive mark or badge on your dress to indicate the arm you belong to. If you go up, you may not be allowed to return, and then," he added, as he shrugged his shoulders indifferently, "you may get killed. But suit yourself."

So I went on. There was very heavy firing to the left of the road in a chaparral of brush and scrubby pines and oaks. There the musketry was a steady roar, and the cheers and yells of the fighters incessant. I left the road and walked through the woods toward the battle-ground, and met many wounded men who were coming out. They were bound for the rear and the hospitals. Then I came on a body of troops lying in reserve—a second line of battle, I suppose. I heard the hum of bullets as they passed over the low trees. Then I noticed that small limbs of trees were falling in a feeble shower in advance of me. It was as though an army of squirrels were at work cutting off nut and pine cone-laden branches preparatory to laying in their winter's store of food. Then, partially obscured by a cloud of powder smoke, I saw a straggling line of men clad in blue. They were not standing as if on parade, but they were taking advantage of the cover afforded by trees, and they were firing rapidly. Their line officers were standing behind them or in line with them. The smoke drifted to and fro, and there were many rifts in it. I saw scores of wounded men. I saw dead soldiers lying on the ground, and I saw men constantly falling on the battle-line. I could not see the Confederates, and, as I had gone to the front expressly to see a battle, I pushed on, picking my way from protective tree to protective tree, until I was about forty yards from the battle line. The uproar was deafening; the bullets flew through the air thickly. Now our line would move forward a few yards, now fall back. I stood behind a large oak tree, and peeped around its trunk. I heard bullets "spat" into this tree, and I suddenly realized that I was in danger. My heart thumped wildly for a minute; then my throat and mouth felt dry and queer. A dead sergeant lay at my feet, with a hole in his forehead just above his left eye. Out of this wound bits of brain oozed, and slid on a bloody trail into his eye, and thence over his cheek to the ground. I leaned over the body to feel of it. It was still warm. He could not have been dead for over five minutes. As I stopped over the dead man, bullets swept past me, and I became angry at the danger I had foolishly gotten into. I unbuckled the dead man's cartridge belt, and strapped it around me, and then I picked up his rifle. I remember standing behind the large oak tree, and dropping the ramrod into the rifle to see if it was loaded. It was not. So I loaded it, and before I fairly understood what had taken place, I was in the rear rank of the battle-line, which had surged back on the crest of a battle billow, bareheaded, and greatly excited, and blazing away at an indistinct, smoke-and-tree-obscured line of men clad in gray and slouch-hatted. As I cooled off in the heat of the battle fire, I found that I was on the Fifth Corps' line, instead of on the Second Corps' line, where I wanted to be. I spoke to the men on either side of me, and they stared at me, a stranger, and briefly said that the regiment, the distinctive number of which I have long since forgotten, was near the left of the Fifth Corps, and that they had been fighting pretty steadily since about ten o'clock in the morning, but with poor success, as the Confederates had driven them back a little. The fire was rather hot, and the men were falling pretty fast. Still it was not anywhere near as bloody as I had expected a battle to be. As a grand, inspiring spectacle, it was highly unsatisfactory, owing to the powder smoke obscuring the vision. At times we could not see the Confederate line, but that made no difference; we kept on firing just as though they were in full view. We gained ground at times, and then dead Confederates lay on the ground as thickly as dead Union soldiers did behind us. Then we would fall back, fighting stubbornly, but steadily giving ground, until the dead were all clad in blue.

Between two and three o'clock the fire in our front slackened. We did not advance. Indeed I saw no general officer on the battle-line to take advantage of any opportunity that the battle's tide might expose to a man of military talent. I had seen some general officer on the battle-line to general officers near the reserves, but none on the front line. I noticed the lack of artillery and saw that the nature of the ground forbade its use. Our line was fed with fresh troops and greatly strengthened. Boxes of cartridges were carried to us, and we helped ourselves. We were standing behind trees or lying on the ground, and occasionally shooting at the Confederate line, or where their line should have been. Some of the old soldiers muttered about things in general and rebel dodges in particular, and darkly hinted that the sudden slackening of the fire in our front boded no good to us. Soon a storm of yells, followed instantly by a roar of musketry, rolled to us from the left, and not distant. Almost instantly it was followed by a cheer and a volley of musketry. We sprang to our feet and in line, but there was nothing in strength ahead of us. To the left the noise increased in volume. The musketry was thunderous. Soon affrighted men rushed through the woods to our rear, not in ones and twos, but in dozens and scores, and as they swept past us they cried loudly:

"We are flanked! Hill's corps has got around our left."

Officers gave commands which I did not understand, but I did as my comrades did, and we were speedily placed at right angles to our original position, which was held by a heavy skirmish line. Many of the men who were running from the battle-field dropped into our line and remained with us until nightfall. I saw men from a dozen different regiments standing in our line. We were dreadfully nervous, and felt around blindly for a few minutes, not knowing what to do. Then we were reassured by seeing a staff officer explaining something to the commander of the regiment, a young major. This officer passed the word along the line that the Second Corps had come up just in time to close up a gap between the two corps, through which the Confederate general, Hill, had endeavored to thrust a heavy column of infantry. Speedily we got back into our original position. In a few minutes we saw a thin line of gray figures, not much heavier than a strong skirmish line, advancing rapidly toward us. They yelled loudly and continuously. We began firing rapidly, and so did they. They came quite close to us, say within seventy-five yards, and covered themselves as well as they could. We could see them fairly well, and shot many of them, and they killed and wounded many Union soldiers. Soon we drove them to cover, and they were comparatively quiet. The noise to the left, where Hancock's corps was fighting, almost drowned the racket we were making. The Confederate charge against the portion of the Fifth Corps where I was fighting was not delivered with vim. It impressed me as a sham. Their line, as I said, was thin, and it lacked momentum. I spoke to my fellows about it, and they all agreed that it was not earnest fighting, but a sham to cover the real attack on our left. There the battle raged with inconceivable fury for about two hours. Then the fight died down, and excepting for picket-firing, the lines were silent.

The wounded soldiers lay scattered among the trees. They moaned piteously. The unwounded troops, exhausted with battle, helped their stricken comrades to the rear. The wounded were haunted with the dread of fire. They conjured the scenes of the previous year, when some wounded men were burned to death, and their hearts well-nigh ceased to beat when they thought they detected the smell of burning wood in the air. The bare prospect of fire running through the woods where they lay helpless, unnerved the most courageous of men, and made them call aloud for help. I saw many wounded soldiers in the Wilderness who hung on to their rifles, and whose intention was clearly stamped on their pallid faces. I saw one man, both of whose legs were broken, lying on the ground with his cocked rifle by his side and his ramrod in his hand, and his eyes set on the front. I knew he meant to kill himself in case of fire—knew it as surely as though I could read his thoughts. The dead men lay where they fell. Their haversacks and cartridges had been taken from their bodies. The battle-field ghouls had rifled their pockets. I saw no dead man that night whose pockets had not been turned inside out.

Soon after dark the story of the fight on our left had been gathered by the newsmongers, and we learned that the Second Corps had saved itself from rout and the army from defeat by the most dogged fighting, and that they had required the aid of Getty's division of the Sixth Corps to enable them to hold their own. That news was sufficient to start me. So I went down the line, walking through the woods, stumbling over the dead and being cursed by the living, until I came to the Second Corps. There I found a regiment, Fortieth New York, if I correctly recall the number, some of whose soldiers I knew. They told me the story of the fight. It was really told by the windrows of dead men, and the loud and continuous shrieks and groans of the wounded. I was still bareheaded, and I fitted myself with a hat from the collection of hats lying near some dead men. And I took a pair of blankets from the shoulders of a dead man and slept in them that night.

Early the next morning, long before sunrise, I had my breakfast, and having seen sufficient of the fighting done by infantry, and strongly impressed with the truth that a light-artillery man had better stay close to his guns, I bade my acquaintances good-by, and walked off, intent on getting to my gun and comparative comfort and safety. But I hung on to my rifle and belt. They were to be trophies of the battle, and I meant to excite the envy of my comrades by displaying them. Stepping into the road I walked along briskly, and saw many other unwounded men rearward bound. A sentinel, with rifle at the carry, halted me, and demanded to see blood. I could show none. I assured him that I belonged to the light artillery, and that I had gone to the front the previous day just to see the battle.

He said: "You have a rifle; you have a belt and a cartridge box. Your mouth is powder-blackened. You have been fighting as an infantryman, and you shall so continue to fight. You go back, or I will arrest you, and then you will be sent back."

I longed to kill him—longed to show the Army of the Potomac one dead provost guard; but I was afraid to shoot him, for fear that his comrades might see me do it. So I turned and hastened back to the front. I determined to fight that day, and go home to the battery the succeeding night.

Away off to the right, toward the Rapidan, the battle rose with the sun. In our front, the Second Corps, there was little movement discernible. But so dense was the cover that we could see but little at a distance of two hundred yards. I saw that the soldiers had thrown up a slight intrenchment during the previous night. About five o'clock we were ordered to advance, and pushed ahead, fighting as we went, and forced Hill's men back, killing many, wounding more, and taking scores of prisoners. We crossed a road, which a wounded Confederate told me was the Brock road. I saw many dead

Confederates during this advance. They were poorly clad. Their blankets were in rolls, hanging diagonally from the left shoulder to the right side, where the ends were tied with a string or a strap. Their canvas haversacks contained plenty of corn-meal and some bacon. I saw no coffee, no sugar, no hard bread in any of the Confederate haversacks I looked into. But there was tobacco in plugs on almost all the dead Confederates. Their arms were not as good as ours. They were poorly shod. The direful poverty of the Confederacy was plainly indicated by its dead soldiers. But they fought.

The Confederates seemed to be fighting more stubbornly, fighting as though their battle-line was being fed with more troops. They hung on to the ground they occupied tenaciously, and resolutely refused to fall back further. Then came a swish of bullets and a fierce exultant yell, as of thousands of infuriated tigers. Our men fell by scores. Great gaps were struck in our lines. There was a lull for an instant, and then Longstreet's men sprang to the charge. It was swiftly and bravely made, and was within an ace of being successful. There was great confusion in our line. The men wavered badly. They fired wildly. They hesitated. I feared the line would break; feared that we were whipped. The line was fed with troops from the reserve. The regimental officers held their men as well as they could. We could hear them close behind us, or in line with us, saying: "Steady, men, steady, steady, steady!" as one speaks to frightened and excited horses. The Confederate fire resembled the fury of hell in intensity, and was deadly accurate. Their bullets swished by in swarms. It seems to me that I could have caught a pot full of them if I had had a strong iron vessel rigged on a pole as a butterfly net. Again our line became wavy and badly confused, and it was rapidly being shot into a skirmish-like order of formation. Speedily a portion of the Ninth Corps came to our assistance and we regained heart. During this critical time, when the fate of the Second Corps was trembling in the balance, many officers rushed to and fro behind us, but I saw no major-generals among them; but then I had sufficient to do to look ahead and fall back without falling down, and they may have been on the battle-line, only I did not see them. The Confederates got a couple of batteries into action, and they added to the deafening din. The shot and shell from these guns cut great limbs off the trees, and these occasionally fell near the battle-line, and several men were knocked down by them. Our line strengthened, we, in our

turn, pushed ahead, and Longstreet's men gave ground slowly before us, fighting savagely for every foot. The wounded
lay together. I saw, in the heat of this fight, wounded men
of the opposing forces aiding each other to reach the protective shelter of trees and logs, and, as we advanced, I saw a
Confederate and a Union soldier drinking in turn out of a
Union canteen, as they lay behind a tree.

There was another lull, and then the charging line of gray
again rushed to the assault with inconceivable fury. We fired
and fired and fired, and fell back fighting stubbornly. We
tore cartridges until our teeth ached. But we could not check
the Confederate advance, and they forced us back and back
and back until we were behind the slight intrenchments
along the Brock road. A better charge, or a more determined, I never saw. We fought savagely at the earthworks.
At some points the timber used in the earthworks was fired,
and our men had to stand back out of the line of flame and
shoot through it at the Confederates, who were fighting in
front of the works. And the woods, through which we had
fallen back, were set on fire, and many wounded soldiers
were burned to death. We beat off the Confederates, and
they, with the exception of the picket line, disappeared. Our
line was straightened, reserves were brought up, and some
of the battle-torn troops were relieved. We had half an
hour's rest, during which time many of us ate and smoked,
and drank out of our canteens; and we talked, though not so
hopefully as in the early morning. Men missed old comrades,
and with only seeming indifference figuratively reckoned
they had "turned up their toes." Firing had almost ceased. It
was as the cessation of the wind before the approach of a
cyclone. A tempest of fire and balls and yells broke out on
the right. We were out of it. The real battle raged furiously
in the woods to the right, while a heavy line of Confederate
skirmishers, who lurked skillfully behind trees and who fired
briskly and accurately, made things decidedly unpleasant
for us, and effectually prevented any men being drawn from
our portion of the line to strengthen the right. How we fret-
ted while this unseen combat raged! We judged that our men
were being worsted as the battle-sounds passed steadily to
our rear. Then the fugitives, the men quick to take alarm and
speedy of foot when faced to the rear, began to pass diagonally through the woods behind us. While we stood quivering with nervous excitement, and gazing anxiously into each
other's eyes we heard a solid roll of musketry, as though a

division had fired together, cheers followed, and then the battle-sound rapidly advanced toward the Confederate line. Then all was quiet, and the fighting on the left of our line was over. Soon word was passed along the line that the charging Confederates had broken through the left of the Ninth Corps, and would have cut the army in twain if General Carroll had not caught them on the flank and driven them back with the Third Brigade of the Second Division of the Second Corps.

The enlisted men supposed the day's fighting was over. And so did our generals. But the Confederates marched swiftly on many parallel roads, and were massed for an attack on our right, the Sixth Corps. They were skilfully launched and ably led, and they struck with terrific violence against Shaler's and Seymour's brigades, which were routed, with a loss of 4,000 prisoners. The Confederates came within an ace of routing the Sixth Corps; but the commanders restored and steadied the lines, and the Confederate charge was first checked and then bloodily repulsed.

The day's offensive fighting on the part of the Confederates, as we, the enlisted men, summed it up, had consisted of two general assaults delivered all along our line, as though to feel of us and discover where we were the weakest, and to promptly take advantage of the knowledge gained, to attack in force and with surprising vim and stanchness first one flank and then the other. Both of the assaults were dangerously near being successful.

The sun sank, and the gloom among the trees thickened and thickened until darkness reigned in the forest where thousands of dead and wounded men lay. The air still smelled of powder-smoke. Many soldiers cleaned out their rifles. We ate, and then large details helped carry their wounded comrades to the road, where we loaded them into ambulances and wagons. I determined to join my battery. I threw away my rifle and belt, and as the first wagons loaded with wounded men moved to the rear, I walked by the side of the column and passed the guards, if there were any stationed on that road, without being challenged. When I was well to the rear, I for the first and last time became a "coffee boiler." I cooked and ate a hearty supper, and then rolled myself in the dead soldier's blankets, which I had hung on to, and slept soundly until morning, when I found the battery I belonged to without much trouble, and was promptly punished for being absent without leave.

That evening the troops began to pour out of the woods in columns. The infantry soldiers marched soberly past the artillery. There were no exultant songs in those columns. The men seemed aged. They were very tired and very hungry. They seemed to be greatly depressed.

There was a gap in the column, and my battery moved on to the road, and other batteries followed us. We marched rapidly and without halting, until we reached a point where another road, which led in the direction of the right of our battle-line, joined the road we were on. Here we met a heavy column of troops marching to the rear, as we were. The enlisted men were grave, and rather low in spirits, and decidedly rough in temper.

"Here we go," said a Yankee private; "here we go, marching for the Rapidan, and the protection afforded by that river. Now, when we get to the Chancellorsville House, if we turn to the left, we are whipped—at least so say Grant and Meade. And if we turn toward the river, the bounty-jumpers will break and run, and there will be a panic."

"Suppose we turn to the right, what then?" I asked.

"That will mean fighting, and fighting on the line the Confederates have selected and intrenched. But it will indicate the purpose of Grant to fight," he replied.

Grant's military standing with the enlisted men this day hung on the direction we turned at the Chancellorsville House. If to the left, he was to be rated with Meade and Hooker and Burnside and Pope—the generals who preceded him. At the Chancellorsville House we turned to the right. Instantly all of us heard a sigh of relief. Our spirits rose. We marched free. The men began to sing. The enlisted men understood the flanking movement. That night we were happy.

May 8, 1864. The bloody battle of the Wilderness was a thing of the past. That dense chaparral in which the unburied dead Union and Confederate soldiers lay scattered thickly was being left behind us as we marched. In the morning the guns of the Fifth Corps notified the Union troops that the Confederates had been found. The Fifth Corps had been in the advance in the flank movement to the left out of the Wilderness, and Longstreet's corps had marched parallel with it, and had taken position behind the river Ny, which was more properly a creek. We were not in this fight, but correctly judged that it was not severe, as at no time did

Spottsylvania: *The bloody struggle at the Salient*

the battle's roar rise to the volume which indicates a fierce engagement. On May 9th the army was clear of the Wilderness. We took position around Spotsylvania Court House. Wherever we went there were heavy earthworks, behind which the veteran Confederate infantry lurked. The day was spent in getting into position and in bloody wrangling between the opposing pickets and in sharpshooting. At intervals would be a crash of musketry and a cheer; then the artillery would open and fire briskly for a few minutes. But there was no real fighting. That night we heard that General Sedgwick, commanding the Sixth Corps, had been killed by a sharpshooter or by a stray ball from the Confederate picket line.

May 10th, and the fighting began. The din of the battle was continuous, and as much of the artillery had been drawn to the battle-line the noise was far louder than it had been in the Wilderness. The troops fought all day. A solid roll of musketry, mingled with the thunderous reports of cannon quickly served, caused the air to quiver. After fighting all day, we spent a large portion of the night in fruitless endeavors to flank the Confederate position. Spent it in following staff officers, to find that we were again in front of earthworks, which were lined with keen-eyed, resolute infantry soldiers. In Spotsylvania we fought by day, we marched by night, and our losses were exceedingly large.

One day the battery I served with was parked for rest near a road down which wounded men were streaming in a straggling column. These men, tired, weakened by loss of blood, and discouraged, tumbled exhausted into the angles of worm fences, and spread their blankets from rail to rail to make a shade. There they rested and patiently waited for their turn at the surgeons' tables. They were a ghastly array. The sight of these poor, stricken men as they helped one another, as they bound one another's wounds, as they painfully hobbled to and fro for water, was a most pathetic one. They lined the roadside for half a mile, a double hedgerow of suffering and death, as men were dying in the fence corners every few minutes. Down the road we heard the stirring music of a martial band. Soon the head of a column of troops came in sight. Officers were riding at the head of the soldiers on horses that pranced. The men were neatly clad, and their brass shoulder-plates shone brightly in the sun.

"The heavy-artillery men from the fortifications around Washington," one of my comrades murmured.

These fresh soldiers were marching beautifully. They were singing loudly and tunefully. They were apparently pleased with the prospect of fighting in defence of their country. For some reason the infantry of the line—the volunteer infantry—did not admire heavy-artillery men. They liked light-artillery men, and were encouraged by the presence of the guns on the battle-line. There was something inspiring in the work of the gunners and in the noisy reports of the cannon; and, then, cannon were deadly, and if well served and accurately aimed, they could and did pulverize charging columns. But heavy-artillery men were soldiers of a different breed. There was a widespread belief among us that these men had enlisted in that arm because they expected to fight behind earthworks or to safely garrison the forts which surrounded Washington. We did not like these troops. The head of the heavy-artillery column, the men armed as infantry, was thrust among the wounded who lined the roadside. These bloody wrecks of soldiers derided the new-comers. Men would tauntingly point to a shattered arm, or a wounded leg, or to bloody wounds on their faces, or to dead men lying in fence corners, and derisively shout: "That is what you will catch up yonder in the woods!" and they would solemnly indicate the portion of the forest they meant by extending arms from which blood trickled in drops. I saw one group of these wounded men repeatedly cover and uncover with a blanket a dead man whose face was horribly distorted, and show the courage-sapping spectacle to the marching troops, and faintly chuckle and cause their pale cheeks to bulge with derisive tongue-thrusts, as they saw the heavy artillery men's faces blanch. Still others would inquire in mock solicitous tones as to the locality of their cannon, and then tenderly inquire of some soldier whose bearing or dress caught their attention: "Why, dearest, why did you leave your earthwork behind you?" And they would hobble along and solemnly assure the men that he had made a serious mistake, and that he should have brought the earthwork along, as he would need it in yonder woods, pointing with outstretched body arms to the forest where the battle's roar resounded. Others assumed attitudes of mock admiration and gazed impudently and contemptuously at the full regiments as they marched by. Long before the heavy-artillery men had passed through the bloody gauntlet their songs were hushed.

The movable fight dragged along until May 12th. We

fought here. We charged there. We accomplished nothing.
But early on the morning of May 12th the Second Corps carried by assault the Confederate works held by Johnston's
division of Ewell's corps, capturing about three thousand
five hundred prisoners and thirty guns. Our troops caught
the battle-exhausted Confederates asleep in their blankets.
The Confederate line was broken. Their army was cut in
twain. But it amounted to nothing. If the advantage had
been intelligently followed up, it might have had decisive
results. As it was, many thousands of enlisted men were
killed and wounded in a furious fight which lasted all day,
and the next morning we found that the Confederates had
fortified a line in rear of the captured works, and our losses
of thousands of brave men resulted in nothing but the capture of twenty guns (ten of these guns which were captured
by the Second Corps were wrested from them by Ewell's
men in the fights that ensued).

That night a wounded Second Corps soldier came into
our battery, and joined me at the fire. He asked for food. I
had plenty, and as the man's right arm was stiff from a
wound, I told him I would cook a supper for him if he would
wait. He greedily accepted the invitation. Soon I had a mess
of pork and hardtack frying and coffee boiling, and as I had
that day found a haversack—truth is that its owner, a heavy-
artilleryman, was asleep when I found it—which contained
a can of condensed milk and half a loaf of light bread, the
wounded soldier and I had a feast. After supper we smoked
and talked.

"The Wilderness," said my wounded guest, "was a
private's battle. The men fought as best they could, and
fought stanchly. The generals could not see the ground, and
if they were on the front line, they could not have seen their
troops. The enlisted men did not expect much generalship to
be shown. All they expected was to have the battle-torn portions of the line fed with fresh troops. There was no chance
for a display of military talent on our side, only for the
enlisted men to fight, and fight, and fight; and that they did
cheerfully and bravely. Here the Confederates are strongly
intrenched, and it was the duty of our generals to know the
strength of the works (we all knew the dogged fighting
capacity of their defenders) before they launched the army
against them." My guest was tired, and first exacting a promise from me that I would give him his breakfast, he lay on

his back behind a tree, and after I had bathed his wounded arm he slept.

We marched to and fro. The infantry were almost constantly engaged in feeling of the Confederate lines to find a weak place, and finding all points stanchly defended. The artillery was pleasantly employed in burying good iron in Confederate earthworks. The list of our killed and wounded and missing grew steadily and rapidly, longer and longer, as their cartridge-boxes grew lighter and lighter. One day a brisk fight was going on in front of us. We were ordered to the top of a hill and told to fire over our infantry into the edge of the woods, where the Confederates lay. The battery swung into action. Below us, in the open, was a pasture field. In it were two batteries and a line of infantry. The former were noisily engaged; the latter were not doing much of anything. The Confederates were behind an earthwork that stood, shadowed by trees, in the edge of the forest, and it was evident that they meant to stay there. Our infantry charged, and at some points they entered the edge of the woods, out of which they speedily came, followed by a disorderly and heavy line of Confederate skirmishers. The batteries in the open were skilfully handled and admirably served, but it was a matter of a very short time for them. As soon as our infantry got out of range in a ravine, the Confederate skirmishers dropped prone on the ground, disappeared behind trees, sank into holes, squatted behind bushes, and turned their attention to the Union batteries, which were within rifle range of the skirmishers, and the guns were almost instantly driven from the field, leaving many horses, and men clad in blue, lying on the ground. Then the Confederate skirmishers ran back to their earthworks and clambered over. The battery I served with was firing three-inch percussion bolts at the Confederate line and doing no harm. One of my comrades spoke to me across the gun, saying: "Grant and Meade are over there," nodding his head to indicate the direction in which I was to look. I turned my head and saw Grant and Meade sitting on the ground under a large tree. Both of them were watching the fight which was going on in the pasture field. Occasionally they turned their glasses to the distant wood, above which small clouds of which smoke marked the bursting shells and the extent of the battle. Across the woods that lay behind the pasture, and behind the bare ridge that formed the horizon, and well within the Confederate lines, a dense column of

dust arose, its head slowly moving to our left. I saw Meade
call Grant's attention to this dust column, which was raised
either by a column of Confederate infantry or by a wagon
train. We ceased firing, and sat on the ground around the
guns watching our general, and the preparations that were
being made for another charge. Grant had a cigar in his
mouth. His face was immovable and expressionless. His eyes
lacked lustre. He sat quietly and watched the scene as
though he was an uninterested spectator. Meade was nervous, and his hand constantly sought his face, which it
stroked. Staff officers rode furiously up and down the hill
carrying orders and information. The infantry below us in
the ravine formed for another charge. Then they started on
the run for the Confederate earthworks, cheering loudly the
while. We sprang to our guns and began firing rapidly over
their heads at the edge of the woods. It was a fine display of
accurate artillery practice, but, as the Confederates lay
behind thick earthworks, and were veterans not to be shaken
by shelling the outside of a dirt bank behind which they lay
secure, the fire resulted in emptying our limber chests, and
in the remarkable discovery that three-inch percussion shells
could not be relied upon to perform the work of a steam
shovel. Our infantry advanced swiftly, but not with the vim
they had displayed a week previous; and when they got within close rifle range of the works, they were struck by a
storm of rifle-balls and canister that smashed the front line to
flinders. They broke for cover, leaving the ground thickly
strewed with dead and dying men. The second line of
battle did not attempt to make an assault, but returned to the
ravine. Grant's face never changed its expression. He sat
impassive and smoked steadily, and watched the short-lived
battle and decided defeat without displaying emotion. Meade
betrayed great anxiety. The fight over, the generals arose and
walked back to their horses, mounted and rode briskly away,
followed by their staff. No troops cheered them. None
evinced the slightest enthusiasm.

Toward evening of the eighth day's fighting a furious attack was made on our right by Ewell's corps. This attack
was repulsed, and then the battle died down to picket-firing
and sharpshooting. Now and then a battery would fire a
few shot into a Confederate earthwork, just to let its defenders know that we still lived. We were strongly intrenched,
and it was evident to the enlisted men that the battles fought
around Spotsylvania belonged to the past. We estimated our

losses up to this time at from forty-five thousand to fifty thousand men, or about two fifths of the men whom Grant took across the Rapidan. I slept from 6 P.M. of the eighth day's fighting until 2 P.M. of the ninth day's fighting. I made up the losses of sleep incurred during the eight days and nights of almost continuous fighting and marching. This sleep was so profound that I barely heard the guns as they occasionally roared over my head. I was easy in mind, as I knew that some hollow-eyed comrade would awaken me if I was needed at the guns or if we moved.

On the morning of May 28, 1864, the Second Corps crossed the Pamunkey River. Close by the bridge on which we crossed, and to the right of it, under a tree, stood Generals Grant, Meade, and Hancock and a little back of them was a group of staff officers. Grant looked tired. He was sallow. He held a dead cigar firmly between his teeth. His face was as expressionless as a pine board. He gazed steadily at the enlisted men as they marched by as though trying to read their thoughts, and they gazed intently at him. He had the power to send us to our deaths, and we were curious to see him. Grant stood silently looking at his troops and listening to Hancock, who was talking and gesticulating earnestly. Meade stood by Grant's side and thoughtfully stroked his own face.

During the afternoon we heard considerable firing in front of us, and toward evening we marched over ground where dead cavalrymen were plentifully sprinkled. The blue and the gray lay side by side, and their arms by them. With the Confederates lay muzzle-loading carbines, the ramrods of which worked upward on a swivel hinge fastened near the muzzle of the weapon. It was an awkward arm and far inferior to the Spencer carbine with which our cavalry was armed. There were ancient and ferocious-looking horse-pistols, such as used to grace the Bowery stage, lying by the dead Confederates. The poverty of the South was plainly shown by the clothing and equipment of her dead. These dead men were hardly stiff when we saw them. All of their pockets had been turned inside out. That night, while searching for fresh, clean water, I found several dead cavalrymen in the woods, where they had probably crawled after being wounded. I struck a match so as to see one of these men plainly, and was greatly shocked to see large black beetles eating the corpse. I looked at no more dead men that night.

The next day the sound of battle arose again. At distant points it would break out furiously and then die down. In our immediate front heavy skirmishing was going on, and wounded men began to drift to the rear in search of hospitals. They said that there was a stream of water, swamps, and a line of earthworks, behind which lay the Confederate infantry, in our front, and that we could not get to the works. At no time did the fire rise to a battle's volume; it was simply heavy and continuous skirmishing, in which our men fought at great disadvantage, and were severely handled. Finding that these works were too strong to be taken by assault, Grant moved the army to the left. On June 1st we heard heavy fighting to our left, and that night we learned that a portion of the Sixth Corps, aided by ten thousand of Butler's men from Bermuda Hundred, had forced the Chickahominy River at a loss of three thousand men, and that they held the ground they had taken. The news-gatherers said that the Confederates were strongly in-trenched, and evidently had no intention of fighting in the open. We knew that a bloody battle was close at hand, and instead of being elated the enlisted men were depressed in spirits. That night the old soldiers told the story of the campaign under McClellan in 1862. They had fought over some of the ground we were then camped on. Some of the men were sad, some indifferent; some so tired of the strain on their nerves that they wished they were dead and their troubles over. The infantry knew that they were to be called upon to assault perfect earthworks, and though they had re-solved to do their best, there was no eagerness for the fray, and the impression among the intelligent soldiers was that the task cut out for them was more than men could accom-plish.

On June 2d the Second Corps moved from the right to the left. We saw many wounded men that day. We crossed a swamp or marched around a swamp, and the battery I belonged to parked in a ravine. There were some old houses on our line of march, but not a chicken or a sheep or a cow to be seen. The land was wretchedly poor. The night of June 2d was spent in getting into battle-line. There was con-siderable confusion as the infantry marched in the darkness. In our front we could see tongues of flames dart forth from Confederate rifles as their pickets fired in the direction of the noise they heard, and their bullets sang high above our heads. My battery went into position just back of a crest of a hill. Behind us was an alder swamp, where good drinking water gushed forth from many springs. Before we slept we talked with some of the Seventh New York Heavy Artillery, and found that they were sad of heart. They knew that they were to go into the fight early in the morning, and they dreaded the work. The whole army seemed to be greatly depressed the night before the battle of Cold Harbor.

Before daybreak of June 3d the light-artillery men were aroused. We ate our scanty breakfast and took our positions around the guns. All of us were loath to go into action. In front of us we could hear the murmurs of infantry, but it was not sufficiently light to see them. We stood leaning against the cool guns, or resting easily on the ponderous wheels, and gazed intently into the darkness in the direction of the Confederate earthworks. How slowly dawn came! Indistinctly we saw moving figures. Some on foot rearward bound, cowards hunting for safety; others on horseback riding to and fro near where we supposed the battle-lines to be; then orderlies and servants came in from out the darkness leading horses, and we knew that the regimental and brigade commanders were going into action on foot. The darkness faded slowly, one by one the stars went out, and then the Confederate pickets opened fire briskly; then we could see the Confederate earthworks, about six hundred yards ahead of us—could just see them and no more. They were apparently deserted, not a man was to be seen behind them; but it was still faint gray light. One of our gunners looked over his piece and said that he could see the sights, but that they blurred. We filled our sponge buckets with water and waited, the Confederate pickets firing briskly at us the while, but doing no damage. Suddenly the Confederate works were manned. We could see a line of slouch hats above the parapet. Smoke in great puffs burst forth from their line, and shell began to howl by us. Their gunners were getting the range. We sprung in and out from the three-inch guns and replied angrily. To our left, to our right, other batteries opened; and along the Confederate line cannon sent forth their balls searching for the range. Then their guns were silent. It was daylight. We, the light-artillery men, were heated with battle. The strain on our nerves was over. In our front were two lines of blue-coated infantry. One well in advance of the other, and both lying down. We were firing over them. The Confederate pickets sprang out of their rifle pits and ran back to their main line of works. Then they turned and warmed the battery with long-range rifle practice, knocking a man over here, killing another there, breaking the leg of a horse yonder, and generally behaving in an exasperating manner. The Confederate infantry was always much more effective than their artillery, and the battery that got under the fire of their cool infantry always suffered severely. The air began to grow hazy with powder smoke. We saw that the line of slouch-hatted heads had disappeared from the Confederate earthworks, leaving heads exposed only at long intervals. Out of the powder smoke came an officer from the battle-lines of infantry. He told us to stop firing, as the soldiers were about to charge. He disappeared to carry the message to other batteries. Our cannon became silent. The smoke drifted off of the field. I noticed that the sun was not yet up. Suddenly the foremost line of our troops, which were lying on the ground in front of us, sprang to their feet and dashed at the Confederate earthworks at a run. Instantly those works were manned. Cannon belched forth a torrent of canister, the works glowed brightly with musketry, a storm of lead and iron struck the blue line cutting gaps in it. Still they pushed on, and on, and on. But, how many of them fell! They drew near the earthworks, firing as they went, and then, with a cheer, the first line of the Red Division of the Second Corps (Barlow's) swept over it. And there in our front lay, sat, and stood the second line, the supports; why did not they go forward and make good the victory? They did not. Intensely excited, I watched the portion of the Confederate line which our men had captured. I was faintly conscious of terrific firing to our right and of heavy and continuous cheering on that portion of our line which was held by the Fifth and Sixth Corps. For once the several corps had delivered a simultaneous assault, and I knew that it was to be now or never. The powder smoke curled lowly in thin clouds above the captured works. Then the firing became more and more thunderous. The tops of many battle-flags could be seen indistinctly, and then there was a heavy and fierce yell, and the thrilling battle-cry of the Confederate infantry floated to us. "Can our men withstand the charge?" I asked myself. Quickly I was answered. They came into sight clambering over the parapet of the captured works. All organization was lost. They fled wildly for the protection of their second line and the Union guns, and they were shot by scores as they ran. The Confederate infantry appeared behind their works and nimbly climbed over, as though intent on following up their success, and their fire was as the fury of hell. We manned the guns and drove them to cover by bursting shell. How they yelled! How they swung their hats! And how quickly their pickets ran forward to their rifle pits and sank out of sight! The swift, brave assault had been bravely met and most bloodily repulsed. Twenty minutes had not passed since the infantry had sprung to their feet, and ten thousand of our men lay dead or wounded on the ground. The men of the Seventh New York Heavy Artillery came back without their colonel. The regiment lost heavily in enlisted men and line officers. Men from many commands sought shelter behind the crest of the hill we were behind. They seemed to be dazed and utterly discouraged. They told of the strength of the Confederate earthworks, and asserted that behind the line we could see was another and stronger line, and all the enlisted men insisted that they could not have taken the second line even if their supports had followed them. These battle-dazed visitors drifted to the rear and to coffee pots. We drew the guns back behind the crest of the hill, and lay down in the sand and waited. I noticed that the sun was now about a half an hour high. Soldiers came to the front from the rear, hunting for their regiments, which had been practically annihilated as offensive engines of war. Occasionally a man fell dead, struck by a stray ball from the picket line. By noon the stragglers were mostly gathered up and had rejoined their regiments, and columns of troops began to move to and fro in our rear in the little valley formed by the alder swamp. A column of infantry marching by fours passed to our right. I watched them, listlessly wondering if they were going to get something to eat, as I was hungry. I saw a puff of smoke between the marchers and myself, heard the report of a bursting shell, and twelve men of that column were knocked to the earth. Their officers shouted, "Close up! close up!" The uninjured men hurriedly closed the gap and marched on. The dead and wounded men lay on the ground, with their rifles scattered among them.

Soon some soldiers came out of the woods and carried the wounded men off, but left the dead where they fell. We buried them that night. Then, as the day wore away, and the troops were well in hand again, I saw staff officers ride along the lines, and then I saw the regimental commanders getting

Cold Harbor: *A Federal charge into Confederate lines*

their men into line. About four o'clock in the afternoon I heard the charging commands given. With many an oath at the military stupidity which would again send good troops to useless slaughter, I sprang to my feet and watched the doomed infantry. Men, whom I knew well, stood rifle in hand not more than thirty feet from me, and I am happy to state that they continued to so stand. Not a man stirred from his place. The army to a man refused to obey the order, presumably from General Grant, to renew the assault. I heard the order given, and I saw it disobeyed. Many of the enlisted men had been up to and over the Confederate works. They had seen their strength, and they knew that they could not be taken by direct assault, and they refused to make a second attempt. That night we began to intrench.

By daylight we had our earthwork finished and were safe. The Seventh New York Heavy Artillery, armed as infantry, were intrenched about eighty yards in front of us. We were on the crest of a ridge; they were below us. Behind us, for supports, were two Delaware regiments, their combined strength being about one hundred and twenty men. Back of us was the alder swamp, where springs of cool water gushed forth. The men in front of us had to go to these springs for water. They would draw lots to see who should run across the dangerous, bullet-swept ground that intervened between our earthworks and theirs. This settled, the victim would hang fifteen or twenty canteens around him; then, crouching low in the rifle-pits, he would give a great jump, and when he struck the ground he was running at the top of his speed for our earthwork. Every Confederate sharpshooter within range fired at him. Some of these thirsty men were shot dead; but generally they ran into the earthwork with a laugh. After filling their canteens, they would sit by our guns and smoke and talk, nerving themselves for the dangerous return. Adjusting their burden of canteens, they would go around the end of our works on a run and rush back over the bullet-swept course, and again every Confederate sharpshooter who saw them would fire at them. Sometimes these water-carriers would come to us in pairs. One day two Albany men leaped into our battery. After filling their canteens, they sat with us and talked of the beautiful city on the Hudson, and finally started together for their rifle-pits. I watched through an embrasure, and saw one fall. Instantly he began to dig a little hollow with his hands in the sandy soil, and instantly the Confederate sharpshooters went to work at him.

The dust flew up on one side of him, and then on the other. The wounded soldier kept scraping his little protective trench in the sand. We called to him. He answered that his leg was broken below the knee by a rifle ball. From the rifle-pits we heard his comrades call to him to take off his burden of canteens, to tie their strings together, and to set them to one side. He did so, and then the thirsty men in the pits drew lots to see who should risk his life for the water. I got keenly interested in this dicing with death, and watched intently. A soldier sprang out of the rifle-pits. Running obliquely, he stooped as he passed the canteens, grasping the strings, turned, and in a flash was safe. Looking through the embrasure, I saw the dust rise in many little puffs around the wounded man, who was still digging his little trench, and, with quickening breath, felt that his minutes were numbered. I noted a conspicuous man, who was marked with a goitre, in the rifle-pits, and recognized him as the comrade of the stricken soldier. He called to his disabled friend, saying that he was coming for him, and that he must rise when he came near and cling to him when he stopped. The hero left the rifle-pits on the run; the wounded man rose up and stood on one foot; the runner clasped him in his arms; the arms of the wounded man twined around his neck, and he was carried into our battery at full speed, and was hurried to the rear and to a hospital. To the honor of the Confederate sharpshooters, be it said, that when they understood what was being done they ceased to shoot.

One day during this protracted Cold Harbor fight, a battery of Cohorn mortars was placed in position in the ravine behind us. The captain of this battery was a tall, handsome, sweet-voiced man. He spent a large portion of his time in our earthworks, watching the fire of his mortars. He would jump on a gun and look over the works, or he would look out through the embrasures. Boy-like, I talked to him. I would have talked to a field-marshal if I had met one. He told me many things relative to mortar practice, and I, in turn, showed him how to get a fair look at the Confederate lines without exposing himself to the fire of the sharpshooters, most of whom we had "marked down." He playfully accused me of being afraid, and insisted that at six hundred yards a sharpshooter could not hit a man. But I had seen too many men killed in our battery to believe that. So he continued to jump on guns and to poke his head into embrasures. One day I went to the spring after water. While walking back I met four men carrying a body in a blanket. "Who is that?" I asked. "The captain of the mortars," was the reply. Stopping, they uncovered his head for me. I saw where the ball had struck him in the eye, and saw the great hole in the back of his head where it had passed out.

The killed and wounded of the first day's fight lay unburied and uncared for between the lines. The stench of the dead men became unbearable, and finally a flag of truce was sent out. There was a cessation of hostilities to bury the dead and to succor the wounded. I went out to the ground in front of our picket line to talk to the Confederate soldiers, and to trade sugar and coffee for tobacco. Every corpse I saw was as black as coal. It was not possible to remove them. They were buried where they fell. Our wounded—I mean those who had fallen on the first day on the ground that lay between the picket lines—were all dead. I saw no live man lying on this ground. The wounded must have suffered horribly before death relieved them, lying there exposed to the blazing southern sun o' days, and being eaten alive by beetles o' nights.

One evening just before sunset I went to the spring to fill some canteens. Having filled them, I loaded my pipe and smoked in silent enjoyment. Looking up, I saw two Confederate infantry soldiers walking slowly down the ravine. They were tall, round-shouldered men. I clasped my knees and stared at them. They walked toward me, then halted, and dropping their musket-butts to the ground, they clasped their hands over the muzzles of their rifles and stared at me as I stared at them. I could not understand what two fully armed Confederate soldiers could be doing within our lines. After gazing at one another in silence for an instant, one of them smiled (I could almost hear the dirt on his face crack, and was agreeably interested in the performance) and inquired kindly, "Howdy?" So I said, still seated and sucking my pipe, "Howdy," as that seemed to be the correct form of salutation in Virginia. Then I asked indifferently what they were doing within our lines. They told me that they had been captured and they were on their way to our rear. That statement struck me as decidedly funny. I did not believe it, and my face expressed my disbelief. They then said that they were lost, that they were afraid to return to the front for fear of being killed, that they were afraid to kept on travelling for fear of running against the Union pickets on the flanks, and that they were out of provisions and were hungry. That last statement appealed strongly to me. I imagined myself prowling between the front and the rear of the Confederate army, with an empty haversack dangling at my side, and nothing to hope for but a Confederate prison, and my heart went out to these men. I opened my haversack and shared my hardtack with them, and then showed them the road which led to our rear.

During the fighting of the fourth day, which was not severe, a headquarters' orderly rode into the battery and delivered an order to our captain. He read it, and then calling me to him, handed me the order to read. With military brevity it commanded him to send Private Frank Wilkeson to army head-quarters at once to report to Adjutant-General Seth Williams. My heart sank. I had been doing a lot of things which I should not have done, and now I was in for it. The captain said: "Wash up and accompany the orderly. Get a horse from the chief of caissons and return promptly."

I ignored the first portion of the order, but secured the horse and rode off, pants in boots, slouch-hatted, flannel-shirted, blouseless, a strap around my waist and supremely dirty. I was tortured with the belief that I was to be punished. A certain sheep, which I had met in a field near Bowling Green, weighed heavily on me. A large bunch of haversacks, which I had found o'nights, dangled before me. I ransacked my memory and dragged forth all my military misdeeds and breaches of discipline and laid them one after the other on my saddle-bow and thoughtfully turned them over and over and looked at them, regretfully at first, then desperately and recklessly. I knew that I ought to be court-martialed and that I deserved to be shot.

I rode into a village of tents, one of which was pointed out to me as General Williams'. Sentinels paced to and fro; nice, clean men they were too. I dismounted, hitched my horse, and walked to Williams' tent. I was halted, sent in my name, and was admitted. I strode in defiant, hat on head, expecting to be abused, and resolved to take a hand in the abuse business myself.

I saw a handsome, kind-faced, middle-aged officer standing before me. He smiled kindly, and inquired, as he extended his hand to me, "Have I the pleasure of addressing Lieutenant Frank Wilkeson?" My hat came off instantly; my heart went out to Seth Williams, and I replied: "No, General; I am Private Frank Wilkeson." He smiled again

and looked curiously at me. How I did wish I had washed
my face and brushed the dirt off of my clothes. He bade me
to be seated, and skilfully set me to talking. He asked me
many questions, and I answered as intelligently as I could.
Growing confidential, I told him that I had been dreadfully
frightened by being summoned to head-quarters, and confessed the matter of the sheep and the haversacks, and my
misconception of his duties. He tried to look severely grave,
but laughed instead, and said pleasantly: "You are not to be
shot. The crimes you have committed hardly deserve that
punishment. I have called you to me to say that Secretary of
War Stanton has ordered your discharge, and that you are to
be appointed a second lieutenant in the Fourth Regiment of
United States Artillery. When you want your discharge,
claim it from your captain. He has the order to discharge
you. When you get it, come to me if you need money to
travel on, and I will lend you sufficient to take you to Washington and to buy you some clothing. When you arrive there,
report to the Secretary of War, and he will tell you what to
do."

Kind Seth Williams! So gracious, and sweet, and sympa-
thetic was he to me, a dirty private, that my eyes filled with
tears, and I could not talk, could not thank him. I returned
to my battery and resumed work on my gun. I thought that
the Army of the Potomac might win the next battle, and end
the war. If it did, I preferred to be a private in a volunteer
battery which was serving at the front, rather than to be a
lieutenant in the United States Artillery, stationed at Camp
Barry, near Washington.

One night, of these six Cold Harbor nights, I was on
guard in the battery. I walked up and down behind the
guns. Voices whispering outside of our work startled me.
Then I heard men scrambling up the face of the earthwork.
In the indistinct light I made out four. They were carrying
something. They stood above me on the parapet, and in
reply to my challenge poked fun at me. They said they loved
me, and had brought me a present. They threw down to me
a dead man, and with a light laugh went off. I called to them
to come back—insisted that they should carry their corpse
and bury it, but they stood off in the darkness and laughed
at me, and insisted that they had made me a present of him.
"You can have him; the battery can have him," and disappeared, leaving the dead man with me.

I was young, and therefore soft; and the lack of good food

and loss of sleep told hard on me. Indeed, I got utterly used up. So one afternoon of this battle that lasted nearly a week, when but little was going on, I said to my sergeant: "I am exhausted, and want a night's sleep. I will dig a trench back here. If possible, let me sleep to-night, or I will be on the sick-list." He promised to let me sleep unless something urgent happened in the night. I ate my supper, wrapped my blanket around me, and lay down in my trench. The guns roared about me, the bullets whistled over me; but, overcome with exhaustion, I fell into a deep sleep. I was awakened with a strong grip on my shoulders, was lifted up and violently shaken, and the earnest voice of the gunner told me to run to my gun. "They have got an enfilading fire on us," the sergeant cried to me. Dazed, half awake, stupid from the deep sleep and coming sickness, I sat on the brink of my trench and wondered where I was. I heard, "Ho, Frank! Yah! No. 1!" sharply screamed. I heard the shot crash into our horses. Still not awake, I started for my gun. I saw the blaze of the fuses of the shells as they whizzed by. I saw countless fireflies; and, in my exhausted, half-awake condition, I confounded the shells and fireflies together, and thought they were all shells. The shock to me, in my weak, nervous condition, when I saw, as I thought, the air actually stiff with shells, required all my pride to stand up under. It woke me up and left me with a fit of trembling that required ten minutes warm work at the guns to get rid of. The enfilading fire did not amount to much, and I soon returned to my trench and deep sleep.

One day four men carrying a pale infantryman stopped for an instant in my battery. The wounded man suffered intensely from a wound through the foot. My sympathy was excited for the young fellow, and as we at the moment were doing nothing, I asked for half an hour's leave. Getting it, I accompanied him back into the woods to one of the Second Corps' field hospitals. Here groaning loudly, he awaited his turn, which soon came. We lifted him on the rude table. A surgeon held chloroform to his nostrils, and under its influence he lay as if in death. The boot was removed, then the stocking, and I saw a great ragged hole on the sole of the foot where the ball came out. Then I heard the coatless surgeon who was making the examination cry out, "The cowardly whelp!" So I edged around and looked over the shoulders of an assistant surgeon, and saw that the small wound on the top of the foot, where the ball entered, was blackened with powder! I too, muttered "The coward" and was really pleased to see the knife and saw put to work and the craven's leg taken off below the knee. He was carried into the shade of a tree, and left there to wake up. I watched the skilful surgeons probe and carve other patients. The little pile of legs and arms grew steadily, while I waited for the object of my misplaced sympathy to recover his senses. With a long breath he opened his eyes. I was with him at once, and looked sharply at him. I will never forget the look of horror that fastened on his face when he found his leg was off. Utter hopelessness and fear that look expressed. I entered into conversation with him; and he, weakened and unnerved by the loss of the leg, and the chloroform, for once told the truth. Lying on his back, he aimed at his great toe, meaning to shoot it off, but being rudely joggled by a comrade at the critical instant, his rifle covered his foot just below the ankle, and an ounce ball went crashing through the bones and sinews. The wound, instead of being a furlough, was a discharge from the army, probably into eternity. Our guns at the front began to howl at the Confederates again, and I was forced to leave the hospital. So I hastened back to my guns. The utter contempt of the surgeons, their change from careful handling to almost brutality, when they discovered the wound was self-inflicted, was bracing to me. I liked it, and rammed home the ammunition in gun No. 1 with vim.

Constantly losing men in our earthwork, shot not in fair fight, but by sharpshooters, we all began to loathe the place. At last one afternoon the captain ordered us to level the corn-hills between the battery and the road, so that we could withdraw the guns without making a noise. At once understanding that a flank movement was at hand, we joyfully gathered up shovels and spades, and went at the obstructions with a will. No. 3 of No. 1 gun, an Albany man, was at my side. I was bent over shoveling. I straightened myself up. He leaned over to sink his shovel, pitched forward in a heap, dead, and an artilleryman beyond him clasped his stomach and howled a death howl. No. 3 was shot from temple to temple. The ball passed through his head and hit the other man in the stomach, fatally wounding him. They were the last men our battery lost at Cold Harbor.

That evening the horses were brought up, and all the guns but mine, No. 1, were taken off. We sat and watched them disappear in the darkness. Soon heavy columns of infantry could be indistinctly seen marching by the alder swamp in our rear. Then all was quiet, excepting the firing of the pickets. We sat and waited for the expected advance of the Confederates; but they did not come. Towards midnight an officer rode into the earthwork and asked lowly who was in command. The sergeant stepped forward and received his orders. Turning to us he whispered, "Limber to the rear." Silently the horses swung around. The gun was limbered, and, with the caisson in the lead, we pulled out of the earthwork, slowly drove across the cornfield, struck into a dusty road in the forest, and marched for the James River and the bloody disasters that awaited us beyond that beautiful stream.

SIDE-SLIPPING TO THE JAMES

THE TWO-DAY BATTLE IN THE WILDERNESS had cost the Army of the Potomac 17,600 casualties, and General Lee's Army of Northern Virginia still barred the road to Richmond. But Grant, breaking a dismal eastern tradition, gave the order to advance rather than retreat. He marched his troops around Lee's right flank, heading for the crossroads at Spotsylvania. He hoped to get there before Lee, thus placing himself between Lee and Richmond. But the Confederates reached Spotsylvania first—they had the shorter interior line of march—and here, as we saw in Wilkeson's selection, a second furious battle was fought.

Catton says, "The fight that started at Spotsylvania lasted for ten uninterrupted days, and it was even worse than the Wilderness fight had been. It was like the Wilderness . . . in that so much of the ground was heavily wooded and the troops had to fight blindly, nobody from commanding general down to private ever being quite sure just where everybody was and what was going on. As the fight developed, Grant's army kept on edging around to the left, trying vainly to get around the Confederate capital. It never quite made it, but in the ten days the two armies swung completely around three quarters of a circle, and on May 12 they had what may have been the most vicious fight of the whole war—a headlong contest for a horseshoe-shaped arc of Confederate trench guarding the principal road crossing, with hand-to-hand fighting that lasted from dawn to dusk, in a pelting rain, over a stretch of breastworks known forever after as the Bloody Angle."*

The losses continued to be huge. But as General Grant says, "During three long years the armies of the Potomac and Northern Virginia had been confronting each other. . . . They had fought more desperate battles than it probably

* Bruce Catton, *This Hallowed Ground*, pp. 326, 327.

ever before fell to the lot of two armies to fight, without materially changing the vantage-ground of either. The Southern press and people, with more shrewdness than was displayed in the North, finding that they had failed to capture Washington and march on to New York, as they had boasted they would do, assumed that they only defended their capital and Southern territory. Hence, Antietam, Gettysburg, and all the other battles that had been fought were by them set down as failures on our part and victories for them. Their army believed this. It produced a morale which could only be overcome by desperate and continuous hard fighting. The battles of the Wilderness, Spotsylvania, North Anna, and Cold Harbor, bloody and terrible as they were on our side, were even more damaging to the enemy, and so crippled him as to make him wary ever after of taking the offensive. His losses in men were probably not so great, owing to the fact that we were, save in the Wilderness almost invariably the attacking party; and when he did attack, it was in the open field."*

Confederate General Law says, "So far as the Confederates were concerned, it would be idle to deny that they (as well as General Lee himself) were disappointed at the result of their efforts in the Wilderness on the 5th and 6th of May, and that General Grant's constant 'hammering' with his largely superior force had, to a certain extent, a depressing effect upon both officers and men. 'It's no use killing these fellows; a half-dozen take the place of every one we kill,' was a common remark in our army. We knew that our resources of men were exhausted, and that the vastly greater resources of the Federal Government, if brought fully to bear even in this costly kind of warfare, must wear us out in the end."†

The story of the fight for Richmond continues from the Confederate side.

* *Battles and Leaders,* IV, 149.
† *Ibid.,* pp. 143–44.

Falling Back to Richmond‡

BY MAJOR ROBERT STILES

THE 10TH OF MAY, '64, was preeminently a day of battle
with the Army of Northern Virginia. I know of course, that
the 12th is commonly regarded as the pivotal day, the great
day, and the Bloody Angle as the pivotal place, the great
place, of the Spotsylvania fights, and that for an hour or so,
along the sides and base of that angle, the musketry fire is
said to have been heavier than it ever was at any other place
in all the world, or for any other hour in all the tide of time.
But for frequency and pertinacity of attack, and repetition
and constancy of repulse, I question if the left of General
Lee's line on the 10th of May, 1864, has ever been surpassed.
I cannot pretend to identify the separate attacks or to distinguish between them, but should think there must have
been at least a dozen of them. One marked feature was that,
while fresh troops poured to almost every charge, the same
muskets in the hands of the same men met the first attack
in the morning and the last at night; and so it was that the
men who in the early morning were so full of fight and fun
that they leaped upon the breastworks and shouted to the
retiring Federals to come a little closer the next time, as they
did not care to go so far after the clothes and shoes and
muskets—were so weary and worn and heavy at night that
they could scarcely be roused to meet the charging enemy.

The troops supporting the two Napoleon guns of the
Howitzers were, as I remember, the Seventh (or Eighth)
Georgia and the First Texas. Toward the close of the day
everything seemed to have quieted down, in a sort of
implied truce. There was absolutely no fire, either of musketry or cannon. Our weary, hungry infantry stacked arms and
were cooking their mean and meagre little rations. Some one
rose up, and looking over the works—it was shading down a
little toward the dark—cried out: "Hello! What's this? Why,
here come our men on a run, from—no, by Heavens! it's the
Yankees!" and before any one could realize the situation, or

‡ From *Four Years Under Marse Robert.*

even start toward the stacked muskets, the Federal column broke over the little work, between our troops and their arms, bayonetted or shot two or three who were asleep before they could even awake, and dashed upon the men crouched over their low fires—with cooking utensils instead of weapons in their hands. Of course they ran. What else could they do?

The Howitzers—only the left, or Napoleon section, was there—sprang to their guns, swinging them around to bear inside our lines, double-shotted them with canister and fairly spouted it into the Federals, whose formation had been broken in the rush and the plunge over the works, and who seemed to be somewhat massed and huddled and hesitating, but only a few rods away. Quicker almost than I can tell it, our infantry supports, than whom there were not two better regiments in the army, had rallied and gotten to their arms, and then they opened out into a V-shape, and fairly tore the head of the Federal column to pieces. In an incredibly short time those who were able to do so turned to fly and our infantry were following them over the intrenchments; but it is doubtful whether this would have been the result had it not been for the prompt and gallant action of the artillery.

There was an old Captain Hunter—it seems difficult to determine whether of the Texas or the Georgia regiment—who had the handle of his frying pan in his hand, holding the pan over the hot coals, with his little slice of meat sizzling in it, when the enemy broke over. He had his back to them, and the first thing he knew his men were scampering past him like frightened sheep. He had not been accustomed to that style of movement among them, and he sprang up and tore after them, showering them with hot grease and hotter profanity, but never letting go his frying pan. On the contrary, he slapped right and left with the sooty, burning bottom, distributing his favors impartially on Federal and Confederate alike—several of his own men bearing the black and ugly brand on their cheeks for a long time after and occasionally having to bear also the captain's curses for having made him lose his meat that evening. He actually led the counter-charge, leaping upon the works, wielding and waving his frying pan, at once as sword and banner.

It is an interesting coincidence that on this very day, the 10th of May, '64, at the point christened two days later as "The Bloody Angle," the Second Howitzers rendered a service even more important and distinguished perhaps than the gallant conduct of the First Company just recorded; a service which, in the opinion of prominent officers thoroughly acquainted with the facts and every way competent and qualified to judge, was deemed to have saved General Lee's army from being cut in twain.

There is one other feature or incident of the closing fight of the 10th of May which may be worthy of record, not alone because of its essentially amusing nature, but also because of a very pleasant after-clap or reminder of it later on. There were two men in the First Howitzers, older than most of us, of exceptionally high character and courage, who, because of the deafness of the one and the lack of a certain physical flexibility and adaptation in the other, were not well fitted for regular places in the detachment or service about the gun. For a time one or both of them took the position of driver, but this scarcely seemed fitting, and finally they were both classed as "supernumeraries," but with special duties as our company ambulance corps, having charge, under the surgeon of the battalion, of our company litters and our other simple medical and surgical outfit. For this and other reasons, the elder of these two good and gritty soldiers was always called "Doctor."

When the break occurred these two men, always on the extremest forward verge of our battle line, were overwhelmed with amazment, not so much at the irruption of the enemy, as at what seemed to be the demoralized rout of the Georgians and Texans. They ran in among them asking explanation of their conduct, then appealing to them and exhorting them—the Doctor in most courteous and lofty phrase: "Gentlemen, what does this mean? You certainly are not flying before the enemy! Turn, for God's sake; turn, and drive them out!" Then, with indignant outburst: "Halt! you infernal cowards!" and suiting the action to the word, these choleric cannoneers tore the carrying poles out of their litters, and sprang among and in front of the fugitives, belaboring them right and left, till they turned, and then turned with them, following up the retreating enemy with their wooden spears.

Some weeks later, after we had reached Petersburg, in the nick of time to keep Burnside out of the town, and had taken up what promised to be a permanent position and were just dozing off into our first nap in forty-eight hours, an infantry command passing by, in the darkness, stumbled over the trail handspikes of our guns and broke out in the usual style:

"Oh, of course! Here's that infernal artillery again; always in the way, blocking the roads by day and tripping us up at night. What battery is this, any way?"

Some fellow, not yet clean gone in slumber, grunted out:

"First Company, Richmond Howitzers."

What a change! Instantly there was a perfect chorus of greetings from the warm-hearted Texans.

"Boys, here are the Howitzers! Where's your old deaf man? Trot out your old Doctor. They're the jockeys for us. We are going to stay right here. We won't get a chance to run if these plucky Howitzer boys are with us."

Billy tells me that he remembers, word for word, the last crisp sentence Colonel Stephen D. Lee uttered the morning he complimented the old battery on the field of Frazier's Farm; that he said, "Men, hereafter when I want a battery, I'll know where to get one!" Two years later, at the base of the Bloody Angle, General Ewell seems to have been of the same opinion. We held our centre, which had just been pierced and smashed and his artillery captured. He wanted guns to stay the rout and steady his men, and he sent to the extreme left for Cabell's Battalion. I do not mean that the old battalion, or either of its batteries, was counted among the most brilliant artillery commands of the army, but I do claim that the command did have and did deserve the reputation of "staying where it was put," and of doing its work reliably and well.

The 11th had been a sort of off-day with us, very little business doing; but the 12th made up for it. As I remember, it was yet early on the morning of the 12th that we were sent for. We went at once, and did not stand upon the order of our going, though I think two guns of the Howitzers led the column, followed by two guns of Carlton's battery, the Troupe Artillery. If I remember correctly, our other guns occupied positions on the line from which they could not be withdrawn. As Colonel Cabell and I rode ahead, as before mentioned in another connection, to learn precisely where the guns were to be placed, we passed General Lee on horseback, or he passed us. He had only one or two attendants with him. His face was more serious than I had ever seen it, but showed no trace of excitement or alarm. Numbers of demoralized men were streaming past him and his voice was deep as the growl of a tempest as he said: "Shame on you, men; shame on you! Go back to your regiments; go back to your regiments!"

I remember thinking at the moment that it was the only time I ever knew his faintest wish not to be instantly responded to by his troops; but something I have since read induces me to question whether he did not refer to some special rendezvous, somewhere in the rear, appointed for the remnants of the shattered commands to rally to. Be this as it may, every soldier of experience knows that when a man has reached a certain point of demoralization and until he has settled down again past that point, it is absolutely useless to attempt to rouse him to a sense of duty or of honor. I have seen many a man substantially in the condition of the fellow who, as he executed a flying leap over the musket of the guard threatening to shoot and crying "Halt!"—called back, "Give any man fifty dollars to halt me, but can't halt myself!"

When we came back to our four guns and were leading them to the lines and the positions selected for them, just as we were turning down a little declivity, we passed again within a few feet of General Lee, seated upon his horse on the crest of the hill, this time entirely alone, not even a courier with him. I was much impressed with the calmness and perfect poise of his bearing, though his centre had just been pierced by forty thousand men and the fate of his army trembled in the balance. He was completely exposed to the Federal fire, which was very heavy. A half dozen of our men were wounded in making this short descent. In this connection I have recently heard from a courier—who, with others, had ridden with the General to the point where we saw him that, observing and remarking upon the peril to which they were subjected, he ordered all his couriers to protect themselves behind an old brick kiln, some one hundred and fifty yards to the left, until their services were required, but refused to go there himself. This habit of exposing himself to fire, as they sometimes thought, unnecessarily, was the only point in which his soldiers felt that Lee ever did wrong. The superb stories of the several occasions during this campaign when his men refused to advance until he retired, and, with tears streaming down their faces, led his horse to the rear, are too familiar to justify repetition, especially as I did not happen to be an eye-witness of either of these impressive scenes.

Our guns were put in at the left base of the Salient, and there, in full sight and but a short distance up the side of the angle, stood two or three of the guns from which our men had been driven, or at which they had been captured. The Howitzers had two clumsy iron three-inch rifles, and Captain McCarthy and I offered, with volunteers from that company, to draw these captured guns back into our lines, provided we were allowed to exchange our two iron guns for two of these, which were brass Napoleons. This would have given the battery a uniform armament and prevented the frequent separation of the sections. There was not at the time a Federal soldier in sight, and some of us walked out to or near these guns without being fired upon. It might have been a perilous undertaking, yet I think General Ewell would have given his consent; but the officer to whose command the guns belonged protested, saying he would himself have them drawn off later in the day. If it ever could have been done, the opportunity was brief; later it became impracticable, and the guns were permanently lost.

Barrett, Colonel Cabell's plucky little courier, rode almost into the works with us, and we had left our horses with him, close up, but in a position which we thought afforded some protection. In a few moments some one shouted that Barrett was calling lustily for me. I ran back where I had left him and was distressed to see my good horse, Mickey, stretched on the ground. Barrett said he had just been killed by a piece of shell which struck him in the head. The poor fellow's limbs were still quivering. I could see no wound of any consequence about the head or anywhere else; while I was examining him he shuddered violently, sprang up, snorted a little blood and was again "as good as new." As soon as practicable, however, we sent Barrett and the three horses behind that brick kiln back on the hill, or to some place near by of comparative safety. I was afraid that Mickey, who seemed to have "gotten his hand in," might keep up this trick of getting "killed," as Barrett said, once too often. I may as well say right here that the noble horse got safely through the war, but was captured with his master at Sailor's Creek.

When our guns first entered the works, or rather were stationed on the line just back of the little trench, there seemed to be comparatively few infantrymen about. One thing that pleased us greatly was, that our old Mississippi brigade, Barksdale's, or Humphreys', was supporting us; but it must have been just the end of their brigade line, and a very thin line it was. We saw nothing of the major-general of our division. General Rodes, of Ewell's corps, was the only major-general we saw. He was a man of very striking appearance, of erect, fine figure and martial bearing. He constantly passed and repassed in rear of our guns, riding a black horse that champed his bit and tossed his head proudly, until his neck and shoulders were flecked with white froth, seeming to be conscious that he carried Cæsar. Rodes' eyes were everywhere, and every now and then he would stop to attend to some detail of the arrangement of his line or his troops, and then ride on again, humming to himself and catching the ends of his long, tawny moustache between his lips.

It had rained hard all night and was drizzling all day, and everything was wet, soggy, muddy, and comfortless. General Ewell made his headquarters not far off, and seemed busy and apprehensive, and we gathered from everything we saw and heard, especially from General Lee's taking his position so near, that he and his generals anticipated a renewal of the attack at or about this point. From the time of our first approach, stragglers from various commands had been streaming past. I noticed that most of them had their arms and did not seem to be very badly shattered, and I tried hard to induce some of them to turn in and reinforce our thin infantry line. But they would not hearken to the voice of the charmer, charming never so wisely, and finally I appealed to General Rodes and asked him for a detail of men to throw off a short line at right angles to the works so as to catch and turn in these stragglers. He readily assented, and we soon had a strong, full line, though at first neither Rodes' own men nor our Mississippians seemed to appreciate this style of reinforcement.

One point more, with regard to our experience at the left base of the Salient, and we have done with the "Bloody Angle." Every soldier who was there, if he opens his mouth to speak or takes up his pen to write, seems to feel it solemnly incumbent upon him to expatiate upon the fearful fire of musketry. What I have to say about the matter will doubtless prove surprising and disappointing to many; but first let me quote Colonel Taylor's account of it . . . so frequently referred to:

> The army was thus cut in twain, and the situation was well calculated to test the skill of its commander and the nerve and courage of the men. Dispositions were im-

mediately made to repair the breach, and troops were moved up to the right and left to dispute the further progress of the assaulting column. Then occurred the most remarkable musketry fire of the war—from the sides of the Salient, in the possession of the Federals, and the new line forming the base of the triangle, occupied by the Confederates, poured forth from continuous lines of hissing fire an incessant, terrific hail of deadly missiles. No living man nor thing could stand in the doomed space embraced within those angry lines; even large trees were felled, their trunks cut in twain by the bullets of small arms.

Every intelligent soldier, on either side, is aware of Colonel Taylor's deserved reputation for careful and unprejudiced observation and investigation, and for correct and accurate statement. General Fitz Lee, in his "Life of General Robert E. Lee," at p. 335, fully agrees with Colonel Taylor, saying: "The musketry fire, with its terrific leaden hail, was beyond comparison the heaviest of the four years of war. In the bitter struggle, trees, large and small, fell, cut down by bullets."

Still, I am bound to say I saw nothing that approached a justification of these vivid and powerful descriptions. Of course the fire was at times heavy, but at no time, *in front of our position,* did it approximate, for example, the intensity of the fire during the great attack at Cold Harbor, a few weeks later. One singular feature of the matter is that we appear to have been at the very place where this fire is said to have occurred, and at the very time; for we were sent for by General Ewell, as I recollect, early on the morning of the 12th, and we remained at the left base of the Salient and within sight of some of the captured guns all that day and until the line was moved back out of the bottom, to the crest of the little ridge above mentioned. The only explanation I can suggest is that the fighting must have been much hotter *further to the right.*

It may be well just here to explain, while we cannot excuse, the existence not alone of the great Salient of Spotsylvania, with its soldier nickname of "Bloody Angle," and its fearful lesson of calamity, but also of other like faulty formations in our Confederate battle lines.

It was noticeable toward the close of the war what skilful, practical engineers the rank and file of the Army of Northern

Virginia had become; how quickly and unerringly they detected and how unsparingly they condemned an untenable line—that is, where they were unprejudiced critics, as for instance, where fresh troops were brought in to reinforce or relieve a command already in position. I seem to hear, even now, their slashing, impudent, outspoken comment:

"Boys, what infernal fool do you reckon laid out this line? Why, any one can see we can't hold it. We are certain to be infiladed on this flank, and the Yankees can even take us in reverse over yonder. Let's fall back to that ridge we just passed!"

But where troops had themselves originally taken position, it was a very different matter. This was one point where Johnny was disposed to be unreasonable and insubordinate—not to consider consequences or to obey orders. He did not like to fall back from any position he had himself established by hard fighting, especially if it was in advance of the general line. So well recognized was his attitude in this regard that it had well nigh passed into a proverb:

"No, sir! *We fought for this dirt, and we're going to hold it.* The men on our right and left ought to be here alongside of us, and would be if they had fought as hard as we did!"

Of course, Johnny would not violate or forget the fundamental maxim of geometry and war, that *a line must be continuous;* that his right must be somebody's left and his left somebody's right; but the furthest he would go in recognition of the maxim was the compromise of bending back his flanks, so as to connect with the troops on his right and left who had failed to keep up. So this was done, he did not seem to care how irregular the general line of battle was. One cannot look at a map of any of our great battles without being impressed with the tortuous character of our lines.

I have myself heard a major-general send a message back to Army Headquarters, by a staff officer of General Lee, that he didn't see why his division should be expected to abandon the position they had fought for just to accommodate General———, whose troops had fallen back where his had driven the enemy. On that very occasion, if my memory serves me, this selfish, stupid obstinacy cost us the lives of hundreds of men.

One word more in connection with the straightening of our lines. Of course we moved after dark, and, as I remember, but a short distance. After we got to our new position I discovered that I had lost my pocketknife, or some such trivial article of personal outfit, but difficult to replace; so, contrary to Colonel Cabell's advice—he didn't forbid my going—I went back, on foot and in the dark, to look or feel for it. I had no difficulty in finding the spot where we had been lying, and began to grope and feel about for the knife, having at the time an unpleasant consciousness that I was running a very foolish and unjustifiable risk, for the Minies were hissing and singing and spatting all about me.

There was a man near me, also on his hands and knees, looking or feeling for something. While glancing at the shape, dimly outlined, I heard the unmistakable thud of a bullet striking flesh. There was a muffled outcry, and the crouching or kneeling figure lay stretched upon the ground. I went to it and felt it. The man was dead.

In a very brief time I was back in our new position and not thinking of pocket-knives.

After feeling our lines, feinting several times, and making, on the 18th, what might perhaps he termed a genuine attack, Grant, on the evening of the 20th, slid off toward Bowling Green; but although he got a little the start of Lee, yet, when he reached his immediate objective, Lee was in line of battle at Hanover Junction, directly across the line of further progress. It is the belief of many intelligent Confederate officers that if Lee had not been attacked by disabling disease, the movements of the two armies about the North Anna would have had a very different termination. Grant ran great risk in taking his army to the southern bank of the river with Lee on the stream between his two wings; it is fair to add that he seems to have realized his peril and to have withdrawn in good time,

General Lee's indisposition about this time, was really serious. Some of us will never forget how shocked and alarmed we were at seeing him in an ambulance. General Early says of this matter:

One of his three corps commanders had been disabled by wounds at the Wilderness, and another was too sick to command his corps, while he himself was suffering from a most annoying and weakening disease. In fact nothing but his own determined will enabled him to keep the field at all; and it was there rendered more manifest than ever that he was the head and front, the very life and soul of his army.

It was about this date that General Lee, as I remember a second time, broached the idea that he might be compelled to retire—an idea which no one else could contemplate with any sort of composure; happily, as soon as the disease was checked his superb physical powers came to his aid, and he soon rallied and regained his customary vigor and spirits.

Perhaps no other position of equal labor and responsibility can be mentioned, nor one which makes such drafts upon human strength and endurance, as the command of a great army in a time of active service. I recall during the force of this general proposition, and with the almost incredible physical powers of General Lee. On two occasions, just before and just after we recrossed the Potomac, I was sent upon an errand which required my visiting army, corps, and division headquarters, and, so far as practicable, seeing the respective commanding officers in person. On the first round I did not find General Lee at his quarters, and was told that he had ridden down the road to the lines. When I reached the lines I heard he had passed out in front. Following him up, I found him in the rain with a single piece of horse artillery, feeling the enemy. My second ride was made largely at night, and, as I remember, every officer I desired to see was asleep, except at Army Headquarters, where I found Colonel Taylor in his tent on his knees, with his prayer-book open before him, and General Lee in his tent, wide-awake, poring over a map stretched upon a temporary table of rough plank, with a tallow candle stuck in a bottle for a light. I remember saying to myself, as I delivered my message and withdrew, "Does he never, never sleep?"

Again General Grant slid to the east, and we moved off upon a parallel line. I think it was during this detour—or it may have been an earlier or a later one—that I was sent ahead, upon a road which led through a tract of country which had not been desolated by the encampments or the battles of armies, to select a night's resting place for the battalion. Forests were standing untouched, farm lands were protected by fences, crops were green and untrampled, birds were singing, flowers blooming—Eden everywhere. Even my horse seemed to feel the change from the crowded roads, the deadly lines, the dust, the dirt, the mud, the blood, the horror. We were passing through a quiet wood at a brisk walk, when suddenly he roused himself and quickened his gait, breaking of his own accord into a long trot, his beautiful, sensitive ears playing back and forth in the unmistakable way which, in a fine horse, indicates that he catches sounds interesting and agreeable to him. It was, perhaps, several hundred yards before we swung around out of the forest into the open land where stood a comfortable farm house, and there in a sweet and sunny corner were several chubby little children chatting and singing at their play. Mickey, dear old Mickey, trotted right up to the little people, with low whinnies of recognition and delight, and rubbed his head against them. They did not seem at all afraid, but pulled nice tufts of grass for him, which he ate with evident relish and gratitude.

If I remember correctly, it was the evening of the same day, after Mickey and I had kissed and left the children, and I had found a beautiful camping ground for the battalion—a succession of little swells of land crowned with pine copses and covered with broom-sedge, with a clear, cool stream flowing between the hills and after the batteries were all up and located in this soldier paradise—guns parked, horses watered and fed and all work done—I say, I think it was after all this, that the bugles of each of the batteries blew such sweet and happy notes as I never heard from any one of them before, and then, while I was lying on the broom-sedge, bathing my soul in this peace, and Mickey was browsing near-by, over across the stream, the Howitzer Glee Club launched out into a song, the first they had sung since we broke camp at Morton's Ford, three weeks before.

As the song ceased and the day was fading into the twilight, I caught, up the road, the low murmur of conversation and the rattle of canteens, and following the sound with my eye, saw two infantrymen, from a command that had followed us and camped further back from the stream, wending their way to water. Just as they came fully within sight and hearing, two of the Howitzer Club struck up "What Are the Wild Waves Saying?"—one of them, in a fine falsetto, taking the sister's part. As the clear, sweet female voice floated out on the still evening air my two infantrymen stood transfixed, one putting his hand upon the other's arm and saying with suppressed excitement, "Stop, man; there's a woman!" They were absolutely silent during the singing of the sister's part, but when the brother took up the song they openly wondered whether she would sing again. "Yes, there she is; listen, listen!"

And so, until the song was done, and they had waited, and it had become evident she would sing no more—and then a deep sigh from both the spell-bound auditors, and one of them, making use of the strongest figure he could command, exclaimed, from the bottom of a full heart, "Well, it beats a furlough hollow!"

We almost began to hope that Grant had gotten enough. Even his apparent, yes, real, success at the Salient did not embolden him to attack again at Spotsylvania. He had retired without any serious fighting at Hanover Junction or North Anna, and after feeling our position about Atlee's, he had once more slipped away from our front. Where was he going? What did he intend to do? Any one of his predecessors would have retired and given it up long ago. Was he about to do so?

The fact is, Grant was waiting for reinforcements. He had been heavily reinforced at Spotsylvania after the 12th of May, but not up to the measure of his desires, or of his needs, either; for he really needed more men—and more, and more. He needed them, he asked for them, and he got them. He had a right to all he wanted. His original contract so provided; it covered all necessary drafts. He wanted especially Baldy Smith and his men from the transports, and they were coming. They were stretching out hands to each other. When they clasped hands, then Grant would attack once more; would make his great final effort. When and where would it be?

When Grant slid away from Lee at Atlee's, we felt satisfied that he was, as usual, making for the south and east, so Hoke was ordered toward Cold Harbor, and Kershaw (now our division general, McLaws never having returned from the West) toward Beulah Church. Colonel Cabell received orders on the evening of the 31st of May, or early on the morning of the 1st of June, to make for the latter point; but he was not upon the same road as Kershaw's division, and our orders said nothing about joining it. They seemed to contemplate our going by the most direct route, and we went—that is, as far as we could. No infantry apparently had received any orders to go with us, certainly one went, and we soon passed beyond the apparent end of our infantry line, at least on the road we were traveling.

Very soon we reached a stout infantry picket, which I interviewed, and they said there were no Confederate troops down that road, unless perhaps a few cavalry videttes.

I was on very intimate terms with my colonel, and I went to him and suggested whether there was not danger in our proceeding as we were, a battalion of artillery unaccompanied by infantry, out and beyond the last picket post. The colonel was a strict constructionist, and he shut me up at once by saying: "Stiles, that is the responsibility of the general officer who sent me my orders. I am ordered to Beulah Church and to Beulah Church I am going. This is the nearest road." I looked up at him in some little surprise, but said no more; having fired, I now fell back on my reserves, in pretty fair order, but slightly demoralized.

My reserves were the officers and men of the battalion, all of whom I think were fond of me. If I mistake not, Frazier's battery led the column. I am certain it did a little later. Calloway, its commanding officer, to whom we have already been introduced, was one of the very best of soldiers, as the reader will soon be prepared to admit. He was the first man I fell in with as I fell back, Colonel Cabell and little Barrett, his courier, being ahead of the column. Calloway asked me if I didn't think we were running some risk, entirely unsupported as we seemed to be, and outside our lines. I told him what had occurred, and he smiled grimly.

Then I fell back further to the old battery. The column was pretty closed up that morning; everybody seemed to feel it well to be so. I was strongly attached to the old company and particularly to the captain, who was a magnificent fellow. It was early on a beautiful summer morning, and we were again passing through a tract of undesolated, undesecrated country—greenness, quiet, the song of birds, the scent of flowers, all about us. Captain McCarthy was on foot, walking among his men, his great arms frequently around the necks of two of them at once—a position which displayed his martial, manly figure to great advantage. I dismounted, one of the fellows mounting my horse, and walked and talked and chatted with the men, and particularly with the captain.

He was altogether an uncommon person, marked by great simplicity, sincerity, kindliness, courage, good sense, personal force, and a genius for commanding men. He had been rather a reckless, pugnacious boy, difficult to manage, impatient of control. The war had proved a real blessing to him.

It let off the surplus fire and fight. Its deep and powerful un-
dertone was just what was needed to harmonize his nature.
His spirit had really been balanced and gentled and sweet-
ened by it. He was not essentially an intellectual man, nor
yet a man of broad education, and he had under him some of
the most intellectual and cultivated young men I ever met,
yet he was easily their leader and commander; in the matter
of control and for the business in hand, "from his shoulders
and upward, taller than any of the people." And these intellectual and cultivated men freely recognized his su-
premacy and admired and loved him. He seemed to be
somewhat subdued and quiet that morning; even more than
ordinarily affectionate and demonstrative, but not cheerful
or chatty. Several of us noticed his unusual bearing and
speculated as to the cause.

As the morning wore on and we were leaving our infantry
further and further behind, my uneasiness returned; and
besides, I had been away long enough from the colonel, so I
remounted and rode forward to the head of the column. He
had been very emphatic in repelling my suggestions, but I
thought it my duty to renew them, and I did. He was even
more emphatic than before, saying he had been ordered to
take that battalion to Beulah Church, and he proposed to do
it, and he even added that when he wanted any advise from
me he would ask it. I felt a nearer approach to heat than ever
before or after, in all my intercourse with my friend and
commander, and I assured him I would not obtrude my advice again.

I reined in my horse, waiting for Calloway, and rode with
him at the head of his battery. I had scarcely joined him,
when Colonels Fairfax and Latrobe, of Longstreet's staff,
and Captain Simonton, of Pickett's dashed by, splendidly
mounted, and disappeared in a body of woods but a few
hundred yards ahead. Hardly had they done so, when *pop!
pop! pop!* went a half dozen carbines and revolvers; and a
moment later the three officers galloped back out of the
forest, driving before them two or three Federal cavalrymen
on foot—Simonton leaning over his horse's head and striking
at them with his riding whip. On the instant I took my
revenge, riding up to Colonel Cabell, taking off my hat with
a profound bow, and asking whether it was still his intention
to push right on to Beulah Church? Meanwhile, Minié balls
began to drop in on us, evidently fired by sharpshooters from
a house a short distance to our left and front. The Colonel

turned toward me with a smile, and said, in a tone that took all the sting out of his former words, if any was ever intended to be in them: "Yes, you impudent fellow, it is my intention, but let's see how quickly you can drive those sharpshooters out of that house!"

Scarce sooner said than done. I sprang from my horse. Calloway's guns were in battery on the instant, I, by his permission, taking charge of his first piece as gunner. Making a quick estimate of the distance, I shouted back to No. 6 at how many seconds to cut the fuse, and the shell reached the gun almost as soon as I did. A moment—and the gun was loaded, aimed and fired; a moment more and the house burst into flame. The shell from the other three guns were exploded among the retiring skirmishers, who ran back toward the woods; while from the side of the house nearest to us two women came out, one very stout and walking with difficulty, the other bearing a baby in her arms and two little children following her. Calling to the gunner to take charge of his piece, I broke for these women, three or four of the men running with me. There was a fence between us and them and could not have been less than four and a half feet high, which I cleared, "hair and hough," while the rest stopped to climb it. I took the baby and dragged the youngest child along with me, telling the other to come on, and sent the younger woman back to help the elder. When the reinforcements arrived we re-arranged convoys, I still keeping the baby. By the time we reached the battery more of the guns were in action, shelling the woods, and I became interested in the firing. The number fives as they ran by me with the ammunition would stop a moment to pat the baby, who was quite satisfied, and seemed to enjoy the racket, cooing and trying to pull my short hair and beard. This thing had been going on for several minutes, and I had not been conscious of any appeal to me, until one of the men ran up, and, pulling me sharply around, pointed to the two women, who were standing back down the hill, and as far as possible out of the line of the bullets, which were still annoying us. There was a rousing laugh and cheer as I started back to deliver the little infant artilleryman to his mother. It turned out that the elder of the two women was the mother of the other, and had been bedridden for several years. We were exceedingly sorry to have burned their little house, but some of the boys suggested that if the cure of the mother proved permanent, the balance, after all, might be considered rather in our favor.

I do not recall the events of the next few hours with any distinctness, or in any orderly sequence, nor how we got into connection with our division, Kershaw's; but we did so without serious mishap; so, perhaps, Colonel Cabell may have been more nearly right than I after all. The first definite recollection I have, after what I have just related, is of the breaking of Colonel Lawrence M. Keitt's big South Carolina regiment, which had just come to the army and been entered in Kershaw's old brigade, and probably outnumbered all the balance of that command. General Kershaw had put this and another of his brigades into action not far from where we had burned the house to dislodge the skirmishers. Keitt's men gave ground, and in attempting to rally them their colonel fell mortally wounded. Thereupon the regiment went to pieces in abject rout and threatened to overwhelm the rest of the brigade. I have never seen any body of troops in such a condition of utter demoralization; they actually groveled upon the ground and attempted to burrow under each other in holes and depressions. Major Goggin, the stalwart adjutant-general of the division, was attempting to rally them, and I did what I could to help him. It was of no avail. We actually spurred our horses upon them, and seemed to hear their very bones crack, but it did no good; if compelled to wriggle out of one hole they wriggled into another.

So far as I recollect, however, this affair was of no real significance. Our other troops stood firm, and we lost no ground. I think none of the guns of the battery were engaged. Meanwhile the three divisions of our corps—the First, since Longstreet's wounding, under command of Major-General R. H. Anderson—had settled into alignment in the following order, beginning from the left: Field, Pickett, Kershaw. On the right of Kershaw's was Hoke's division, which had been under Beauregard and had joined the Army of Northern Virginia only the night before. The ground upon which our troops had thus felt and fought their way into line was the historic field of Cold Harbor, and the day was the first of June, 1864.

In the afternoon a furious attack was made on the left of Hoke and right of Kershaw; and Clingman's, the left brigade of Hoke, and Wofford's, the right brigade of Kershaw, gave way and the Federal troops poured into the gap over a marshy piece of ground which had not been properly cov-

ered by either of these two brigades. Both Field and Pickett
sent aid to Kershaw, and several of the guns of our battalion
—I am not sure of which batteries, though I think two belonged to the Howitzers, came into battery on the edge of a
peach orchard which sloped down to the break, and poured
in a hot infilade fire on the victorious Federals, who, after a
manly struggle, were driven back, though we did not quite
regain all we had lost, and our lines were left in very bad
shape.

While Wofford was bending back the right of his line to
connect with Hoke, who, even with the aid sent him, had
not quite succeeded in regaining his original position, Kershaw's old brigade, which had more perfectly recovered
from its little contretemps, was pressing and driving the
enemy, both advancing and extending its line upon higher
and better ground, a feat it would never have been able to
accomplish but for the aid of one of Calloway's guns, which,
under command of Lieutenant Robert Falligant, of Savannah, Ga., held and carried the right flank of the brigade,
coming into battery and fighting fiercely whenever the
enemy seemed to be holding the brigade in check, and lim-
bering up and moving forward with it, while it was advancing; and this alternate advancing and firing was kept up until a fresh Federal force came in and opened fire on the right
flank, and all of Falligant's horses fell at the first volley. The
enemy made a gallant rush for the piece, but they did not
get it. It was in battery in a moment, belching fire like a volcano, and very hot shot, too. The brigade, whose flank it had
held, now sprang to its defense, and after a furious little
fight the gun was for the present safe, and every one began
to dig and to pile up dirt.

The brigade did not, however, advance one foot after
Falligant's horses were shot; but it was already considerably
in advance of Wofford's left, with which it was not connected at all, until the entire line was rectified on the night
of the 2d—nor was there at any time a Confederate infantry
soldier to the right of this piece, nor a spadeful of earth, except the lattle traverse we threw up to protect the right of
the gun. It may just as well be added now that this lone gun
held the right of Kershaw's brigade line that evening and
night—it was getting dark when the extreme advanced position was reached—and all the next day, and was moved
back by hand the night of the 2d of June. I have no hesita-
tation in saying that in all my experience as a soldier I never

witnessed more gallant action than this of Lieutenant Falligant and his dauntless cannoneers, nor do I believe that any officer of his rank made a more important contribution than he to the success of the Confederate arms in the great historic battle.

Both sides anticipated battle on the 3rd, as it really occurred. General Grant in his memoirs says in express terms, "The 2d of June was spent in getting troops into position for attack on the 3d"; and the "Official Journal" of our corps says, under date of June 3d, "The expected battle begins early." This journal also notes the weakness of "Kershaw's Salient," and that the enemy was aware of it, and was "massing heavily" in front of it. Three brigades were sent to support Kershaw—Anderson's, Gregg's, and Law's. We also set to work to rectify the lines about this point. General E. M. Law, of Alabama, is probably entitled to the credit of this suggestion, which had so important a bearing upon our success. He laid off the new line with his own hand and superintended the construction of it during the night of the 2d. The record of the 3d might have been a very different one if this change had not been made. Under Colonel Cabell's instructions and with the aid of the division pioneer corps, I opened roads through the woods for the more rapid and convenient transmission of artillery ammunition, and put up two or three little bridges across ravines with the same view.

While I was superintending this work, the fire at the time being lively, I heard some one calling in a most lugubrious voice, "Mister, Mister, won't you please come here!" I glanced in the direction of the cry and saw a man standing behind a large tree in a very peculiar attitude, having the muzzle of his musket under his left shoulder and leaning heavily upon it. Supposing he was wounded, I went to him and asked what he wanted. He pointed to the butt of his gun, under which a large, vigorous, venomous copperhead snake was writhing; and the wretched skulker actually had the face to whine to me, "Won't you please, sir, kill that snake!" I knew not what to say to the creature, and fear what I did say was neither a very Christian nor a very soldierly response; but no one who has not seen a thoroughly demoralized man can form the slightest conception of how repulsive a thing such a wretch is.

The headquarters of General Kershaw at Cold Harbor was close up to the lines and just back of the position of some of our guns. It was but a short distance, too, from where the caissons bringing in ammunition turned to the right, on a road I had cut, running along the slope of a declivity at the crest of which our guns were stationed, some of them before and all of them after the lines were rectified. He might have found a safer place, but none nearer the point of peril and the working point of everything. The position, however, was so exposed that he found himself compelled to protect it, which he did by putting up a heavy wall of logs, back of which the earth was cut away and pitched over against the face, which was toward the lines. His quarters were thus cut deep into the hillside, and had besides, above the surface and toward the enemy, this wall of logs faced with earth. Thus he had a place where he and his officers could safely confer and at a very short distance from their commands; but it was after all a ghastly place, and very difficult and dangerous of approach. All the roads or paths leading to it were not only swept by an almost continuous and heavy fire of musketry, but I had to keep a force of axe-men almost constantly at work cutting away trees felled across the ammunition roads by the artillery fire of the enemy. Colonel Charles S. Venable, reputed to be one of the roughest and most daring riders on General Lee's staff—later, professor of mathematics at the University of Virginia, and chairman of the faculty—told me he believed this headquarter position of Kershaw's at Cold Harbor was the worst place he was ever sent to. Colonel Cabell was necessarily a great part of the time at these headquarters, and I also, when not engaged at some special work, or with some of the guns, or on the way from one to another. At Cold Harbor these journeys had to be made on foot, and necessarily consumed a good deal of time, an artillery battalion frequently covering, say, half a mile of the line.

Up to the night of the 2d of June, when it was moved back, every time Falligant's gun fired while I was at headquarters, General Kershaw would repeat his admiration of his courage, and ask me to explain to him again and again the isolated and exposed position of the piece, and then he would express his determination that Falligant's gallantry and services should receive their merited reward. Once when I happened to be there, a soldier from a South Carolina regiment in Kershaw's old brigade, one of those supporting Falligant's gun, came in, reporting that his part of the line was almost out of ammunition, and asking that some be sent in at once. He may have had a written order,

but at all events he represented that the case was urgent;
that they could not trust to getting it into the line at some
safe point and having it passed along by hand, because it
would take too long, and besides all the troops were scantily
supplied and it would never get to his regiment; and lastly,
because the officer who sent him had ordered him to bring it
himself. The man was intelligent, self-possessed, and determined. I well remember, too, how pale and worn and
powder-begrimed he looked. He confirmed all I had said as
to the position and services of Falligant's gun, and was en-
thusiastic about him and his detachment.

I told him I was going down there and would help him.
Boxes of ammunition were piled up in a corner of the cellar,
as it might be called, in which we were sitting, and we
knocked the top from one or more, and putting two good,
strong oilcloths together, poured into them as many cartridges as either of us could conveniently carry at a pretty
good rate of speed. We then tied up the cloths, making a bag
of double thickness and having two ends to hold by.
Together we could run quite rapidly with it, and in case
either of us should be killed or wounded, the other could get
along fairly well. We then took the course I had already
several times taken in reaching the gun—that is, we went
down behind Wofford's left flank, and from that point ran
across a field covered with scattering sassafras bushes, to a
point on Kershaw's line, a little to the left of our gun. This
route afforded the best protection, but after we left
Wofford's position the "protection" amounted to nothing.
The sharpshooters had two-thirds of a circle of fire around
the piece, and they popped merrily at us as we stepped
across the field, but they never touched either of us; we got
in safe and each of us "counted a *coup*," as the French Cana-
dian trappers used to say.

After shaking hands with the infantry, hearing my plucky
comrade complimented on his quick and successful trip, and
seeing the men draw their rations of powder and ball, I
made my way to the gun, told Bob and his gallant detachment what the General had said about them, looked to their
fortification and ammunition, and was just about to take the
perilous trip back again when the enemy began to press us in
a very determined way. There was heavy timber immediately in front, and their mode of attack was to thicken a
skirmish line into a line of battle behind the trees, and then
try to rush us at very short range. The infantry ammunition

had been replenished just in time, but it must be remembered there was not an infantry soldier to our right. If the woods had been as close upon us in that direction they would undoubtedly have captured the piece, but they did not relish coming out into the open.

I was struck with the splendid fighting spirit of Campbell, the tall, lean, keen-eyed, black-haired gunner of the piece; but he was entirely too reckless, standing erect except when bending over the handspike in sighting the piece, and not much "sighting" is done at such short range. Every time the gun belched its deadly contents into the woods Campbell would throw his Glengarry around his head and yell savagely. I cautioned him again and again, reminding him that the other men of the detachment were fighting, and fighting effectively, on their hands and knees. When his commanding officer or I ordered him to "get down" he would do so for a moment, but spring up again when the gun fired. Suddenly I heard the thud of a Minié striking a man, and Campbell's arms flew up as he fell backward, ejaculating, "O God! I'm done forever!" We lifted the poor fellow around, across the face of the little work, under the mouth of the piece, and Falligant kneeled by him and pressed his finger where the blood was spouting, while I took the gunner's place at the trail. Every time the gun was discharged I noticed how Campbell's face—which was almost directly under the bellowing muzzle—was contorted, but he urged me to keep up the fire, until finally, observing a sort of lull in the fight, I proposed to cease firing and note the effect, and the poor fellow said brokenly, "Well, if you think it's safe, Adjutant!" Then he added, "Tell my mother I died like a soldier"—and he was gone.

During this flurry one of the enemy bounded over the work and landed right in among us; but he ran on toward the rear and brought up in a sitting posture on a pile of earth one of the infantry had thrown out of a hole he had dug to cook in—a sort of safety-kitchen. The man's back was turned toward us, his elbows were on his knees, and his head sunk in his hands. After Campbell's death, as he was still sitting there, thinking he must be wounded, I proposed to one of the men to run out with me and bring him back into the work. We tried it, but he cast off our hands and we had to leave him to his fate. In a few moments he was shot in the head and tumbled in upon the cook in the kitchen—dead.

The 2d of June, 1864, was the heaviest, the hardest-

worked and the most straining day of my life. Not only did I
have my ordinary duties of a day of battle to perform, but I
had, in addition, to open and to keep open roads for getting
in ammunition, to bridge two or three ravines, to visit
Falligant's gun several times and to keep it supplied with
ammunition, which had to be passed along the infantry line
by hand for quite a long distance. When night came I
believe I was more nearly worn out than on any other occasion during the entire war. Colonel Cabell insisted I should
go back to our headquarters camp, which was about mid-
way between the lines and the drivers' camp, and sleep;
and, in view of what impended on the morrow, I consented
to do so. But first, and just before dark, I took Calloway over
all the obscure and confusing part of the road to Falligant's
gun, the road by which he was to bring it out later. I omitted
to say that General Kershaw highly approved our determination to save that piece, if at all possible. I greatly
disliked not going with the party to fetch the gun out, but
Calloway and every one concerned insisted that I must not
think of attempting it, fearing that I would utterly give way
if I did so. So I yielded, and after showing and explaining
everything to Calloway, I went back to camp and lay down.

I had scarcely gotten to sleep when I had to get up to pilot
an officer who had important orders for General Kershaw,
and had been unable to find his headquarters. Once more I
stretched out and dozed off. How long I dozed or slept I
cannot say, but I was awakened by Calloway bending over
me and saying, "Adjutant, I never was so sorry about anything, but in those woods it is now as dark as Erebus! Nobody but yourself can find and keep the road you showed
me, and I don't believe even you can do it."

The noble fellow was evidently much mortified and troubled at being compelled to rouse me, but he well knew I had
much rather this should be done than that the chance of saving the gun should be abandoned. So I got up and mounted
Mickey, and off we started.

It was very dark. Just before reaching the point where the
road turned to the right along the slope of the hill, we found
the gun horses and drivers, Calloway and I passing and
directing them to follow us, and to keep absolutely quiet. I
experienced little difficulty in finding the road, having
superintended the cutting of it and being very familiar with
it, and we passed on over the little bridge, and were just
passing out from behind Wofford's left flank and heading for

Kershaw's line, when some one seized my bridle rein and abruptly stopped my horse; at the same time asking who I was and what I intended to do, and what I meant by bringing artillery horses through his lines without his permission.

The manner and tone of this address was irritating, but suspecting who my interlocutor was and knowing something of his temperament, I answered quietly that I was adjutant of Cabell's Battalion of Artillery, and that the commanding officer of one of our batteries was with me; that the gun out there, which had protected this part of the line all day, belonged to this battery; that we proposed to save it, and that we had brought the horses for the purpose of hauling it off. I could see nothing, but by this time my suspicion had become conviction and I felt sure I was talking with General Wofford. He positively forbade the attempt, and did not seem disposed to yield until my cousin, Colonel Edward Stiles, of the Sixteenth Georgia, of his brigade, who knew the General well, joined us and suggested as a compromise that we should make the attempt without taking the horses any further; to which I agreed, upon condition that he would furnish me with, say, twenty men, to get the gun off by hand, and that in the event of their failing I should then make the effort with the horses, as we had General Kershaw's positive orders to save the gun if possible.

We got the men and started up the hill, leaving drivers and horses to await our return. It was now absolutely dark. I remember putting my hand before my face and being unable to see it. Calloway and I rode side by side, inclining to the left, so as to guard against running out into the enemy through the gap in the lines. There was absolute stillness, save the soft tread of our horses' feet in the sandy soil. In a few moments their heads rustled against dry leaves—the leafy screen which the troops had put up to protect themselves from the baking sun. We knew we were at the infantry line and turned to the right and toward the gun. There was a good deal of smoke in the air from the woods afire out in front, and we soon became conscious of an insufferable odor of burning flesh. My horse being a rapid walker, I kept a little ahead of Calloway, and very soon was stopped again, by some one who spoke almost in a stage whisper. It turned out to be the commanding officer of Kershaw's old brigade, and he, too, forbade our attempt and ordered us back; but the direct authority of his major-general satisfied him, and he begged only that we should wait until his men could be

thoroughly roused and ready to resist any attack that might
be made; adding that the poor fellows were utterly exhausted
by the unrelieved strain of the past thirty-six hours. All true;
yet it was fearful to contemplate the risk they ran in sleeping. The colonel told us, too, what we already suspected, that
the odor which so offended our nostrils was that of human
bodies roasting in the forest fires in front. We plainly heard
the officers passing along the lines and rousing the men, and
we feared the enemy heard it, too; but preferred this risk to
that of a sudden rush upon a slumbering brigade just as we
were drawing the gun off.

Soon after we started again, my horse snorted and sprang
aside. I knew this meant we had reached the dead horses,
and told Calloway we were almost upon the gun. He dismounted, handing his bridle rein to me, and I heard him enter the little trench and feel and fumble his way along it for a
few steps, and then heard him call, in a low tone, "Falligant,
Falligant!" Then I heard the sort of groan or grumble a tired
man gives out when he is half roused from a sound sleep,
and after that a low hum of conversation. Then Calloway
came up out of the trench, and, groping his way to me, said:
"Adjutant, do you know every man in that detachment was
fast asleep and the enemy is lying down in line of battle between here and that low fire out there!" I said he must be
mistaken, that I could toss a cracker into that fire. He insisted he was right and urged me to dismount and go into
the trench and stoop till I could see under the smoke. I did
so, and there, sure enough, was a continuous line of blue
which the flickering of the flames beyond enabled me to see.
My heart stopped beating at the sight, but this was no time
for indulgence of over-sensibility, physical or emotional.

As quietly and rapidly as possible we got everything
ready for fight or retreat. Our twenty men had brought their
muskets and Kershaw's brigade was up in the trench and on
their knees. The gun was backed out of the little work, limbered up, and the ammunition chest replaced; some of the
men took hold of the wheels and some of the tongue, and the
piece was soon moving after us, almost noiselessly, along the
sassafras field toward Wofford's line. In a few moments we
reached the goal, returning our thanks to the General, and to
my cousin and the sturdy, gallant men they lent us; the
horses were hitched up and we were rolling over the little
bridges and up to the new line and the position selected for
this now distinguished piece.

I trust I am not small enough to indulge in any vulgar pride in my part of the trying experiences of this day; yet I scarce recall another day for which I so thank God, or which has had a greater influence on my life. Often, when depressed and disposed to question whether there is, or ever was, in me the salt of a real manhood, I have looked back to the first three days of June, 1864, and felt the revival of a saving self-respect and the determination not to do or suffer anything unworthy of this heroic past of which I was a part.

There were two battles at Cold Harbor, one in '62 and one in '64. In '62 the Confederates attacked and drove the Federals from their position; in '64 the Federals attacked, but were repulsed with frightful slaughter. It is undisputed that both McClellan's army and Grant's outnumbered Lee's—Grant's overwhelmingly—and it is asserted that the position occupied by the Federals in '62 and the Confederates in '64 was substantially the same.

We were in line of battle at Cold Harbor of '64 from the 1st to the 12th of June—say twelve days; the battle proper did not last perhaps that many minutes. In some respects, at least, it was one of the notable battles of history—certainly in its brevity measured in time, and its length measured in slaughter—as also in the disproportion of the losses. A fair epitome of it in these respects would be that in a few moments more than thirteen thousand men were killed and wounded on the Federal side and less than thirteen hundred on the Confederate. As to the time consumed in the conflict, the longest duration assigned is sixty minutes and the shortest less than eight. For my own part, I could scarcely say whether it lasted eight or sixty minutes, or eight or sixty hours—to such a degree were all my powers concentrated upon the one point of keeping the guns fully supplied with ammunition.

The effect of the fighting was not at all appreciated on the Confederate side at the time. Why we did not at least suspect it, when the truce was asked and granted to allow the removal of the Federal dead and wounded, I cannot say, although I went myself with the officers on our side, detailed to accompany them, on account of my familiarity with the lines. I presume the ignorance, and even incredulity, of our side as to the overwhelming magnitude of the Federal losses resulted from two causes mainly—our own loss was so trivial, so utterly out of proportion, and the one characteristic feature of the fight on the Federal side was not then generally known or appreciated by us, namely, that Grant had attacked in column, in phalanx, or in mass. The record of the Official Diary of our corps (Southern Historical Society Papers, Vol. VII., p. 503), under date of June 3, 1864, is very peculiar and in part in these words: "Meantime the enemy is heavily massed in front of Kershaw's salient. Anderson's, Law's, and Gregg's brigades are there to support Kershaw. Assault after assault is made, and each time repulsed with severe loss to the enemy. At 8 o'clock A.M., fourteen had been made and repulsed (this, means, I suppose, fourteen lines advanced)."

This is obviously a hurried field note by one officer, corrected later by another, in accordance with the facts known to the writer, that is, to the officer who made the later note, but not generally known at the time to the public. We suppose, however, it will to-day be admitted by all that there was *but one attack* upon Kershaw up to 8 A.M., and that at that hour the order was issued to the Federal troops to renew the attack, but they failed to advance; that this order was repeated in the afternoon, when the troops again refused to obey, and that at least some of Grant's corps generals approved of this refusal of their men to repeat the useless sacrifice.

Here, then, is the secret of the otherwise inexplicable and incredible butchery. A little after daylight on June 3, 1864, along the lines of Kershaw's salient, his infantry discharged their bullets and his artillery fired case-shot and double shotted canister, at very short range, into a mass of men twenty-eight (28) deep, who could neither advance nor retreat, and the most of whom could not even discharge their muskets at us. We do not suppose that the general outline of these facts will be denied to-day, but it may be as well to confirm the essential statements by a brief extract from Swinton's "Army of the Potomac":

The order was issued through these officers to their subordinate commanders, and from them descended through the wonted channels, but no man stirred and the immobile lines pronounced a verdict, silent, yet emphatic, against further slaughter. The loss on the Union side in this sanguinary action was over thirteen thousand, while on the part of the Confederates it is doubtful whether it reached that many hundreds.

To like effect, as to the amount and the disproportion of the carnage, is the statement of Colonel Taylor, on page 135 of his book, that:

I well recall having received a report after the assault from General Hoke—whose division reached the army just previous to this battle—to the effect that the ground in his entire front over which the enemy had charged was literally covered with their dead and wounded, and that up to that time he had not had a single man killed.

So much for the amount, the disproportion, and the cause of the slaughter. A word now as to the effect of it upon the Federal leaders and the Northern people. Is it too much to say that even Grant's iron nerve was for the time shattered? Not that he would not have fought again if his men would, but they would not. Is it not true that he so informed President Lincoln; that he asked for another army; that, not getting it, or not geting it at once, he changed his plan of campaign from a fighting to a digging one? Is it reasonable to suppose that when he attacked at the Bloody Angle or at Cold Harbor, he really contemplated the siege of Petersburg and regarded those operations as merely preparatory? Is it not true that, years later, Grant said—looking back over his long career of bloody fights—that Cold Harbor was the only battle he ever fought that he would not fight over again under the same circumstances? Is it not true that when first urged, as President, to remove a certain Democratic office holder in California, and later, when urged to give a reason for his refusal, he replied that the man had been a standard-bearer in the Army of the Potomac, and that he would—allow something very unpleasant to happen to him—before he would remove the only man in his army who even attempted to obey his order to attack a second time at Cold Harbor? Is it not true that General Meade said the Confederacy came nearer to winning recognition at Cold Harbor than at any other period during the war? Is it not true that, after Grant's telegram, the Federal Cabinet resolved at least upon an armistice, and that Mr. Seward was selected to draft the necessary papers, and Mr. Swinton to prepare the public mind for the change? And finally, even if none of these things be true, exactly as propounded—yet is it not true, that Cold Harbor shocked and depressed the Federal Government and the northern public more than any other single battle of the war?

A few words as to some of the prominent features, physical and otherwise, of fighting in "the lines," as we began regularly to do in this campaign of '64, particularly at Cold Harbor. Something of this is necessary to a proper understanding and appreciation of some of the incidents that occurred there. And first, as to "the works" of which I have so often spoken. What were they? I cannot answer in any other way so well as by the following vivid quotation from my friend Willy Dame's "Reminiscences":

Just here I take occasion to correct a very wrong impression about the field works the Army of Northern Virginia fought behind in this campaign. All the Federal writers who have written about these battles speak about our works as "formidable earthworks," "powerful fortifications," impregnable lines"; such works as no troops could be expected to take and *any troops* should be expected to hold.

Now about the parts of the line distant from us, I couldn't speak so certainly—though I am sure they were all very much the same—but about the works all along our part of the line I can speak with exactness and certainty. I saw them, I helped with my own hands to make them, I fought behind them, I was often on top of them and both sides of them. I know all about them. I got a good deal of the mud off them on me (not for purposes of personal fortification, however). Our works were a single line of earth about four feet high and three to five feet thick. It had no ditch or obstruction in front. It was nothing more than a little heavier line of "rifle pits." There was no physical difficulty in men walking right over that bank. I did it often myself, saw many others do it, and twice saw a line of Federal troops walk over it, and then saw them walk *back* over it with the greatest ease, at the rate of forty miles an hour; i.e. except those whom we had persuaded to stay with us, and those the angels were carrying to Abraham's bosom at a still swifter rate. Works they could go over like that couldn't have been much obstacle! They couldn't have made better time on a dead level.

Such were our works actually, and still they seemed to "loom large" to the people in front. I wonder what could have given them such an exaggerated idea of the strength of those modest little works! I wonder if it could have been the *men* behind them! There wasn't a great many of these men! It was a very thin gray line along them, back of a thin red line of clay. But these lines stuck together, very hard, and were very hard indeed to separate. The red clay was "sticky" and the men were just as "sticky," and as the two lines "stuck" together so closely, it made the whole very strong indeed. Certainly it seems they gave to those who tried to force them apart an impression of great strength.

Yes, it must have been the *men!* A story in point comes to my aid here. A handsome, well dressed lady sweeps with a great air past two street boys. They are much struck. "My eye, Jim, but ain't that a stunning dress?" Says Jim with a superior air, "Oh, get out, Bill, the dress ain't no great shakes; it's the woman in it that makes it so killing!" That was the way with the Spotsylvania earthworks. The "works wa'n't no great shakes." It was the men in 'em that made them so "killing."

The original intent of such "works" is to afford protection against regular attack by the full line of battle of the opposite side, advancing out of their works to attack yours. This, of course, every one understands. But this is only an occasional and comparatively rare thing. The constant and wearing feature of "the lines" is the sharpshooting, which never ceases as long as there is light enough to see how to shoot; unless the skirmishers or sharpshooters of the two sides proclaim, or in some way begin, a temporary truce, as I have known them to do. I have also known them to give explicit warning of the expiration of such a truce.

Sharpshooting, at best, however, is a fearful thing. The regular sharpshooter often seemed to me little better than a human tiger lying in wait for blood. His rifle is frequently trained and made fast bearing upon a particular spot—for example, where the head of a gunner must of necessity appear when sighting his piece—and the instant that object appears and, as it were, "darkens the hole," crash goes a bullet through his brain.

The consequence of the sharpshooting is the "coveredway," which, when applied to these rough and ready temporary lines, means any sort of protection—trenches, ditches, traverses, piles of earth, here and there, at what have proved to be the danger points designed and placed so as to protect as far as possible against the sharpshooters. Only in regular and elaborate lines of "siege," such as we had later about Petersburg, is seen the more perfect protection of regularly covered galleries and ways for passing from one part of the line to another inside; just as, outside and on the face toward the enemy, such elaborate and permanent lines of works are protected by ditches, abatis or felled trees, friezes or sharpened stakes, to make the "works" more difficult of approach, of access, and of capture.

One can readily understand, now, the supreme discomfort and even suffering of "the lines." Thousands of men cramped up in a narrow trench, unable to go out, or to get up, or to stretch or to stand, without danger to life and limb; unable to lie down, or to sleep, for lack of room and pressure of peril; night alarms, day attacks, hunger, thirst, supreme weariness, squalor, vermin, filth, disgusting odors everywhere; the weary night succeeded by the yet more weary day; the first glance over the way, at day dawn, bringing the sharpshooter's bullet singing past your ear or smashing through your skull, a man's life often exacted as the price of a cup of water from the spring. But I will not specify or elaborate further; only, upon the canvas thus stretched, let me paint for you two or three life and death pictures of Cold Harbor of '64.

The reader may recall our "Old Doctor," the chief of our ambulance corps, who helped to rally the Texans and Georgians on the 10th of May at Spotsylvania, first exhorting them as "gentlemen," then berating and belaboring them as "cowards." No man who was ever in the Howitzers but will appreciate the grim absurdity of this man's feeling a lack of confidence in his own nerve and courage; but he did feel it. When the war broke out he was in Europe enjoying himself, but returned to his native State, serving first in some, as he considered it, "non-combatant" position, until that became unendurable to him, and then he joined the Howitzers as a private soldier; and that final flurry of the 10th of May was the first real fight he ever got into. Hearing some one say just as it was over that it had been "pretty hot work," he asked with the greatest earnestness whether the speaker really meant what he said, and when assured that he did, he asked two or three others of his comrades, whom he regarded as experienced soldiers, whether they concurred in this view of the matter, and on their expressing emphatic concurrence, he expressed intense satisfaction at having at last a standard in his mind, and a relieving standard to that; saying that he had feared he would disgrace his family by exhibiting a lack of courage; but if that was really "hot work," he felt that he would be able to maintain himself and do his duty. The story is almost too much for belief, but it is the sober truth and vouched for by gentlemen of the highest character.

I think it was the evening after the big fight at Cold Harbor that I was sitting in the works, with one of the Howitzer detachments, when the Doctor announced his intention of going to the spring for water. I reminded him that it was not quite dark and the sharpshooters would be apt to pay their respects to him; but he said he must have some water, and offered to take down and fill as many canteens as he could carry. His captain was present and I said no more. He was soon loaded up and started off, stepping right up out of the trench on the level ground. I could not help urging him to take the "covered way," but he replied, "I can't do it, Adjutant. It is dirty; a gentleman can't walk in it, sir."

Away he went, walking bolt upright and with entire nonchalance, down the hill; to my great relief reaching the spring in safety, where he was pretty well protected. In due time he started back, loaded with the full canteens and having a tin cup full of water in his right hand. I heard the sharp report of a rifle and saw the Doctor start forward or stumble, and sprang up to go to his relief, but he steadied himself and came right on up the hill without further attention from the sharpshooters, and stepped down into the work. As he did so he handed the captain the cup of water, in the quietest manner apologizing for having spilled part of it, adding that he had met with a trivial accident. The upper joint of his thumb had been shot away, yet he had not dropped the cup. Then he turned to me and asked my pardon for his disregard of my warning and his imprudence in getting shot, protesting still, however, that it was very hard indeed for a gentleman to walk in those filthy, abominable covered ways.

The spring was perhaps the point of greatest power and pathos in all the weird drama of "The Lines." About this date, or very soon after, a few of us were sitting in the part of the trenches occupied by the Twenty-first Mississippi, of our old brigade—Barksdale's, now Humphreys'—which was supporting our guns. There had been a number of Yale men in the Twenty-first—the Sims, Smiths, Brandon, Scott, and perhaps others. A good many were "gone," and those of us who were left were talking of them and of good times at Old Yale, when some one said, "Scott, isn't it your turn to go to the spring?" "Yes," said Scott, submissively, "I believe it is. Pass up your canteens," and he loaded up and started out. There was a particularly exposed spot on the way to water, which we had tried in vain to protect more perfectly, and we heard, as usual, two or three rifle shots as Scott passed that point. In due time we heard them again as he returned, and one of the fellows said, "Ha! they are waking up old Scott, again, on the home stretch."

The smile had not died upon our faces when a head appeared above the traverse and a business-like voice called: "Hello, Company I; man of yours dead out here!" We ran around the angle of the work, and there lay poor Scott, prone in the ditch and almost covered with canteens. We picked him up and bore him tenderly into the trench, and, as we laid him down and composed his limbs, manly tears dropped upon his still face. Each man disengaged and took his own canteen from the slumbering water-carrier. We did not "pour the water out unto the Lord," as David did when the "three mightiest brake through the host of the Philistines and drew water out of the well of Bethlehem that was by the gate"—albeit, in a truer sense than David spoke, this water was the very "blood of this man."

It was about six o'clock in the evening of one of the days that followed close upon the great fight that there befell the company the very saddest loss it had yet experienced. An order had come to Captain McCarthy, from General Alexander, commanding the artillery corps, directing that the effect of the fire of several howitzers, which were operating as mortars, from a position immediately back of the Howitzer guns, should be carefully observed and reported to him. The captain, appreciating at once the responsibility and the peril of the work, with characteristic chivalry, determined to divide it between himself and one of the most competent and careful men in the company. He was not the man to shrink, or slur over, or postpone his own part in any duty, and immediately stationed himself where he could thoroughly discharge it. He had taken his stand but a few moments when he fell back among his men, his brain pierced by a sharpshooter's bullet. The detachment sprang to his aid, but too late even to prevent his fall. His broad breast heaved once or twice as they knelt about him and it was all over. The men broke down utterly and sobbed like children.

We never found his hat. While his boys were still gazing at him through their tears a Mississippi soldier came working his way along the lines, from a point a hundred feet or more to the right, holding in his hand a little piece of brass, and as he approached the group said: "This here thing has just fell at my feet. I reckon it belongs to some of you artillery fellows"; and then, looking at the noble figure stretched upon the ground, he asked in the dry, matter-of-fact soldier style, "Who's that's dead?" When we told him Captain McCarthy, of the Howitzers, he said musingly: "McCarthy, McCarthy; why, that's the name of the folks that took care o' me, when I was wounded so bad last year. Well, here's the cannons from his hat." And so it was; his hat, as we suppose, had gone over the works, and his badge of cross cannon, dislodged from it by the shock, had fallen at the feet of a man who had been nursed back to life by his mother and sisters in his boyhood's home.

My younger brother was a great favorite in the company. As he had been a sailor, and as we had come from New England to Virginia, he was nicknamed "Skipper." He had a beautiful tenor voice and a unique repertoire of songs from almost every clime and country. Whenever "Skipper" deigned to sing, "the Professor," the trainer of the Glee Club, would enforce absolute silence throughout the camp, under penalty of a heavy battery of maledictions.

The day after Captain McCarthy's death, my brother, being in almost the exact position the Captain occupied when killed, was shot in the left temple, and fell just where the captain had fallen. I was not present at the moment, but the boys reported that as they bent over him, thinking him dead, he raised his head and said, "If you fellows will stand back and give me some air, I'll get up!"—which he not only did, but walked out to the hospital camp, refusing a litter. He also refused to take chloroform, and directed the surgeons in exploring the track of the ball, which had crushed up his temple and the under half of the socket of his eye, and lodged somewhere in behind his nose. After they had extracted the ball and a great deal of crushed bone, he declared there was something else in his head which must come out. The surgeons told him it was more crushed bone which would come away of itself after awhile, but he insisted it was something that did not belong there, and that they must take it away immediately. They remonstrated, but he would not be satisfied, and finally they probed further and drew out a piece of his hat brim, cut just the width of the ball and jammed like a wad into his head; after that he was much easier. I omitted to say we never found his hat, either.

He was blind in the left eye from the moment the ball struck him, and became for a time blind in the other eye also. While in utter darkness he sang most of the time, and I remember our dear mother was troubled by a fancy that, like a mockingbird she once had that went blind in a railroad train, he might sing himself to death. But he recovered the sight of his right eye after a time, and the marvel is that the left eye did not shrink away and was not even discolored. The bony formation of the under-socket of the eye grew up and rectified itself almost entirely, and a lock of his curly hair covered the desperate-looking wound in the temple. It was a wonderful recovery.

THE VALLEY AGAIN

NEITHER LEE NOR GRANT was happy to have his army settle in for a siege of Richmond. Grant had hoped to get flanking forces around to Lee's rear to cut the railroads supplying Richmond. And Lee knew that time was an enemy: time would enable the Federals to increase their strength to a point where sheer numbers would overwhelm the Confederates. There were no new troops to be found for Lee, and supplies were getting shorter and shorter. One faint hope still existed, a hope based on an old tactic that had always worked in the past—an attack force marching up the Shenandoah Valley to threaten Washington. Always before, any threat to Washington had relieved the pressure on Richmond.

In July, General Jubal Early started up the Valley with 14,000 troops; they drove north to within sight of the outlying defenses of the capital. Fortunately for the Federals, Grant rushed a corps up to the city in the nick of time. After only a light skirmish, Early retreated to the Valley.

To clear the Valley, once and for all, General Grant sent General Sheridan into the Valley with about 43,000 men.

"Up to the summer of 1864 the Shenandoah Valley had not been to the Union armies a fortunate place either for battle or for strategy. A glance at the map will go far toward explaining this. The Valley has a general direction from southwest to north-east. The Blue Ridge Mountains, forming its eastern barrier, are well defined from the James River above Lynchburg to Harper's Ferry on the Potomac. Many passes (in Virginia called 'gaps') made it easy of access from the Confederate base of operations; and, bordered by a fruitful country filled with supplies, it offered a tempting highway for an army bent on a flanking march on Washington or the invasion of Maryland or Pennsylvania. For the Union armies, while it was an equally practicable highway, it led away from the objective, Richmond, and was exposed to flank attacks through the gaps from vantage-ground and perfect cover.

"It was not long after General Grant completed his first campaign in Virginia, and while he was in front of Petersburg, that his attention was called to this famous seat of side issues between Union and Confederate armies. With quick military instinct he saw that the Valley was not useful to the Government for aggressive operations. He decided that it must be made untenable for either army. In doing this he reasoned that the advantage would be with us, who did not want it as a source of supplies, nor as a place of arms, and against the Confederates, who wanted it for both."*

At Winchester on September 19, Sheridan defeated Early and the Union won, for the first time, a clear-cut victory in the Valley. The next month Early surprised Sheridan's troops at Cedar Run and put them to rout. Only the arrival of Sheridan from Winchester could turn the tide.

Sheridan's Ride†

BY MAJOR GEORGE A. FORSYTH

IN THE MORNING, ABOUT DAYLIGHT, word was brought from the picketline south of Winchester of heavy firing at the front. General Sheridan interviewed the officer who brought the information, and decided that it must be the result of the reconnoissance that General Wright had notified him the night before was to take place this morning. Little apprehension was occasioned by the report. After breakfast, probably nearly or quite nine o'clock, we mounted and rode at a walk through the town of Winchester to Mill Creek, a mile south of the village, where we found our escort awaiting us.

We could occasionally hear the far-away sound of heavy guns, and as we moved out with our escort behind us I thought that the general was becoming anxious. He leaned forward and listened intently, and once he dismounted and

---

* From General Wesley Merritt, "Sheridan in the Shenandoah Valley," *Battles and Leaders,* Vol. IV.
† From *Thrilling Days in Army Life.*

placed his ear near the ground, seeming somewhat disconcerted as he rose again and remounted. We had not gone far, probably not more than a mile, when, at the crest of a little hill on the road, we found the pike obstructed by some supply-trains which had started on their way to the army. They were now halted, and seemingly in great confusion. Part of the wagons faced one way, part the other; others were half turned round, in position to swing either way, but were huddled together, completely blocking the road.

Turning to me, the general said, "Ride forward quickly and find out the trouble here, and report promptly." I rode rapidly to the head of the train and asked for the quartermaster in charge, and was told he had gone up the road a short distance.

On reaching him, I found him conversing with a quartermaster-sergeant. They informed me that an officer had come from the front and told them to go back at once, as our army had been attacked at daylight, defeated, and was being driven down the valley. The officer, they said, had gone back towards the front after warning them to come no further.

Galloping back, I made my report. "Pick out fifty of the best-mounted men from the escort," was the response. Riding down the column, with the aid of one of the officers of the regiment, this was soon accomplished, and I reported with the selected men. Turning to his chief of staff, Colonel J. W. Forsyth, the general said something regarding certain instructions he had evidently been giving him, and then said to me, "You and Captain O'Keeffe will go with me"; and nodding good-bye to the other gentlemen of our party, with whom he had probably been conferring while I was making up the cavalry detail, he turned his horse's head southward, tightening the reins of his bridle, and with a slight touch of the spur he dashed up the turnpike and was off. A yard in rear, and side by side, Captain O'Keeffe and myself swept after him, while the escort, breaking from a trot to a gallop, came thundering on behind.

The distance from Winchester to Cedar Creek, on the north bank of which the Army of the Shenandoah lay encamped, is a little less than nineteen miles. The general direction was west of south, and the road to it, by way of the valley pike, ran directly through the road-side hamlets of Milltown, Kearnstown, Newtown, and Middletown. Our army was encamped four miles south of Middletown. The

Shenandoah Valley turnpike, over which we were now
speeding, was formerly a well-built macadamized road, laid
in crushed limestone, and until the advent of the war had
been kept in excellent condition. Even now, though worn for
three years past by the tread of contending armies with all
the paraphernalia of war as they swept up and down the
valley, it was a fairly good road; but the army supply-trains,
ammunition-wagons, and artillery had worn it into deep ruts
in places, and everywhere the dust lay thick and heavy on its
surface, and powdered the trees and bushes that fringed its
sides, so that our galloping column sent a gray cloud
swirling behind us. It was a golden sunny day that had succeeded a densely foggy October morning. The turnpike
stretched away, a white, dusty line, over hill and through
dale, bordered by fenceless fields, and past farm-houses and
empty barns and straggling orchards. Now and then it ran
through a woody copse, with here and there a tiny stream of
water crossing it, or meandering by its side, so clear and lim-
pid that it seemed to invite us to pause and slake our thirst as
we sped along our dusty way. On either side we saw,
through the Indian-summer haze, the distant hills covered
with woods and fairly ablaze with foliage; and over all was
the deep blue of a cloudless Southern sky, making it a day on
which one's blood ran riot and he was glad of health and life.

Within a mile we met more supply-trains that had turned
back, and the general stopped long enough to order the
officer in charge to halt, park his trains just where he was,
and await further instructions. Then on we dashed again,
only to meet, within a few moments, more supply-trains hurrying to the rear. The general did not stop, but signalling the
officer in charge to join him, gave him instructions on the
gallop to park his train at once, and use his escort to arrest
and stop all stragglers coming from the army, and to send
back to the front all well men who might drift to him, under
guard if necessary.

Scarcely had we parted from him and surmounted the
next rise in the road when we came suddenly upon in-
dubitable evidence of battle and retreat. About a mile in advance of us the road was filled and the fields dotted with
wagons and men belonging to the various brigade, division,
and corps headquarters, and in among them officers' servants with led horses, and here and there a broken ambulance, sutlers' supply-trains, a battery forge or two, horses
and mules hastily packed with officers' mess kits, led by their

cooks, and now and then a group of soldiers, evidently detailed enlisted men attached to the headquarters trains. In fact, this was the first driftwood of a flood just beyond and soon to come sweeping down the road. Passing this accumulation of debris with a rush by leaving the pike and galloping over the open fields on the side of the road, we pushed rapidly on; but not so quickly but that we caught an echoing cheer from the enlisted men and servants, who recognized the general, and shouted and swung their hats in glee.

Within the next few miles the pike and adjacent fields began to be lined and dotted everywhere with army wagons, sutlers' outfits, headquarters supply-trains, disabled caissons, and teamsters with led mules, all drifting to the rear; and now and then a wounded officer or enlisted man on horseback or plodding along on foot, with groups of straggling soldiers here and there among the wagon-trains, or in the fields, or sometimes sitting or lying down to rest by the side of the road, while others were making coffee in their tin cups by tiny camp-fires. Soon we began to see small bodies of soldiers in the fields with stacked arms, evidently cooking breakfast. As we debouched into the fields and passed around the wagons and through these groups, the general would wave his hat to the men and point to the front, never lessening his speed as he pressed forward. It was enough; one glance at the eager face and familiar black horse and they knew him, and starting to their feet, they swung their caps around their heads and broke into cheers as he passed beyond them; and then, gathering up their belongings and shouldering their arms, they started after him for the front, shouting to their comrades further out in the fields, "Sheridan! Sheridan!" waving their hats, and pointing after him as he dashed onward; and they too comprehended instantly, for they took up the cheer and turned back for the battlefield.

To the best of my recollection, from the time we met the first stragglers who had drifted back from the army, his appearance and his cheery shout of "Turn back, men! turn back! Face the other way!" as he waved his hat towards the front, had but one result: a wild cheer of recognition, an answering wave of the cap. In no case, as I glanced back, did I fail to see the men shoulder their arms and follow us. I think it is no exaggeration to say that as he dashed on to the field of battle, for miles back the turnpike was lined with men pressing forward after him to the front.

So rapid had been our gait that nearly all of the escort, save the commanding officer and a few of his best-mounted men, had been distanced, for they were more heavily weighted, and ordinary troop horses could not live at such a pace. Once we were safe among our own people, their commander had the good sense to see that his services were no longer a necessity, and accordingly drew rein and saved his horses by following on at a slow trot. Once the general halted a moment to speak to an officer he knew and inquire for information. As he did so he turned and asked me to get him a switch; for he usually rode carrying a light riding-whip, and furthermore he had broken one of the rowels of his spurs. Dismounting, I cut one from a near-by way-side bush, hastily trimmed it, and gave it him. "Thanks, Sandy," said he, and as we started again he struck his splendid black charger Rienzi a slight blow across the shoulder with it, and he at once broke into that long swinging gallop, almost a run, which he seemed to maintain so easily and so endlessly—a most distressing gait for those who had to follow far. These two words of thanks were nearly the only ones he addressed to me until we reached the army; but my eyes had sought his face at every opportunity, and my heart beat high with hope from what I saw there. As he galloped on his features gradually grew set, as though carved in stone, and the same dull red glint I had seen in his piercing black eyes when, on other occasions, the battle was going against us, was there now. Occasionally Captain O'Keeffe and myself exchanged a few words, and we waved our hats and shouted to the men on the road and in the fields as we passed them, pointing to the general and seconding as best we could his energetic shout: "Turn back, men! turn back! Face the other way!" Now and then I would glance at the face of my companion, Captain O'Keeffe, whose gray-blue eyes fairly danced with excitement at the prospect of the coming fray; for if ever a man was a born soldier and loved fighting for chivalry's sake, it was that gallant young Irish gentleman, Joe O'Keeffe.

Each moment that we advanced the road became more closely clogged with stragglers and wounded men, and here the general suddenly paused to speak to one of the wounded officers, from whom I judge he got his only correct idea of the attack by the enemy at dawn, the crushing of our left, and the steady outflanking that had forced our army back to where it was at present, for I caught something of what the officer said, and his ideas seemed to be clear and concise. This pause was a piece of rare good fortune for me, for my orderly happened to be by the side of the road with my led horse, and in a trice he changed my saddle, and I rejoined the general ere he was a hundred yards away, with all the elation that a fresh mount after a weary one inspires in the heart of a cavalryman.

Within a comparatively short distance we came suddenly upon a field-hospital in a farm-house close to the road beyond Newton, where the medical director had established part of his corps. Just ahead of us the road was filled with ambulances containing wounded men, who were being carried into the house to be operated upon, while outside of the door along the foot-path lay several dead men, who had been hastily placed there on being taken from the stretchers. The vicinity was dotted with wounded men, sitting or lying down or standing around, waiting to have their wounds dressed, while the surgeons were flitting here and there doing their best and straining every nerve to meet their necessities. Giving the place a wide berth, after the first glance, and galloping around the line of ambulances that filled the pike, we passed through a fringe of woods, up a slight eminence in the road, and in a flash we were in full view of the battle-field. It was a gruesome sight to meet the eyes of a commanding general who, three short days before, had left it a triumphant host lying quietly in camp, resting securely on its victories, and confident in its own strength. And now!

In our immediate front the road and adjacent fields were filled with sections of artillery, caissons, ammunition-trains, ambulances, battery-wagons, squads of mounted men, led horses, wounded soldiers, broken wagons, stragglers, and stretcher-bearers—in fact, all that appertains to and is part of the rear of an army in action. One hasty glance as we galloped forward and we had taken in the situation. About half or three-quarters of a mile this side of Middletown, with its left resting upon the turnpike, was a division of infantry in line of battle at right angles to the road, with its standards flying, and evidently held well in hand. Near the turnpike, and just to its left, one of our batteries was having a savage artillery duel with a Confederate battery, which was in position on a little hill to the left and rear of Middletown as we faced it. To the left of this battery of ours were the led horses of a small brigade of cavalry, which was holding the ground to the left of the pike, and both the infantry and cavalry dismounted skirmishers were in action with those of the enemy. Further to the left, and slightly to the rear, on a bit of rising ground, was another of our batteries in action. Half a mile to the right, and somewhat to the rear of the division of infantry which was in line of battle, could be seen a body of infantry in column slowly retiring and tending towards the pike; and just beyond these troops was another body of infantry, also in column, and also moving in the same general direction. Further to the right, across a small valley, and more than a mile away from these last-mentioned troops, was a still larger force of infantry, on a side-hill, facing towards the enemy, in line of battle, but not in action. I looked in vain for the cavalry divisions, but concluded rightly that they were somewhere on the flanks of the enemy.

Skirting the road, and avoiding as best we might the impedimenta of battle, the general, O'Keefe, and myself spurred forward. Finally, on the open road and just before we reached the troops in line, which was Getty's division of the Sixth Army Corps, I asked permission to go directly down to the skirmish-line to see the actual condition of things. "Do so," replied the general, "and report as soon as possible." Just then we reached the line, and as I glanced back I saw the chief draw rein in the midst of the division, where he was greeted by a storm of cheers and wild cries of "Sheridan! Sheridan!" while standards seemed to spring up out of the very earth to greet him. A few seconds later and I was on the skirmish-line by the side of Colonel Charles R. Lowell, commanding the regular cavalry brigade.

"Is Sheridan here?"

"Yes."

"Thank goodness for that!"

At this moment Mr. Stillson, the war correspondent of one of the New York newspapers (who had risked his life for news more than once, and in fact was doing it now), rode up and made the same inquiry.

"He is here," was my reply.

"Well? What is he going to do about it?"

"He's going to whale blank out of them."

"He can't do it," shaking his head.

"Wait, and you'll see."

"I wish I may," said the plucky correspondent, "but I doubt it," and he turned and rode back to find the general.

Turning again to Colonel Lowell, I eagerly asked for the facts about the battle, well knowing that there was no cooler head or better brain in all the army, nor one to be more absolutely relied upon. As we rode along the skirmish-line, that I might get a better view of the enemy, he gave me the details as he knew them. Then, as we watched the enemy forming his battalions in the distance for another advance, I put the question:

"Can you hold on here forty minutes?"

"Yes."

"Can you make it sixty?"

"It depends; you see what they are doing. I will if I can."

"Hold on as long as possible," said I; and turning, I rode rapidly back to my chief, whom I found dismounted, surrounded by several general officers, and in the midst of those of his staff who had not gone with us to Washington. Dismounting, I saluted. Stepping on one side from the group, he faced me, and said,

"Well?"

"You see where we are?" (A nod.) "Lowell says that our losses, killed, wounded, and missing, are between three and five thousand, and more than twenty guns, to say nothing of transportation. He thinks he can hold on where he is for forty minutes longer, possibly sixty."

I can see him before me now as I write, erect, looking intently in my eyes, his left hand resting, clinched savagely, on the top of the hilt of his sabre, his right nervously stroking his chin, his eyes with that strange red gleam in them, and his attenuated features set as if cast in bronze. He stood mute and absolutely still for more than ten seconds; then, throwing up his head, he said:

"Go to the right and find the other two divisions of the Sixth Corps, and also General Emory's command [the two divisions of the Nineteenth Corps]. Bring them up, and order them to take position on the right of Getty. Lose no time." And as I turned to mount, he called out: "Stay! I'll go with you!" And springing on his horse, we set off together, followed by the staff.

Riding up closely to him, I said, "Pardon me, general, but I think if I had control of a division I could do good work here."

Looking at me squarely in the eyes for a few seconds, he

replied: "Do you? Perhaps I'll give you control of more than that."

Not another word was said, and in a few moments we had reached the head of the nearest division we were seeking. It was ordered on the line—I think by the general himself; and as I started for the head of the other division, he ordered me to ride directly over to General Emory's command (two divisions of the Nineteenth Corps), and order it up, to take position in line of battle on the right of the Sixth Corps. I rode over to General Emory's line, which was about a mile away, and found his troops in good condition though somewhat shattered by the fortunes of the day, facing towards the enemy, and half covered by small ledges of rock that cropped out of the hill-side. On receiving the order, he called my attention to the fact that in case the enemy advanced on the Sixth Corps, he would be nearly on their flank, and thought best that I apprise the commanding general of the fact, as it might induce him to modify the order. Galloping back, I gave his suggestion to the general.

"No, no!" he replied. "Get him over *at once—at once!* Don't lose a moment!"

I fairly tore back, and the troops were promptly put in motion for their new position, which they reached in due time, and were formed in line of battle in accordance with General Sheridan's orders.

After the whole line was thoroughly formed, I rode over to my chief and urged him to ride down it, that all the men might see him, and know without doubt that he had returned and assumed command. At first he demurred, but I was most urgent, as I knew that in some instances both men and officers who had not seen him doubted his arrival. His appearance was greeted by tremendous cheers from one end of the line to the other, many of the officers pressing forward to shake his hand. He spoke to them all, cheerily and confidently, saying: "We are going back to our camps, men, never fear. I'll get a twist on these people yet. We'll raise them out of their boots before the day is over."

At no time did I hear him utter that "terrible oath" so often alluded to in both prose and poetry in connection with this day's work.

As we turned to go back from the end of the line, he halted on the line of the Nineteenth Corps and said to me: "Stay here and help fight this corps. I will send orders to

General Emory through you. Give orders in my name, if necessary. Stay right on this line with it."

"Very good, general," was my reply; and the general and staff left me there and galloped towards the pike.

It must have been nearly or quite half-past twelve o'clock by this time, and as soon as the skirmishers were thrown forward the troops were ordered to lie down; an order gladly obeyed, for they had been on their feet since daylight, fighting and without food. They were to have but a short period of rest, however, for in a few moments the low rustling murmur, that presages the advance of a line of battle through dense woods (the Nineteenth Corps was formed just at the outer edge of a belt of heavy timber) began to make itself felt, and in a moment the men were in line again. A pattering fire in front, and our skirmishers came quickly back through the woods, and were absorbed in the line; then there was a momentary lull, followed by a rustling, crunching sound as the enemy's line pressed forward, trampling the bushes under foot, and crowding through bits of underbrush.

In a flash we caught a glimpse of a long gray line stretching away through the woods on either side of us, advancing with waving standards, with here and there a mounted officer in rear of it. At the same instant the dark blue line at the edge of the woods seemed to burst upon their view, for suddenly they halted, and with a piercing yell poured in a heavy volley, that was almost instantly answered from our side, and then volleys seemed fairly to leap from one end to the other of our line, and a steady roar of musketry from both sides made the woods echo again in every direction. Gradually, however, the sounds became less heavy and intense, the volleys slowly died away, and we began to recognize the fact that the enemy's bullets were no longer clipping the twigs above us, and that their fire had about ceased, while a ringing cheer along our front proclaimed that for the first time that day the Confederate army had been repulsed.

During the attack my whole thought, and I believe that of every officer on the line, had been to prevent our troops from giving way. In one or two places the line wavered slightly, but the universal shout of "Steady, men, *steady, steady!*" as the field-officers rode up and down the line, seemed to be all that was needed to inspire the few nervous ones with renewed courage and hold them well up to their work. As for myself, I was more than satisfied, for only years of personal

experience in war enable a man to appreciate at its actual
value the tremendous gain when a routed army turns, faces,
and checks a triumphant enemy in the open field. It is a
great thing to do it with the aid of reinforcements; it is a
glorious thing to do it without.

For a few moments the men stood leaning on their arms,
and some of us mounted officers rode slowly forward, anxiously peering through the trees, but save for a dead man or
two there was no sign of the enemy; the Confederates had
fallen back. Word was passed back to the line, and the men
were ordered to lie down, which they willingly did. I rode
slowly up and down the line of the Nineteenth Corps, and
after a few moments grew impatient for orders, for as a
cavalryman my first thought, after the repulse of the enemy,
was a countercharge. The minutes crept slowly by, and nothing came, not even an aide for information. Twenty
minutes elapsed, thirty, forty, fifty, and I could wait no
longer, but galloped to army headquarters, which I found to
the right of the turnpike, about two hundred yards in rear of
the Sixth Corps. Dismounting, I went up and saluted the
commanding general, who was half lying down, with his
head resting on his right hand, his elbow on the ground, and
surrounded by most of his staff. Colonel J. W. Forsyth, his
chief of staff, as well as Colonels Alexander and Thom of the
Engineer Corps, were with him, having reached the field
since I had been on the line with the Nineteenth Corps.

"Well, what is it?" said the general.

"It seems to me, general, that we ought to advance; I have
come hoping for orders." He half sat up, and the black eyes
flashed. I realized that I had laid myself open to censure; but
gradually an amused look overshadowed the anxious face,
and the chief slowly shook his head.

"Not yet, not yet; go back and wait."

I saluted, mounted, and rode leisurely back, cogitating as
I went. I knew that there must be some good reason for the
delay, but as yet I was unable to fathom it. Reaching the
rear of the centre of the Nineteenth Corps, I found a shady
spot, and dismounting, sat down on the ground just back of
the line, holding my horse's bridle in my hand, for I had no
orderly with me. Very soon I became interested in watching
the various phases of the situation as they developed before
me, and I soon saw one reason for delay, and that was that
we were steadily growing stronger. The tired troops had
thrown themselves on the ground at the edge of the woods,

and lay on their arms in line of battle, listlessly and sleepily. Every now and then stragglers—sometimes singly, oftener in groups—came up from the rear, and moving along back of the line, dusty, heavy-footed, and tired, found and rejoined their respective companies and regiments, dropping down quietly by the side of their companions as they came to them, with a gibe or a word or two of greeting on either side, and then they, too, like most of the rest, subsided into an appearance of apathetic indifference. Here and there men loaded with canteens were sent to the rear in search of water; and every few yards soldiers lay munching a bit of hardtack, the first food many of them had had during the day, for they were driven from their camps at daylight.

Little was said by officers or men, for the truth was that nearly all were tired, troubled, and somewhat disheartened by the disaster that had so unexpectedly overtaken them; for even in the light of existing events the Confederates had triumphed. They had been routed from their position, their left overwhelmed, crushed, and driven in upon the centre, and the whole army repeatedly outflanked and forced back beyond Middletown, a distance of nearly five miles, where they now were, with the loss of many cannon, most of their wounded, thousands of prisoners, and quantities of transportation—this, too, by a foe whom they believed practically vanquished, and whom they had defeated in pitched battle twice within the last thirty days. This unpalatable fact burned inself into their brain as they lay prone on the ground, with their rifles beside them, trying to snatch a few moments' troubled sleep for their heavy eyes and weary bodies. It must have been a bitter cud to chew.

As the moments continued to pass with no orders from headquarters I grew impatient again, not withstanding the fact that the delay was increasing our strength by the return of stragglers and the reorganization of scattered regiments, as well as giving a much-needed rest to the whole army. For the foe was also resting, and probably gaining strength in the same manner, so I mounted and passed through our line, and rode out towards the enemy as far as I could with reasonable safety. Owing to the woods and the conformation of the ground, I could not accurately determine anything, so I came back and went again to army headquarters. I reported my actions, and told the general how I had not been able to satisfy myself as to the present location of the enemy's line, but I thought the men were sufficiently rested to advance in good heart. He did not reply immediately, but seemed thoughtful and perplexed.

Finally he shook his head, and said, "Not yet, not yet; go back and wait patiently."

Riding back to my former location, I dismounted and sat down again, much puzzled to know the reason for this inaction, as it was so unlike what I had seen of my chief, who was always so quick to see and prompt to act, especially on the field of battle. I think it must have been nearly an hour when I again passed to the front of our line, gave my horse to one of the skirmishers, and cautiously stole through the woods, till, on surmounting a slight rise, I distinctly heard sounds that indicated the vicinity of the enemy, and by crawling forward I saw his line in the distance, and made out that the Confederates were piling up stones and rails on the prolongation of a line of stone fences, evidently expecting an advance from our side and preparing for it.

I returned at once, and for the third time reported at army headquarters. As I came up I noticed that the general had evidently just received a report of some kind from an officer who was riding off as I made my appearance. Reporting what I had heard and seen, he glanced up brightly and said:

"It's all right now! I have been kept back by a report of troops coming down in our rear by way of the Front Royal pike. It's not so, however." Then, turning to one of his staff officers, he asked for the time of day.

"Twenty minutes to four," was the reply.

"So late!" said the general. "Why, that's later than I thought!" And then, turning again to me, he said: "Tell General Wright to move forward the Sixth Corps and attack at once, keeping his left on the pike; then tell General Emory to advance at the same time, keeping the left of the Nineteenth Corps well closed on the right of the Sixth Corps; if opportunity offers, swing the right division of the Nineteenth Corps to the left, and drive the enemy towards the pike. I will put what is available of General Crook's forces on the left of the pike and General Merritt's cavalry also, and send Custer well out on Emory's right to cover that flank. Do you clearly comprehend?"

"Certainly! The Sixth and Nineteenth Corps attack, with Merritt's cavalry on the left and Custer's on the right, the right division of the Nineteenth to try and outflank the enemy and swing towards the pike."

"Good!" said the general, with a quick nod, and I saluted

and sprang to my saddle with a feeling of elation difficult for one not a soldier to adequately comprehend.

I found General Wright just in rear of his corps, lying on the ground. He sat up as I reported, and I saw that his beard was clotted with blood and his neck and chin swollen, and he spoke with something of an effort. He had been shot just under the chin early in the day, but had retained command of the army until General Sheridan's arrival, and then assumed command of his own corps. On receiving General Sheridan's order, he said:

"Do I understand that General Emory's troops connect with my right flank?"

"Certainly!"

"And General Crook's forces will be on the left of the pike?"

"Yes, and General Merritt's cavalry also."

"Very well."

And as I saluted and turned away he was already giving orders to his aides. I rode rapidly to General Emory and repeated the commanding general's instructions, and then returned to my former station in rear of the right centre of the Nineteenth Corps.

In a few moments the news ran down the line that we were to advance. Springing to their feet at the word of command, the tired troops stood to arms and seemed to resolutely shake off the depression that had sat so heavily upon them, and began to pull themselves together for the coming fray. Everywhere along the line of battle men might be seen to stoop and retie their shoes; to pull their trousers at the ankle tightly together and then draw up their heavy woollen stockings over them; to rebuckle and tighten their waist-belts; to unbutton the lids of their cartridge-boxes and pull them forward rather more to the front; to rearrange their haversacks and canteens, and to shift their rolls of blankets in order to give freer scope to the expansion of their shoulders and an easier play to their arms; to set their forage-caps tighter on their heads, pulling the vizor well down over their eyes; and then, almost as if by order, there rang from one end of the line to the other the rattle of ramrods and snapping of gunlocks as each man tested for himself the condition of his rifle, and made sure that his weapon was in good order and to be depended upon in the emergency that was so soon to arise. Then, grounding arms, they stood at ease, half leaning on their rifles, saying little, but quietly awaiting orders and grimly gazing straight towards the front. In front of the battalions, with drawn swords and set lips, stood their line-officers, slightly craning their heads forward and looking into the woods, as if trying to catch a glimpse of the enemy they knew to be somewhere there, but whom as yet they could not see.

I push through the line slightly forward of the nearest brigade, and in a moment the sharp command, "Attention!" rings down the line. "Shoulder arms! Forward! *March!*" And with martial tread and floating flags the line of battle is away. "Guide left!" shout the line-officers. "Guide left—*left!*" and that is the only order I hear as we press forward through the thick trees and underbrush. I lean well forward on my horse's neck, striving to catch if possible a glimpse of the Confederate line; but hark! Here comes the first shot. "Steady! *Steady,* men!" Another, and now a few scattering bullets come singing through the woods. The line does not halt or return the fire, but presses steadily on to the oft-repeated command of "Forward! *forward!*" that never ceases to ring from one end to the other of the advancing line. Soon the woods become less dense, and through the trees I see just beyond us an open field partly covered with small bushes, and several hundred yards away, crowning a slight crest on its further side, a low line of fence-rails and loose stones, which, as we leave the edge of the woods, and come into the open, suddenly vomits flame and smoke along its entire length, and a crashing volley tells us that we have found the enemy. For an instant our line staggers, but the volley has been aimed too high and few men fall. "Steady —steady, men!" shout the officers. "*Aim!*" and almost instinctively the whole line throw forward their pieces. "*Fire!*" and the next instant a savage volley answers that of the Confederates. I can see that it has told, too, for in several places along the opposite crest men spring to their feet as if to fall back, but their officers promptly rally them. "Pour it into them, men!" shout our officers. "Let them have it. It's our turn now!" for brute instinct has triumphed and the savage is uppermost with all of us. For a moment or two the men stand and fire at will, as rapidly as it is possible to reload, and then the Confederate fire seems to slowly slacken; so, with a universal shout of "Forward! *forward!*" we press towards the enemy's line. Before we are much more than half way across the field, however, they seem to have abandoned our front, for I cannot see anything ahead of us, though I stand up in my stirrups and look eagerly forward. But what—what is that? *Crash! crash!* and from a little bush-covered plateau on our right the enemy sends a couple of rattling volleys on our exposed flank that do us great harm, and I realize that *we are the outflanked!*

For an instant the line gives way, but every mounted officer in the vicinity, among whom I recognize General Fessenden, seems to be instantly on the spot trying to rally the troops and hold the line. *"Steady! steady! Right wheel!"* is the shout, and the men, after the first flush of surprise, behave splendidly, one young color-bearer rushing to the right and waving his flag defiantly in the new direction from which the enemy's fire is now coming. I ask him to let me take it, as I am mounted and it can be seen better, as there is some undergrowth at this particular spot in the field. At first he demurs, but seeing the point, yields. Holding on to my saddle, the color-bearer accompanies me towards a slight hillock. The line catches sight of it, and the left begins to swing slowly round, the men in our immediate vicinity loading and firing as rapidly as they can in the direction from which the enemy is now advancing. The Confederates are giving it to us hot, and we realize that we have lost the continuity of our line on both flanks.

Suddenly peal on peal of musketry broke out on our right, and the copse in front of us was fairly bullet-swept by repeated volleys. The next moment a portion of one of McMillan's brigades, which he had promptly swung round and faced to the right, dashed forward, and together we moved up to the position just held by the enemy, to find that he was in headlong retreat. One hasty look and I saw that we had pierced the enemy's line, and that his extreme left was cut off and scattered. But I could not see any troops nor anything of his line over in the direction of the pike, as there was a dense belt of woods that shut out the view. Nevertheless, the steady roar of artillery and peals of musketry told us that heavy fighting was going on in that part of the field. General McMillan was already re-forming his men to move over and take up the line and our former direction to the left, when General Sheridan, riding his gray charger Breckenridge, and surrounded by his staff, came out of the woods and dashed up. One glance and he had the situation. "This is all right! this is all right!" was his sole comment. Then turning to General McMillan, he directed him to con-

tinue the movement and close up to the left and complete
our line of battle as it originally was.

He told me, however, to hold the troops until I saw that
Custer had driven the enemy's cavalry from our flank. This
we could easily see, as the country was open and the ground
lower than where we were. Having given these instructions,
the general, followed by his staff, galloped rapidly to the left
and rear through the woods, evidently making for the pike,
where, judging from the continued roar of field-guns and
musketry, the Sixth Corps was having savage work.

As soon as we saw General Custer's squadrons charge
across the field and engage the enemy's cavalry, General
McMillan ordered the advance, and we pushed forward,
driving the enemy ahead of us through the wood, and came
out to the left and rear of the Confederate line, enabling our
left to pour in a fearful fire on their exposed flank. The
enemy was gallantly holding his line behind some stone
fences, but "flesh that is born of woman" could not stand
such work as this, and the cavalry, having got well in on
their right flank about this time, gave way in retreat.

Our whole army now pressed rapidly forward, not stopping to re-form, but driving them from each new line of
fence; but it was no walk-over even then, for the Confederates fought splendidly—desperately even. They tried
to take advantage of every stone fence, house, or piece of
woods on which to rally their men and retard our advance.
Their batteries were served gallantly and handled
brilliantly, and took up position after position; but it was all
in vain, for we outnumbered them, both cavalry and infantry, and their men must have comprehended the fact that
our cavalry was turning both their flanks. They made their
last stand on the hills just this side of Cedar Creek, occupying the reverse side of some of our own earthworks; and
when the infantry I was with came up to Belle Plain, which
was the house General Sheridan had occupied as headquarters prior to his departure for Washington, it was already
getting quite dark. I dismounted here and ran in a moment
to see whether Colonel Tolles and Dr. Ohlenschlaeger, two
of General Sheridan's staff who had been wounded by
guerillas, were still living. They were still alive, but unconscious, and some one (a Confederate, I think), fearing
that the house might be shelled during the action, had
placed their mattresses on the floor to keep them as far out of

harm's way as possible. Hurrying out, I pushed on with the infantry.

For a few moments the Confederates held their position on the hills, but suddenly abandoned it in haste and sought safety in flight, for some of General Custer's cavalry had crossed the creek at the ford below and were getting in their rear, and to remain was to be captured. I soon caught up with some of our cavalry regiments, and we started in full cry after the enemy. It was no use for them to attempt anything but flight from this on, and they abandoned everything and got away from our pursuing squadrons as best they might, hundreds of them leaving the pike and scattering through the hills. On we went, pell-mell, in the dark. Two regiments, the Fifth New York Cavalry and the First Vermont Cavalry, to the best of my recollection, were the only regimental organizations that went beyond Strasburg. The road was literally crammed with abandoned wagons, ambulances, caissons, and artillery.

At a small bridge, where a creek crosses the road some distance south of the town, we were fired upon from the opposite side by what I thought was the last organized force of General Early's army. I now believe it to have been his provost guard with a large body of our prisoners captured by the enemy early in the day. The planks of this bridge were torn up to prevent the enemy from coming back during the night and carrying off any of the captured property. I then started to return to headquarters, counting the captured cannon as I went. It soon occurred to me that as it was so dark I might mistake a caisson for a gun, so I dismounted and placed my hand on each piece. I reached headquarters about half-past eight or possibly nine o'clock. Camp-fires were blazing everywhere. I went up to the chief, who was standing near a bright fire surrounded by a group of officers and saluted, reporting my return.

"Where do you come from?"

"Beyond Strasburg."

"What news have you?"

"The road is lined with transportation of almost every kind, and we have captured forty-four pieces of artillery."

"How do you *know* that we have forty-four pieces?"

"I have placed my hand on each and every gun."

Standing there in the firelight I saw my chief's face light up with a great wave of satisfaction.

BEFORE PETERSBURG

A STALEMATE OCCURRED AT COLD HARBOR and lasted for about two weeks. Grant could not break the Confederate lines by frontal assault, nor could he continue to sideslip around Lee's right flank; such a maneuver would simply take Grant farther away from Richmond. Instead, he marched south, bearing slightly to the east, toward the banks of the James River where he hoped to make a crossing before Lee could get at him.

Grant made "careful preparations for the formidable movement he was about to undertake, for he was fully impressed by its hazardous nature. The army had to be withdrawn so quietly from its position that it would be able to gain a night's march before its absence could be discovered. The fact that the lines were within thirty to forty yards of each other at some points made this an exceedingly delicate task. Roads had to be constructed over the marshes leading to the lower Chickahominy, and bridges thrown over that stream preparatory to crossing. The army was then to move to the James and cross upon pontoon bridges and improvised ferries. This would involve a march of about fifty miles. . . . Lee, holding interior lines, could arrive there by a march of less than half that distance."*

The maneuver was a great success. By June 16 Grant had the army with all its artillery safely across. A great opportunity to capture Petersburg—an important rail center twenty-two miles south of Richmond, by which the Southern capital was supplied—was missed when two corps of Grant's army failed to coordinate their attack on Beauregard's very thin defenses. On June 20 Lee moved the Army of Northern Virginia into the fortifications around Richmond, and Petersburg was secure. The war could have been shortened by the capture of Petersburg, but at long last

* From Horace Porter, *Campaigning with Grant.*

Grant had won an important tactical advantage over Lee: he had forced the Confederate general into a siege position, thus depriving the Army of Northern Virginia of its awesomely effective mobility.

Frontal assaults on the Confederate fortifications were launched from time to time, but more as probes than attempts to provoke a major battle. Grant dug and strengthened trenches and continued to extend them to the west, hoping to secure a position from which to cut the two railroads still open to Richmond. The most famous attempt to break through the Petersburg defenses was by mine explosion. The mine-blast planner, Colonel Pleasants, had little help from the army engineers, but he refused to be discouraged. He says:

"My regiment was only about four hundred strong. At first I employed but a few men at a time, but the number was increased as the work progressed, until at last I had to use the whole regiment—non-commissioned officers and all. The great difficulty I had was to dispose of the material got out of the mine. I found it impossible to get any assistance from anybody; I had to do all the work myself. I had to remove all the earth in old cracker-boxes; I got pieces of hickory and nailed on the boxes in which we received our crackers, and then iron-clad them with hoops of iron taken from old pork and beef barrels. . . . Whenever I made application I could not get anything, although General Burnside was very favorable to it. The most important thing was to ascertain how far I had to mine, because if I fell short of or went beyond the proper place, the explosion would have no practical effect. Therefore I wanted an accurate instrument with which to make the necessary triangulations. I had to make them on the farthest front line, where the enemy's sharp-shooters could reach me. I could not get the instrument I wanted, although there was one at army headquarters, and General Burnside had to send to Washington and get an old-fashioned theodolite, which was given to me. . . . General Burnside told me that General Meade and Major Duane, chief engineer of the Army of the Potomac, said the thing could not be done—that it was all clap-trap and nonsense; that such a length of mine had never been excavated in military operations, and could not be; that I would either get the men smothered, for want of air, or crushed by the falling of the earth; or the enemy would find it out and it would amount to nothing. I could get no boards or lumber supplied to me for my operations. I had to get a pass and send two companies of my own regiment, with wagons, outside of our lines to rebel saw-mills, and get lumber in that way, after having previously got what lumber I could by tearing down an old bridge."*

The mine was finished by July 22; an attack was to be coordinated with the explosion early on the thirtieth. "Immediately after the explosion two brigades were to pass through the opening made in the enemy's works, in two columns, one to turn to the right, and the other to the left. Three other divisions would charge directly for the summit of the hill. After them would advance the 18th Corps, and our success seemed assured. Once established on the hill, Petersburg would be ours on July 30th.

"The hour set for the explosion was half past three in the morning. Everyone was up, the officers watch in hand, eyes fixed on the fated redan. From after three the minutes were counted. . . . It is still too dark, it was said. . . . At four o'clock it was daylight; nothing stirred as yet. At a quarter past four a murmur of impatience ran through the ranks. What has happened? Has there been a counterorder or an accident?

"What had happened was that the fuse, which was ninety feet long, had gone out at a splice about halfway of its length. Two intrepid men volunteered to relight it. Suddenly the earth trembled under our feet. An enormous mass sprang into the air. Without form or shape, full of red flames and carried on a bed of lightning flashes, it mounted toward heaven with a detonation of thunder. It spread out like an immense mushroom whose stem seemed to be of fire and its head of smoke.

"Then everything appeared to break up and fall back in a rain of earth mixed with rocks, beams, timbers and mangled human bodies, leaving floating in the air a cloud of white smoke and a cloud of grey dust, which fell slowly toward the earth. The redan had disappeared. In its place had opened a gaping gulf more than 200 feet long and 50 wide and 25 to 30 feet deep.

"All our batteries opened at once on the enemy's entrenchments, and the 1st Brigade advanced to the assault.

"It had nothing in front of it. The Confederate troops occupying the lines in the immediate vicinity of the mine had fled precipitately. The way was completely open to the summit of the hill.

* From *Battles and Leaders*, Vol. IV.

"The column marched to the crater but instead of turning around it, descended into it. Once at the bottom, finding itself sheltered, it stayed there. The general commanding the division had remained within our lines, in a bombproof.

"The 2nd Brigade was soon mixed up with the other. Several regiments descended into the crater, but only one brigade succeeded in making its way through so as to advance beyond. It found itself then engaged in ground cut up by trenches, by covered ways, by sheltered pits dug in the ground. Worse than that, the enemy, recovering from his surprise, had already placed his guns in position and formed his infantry so as to throw a concentrated fire upon the opening made in his works. The brigade, seeing that it was neither supported nor reinforced, was compelled to fall back with loss.

"The 3rd Brigade had not even made a like attempt. Mingling with the first, it had simply increased the confusion.

"Toward seven o'clock a colored brigade received orders to advance in its turn. The Negroes advanced resolutely, passed over the passive mass of white troops, not a company of whom followed them, and charged under a deadly fire of artillery and musketry, which reached them from all sides at once. They even reached the enemy, took from him 250 prisoners, captured a flag and recovered one of ours taken by him. But they were not sustained. They were driven back by a countercharge and returned running in confusion to our lines where, by this time, a large number of the white troops were eager to return with them.

"In a moment it was a general devil-take-the-hindmost, a confused rush in which those who could run fast enough and escape the Rebel fire returned to our lines. Those who endeavored to resist, or were delayed, were taken prisoners.

"Thus passed away the finest opportunity which could have been given us to capture Petersburg."*

There was heavy skirmishing throughout the rest of the summer into the early fall. Grant continued to extend his lines westward, while Lee countered by sidestepping with him. Eventually the fortifications stretched more than fifty miles.

The winter months went by, spring came, and still the siege held. Then on April 1, Grant struck a major blow. For

* From Regis de Trobriand, *Four Years with the Army of the Potomac*.

Petersburg: *Slaughter at the Crater*

the first time since the opening of the campaign he managed to turn Lee's right flank. "The next day Grant ordered an assault all along the main lines. General Horatio Wright and his VI Corps found a place where Lee's force had been stretched too thin and broke it—losing two thousand men in the assault, for even when they were woefully undermanned these Petersburg lines were all but invulnerable—punching a wide hole that could not be repaired. On the evening and night of April 2 Lee evacuated Petersburg and Richmond and began his final retreat.

"A great fire burned in Richmond when Union troops marched in. Retreating Confederates had fired various warehouses full of goods they could not take with them, and in the wild confusion of defeat these flames got out of hand; the victorious Unionists, coming at last into the capital city of the Confederacy, spent their first hours there as a fire brigade, putting out flames, checking looting, and bringing order back to the desolate town. Lincoln himself came up the James River in a gun-boat—he had been at City Point, unable to tear himself away from the military nerve center while the climactic battle was being fought—and he walked up the streets of Richmond with a handful of sailors for an escort, dazed crowds looking on in silence; went to the Confederate White House, sat for a time at Jefferson Davis's desk, and saw for himself the final collapse of the nation he had sworn to destroy.

"Most of Grant's army never got into Richmond, and neither did Grant himself. They were on the road, pushing along furiously to head Lee off and drive him into a pocket where he could be forced to surrender."*

Lee Retreats†

BY MAJOR ROBERT STILES

ON SUNDAY, THE 2D OF APRIL, I stood almost all day on our works overhanging the river, listening to the fire about Petersburg, and noting its peculiar character and progres-

* Bruce Catton, *This Hallowed Ground*. p. 384.
† From *Four Years Under Marse Robert*.

sion. I made up my mind what it meant, and had time and space out there alone with God and upon His day to commit myself and mine to Him, and to anticipate and prepare for the immediate future. Late in the afternoon I walked back to my quarters, and soon after, George Cary Eggleston, who was then in a command that held a part of the line near us, dropped in. He tells me now that I asked him then what effect he thought it would have upon our cause if our lines should be broken and we compelled to give up Petersburg and Richmond; and that he declined to answer the question because, as he said, that supposed facts were out of the plane of the practical, and would not and could not happen. Now, years afterwards, recalling the peculiar expression and manner with which I propounded this interrogatory, he asks whether I had then received any official information, and I answer in the negative—no, none whatever. Up to the time Eggleston left my camp for his I knew nothing beyond what my tell-tale ears and prescient soul had told me.

Indeed, we went into our meeting that night without any other information; but I had directed the acting-adjutant to remain in his office and to bring at once to me, in the church, any orders that might come to hand. Our service was one of unusual power and interest. I read with the men the "Soldier Psalm," the ninety-first, and exhorted them, in any special pressure that might come upon us in the near future—the "terror by night" or the "destruction . . . at noon-day"—to abide with entire confidence in that "Stronghold," to appropriate that "Strength."

As I uttered these words, I noticed a well-grown, fine-looking country lad named Blount, who was leaning forward, and gazing at me with eager interest, while tears of sympathy and appreciation were brimming his eyes. The door opened and the adjutant appeared. I told him to stand a moment where he was, and as quietly as possible told the men what I was satisfied was the purport of the paper he held in his hand, and why I was so satisfied. And then we prayed for the realization of what David had expressed in that Psalm—for faith, for strength, for protection. After the prayer I called for the paper and read it over, first silently and then aloud, gave brief directions to the men and dismissed them—first calling upon such officers and non-commissioned officers as had special duties to perform in connection with the magazines, etc., to remain a few moments. The men were ordered to rendezvous at a given hour, and to fall in by companies on the parade, and the company officers were ordered to see that they brought with them only what was absolutely necessary, and a brief approximate list was given of the proper campaign outfit. But the poor fellows had been many months in garrison, and it was maddening work within a short and fixed time, to select from their motley accumulations what was really necessary in the changed conditions ahead of us.

The orders were, in general, that the men of the fleet and of the James River defenses should leave the river about midnight of the 2d of April, exploding magazines and ironclads, and join the Army of Northern Virginia in its retreat. Orders such as these were enough to try the mettle even of the best troops, in the highest condition, but for my poor little battalion they were overwhelming, well-nigh stupefying. The marvel is that they held together at all and left the Bluff, as they did, in pretty fair condition. A few months earlier I question whether they would have been equal to it.

I said they left in pretty fair condition, and so they did, except that they had more baggage piled upon their backs than any one brigade, perhaps I might say division, in General Lee's army was bearing at the same moment. I could hardly blame them, and there was no time to correct the folly; besides, I knew it would correct and adjust itself, as it had done pretty well by morning.

The explosions began just as we got across the river. When the magazines at Chaffin's and Drury's Bluffs went off, the solid earth shuddered convulsively; but as the ironclads—one after another—exploded, it seemed as if the very dome of heaven would be shattered down upon us. Earth and air and the black sky glared in the lurid light. Columns and towers and pinnacles of flame shot upward to an amazing height, from which, on all sides, the ignited shells flew on arcs of fire and burst as if bombarding heaven. I distinctly remember feeling that after this I could never more be startled—no, not by the catastrophes of the last great day.

I walked in rear of the battalion to prevent straggling and, as the successive flashes illumined the darkness, the blanched faces and staring eyes turned backward upon me spoke volumes of nervous demoralization. I felt that a hare might shatter the column. No Confederate soldier who was on and of that fearful retreat can fail to recall it as one of the most trying experiences of his life. Trying enough, in the mere fact that the Army of Northern Virginia was flying before its foes, but further trying, incomparably trying, in lack of food and rest and sleep, and because of the audacious pressure of the enemy's cavalry. The combined and continued strain of all this upon soft garrison troops, unenured to labor and hardship and privation and peril, can hardly be conceived and cannot be described. Its two most serious effects were *drowsiness and nervousness*. We crossed and left James River at midnight on Sunday. . . .

The somewhat disorganized condition of the troops and the crowded condition of the roads necessitated frequent halts, and whenever these occurred—especially after night-fall—the men would drop in the road, or on the side of it, and sleep until they were roused, and it was manifestly impossible to rouse them all. My two horses were in almost constant use to transport officers and men who had given out, especially our doctor, whose horse was for some reason unavailable. Besides, I preferred to be on foot, for the very purpose of moving around among the men and rousing them when we resumed the march. With this view I was a good part of the time at the rear of the battalion; but notwithstanding my efforts in this respect, individually and through a detail of men selected and organized for the purpose of waking the sleepers, we lost, I am satisfied, every time we resumed the march after a halt at night—men who were not found or who could not be roused.

The nervousness resulting from this constant strain of starvation, fatigue, and lack of sleep was a dangerous thing, at one time producing very lamentable results, which threatened to be even more serious than they were. One evening an officer, I think of one of our supply departments, passed and repassed us several times, riding a powerful black stallion, all of whose furnishings—girths, reins, etc.,—were very heavy, indicating the unmanageable character of the horse. When he rode ahead the last time, about dark, it seems that he imprudently hitched his horse by tying his very stout tie rein to a heavy fence rail which was part of the road fence. Something frightened the animal and he reared back, pulling the rail out of the fence and dragging it after him full gallop down the road crowded with troops, mowing them down like the scythe of a war chairot. Someone, thinking there was a charge of cavalry, fired his musket and, on the instant, three or four battalions, mine among them, began firing into each other.

I was never more alarmed. Muskets were discharged in my very face, and I fully expected to be shot down; but after the most trying and perilous experience, the commanding officers succeeded in getting control of their men and getting them again into formation. But while we were talking to them, suddenly the panic seized them again, and they rushed in such a wild rout against the heavy road fence that they swept it away, and many of them took to the woods, firing back as they ran. A second time the excitement was quieted and a third time it broke out. By this time, however, I had fully explained to my men that we had just put out fresh flankers on both sides of the road, that we could not have an attack of cavalry without warning from them, and that the safe and soldierly thing to do was to lie down until everything should become calm. I was much pleased that this third time my command did not fire a shot, while the battalions in our front and rear were firing heavily. A field officer and a good many other officers and men were killed and wounded in these alarms, just how many I do not believe was ever ascertained.

When we next halted for any length of time, during daylight, I formed my men and talked to them fully and quietly about these alarms explaining the folly of their firing, and impressing upon them simply to lie down, keep quiet, and attempt to catch and obey promptly any special orders I might give. I complimented them upon their having resisted the panicky infection the last time it broke out, and felt that, upon the whole, my men had gained rather than lost by the experience.

On Thursday afternoon we had descended into a moist, green little valley, crossed a small stream called Sailor's Creek, and, ascending a gentle, grassy slope beyond it, had halted, and the men were lying down and resting in the edge of a pine wood that crowned the elevation. A desultory fire was going on ahead and bullets began to drop in. I was walking about among the men seeing that everything was in order and talking cheerfully with them, when I heard a ball strike something hard and saw a little commotion around the battalion colors. Going there, I found that the flag-staff had been splintered, and called out to the men that we were beginning to make a record.

Next moment I heard an outcry—"There, Brookin is killed!"—and saw one of the men writhing on the ground. I went to him. He seemed to be partially paralyzed below the waist, but said he was shot through the neck. I saw no blood anywhere. He had on his roll of blankets and, sure enough, a ball had gone through them and also through his jacket and flannel shirt; but there it was, sticking in the back of his neck, having barely broken the skin. I took it out and said: "Oh, you are not a dead man by a good deal. Here"—handing the ball to him—"take that home and give it to your sweetheart. It'll fix you all right." Brookin caught at the ball and held it tightly clasped in his hand, smiling faintly, and the men about him laughed.

Just then I heard a shell whizzing over us, coming from across the creek, and we were hurried into line facing in that direction, that is, *to the rear*. I inferred, of course, that we were surrounded, but could not tell how strong the force was upon which we were turning our backs.

I remember, in all the discomfort and wretchedness of the retreat, we had been no little amused by the Naval Battalion, under that old hero, Admiral Tucker. The soldiers called them the "Aye, Ayes," because they responded "aye, aye" to every order, some times repeating the order itself, and adding, "Aye, aye, it is, sir!" As this battalion, which followed immediately after ours, was getting into position and seaman's and landsman's jargon and movements were getting a good deal mixed in the orders and evolutions—all being harmonized, however, and licked into shape by the "aye, aye"—a young officer of the division staff rode up, saluted Admiral Tucker, and said: "Admiral, I may possibly be of assistance to you in getting your command into line." The Admiral replied: "Young man, I understand how to talk to my people"; and thereupon followed "a grand moral combination" of "right flank" and "left flank," "starboard" and "larboard," "aye, aye" and "aye, aye"—until the battalion gradually settled down into place.

By this time a large Federal force had deployed into line on the other slope beyond the creek, which we had left not long since; two or three lines of battle, and a heavy park of artillery, which rapidly came into battery and opened an accurate and deadly fire, we having no guns with which to reply and thus disturb their aim. My men were lying down and were ordered not to expose themselves. I was walking backward and forward just back of the line, talking to them whenever that was practicable, and keeping my eye upon everything, feeling that such action and exposure on my part were imperatively demanded by the history and condition of the command and my rather peculiar relations to it. A good many had been wounded and several killed when a twenty-pounder Parrott shell struck immediately in my front, on the line, nearly severing a man in twain, and hurling him bodily over my head, his arms hanging down and his hands almost slapping me in the face as they passed.

In that one awful moment I distinctly recognized young Blount, who had gazed into my face so intently Sunday night; and but for that peculiar paralysis which in battle some times passes upon a man's entire being—excepting only his fighting powers—the recognition might have been too much for me.

In a few moments the artillery fire ceased and I had time to glance about me and note results a little more carefully. I had seldom seen a fire more accurate, nor one that had been more deadly, in a single regiment, in so brief a time. The expression of the men's faces indicated clearly enough its effect upon them. They did not appear to be hopelessly demoralized, but they did look blanched and haggard and awe-struck.

The Federal infantry had crossed the creek and were now coming up the slope in two lines of battle. I stepped in front of my line and passed from end to end, impressing upon my men that no one must fire his musket until I so ordered; that when I said *"ready"* they must all rise, kneeling on the right knee; that when I said *"aim"* they must all aim about the knees of the advancing line; that when I said *"fire"* they must all fire together, and that it was all-important they should follow these directions exactly, and obey, implicitly and instantly, any other instructions or orders I might give.

The enemy was coming on and everything was still as the grave. My battalion was formed upon and around a swell of the hill, which threw it farther to the front than any other command in the division, so that, being likely first to meet the enemy and having received no special orders, I was compelled, as to details, to shape my own course. The Federal officers knowing, as I suppose, that we were surrounded and appreciating the fearful havoc their artillery fire had wrought, probably entertained the hope that we would surrender—some of them, as I remember, having their white handkerchiefs in their hands and waving them toward us as if suggesting that course—and yet they never ceased their advance upon our position, nor sent forward a flag of truce, nor even made any demand or call upon us to surrender; nor, so far as I know or believe or have ever heard, were any white flags or indications of surrender exhibited anywhere in our lines. I do not recall any exact parallel to these circumstances.

I dislike to break the flow and force of the narrative by repeated modifying references to recollection and memory; but it is not safe for a man, so many years after the event, to be positive with regard to details, unless there was special reason why they should have been impressed upon him at the time. I will say, then, that my memory records no musket shot on either side up to this time, our skirmishers having retired upon the main line without firing. The enemy showed no disposition to break into the charge, but continued to advance in the same measured and even hesitating manner, and I allowed them to approach very close—I should be afraid to say just how close—before retiring behind my men, who, as before stated, were lying down. I had continued to walk along their front for the very purpose of preventing them from opening fire; but now I stepped through the line and stationing myself about the middle of it, called out my orders deliberately—everything being in full sight of both parties, and the enemy, as I have every reason to believe, hearing every word. *"Ready!"* To my great relief, the men rose, all together, like a piece of mechanism, kneeling on their right knees and their faces set with an expression that meant —everything. *"Aim!"* The musket barrels fell to an almost perfect horizontal line leveled about the knees of the advancing front line, *"Fire!"*

I have never seen such an effect, physical and moral, produced by the utterance of one word. The enemy seemed to have been totally unprepared for it, and, as the sequel showed, my own men scarcely less so. The earth appeared to have swallowed up the first line of the Federal force in our front. There was a rattling supplement to the volley and the second line wavered and broke.

The revulsion was too sudden. On the instant every man in my battalion sprang to his feet, and, without orders, they rushed, bareheaded and with unloaded muskets, down the slope after the retreating Federals. I tried to stop them, but in vain, although I actually got ahead of a good many of them. They simply bore me on with the flood.

The standard-bearer was dashing by me, colors in hand, when I managed to catch his roll of blankets and jerk him violently back, demanding what he meant, advancing the battalion colors without orders. As I was speaking, the artillery opened fire again and he was hurled to the earth, as I supposed, dead. I stopped to pick up the flag, when his brother, a lieutenant, a fine officer and a splendid-looking fellow, stepped over the body, saying: "Those colors belong to me, Major!" at the same time taking hold of the staff. He was shot through the brain and fell backward. One of the color guard sprang forward, saying: "Give them to me, Major!" But by the time his hand reached the staff he was down. There were at least five men dead and wounded lying close about me, and I did not see why I should continue to make a target of myself. I therefore jammed the color staff down through a thick bush, which supported it in an upright position, and turned my attention to my battalion, which was scattered over the face of the hill firing irregularly at the Federals, who seemed to be reforming to renew the attack. I managed to get my men into some sort of formation and their guns loaded, and then charged the Federal line, driving it back across the creek, and forming my command behind a little ridge, which protected it somewhat.

I ran back up the hill and had a brief conversation with General Curtis Lee—commanding the division, our brigade commander having been killed—explaining to him that I had not ordered the advance and that we would be cut off if we remained long where we were, but that I was satisfied I could bring the battalion back through a ravine, which would protect them largely from the fire of the enemy's artillery, and reform them on the old line, on the right of the naval battalion, which had remained in position. He expressed his doubts as to this, but I told him I believed my battalion would follow me anywhere, and with his permission I would try it. I ran down the hill again and explained to my men that, when I got to the left of the line and shouted to them, they were to get up and follow me, on a run and without special formation, through a ravine that led back to the top of the hill. Just because these simple-hearted fellows knew only enough to trust me, and because the enemy was not so far recovered as to take advantage of our exposure while executing the movement to the rear and reforming, we were back in the original lines in a few moments—that is, all who were left of us.

It was of no avail. By the time we had well settled into our old position we were attacked simultaneously, front and rear, by overwhelming numbers, and quicker than I can tell it the battle degenerated into a butchery and a confused melee of brutal personal conflicts. I saw numbers of men kill each other with bayonets and the butts of muskets, and even bite each others' throats and ears and noses, rolling on the ground like wild beasts. I saw one of my officers and a Federal officer fighting with swords over the battalion colors, which we had brought back with us, each having his left hand upon the staff. I could not get to them, but my man was a very athletic, powerful seaman, and soon I saw the Federal officer fall.

I had cautioned my men against wearing "yankee overcoats," especially in battle, but had not been able to enforce the order perfectly—and almost at my side I saw a young fellow of one of my companies jam the muzzle of his musket against the back of the head of his most intimate friend, clad in a Yankee overcoat, and blow his brains out. I was wedged in between fighting men, only my right arm free. I tried to strike the musket barrel up, but alas, my sword had broken in the clash and I could not reach it. I well remember the yell of demoniac triumph with which that simple country lad of yesterday clubbed his musket and whirled savagely upon another victim.

I don't think I ever suffered more than during the few moments after I saw that nothing could affect or change the result of the battle. I could not let myself degenerate into a mere fighting brute or devil, because the lives of these poor fellows were, in some sense, in my hand, though there was nothing I could do just then to shield or save them. Suddenly by one of those inexplicable shiftings which take place on a battle-field, the fighting around me almost entirely creased, and whereas the moment before the whole environment seemed to be crowded with the enemy, there were now few or none of them on the spot, and as the slaughter and the firing seemed to be pretty well over, I concluded I would try to make my escape, I had always considered it likely I should be killed, but had never anticipated or contemplated capture.

I think it was at this juncture I encountered General Curtis Lee, but it may have been after I was picked up. At all events, selecting the direction which seemed to be most free from Federal soldiers and to offer the best chance of escape, I started first at a walk and then broke into a run; but in a short distance ran into a fresh Federal force, and it seemed the most natural and easy thing in the world to be simply arrested and taken in. My recollection is that General Lee asked to be carried before the Federal general commanding on that part of the line, who, at his request, gave orders putting a stop to the firing, there being no organized Confederate force on the field. Thus ended my active life as a Confederate soldier, my four years' service under Marse Robert, and I was not sorry to end it thus, in red-hot battle, and to be spared the pain, I will not say humiliation of Appomattox.

I must, however, mention an incident to which I have already briefly referred, to which it would perhaps have been more delicate not to refer at all; but the reader of this chapter can scarcely have failed to perceive that one of the most deeply stirring episodes in my soldier-life was the struggle I made to lift my battalion out of the demoralization in which I found it; to make my men trust and love me and to rouse and develop in them the true conception of soldierly duty and devotion, courage and endurance.

Looking back upon the teeming recollections of this first and last retreat and this final battle of the Army of Northern Virginia, amid all the overpowering sadness and depression of defeat, I already felt the sustaining consciousness of a real and a worthy success; but it is impossible to express how this consciousness was deepened and heightened when General Ewell sent for me on the field, after we were all captured, and in the presence of half a dozen generals said that he had summoned me to say, in the hearing of these officers, that the conduct of my battalion had been reported to him and that he desired to congratulate me and them upon the record they had made.

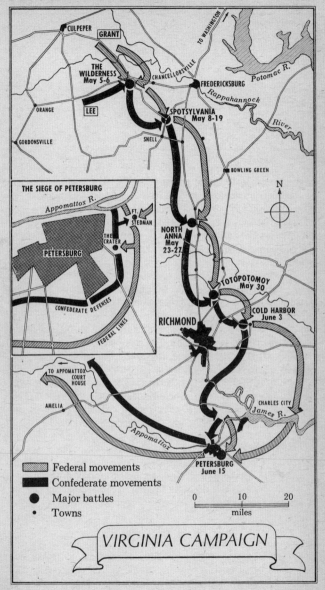

THE SIEGE OF PETERSBURG

Federal movements
Confederate movements
Major battles
Towns

0   10   20
miles

VIRGINIA CAMPAIGN

THE LAST DAY

ON APRIL 9, SHERIDAN, WITH A CORPS OF INFANTRYMEN, cut across Lee's last escape corridor to North Carolina. One of the officers in the infantry corps was Major General J. L. Chamberlain, who describes the last hours:

"By sunrise we had reached Appomattox Station. A staff officer was here to turn us to the Appomattox River, where we might cut Lee's retreat. . . . It had come at last—the supreme hour.

"Dashing out of a woods road came a cavalry staff officer. With sharp salutation he exclaimed, 'General Sheridan wishes you to come to his support. The Rebel infantry is pressing him hard.'

"At cavalry speed we pushed through the woods, right on Sheridan's battle flag gleaming in an open field. Right before us our cavalry gallantly was stemming the surges of the old Stonewall Brigade, desperate to beat its way through. . . . In a few minutes the tide was turned: the incoming wave was at high flood; it receded. Their last hope was gone. . . . They were now giving way but kept a good front by force of old habit. Halfway up the slope they made a stand, with what perhaps they thought a good omen—behind a stone wall.

"Suddenly rose to sight another form—a soldierly young figure, a Confederate staff officer undoubtedly, to whom someone in my advanced line seemed to be pointing out my position. Now I saw the white flag. . . . The messenger drew near, dismounted, 'Sir, I am from General Gordon. General Lee desires a cessation of hostilities until he can hear from General Grant as to the proposed surrender.'

"One o'clock came. I turned about. There behind me appeared a commanding form superbly mounted, richly accoutered, of imposing bearing, noble countenance with expression of deep sadness overmastered by deeper strength. It was no other than Robert E. Lee. . . .

"Not long after, by another road, appeared another form—plain, unassuming, simple and familiar to our eyes, but as awe-inspiring as Lee in his splendor and sadness. It was Grant. Slouched hat without cord; common soldier's blouse, unbuttoned on which, however, were four stars; high boots mudsplashed to the top, trousers tucked inside; no sword, but the sword hand deep in the pocket; sitting his saddle with the ease of a born master; taking no notice of anything, all his faculties gathered into intense thought. He seemed greater than I had ever seen him—a look as of another world about him.

"Staff officers were flying about crying, 'Lee surrenders!' "*

The Surrender
at Appomattox Court House**
BY GENERAL HORACE PORTER

ABOUT ONE O'CLOCK the little village of Appomattox Court House, with its half-dozen houses, came in sight, and soon we were entering its single street. It is situated on some rising ground, and beyond the country slopes down into a broad valley. The enemy was seen with his columns and wagon trains covering the low ground. Our cavalry, the Fifth Corps, and part of Ord's command were occupying the high ground to the south and west of the enemy, heading him off completely. Generals Sheridan and Ord, with a group of officers around them, were seen in the road, and as our party came up General Grant said: "How are you Sheridan?" "First-rate, thank you; how are you" cried Sheridan, with a voice and look that seemed to indicate that on his part he was having things all his own way. "Is Lee over there?" asked General Grant, pointing up the street, having heard a rumor that Lee was in that vicinity. "Yes, he is in that brick house," answered Sheridan. "Well, then, we'll go over," said Grant.

* From "Personal Recollections of the War of the Rebellion," published in the *New York Commandery*, Third Series.
** From *Battles and Leaders*, Vol. IV.

The general-in-chief now rode on, accompanied by Sheridan, Ord, and some others, and soon colonel Babcock's orderly was seen sitting on his horse in the street in front of a two-story brick house, better in appearance than the rest of the houses. He said General Lee and Colonel Babcock had gone into this house a short time before, and he was ordered to post himself in the street and keep a lookout for General Grant, so as to let him know where General Lee was.

The house had a comfortable wooden porch with seven steps leading up to it. A hall ran through the middle from front to back, and on each side was a room having two windows, one in front and one in rear. Each room had two doors opening into the hall. The building stood a little distance back from the street, with a yard in front, and to the left was a gate for carriages and a roadway running to a stable in rear. We entered the grounds by this gate and dismounted. In the yard were seen a fine large gray horse, which proved to be General Lee's, and a good-looking mare belonging to Colonel Marshall. An orderly in gray was in charge of them, and had taken off their bridles to let them nibble the grass.

General Grant mounted the steps and entered the house. As he stepped into the hall Colonel Babcock, who had seen his approach from the window, opened the door of the room on the left, in which he had been sitting with General Lee and Colonel Marshall awaiting General Grant's arrival. The general passed in, while the members of the staff, Generals Sheridan and Ord, and some general officers who had gathered in the front yard, remained outside, feeling that he would probably want his first interview with General Lee to be, in a measure, private. In a few minutes Colonel Babcock came to the front door and, making a motion with his hat toward the sitting-room, said: "The general says, come in." It was then about half-past one of Sunday, the 9th of April. We entered, and found General Grant sitting at a marble-topped table in the center of the room, and Lee sitting beside a small oval table near the front window, in the corner opposite to the door by which we entered, and facing General Grant. Colonel Marshall, his military secretary, was standing at his left. We walked in softly and ranged ourselves quietly about the sides of the room, very much as people enter a sick-chamber when they expect to find the patient dangerously ill. Some found seats on the sofa and the few chairs which constituted the furniture, but most of the party stood.

The contrast between the two commanders was striking, and could not fail to attract marked attention as they sat ten feet apart facing each other. General Grant, then nearly forty-three years of age, was five feet eight inches in height, with shoulders slightly stooped. His hair and full beard were a nut-brown, without a trace of gray in them. He had on a single-breasted blouse, made of dark-blue flannel, unbuttoned in front, and showing a waistcoat underneath. He wore an ordinary pair of top-boots, with his trousers inside, and was without spurs. The boots and portions of his clothes were spattered with mud. He had had on a pair of thread gloves, of a dark-yellow color, which he had taken off on entering the room. His felt "sugarloaf" stiff-brimmed hat was thrown on the table beside him. He had no sword, and a pair of shoulder-straps was all there was about him to designate his rank. In fact, aside from these, his uniform was that of a private soldier.

Lee, on the other hand, was fully six feet in height, and quite erect for one of his age, for he was Grant's senior by sixteen years. His hair and full beard were a silver-gray, and quite thick, except that the hair had become a little thin in front. He wore a new uniform of Confederate gray, buttoned up to the throat, and at his side he carried a long sword of exceedingly fine workmanship, the hilt studded with jewels. It was said to be the sword that had been presented to him by the State of Virginia. His top-boots were comparatively new, and seemed to have on them some ornamental stitching of red silk. Like his uniform, they were singularly clean, and but little travel-stained. On the boots were handsome spurs, with large rowels. A felt hat, which in color matched pretty closely that of his uniform, and a pair of long buckskin gauntlets lay beside him on the table. We asked Colonel Marshall afterward how it was that both he and his chief wore such fine toggery, and looked so much as if they had turned out to go to church, while with us our outward garb scarcely rose to the dignity even of the "shabby-genteel." He enlightened us regarding the contrast, by explaining that when their headquarters wagons had been pressed so closely by our cavalry a few days before, and it was found they would have to destroy all their baggage, except the clothes they carried on their backs, each one, naturally, selected the newest suit he had, and sought to propitiate the god of destruction by a sacrifice of his second-best.

General Grant began the conversation by saying: "I met you once before, General Lee, while we were serving in Mexico, when you came over from General Scott's headquarters to visit Garland's brigade, to which I then belonged. I have always remembered your appearance, and I think I should have recognized you anywhere." "Yes," replied General Lee, "I know I met you on that occasion, and I have often thought of it and tried to recollect how you looked but I have never been able to recall a single feature." After some further mention of Mexico, General Lee said: "I suppose, General Grant, that the object of our present meeting is fully understood. I asked to see you to ascertain upon what terms you would receive the surrender of my army." General Grant replied: "The terms I propose are those stated substantially in my letter of yesterday—that is, the officers and men surrendered to be paroled and disqualified from taking up arms again until properly exchanged, and all arms, ammunition, and supplies to be delivered up as captured property." Lee nodded an assent, and said: "Those are about the conditions which I expected would be proposed." General Grant then continued: "Yes, I think our correspondence indicated pretty clearly the action that would be taken at our meeting; and I hope it may lead to a general suspension of hostilities and be the means of preventing any further loss of life."

Lee inclined his head as indicating his accord with this wish, and General Grant then went on to talk at some length in a very pleasant vein about the prospects of peace. Lee was evidently anxious to proceed to the formal work of the surrender, and he brought the subject up again by saying:

"I presume, General Grant, we have both carefully considered the proper steps to be taken, and I would suggest that you commit to writing the terms you have proposed, so that they may be formally acted upon."

"Very well," replied General Grant, "I will write them out." And calling for his manifold order-book, he opened it on the table before him and proceeded to write the terms. The leaves had been so prepared that three impressions of the writing were made. He wrote very rapidly, and did not pause until he had finished the sentence ending with "officers appointed by me to receive them." Then he looked toward Lee, and his eyes seemed to be resting on the handsome sword that hung at that officer's side. He said afterward that this set him to thinking that it would be an unnecessary humiliation to require the officers to surrender their swords, and a great hardship to deprive them of their personal baggage and horses, and after a short pause he wrote the sentence: "This will not embrace the side-arms of the officers, nor their private horses or baggage." When he had finished the letter he called Colonel (afterward General) Ely S. Parker, one of the military secretaries on the staff, to his side and looked it over with him and directed him as they went along to interline six or seven words and to strike out the word "their," which had been repeated. When this had been done, he handed the book to General Lee and asked him to read over the letter. It was as follows:

APPOMATTOX CT. H., VA.
April 9, 1865

GENERAL R. E. LEE, Commanding C. S. A.
GENERAL:

In accordance with the substance of my letter to you of the 8th inst., I propose to receive the surrender of the Army of Northern Virginia on the following terms, to wit: Rolls of all the officers and men to be made in duplicate, one copy to be given to an officer to be designated by me, the other to be retained by such officer or officers as you may designate. The officers to give their individual paroles not to take up arms against the Government of the United States until properly [exchanged], and each company or regimental commander to sign a like parole for the men of their commands. The arms, artillery, and public property to be parked, and stacked, and turned over to the officers appointed by me to receive them. This will not embrace the side-arms of the officers, nor their private horses or baggage. This done, each officer and man will be allowed to return to his home, not to be disturbed by the United States authorities so long as they observe their paroles, and the laws in force where they may reside.

Very respectfully,   U. S. GRANT, Lieutenant-General

Lee took it and laid it on the table beside him, while he drew from his pocket a pair of steel-rimmed spectacles and wiped the glasses carefully with his handkerchief. Then he crossed his legs, adjusted the spectacles very slowly and deliberately, took up the draft of the letter, and proceeded to read it attentively. It consisted of two pages. When he reached the top line of the second page, he looked up, and said to General Grant: "After the words 'until properly,' the word 'exchanged' seems to be omitted. You doubtless intended to use that word."

"Why, yes," said Grant; "I thought I had put in the word 'exchanged.' "

"I presumed it had been omitted inadvertently," continued Lee, "and with your permission I will mark where it should be inserted."

"Certainly," Grant replied.

Lee felt in his pocket as if searching for a pencil, but did not seem to be able to find one. Seeing this and happening to be standing close to him, I handed him my pencil. He took it, and laying the paper on the table noted the interlineation. During the rest of the interview he kept twirling this pencil in his fingers and occasionally tapping the top of the table with it. When he handed it back it was carefully treasured by me as a memento of the occasion. When Lee came to the sentence about the officers' side-arms, private horses, and baggage, he showed for the first time during the reading of the letter a slight change of countenance, and was evidently touched by this act of generosity. It was doubtless the condition mentioned to which he particularly alluded when he looked toward General Grant as he finished reading and said with some degree of warmth in his manner: "This will have a very happy effect upon my army."

General Grant then said: "Unless you have some suggestions to make in regard to the form in which I have stated the terms, I will have a copy of the letter made in ink and sign it."

"There is one thing I would like to mention," Lee replied after a short pause. "The cavalrymen and artillerists own their own horses in our army. Its organization in this respect differs from that of the United States." This expression attracted the notice of our officers present, as showing how firmly the conviction was grounded in his mind that we were two distinct countries. He continued: "I would like to understand whether these men will be permitted to retain their horses?"

"You will find that the terms as written do not allow this," General Grant replied; "only the officers are permitted to take their private property."

Lee read over the second page of the letter again, and then said:

"No, I see the terms do not allow it; that is clear." His face showed plainly that he was quite anxious to have this concession made, and Grant said very promptly without giving Lee time to make a direct request:

"Well, the subject is quite new to me. Of course I did not know that any private soldiers owned their animals, but I think this will be the last battle of the war—I sincerely hope so—and that the surrender of this army will be followed soon by that of all the others, and I take it that most of the men in the ranks are small farmers, and as the country has been so raided by the two armies, it is doubtful whether they will be able to put in a crop to carry themselves and their familes through the next winter without the aid of the horses they are now riding, and I will arrange it in this way: I will not change the terms as now written, but I will instruct the officers I shall appoint to receive the paroles to let all the men who claim to own a horse or mule take the animals home with them to work their little farms."

Lee now looked greatly relieved, and though anything but a demonstrative man, he gave every evidence of his appreciation of this concession, and said, "This will have the best possible effect upon the men. It will be very gratifying and will do much toward conciliating our people." He handed the draft of the terms back to General Grant, who called Colonel T. S. Bowers of the staff to him and directed him to make a copy in ink. Bowers was a little nervous, and he turned the matter over to Colonel (afterward General) Parker, whose handwriting presented a better appearance than that of any one else on the staff. Parker sat down to write at the table which stood against the rear side of the room. Wilmer McLean's domestic resources in the way of ink now became the subject of a searching investigation, but it was found that the contents of the conical-shaped stoneware inkstand which he produced appeared to be participating in the general breaking up and had disappeared. Colonel Marshall now came to the rescue, and pulled out of his pocket a small boxwood inkstand, which was put at Parker's service, so that, after all, we had to fall back upon the resources of the enemy in furnishing the stage "properties" for the final scene in the memorable military drama.

Lee in the meantime had directed Colonel Marshall to draw up for his signature a letter of acceptance of the terms of surrender. Colonel Marshall wrote out a draft of such a letter, making it quite formal, beginning with "I have the honor to reply to your communition," etc. General Lee took it, and, after reading it over very carefully, directed that these formal expressions be stricken out and that the letter be otherwise shortened. He afterward went over it again and seemed to change some words, and then told the colonel to make a final copy in ink. When it came to providing the paper, it was found we had the only supply of that important ingredient in the recipe for surrendering an army, so we gave a few pages to the colonel. The letter when completed read as follows:

HEADQUARTERS, ARMY OF NORTHERN VIRGINIA
April 9th, 1865

GENERAL:

I received your letter of this date containing the terms of the surrender of the Army of Northern Virginia as proposed by you. As they are substantially the same as those expressed in your letter of the 8th inst., they are accepted. I will proceed to designate the proper officers to carry the stipulations into effect.

R. E. LEE, General

LIEUTENANT-GENERAL U. S. GRANT

While the letters were being copied, General Grant introduced the general officers who had entered, and each member of the staff, to General Lee. The General shook hands with General Seth Williams, who had been his adjutant when Lee was superintendent at West Point, some years before the war, and gave his hand to some of the other officers who had extended theirs, but to most of those who were introduced he merely bowed in a dignified and formal manner. He did not exhibit the slightest change of features during this ceremony until Colonel Parker of our staff was presented to him. Parker was a full-blooded Indian, and the reigning Chief of the Six Nations. When Lee saw his swarthy features he looked at him with evident surprise, and his eyes rested on him for several seconds. What was passing in his mind probably no one ever knew, but the natural surmise was that he at first mistook Parker for a Negro, and was struck with astonishment to find that the commander of the Union armies had one of that race on his personal staff.

Lee did not utter a word while the introductions were

going on, except to Seth Williams, with whom he talked quite cordially. Williams at one time referred in rather jocose a manner to a circumstance which occurred during the former service together, as if he wanted to say something in a good-natured way to break up the frigidity of the conversation, but Lee was in no mood for pleasantries, and he did not unbend, or even relax the fixed sternness of his features. His only response to the allusion was a slight inclination of the head. General Lee now took the initiative again in leading the conversation back into business channels. He said:

"I have a thousand or more of your men as prisoners, General Grant, a number of them officers whom we have required to march along with us for several days. I shall be glad to send them into your lines as soon as it can be arranged, for I have no provisions for them. I have, indeed, nothing for my own men. They have been living for the last few days principally upon parched corn, and we are badly in need of both rations and forage. I telegraped to Lynchburg, directing several train-loads of rations to be sent on by rail from there, and when they arrive I should be glad to have the present wants of my men supplied from them."

At this remark all eyes turned toward Sheridan, for he had captured these trains with his cavalry the night before, near Appomattox Station. General Grant replied: "I should like to have our men sent within our lines as soon as possible. I will take steps at once to have your army supplied with rations, but I am sorry we have no forage for the animals. We have had to depend upon the country for our supply of forage. Of about how many men does your present force consist?"

"Indeed, I am not able to say," Lee answered after a slight pause. "My losses in killed and wounded have been exceedingly heavy, and, besides, there have been many stragglers and some deserters. All my reports and public papers, and, indeed, my own private letters, had to be destroyed on the march, to prevent them from falling into the hands of your people. Many companies are entirely without officers, and I have not seen any returns for several days; so that I have no means of ascertaining our present strength."

General Grant had taken great pains to have a daily estimate made of the enemy's forces from all the data that could be obtained, and, judging it to be about 25,000 at this time, he said: "Suppose I send over 25,000 rations, do you think that will be a sufficient supply?" "I think it will be ample," remarked Lee, and added with considerable earnestness of manner, "and it will be a great relief, I assure you."

General Grant now turned to his chief commissary, Colonel (now General) M. R. Morgan, who was present, and directed him to arrange for issuing the rations. The number of officers and men surrendered was over 28,000. As to General Grant's supplies, he had ordered the army on starting out to carry twelve days' rations. This was the twelfth and last day of the campaign.

Grant's eye now fell upon Lee's sword again, and it seemed to remind him of the absence of his own, and by way of explanation he said to Lee:

"I started out from my camp several days ago without my sword, and as I have not seen my headquarters baggage since, I have been riding about without any side-arms. I have generally worn a sword, however, as little as possible, only during the actual operations of a campaign." "I am in the habit of wearing mine most of the time," remarked Lee; "I wear it invariably when I am among my troops, moving about through the army."

General Sheridan now stepped up to General Lee and said that when he discovered some of the Confederate troops in motion during the morning, which seemed to be a violation of the truce, he had sent him (Lee) a couple of notes protesting against this act, and as he had not had time to copy them he would like to have them long enough to make copies. Lee took the notes out of the breast-pocket of his coat and handed them to Sheridan with a few words expressive of regret that the circumstance had occurred, and intimating that it must have been the result of some misunderstanding.

After a little general conversation had been indulged in by those present, the two letters were signed and delivered, and the parties prepared to separate. Lee before parting asked Grant to notify Meade of the surrender, fearing that fighting might break out on that front and lives be uselessly lost. This request was complied with, and two Union officers were sent through the enemy's lines as the shortest route to Meade—some of Lee's officers accompanying them to prevent their being interfered with. At a little before four o'clock General Lee shook hands with General Grant, bowed to the other officers, and with Colonel Marshall left the room. One after another we followed, and passed out to the porch. Lee signaled to his orderly to bring up his horse, and while the animal was being bridled the general stood on the lowest step and gazed sadly in the direction of the valley beyond where his army lay—now an army of prisoners. He smote his hands together a number of times in an absent sort of a way; seemed not to see the group of Union officers in the yard who rose respectfully at his approach, and appeared unconscious of everything about him. All appreciated the sadness that overwhelmed him, and he had the personal sympathy of every one who beheld him at this supreme moment of trial. The approach of his horse seemed to recall him from his reverie, and he at once mounted. General Grant now stepped down from the porch, and, moving toward him, saluted him by raising his hat. He was followed in this act of courtesy by all our officers present; Lee raised his hat respectfully, and rode off to break the sad news to the brave fellows whom he had so long commanded.

General Grant and his staff then mounted and started for the headquarters camp, which, in the meantime, had been pitched near by. The news of the surrender had reached the Union lines, and the firing of salutes began at several points, but the general sent orders at once to have them stopped, and used these words in referring to the occurrence: "The war is over, the rebels are our countrymen again, and the best sign of rejoicing after the victory will be to abstain from all demonstrations in the field."

Mr. McLean* had been charging about in a manner which indicated that the excitement was shaking his system to its nervous center, but his real trials did not begin until the departure of the chief actors in the surrender. Then the relic-hunters charged down upon the manner-house and made various attempts to jump Mr. McLean's claims to his own furniture. Sheridan set a good example, however, by paying the proprietor twenty dollars in gold for the table at which Lee sat, for the purpose of presenting it to Mrs. Custer, and handed it over to her dashing husband, who started off for camp bearing it upon his shoulder. Ord paid forty dollars for the table at which Grant sat, and afterward presented it to Mrs. Grant, who modestly declined it, and insisted that Mrs. Ord should become its possessor. Bargains were at once struck for all the articles in the room, and it is even said that some mementos were carried off for which no coin of the realm was ever exchanged.

* Owner of the brick house in which the surrender was signed.

Before General Grant had proceeded far toward camp he was reminded that he had not yet announced the important event to the Government. He dismounted by the roadside, sat down on a large stone, and called for pencil and paper. Colonel (afterward General) Badeau handed his orderbook to the general, who wrote on one of the leaves the following message, a copy of which was sent to the nearest telegraph station. It was dated 4:30 P.M.:

HON. E. M. STANTON, Secretary of War, Washington:
General Lee surrendered the Army of Northern Virginia this afternoon on terms proposed by myself. The accompanying additional correspondence will show the conditions fully.

U. S. GRANT, Lieut.-General.

Upon reaching camp he seated himself in front of his tent, and we all gathered around him, curious to hear what his first comments would be upon the crowning event of his life. But our expectations were doomed to disappointment, for he appeared to have already dismissed the whole subject from his mind, and turning to General Rufus Ingalls, his first words were: "Ingalls, do you remember that old white mule that so-and-so used to ride when we were in the city of Mexico?" "Why, perfectly," said Ingalls, who was just then in a mood to remember the exact number of hairs in the mule's tail if it would have helped to make matters agreeable. And then the general-in-chief went on to recall the antics played by that animal during an excursion to Popocatepetl. It was not until after supper that he said much about the surrender, when he talked freely of his entire belief that the rest of the rebel commanders would follow Lee's example, and that we would have but little more fighting, even of a partisan nature. He then surprised us by announcing his intention of starting to Washington early the next morning. We were disappointed at this, for we wanted to see something of the opposing army, now that it had become civil enough the first time in its existence to let us get near it, and meet some of the officers who had been acquaintances in former years. The general, however, had no desire to look at the conquered, and but little curiosity in his nature, and he was anxious above all things to begin the reduction of the military establishment and diminish the enormous expense attending it, which at this time amounted to about four millions of dollars a day. When he considered that the railroad was being rapidly put in condition and that he would lose no time by waiting till noon of the next day, he made up his mind to delay his departure.

That evening I made full notes of the occurrences which took place during the surrender, and from these the above account has been written.

There were present at McLean's house, besides Sheridan, Ord, Merritt, Custer, and the officers of Grant's staff, a number of other officers and one or two citizens who entered the room at different times during the interview.

About nine o'clock on the morning of the 10th General Grant with his staff rode out toward the enemy's lines, but it was found upon attempting to pass through that the force of habit is hard to overcome, and that the practice which had so long been inculcated in Lee's army of keeping Grant out of his lines was not to be overturned in a day, and he was politely requested at the picket-lines to wait till a message could be sent to headquarters asking for instructions. As soon as Lee heard that his distinguished opponent was approaching, he was prompt to correct the misunderstanding at the picket-line, and rode out at a gallop to receive him. They met on a knoll that overlooked the lines of the two armies, and saluted respectfully, by each raising his hat. The officers present gave a similar salute, and then grouped themselves around the two chieftains in a semicircle, but withdrew out of ear-shot. General Grant repeated to us that evening the substance of the conversation, which was as follows:

Grant began by expressing a hope that the war would soon be over, and Lee replied by stating that he had for some time been anxious to stop the further effusion of blood, and he trusted that everything would now be done to restore harmony and conciliate the people of the South. He said the emancipation of the Negroes would be no hindrance to the restoring of relations between the two sections of the country, as it would probably not be the desire of the majority of the Southern people to restore slavery then, even if the question were left open to them. He could not tell what the other armies would do or what course Mr. Davis would now take, but he believed it would be best for their other armies to follow his example, as nothing could be gained by further resistance in the field. Finding that he entertained these sentiments, General Grant told him that no one's influence in the South was so great as his, and suggested to him that he should advise the surrender of the remaining armies and thus exert his influence in favor of immediate peace. Lee said he could not take such a course without consulting President Davis first. Grant then proposed to Lee that he should do so, and urge the hastening of a result which was admitted to be inevitable. Lee, however, was averse to stepping beyond his duties as a soldier, and said the authorities would doubtless soon arrive at the same conclusion without his interference.

After the conversation had lasted a little more than half an hour and Lee had requested that such instructions be given to the officers left in charge to carry out the details of the surrender, that there might be no misunderstanding as to the form of paroles, the manner of turning over the property, etc., the conference ended. The two commanders lifted their hats and said good-bye. Lee rode back to his camp to take a final farewell of his army, and Grant returned to McLean's house, where he seated himself on the porch until it was time to take his final departure. During the conference Ingalls, Sheridan, and Williams had asked permission to visit the enemy's lines and renew their acquaintance with some old friends, classmates, and former comrades in arms who were serving in Lee's army. They now returned, bringing with them Cadmus M. Wilcox, who had been General Grant's groomsman when he was married; Longstreet, who had also been at his wedding; Heth, who had been a subaltern with him in Mexico, besides Gordon, Pickett, and a number of others. They all stepped up to pay their respects to General Grant, who received them very cordially and talked with them until it was time to leave. The hour of noon had now arrived, and General Grant, after shaking hands with all present who were not to accompany him, mounted his horse, and started with his staff for Washington without having entered the enemy's lines. Lee set out for Richmond, and it was felt by all that peace had at last dawned upon the land. The charges were now withdrawn from the guns, the camp-fires were left to smolder in their ashes, the flags were tenderly furled—those historic banners, battle-stained, bullet-riddled, many of them but remnants of their former selves, with scarcely enough left of them on which to imprint the names of the battles they had seen—and the Army of the Union and the Army of Northern Virginia turned their backs upon each other for the first time ur long, bloody years.